Advancing Electoral Integrity

Advancing Electoral Integrity

EDITED BY PIPPA NORRIS, RICHARD W. FRANK,
and
FERRAN MARTÍNEZ I COMA

OXFORD
UNIVERSITY PRESS

OXFORD

UNIVERSITY PRESS

Oxford University Press is a department of the University of
Oxford. It furthers the University's objective of excellence in research,
scholarship, and education by publishing worldwide.

Oxford   New York

Auckland   Cape Town   Dar es Salaam   Hong Kong   Karachi
Kuala Lumpur   Madrid   Melbourne   Mexico City   Nairobi
New Delhi   Shanghai   Taipei   Toronto

With offices in

Argentina   Austria   Brazil   Chile   Czech Republic   France   Greece
Guatemala   Hungary   Italy   Japan   Poland   Portugal   Singapore
South Korea   Switzerland   Thailand   Turkey   Ukraine   Vietnam

Oxford is a registered trademark of Oxford University Press
in the UK and certain other countries.

Published in the United States of America by
Oxford University Press
198 Madison Avenue, New York, NY 10016

© Oxford University Press 2014

Library of Congress Cataloging-in-Publication Data
Advancing electoral integrity / edited by Pippa Norris, Richard W. Frank and Ferran Martínez i Coma.
pages cm
Includes bibliographical references and index.
ISBN 978-0-19-936870-9 (hardcover : alk. paper)—ISBN 978-0-19-936871-6
(pbk. : alk. paper)   1. Elections—Management.   2. Elections—Corrupt practices.   3. Election
monitoring.   4. Elections—Management—Case studies.   5. Elections—Corrupt practices—Case
studies.   6. Election monitoring—Case studies.   I. Norris, Pippa.   II. Frank, Richard W.   III. Martínez
i Coma, Ferran, 1977-
JF1001.A27 2014
324.6—dc23
2013040844

1 3 5 7 9 8 6 4 2
Printed in the United States of America
on acid-free paper

CONTENTS

WHEN DO ELECTIONS FAIL? STANDARDS AND EVIDENCE

DO INSTITUTIONS MATTER? MANAGING ELECTIONS

LIST OF TABLES

LIST OF FIGURES

PREFACE AND ACKNOWLEDGMENTS

This book is part of the Electoral Integrity Project (EIP), a six-year research project generously funded by the Australian Research Council's Laureate Award as well as the support of many other agencies and partners. The project focuses on the challenges of electoral integrity around the world, including why it matters, why electoral integrity fails, and what can be done to address these problems. Work on the project started in June 2012, with the official launch workshop held in Madrid, in conjunction with the International Political Science Association World Congress.

As always, this book also owes immense debts to many friends and colleagues. The EIP project is located in the Department of Government and International Relations at the University of Sydney, and we are deeply indebted to Michael Spence, Duncan Ivison, Simon Tormey, Allan McConnell, and Graeme Gill for facilitating the arrangement, as well as to all colleagues in the department. The book would not have been possible without the research team and visiting fellows at Sydney who have played an essential role in stimulating ideas, providing critical feedback and advice, generating related publications, and organizing events, especially developing the Perception of Electoral Integrity (PEI) dataset. In particular, we greatly appreciate the contribution of Max Grömping and Sandra Urquiza, who helped with research on the project as they pursued their doctoral studies, as well as Carolien van Ham and Larry LeDuc, who were visiting fellows during this book's gestation.

Draft papers, which formed the basis for these chapters, were originally presented at the Harvard Workshop on Challenges of Electoral Integrity at the Weatherhead Center for International Affairs in Cambridge, MA, on June 3–4, 2013. This workshop was generously facilitated by the award of the Kathleen Fitzpatrick Australian Laureate from the Australian Research Council, and at Harvard by support from the Weatherhead Center for International Affairs, the Roy and Lila Ash Center for Democratic Governance and Innovation, and the Australian Studies Committee. We would also like to thank Beth Simmons for opening the workshop, all the paper discussants and the workshop participants who provided such lively and stimulating comments, as well as Marina Ivanova, Julie de Benedictus, and Sarah Doyle at Harvard, for helping with the local arrangements.

The editors would also like to express appreciation for invaluable feedback from presentations of related project papers on electoral integrity at several international workshops and meetings, including the Madrid pre-IPSA Workshop on Electoral Integrity in June 2012, the American Political Science Association annual meeting and EIP workshop in Chicago in August 2013, the Australian Political Studies Association annual meeting in Perth in September 2013, and from faculty seminars at Harvard's Kennedy School of Government and the Department of Government and International Relations at Sydney University. Finally, the support and enthusiasm of Angela Chnapko at Oxford University Press has proved invaluable, as were the helpful comments of the reviewers.

Harvard University and the University of Sydney

NOTES ABOUT CONTRIBUTORS

Eric Bjornlund is co-founder and principal of Democracy International. A lawyer and development professional with two decades of international experience, Mr. Bjornlund has designed, managed, and evaluated democratic development programs in 30 countries in Africa, Asia, Europe, Eurasia, and the Middle East. He is author of *Beyond Free and Fair: Monitoring Elections and Building Democracy* (2004). Mr. Bjornlund holds a J.D. from Columbia University, an M.P.A. from John F. Kennedy School of Government at Harvard University, and a BA magna cum laude from Williams College.

David J. Carroll leads the Carter Center's initiative on developing standards and best practices in international election observation. He has managed or participated in more than 30 Carter Center projects to strengthen democracy and electoral processes. He joined the Carter Center in 1991 as assistant director of the Latin American and Caribbean Program and since 2003 has directed the Democracy Program. He received his Ph.D. in international relations from the University of South Carolina, has published articles and book chapters on development and democratization, and has taught at Georgia State University and the University of the South.

Alistair Clark is Senior Lecturer in Politics at Newcastle University. His research interests revolve around electoral integrity and administration, political parties and party organizations, and devolved and urban/local politics. He has previously held posts at Queen's University Belfast and at University of Birmingham. He is author of *Political Parties in the UK* (2012), co-editor (with Liam Weeks) of *Radical or Redundant: Minor Parties in Irish Politics* (2012), and has published widely in journals such as *Party Politics, Journal of Elections, Public Opinion and Parties, Parliamentary Affairs,* and *PS: Political Science and Politics.*

Svitlana Chernykh is a Postdoctoral Research Fellow at the University of Oxford. She received her PhD in Political Science at the University of Illinois at

Urbana-Champaign, where she also worked as a senior researcher and project manager of the Comparative Constitutions Project at the Cline Centre for Democracy. Her research interests focus on the political determinants and consequences of post-election protests, constitutional design, and democratic performance. She has published in the *Journal of Politics, Comparative Political Studies, and Constitutional Political Economy.*

Staffan Darnolf is Director, Program Development and Innovation at the International Foundation for Electoral Systems, (IFES), Washington DC. He has 20 years of experience as a scholar and practitioner in the field of democratization and electoral processes. He specializes in electoral reform in emerging democracies and post-conflict societies and he has published books, articles, and chapters in peer-reviewed scholarly journals throughout his career. Darnolf has been engaged as an elections expert in over 20 countries. He holds a PhD in political science with a focus on elections in emerging democracies from Goteborg University, Sweden.

Avery Davis-Roberts manages the Center's Democratic Election Standards Projects, which seeks to build consensus on the components of democratic elections. She supported the Center's collaborative effort with the National Democratic Institute and the U.N. Electoral Assistance Division on principles for international election observation and has worked on Carter Center election observation missions in Asia, Africa, South America, and the Middle East. Before joining the Center, Ms. Davis-Roberts was a research consultant in London. She gained a joint honors bachelor's degree in Arabic and law and a Master of Laws degree (LL.M.) in international human rights law, both from the School of Oriental and African Studies at the University of London.

Ursula Daxecker is Assistant Professor in Political Science at the University of Amsterdam. Her research focuses on civil war, election violence, maritime piracy, and terrorism. Major articles have appeared in *British Journal of Political Science, Journal of Conflict Resolution,* and the *Journal of Peace Research.* Current research is funded by the Dutch Science Foundation, the European Commission's Marie Curie actions, and the U.S. Department of Defense Minerva Initiative.

Zachary Elkins is Associate Professor of Government at the University of Texas at Austin. His research focuses on issues of democracy, institutional reform, research methods, and national identity, with an emphasis on Latin America. He co-directs the Comparative Constitutions Project. Elkins earned his BA from Yale University, an MA from the University of Texas at Austin, and his PhD from the University of California, Berkeley.

Jørgen Elklit is Professor of Political Science at Aarhus University, Denmark. His main professional interests are electoral behavior, electoral systems, election administration, political parties, and Danish politics. He also has considerable experience as advisor on democratization and elections in a number of countries in

Europe, Africa, and Asia. His most recent book is a co-edited volume on the 2009 local elections in Denmark.

Annette Monika Fath-Lihic is the Senior Programme Manager for Electoral Processes with International IDEA. She holds a PhD in Modern History and International Humanitarian Law from the University of Mannheim in Germany. She has worked in many conflict zones such as the Balkans, Sudan, Liberia, and the Occupied Palestinian Territories, since 1994 for IOM, EU, OSCE, and the UN, among others.

Aleida Ferreyra is a Research Analyst at the Democratic Governance Group in UNDP's Bureau for Development Policy in New York. She has been involved with several publications on electoral assistance and governance, including the *Electoral Assistance Implementation Guide, Making Democracy Deliver: Innovative Governance for Human Development,* and *Governance for the Future: Democracy and Development in the Least Developed Countries.* She holds a MA and MPhil in Political Science and Government from the New School for Social Research in New York.

Richard W. Frank is the Electoral Integrity Project Manager and Research Fellow. His research focuses on the causes of electoral violence, civil conflict, and human trafficking. Richard received his PhD. from Binghamton University, and his work has appeared in the *Journal of Democracy, Journal of Peace Research, Conflict Management* and *Peace Science,* and *International Interactions.*

Tom Ginsburg, Leo Spitz Professor of International Law, Ludwig and Hilde Wolf Research Scholar, and Professor of Political Science at the University of Chicago, focuses on comparative and international law from an interdisciplinary perspective. He holds BA, JD, and PhD degrees from the University of California at Berkeley. His books include *Judicial Review in New Democracies* (2003); *The Endurance of National Constitutions* (2009); *Rule by Law: The Politics of Courts in Authoritarian Regimes* (2008), and *Comparative Constitutional Design* (2011). He currently co-directs the Comparative Constitutions Project.

Thad E. Hall is the Director of Graduate Studies at the Political Science Department at the University of Utah. He is the Director of the Master of Public Administration Program at the College of Social and Behavioral Science, an Associate Professor at the Political Science Department, and a Research Fellow at the Institute of Public and International Affairs at the University of Utah. His publications include: *Evaluating Elections: A Handbook of Methods and Standards* and *Confirming Elections: Creating Confidence and Integrity Through Election Auditing,* among many others.

Toby S. James is a Lecturer at the University of East Anglia, Norwich, United Kingdom. His research focuses on electoral management/administration, the policy process and political leadership. He is the author of *Elite Statecraft and Election Administration* (Palgrave, 2012) and has recently published in journals such as *Electoral Studies, Parliamentary Affairs* and *Government and Opposition.*

Nicholas Kerr is Assistant Professor in the Department of Political Science at University of Alabama. His research interests include comparative electoral institutions, electoral integrity, democratization, and African politics. His current research project explores the factors that influence the design of electoral commissions in Africa, and how the design and performance of these institutions influence electoral integrity.

Arturo Maldonado is a PhD Candidate at Vanderbilt University and Research Assistant in the Latin American Public Opinion Project (LAPOP). He received a BA in Sociology from the Pontificia Universidad Católica del Perú. His dissertation topic is about the effects of compulsory voting on political behavior in Latin American countries and his areas of interest also include voting behavior, turnout, elections, and experiments in political science.

Ferran Martínez i Coma is Research Associate at The Electoral Integrity Project in the Department of Government and International Relations at the University of Sydney. He has published in *Electoral Studies, the Journal of Democracy,* and *Party Politics.* Prior to arriving in Sydney, Ferran worked at the Ministry of Interior, in the General Direction of Interior Policy, in charge of organizing the elections, and the Prime Minister's Office. He was an Assistant Professor at Centro de Investigacion y Docencias Economicas (CIDE) in Mexico City. Ferran is a member of the Juan March Institute in Madrid.

Robert Mattes is Professor of Political Studies and Director of the Democracy in Africa Research Unit at the University of Cape Town. He is also a co-founder and co-director of the Afrobarometer, a regular survey of public opinion in 18 African countries. His research has focused on the development of democratic attitudes and practices in South Africa and across the continent. He is the co-author (with Michael Bratton and E. Gyimah-Boadi) of *Public Opinion, Democracy and Markets In Africa* (2004) and has authored or co-authored articles in journals such as the *American Journal of Political Science, British Journal of Political Science, World Development, Journal of Democracy, Democratization,* and *Party Politics.* He holds a PhD in Political Science from the University of Illinois, Urbana-Champaign (1992).

James Melton lectures in the Department of Political Science and he is a Researcher in the Constitution Unit at University College London (UCL). Prior to this, he was an Assistant Professor (2009-2012) at the IMT Institute for Advanced Studies in Lucca, Italy. He holds a BA from Illinois Wesleyan University and an MA and PhD from the University of Illinois. His research and teaching interests focus on comparative constitutional design.

Betilde Muñoz-Pogossian is the Director of the Department of Electoral Cooperation and Observation at the Organization of American States. She has authored and co-authored numerous publications on democracy, elections, and gender mainstreaming in election observation, including a book on *Electoral*

Rules and Transformation of Bolivian Politics: The Rise of Evo Morales (2008). Dr. Muñoz-Pogossian holds a PhD in Political Science from Florida International University of Miami.

Pippa Norris is the McGuire Lecturer in Comparative Politics at the John F. Kennedy School of Government, Harvard University, where she has taught for more than twenty years, Laureate Fellow and Professor of Government and International Relations at the University of Sydney, and Director of the Electoral Integrity Project. Her research compares election and public opinion, political communications, and gender politics, and in 2011 she received the Johan Skytte award. Prize-winning author of more than forty books, her latest volume is *Why Electoral Integrity Matters* (Cambridge University Press 2014). She also served as Director of the Democratic Governance Group in United Nations Development Programme, NY, and as an expert consultant to many international organizations.

Andrew Reynolds is an Associate Professor of Political Science at UNC Chapel Hill and the Chair of Global Studies. He is collaborating with the Electoral Integrity Project in designing and implementing the expert survey of Perceptions of Electoral Integrity (with Professor Elklit). He received his MA from the University of Cape Town and his PhD from the University of California, San Diego. His research and teaching focus on democratization, constitutional design, and electoral politics. His publications include *Designing Democracy in a Dangerous World* (2011), *The Architecture of Democracy* (2002), *Electoral Systems and Democratization in Southern Africa* (1999), and *Elections and Conflict Management in Africa* (1998).

Gerald Schneider is Professor of International Politics at the University of Konstanz and President of the European Political Science Association (2013–2015). He has published around 140 articles on European integration, the causes of violent conflict, conflict management, and other issues. Schneider is also Executive Editor of *European Union Politics* and co-editor of *International Interactions*.

Mitchell Seligson is the Centennial Professor of Political Science and Professor of Sociology at Vanderbilt University and founding Director of the Latin American Public Opinion Project (LAPOP). LAPOP regularly conducts the AmericasBarometer survey, covering twenty-six nations and over 40,000 interviews each round. His most recent books are *The Legitimacy Puzzle in Latin America* (2009) and *Development and Underdevelopment: the Political Economy of Global Inequality, Fifth edition, 2014* and he is currently on the editorial boards of the *European Political Science Review, Comparative Political Studies*, the *Journal of Democracy en Español, ROP: Revista Opinião Pública*, the *Political Analysis* series, Palgrave Macmillan and *Estudios Interdisciplinarios de América Latina y el Caribe*.

Charles Stewart III is the Kenan Sahin Distinguished Professor of Political Science at MIT, where he has taught since 1985. His research and teaching areas include congressional politics, elections, and American political development. His current research about Congress touches on the historical development of committees, party leadership, and Senate elections. Since 2001, Professor Stewart has been a member of the Caltech/MIT Voting Technology Project, a leading research effort that applies scientific analysis to questions about election technology, election administration, and election reform. He received his BA in political science from Emory University, and SM and PhD from Stanford University.

Antonio Ugues Jr. is Assistant Professor of Political Science at St. Mary's College of Maryland. His primary areas of expertise include democracy, democratization, and electoral integrity, especially in Mexico and Central America. He has published in the *Journal of Legislative Studies*, the *Journal of Elections, Public Opinion, and Parties*, and *Latin American Politics and Society*. He received his PhD in Political Science at the University of California, Riverside.

Chad Vickery is based at the International Foundation for Electoral Systems, Washington DC. He has 17 years of legal and international election administration experience, especially strengthening democracy and governance in transitioning societies. He also has extensive experience in designing and managing election complaint adjudication programs; providing comparative legal analysis; working on elections; and rule of law programs throughout South Asia, Southeast Asia, Eurasia and the Middle East. He holds a master's degree in international relations from Georgetown University; a Juris Doctorate from the Catholic University of America with a concentration in comparative and international law; and a bachelor's degree in political science from the University of Washington.

Advancing Electoral Integrity

WHEN DO ELECTIONS FAIL?
STANDARDS AND EVIDENCE

1

Introduction

Challenges of Electoral Integrity

PIPPA NORRIS

Many elections fail. The most overt malpractices used by rulers include imprisoning dissidents, harassing adversaries, coercing voters, vote-rigging counts, and finally, if losing, blatantly disregarding the people's choice. Such actions have triggered protests and been widely condemned by the international community. Administrative flaws such as inaccurate electoral registers, ballot miscounts, and security defects are also common.

It is timely to take stock of these developments. This book seeks to bring together international experts to address three related themes: (i) what normative standards and empirical evidence help to determine when elections fail? (ii) What strengthens effective, impartial, and independent electoral authorities? And, (iii) what are the consequences of lack of electoral integrity for trust and confidence in elections and thus, political legitimacy?

Chapters bring new concepts, theories, and evidence to illuminate these issues, drawing upon cases in established democracies such as Britain and the United States, newer democracies in Central and Latin America, and diverse regimes in Sub-Saharan Africa and the Middle East.

Before laying out the reasons for growing concern about challenges of electoral integrity, the core concepts, and the overall plan of the book, a case study of the Cambodian elections helps to illustrate some of the core challenges facing contemporary elections.

The Cambodian Elections

In the Cambodian general election to the National Assembly on July 28, 2013, the ruling Cambodian People's Party (CPP) won 49 percent of the vote, holding on to its parliamentary majority with 68 seats. The government won around 290,000 more ballots than the opposition. Meanwhile, under the list PR electoral system, the opposition Cambodia National Rescue Party (CNRP) nearly doubled its representation, to 55 seats, with 44 percent of the vote.[1]

Immediately following the announcement of results, the opposition leader, Sam Rainsy, held a press conference alleging widespread irregularities: "The ruling party organized the election in such a way as to secure victory even before voting day."[2] He claimed problems of duplicate names on the official electoral register, 1.3 million names missing from the list (many opposition supporters), and intimidation used by the security forces. Residents in Phnom Penh told local media that the authorities forced them to sign statements saying they supported the provisional election result and promising not to join any protests.[3] Documentation by poll monitors before the election demonstrated that the ink identifying that people had already voted could be washed off simply using bleach or lime juice in minutes upon drying, allowing multiple voting.[4] The opposition claimed that local irregularities mattered; immediately after polling day, based on agents in each polling station, the opposition CNRP announced that they had won 63 seats to the CPP's 60.[5]

What was the evidence supporting claims of malpractice? The National Election Committee, with members nominated by the Ministry of the Interior and appointed by a majority of the ruling party in the National Assembly, was tasked with running the contest (motto, "Independence. Truthfulness, Neutrality. Justice and Transparency."). The agency received almost 500 complaints during the campaign and polling day, but, after examination, they concluding blandly that "irregularities did not have any serious impact."[6] Contrary to this statement, the largest domestic election watchdog group COMFREL documented more than 10,000 cases of irregularities occurring in more than 2,000 different polling stations.[7] In total, around 40,000 observers from 35 organizations oversaw activity in approximately 19,000 polling stations.[8] Cambodian civil society mobilized a substantial number of domestic election monitors, perhaps 15,000 volunteers in total, coordinated by COMFREL, who also conducted a parallel vote tabulation. The COMFREL situation room gathered and publicized a plethora of anecdotes about irregularities, although they lacked the capacity to generate more systematic analysis.[9] The EU was not invited to send a monitoring mission. Instead, almost 300 observers from the Centrist Asia Pacific Democrats International and the International Conference of Asian Political Parties, who were invited by the National Election Commission to monitor the contest, declared that the election met democratic standards as "free, fair and transparent, and, above all, peaceful, non-violent and smooth."[10] Not a single international election observer reported witnessing any serious misconduct on polling day, according to the official government report.[11]

Despite these assurances, Sam Rainsy demanded an independent bipartisan committee to investigate the allegations and find a solution—either by holding new polls in the most severely affected provinces or by rerunning the entire election. Several international organizations, including Human Rights Watch, the US State Department, and Transparency International, along with Ban Ki-Moon, secretary general of the UN, welcomed a peaceful outcome but reinforced the call for authorities to investigate and adjudicate claims of electoral fraud and voting irregularities fairly and transparently.[12] "Senior ruling party officials appear to have been involved in issuing fake election documents and fraudulently registering voters in multiple provinces," Human Rights Watch concluded, with thousands of soldiers issued fake identity documents and shipped to vote in provinces where they did not reside.[13] Ignoring these claims, the government rejected demands for a commission of inquiry, arguing that there were many positive assessments of the process: "The UN Secretary General, Ban Ki-Moon, the State Department of the United States of America, the European Union and others expressed satisfaction with the conduct of the election."[14] The opposition lodged further appeals with the Constitutional Court, but many in the judiciary are close to the ruling party. The prolonged crisis generated mass protests and rallies, some violent clashes with security forces, and political stalemate. In September, opposition parties, continuing to demand an investigation, boycotted the opening of parliament. While the ruling party confirmed Hun Sen for another five-year term as prime minister, continuing his almost three decades in power, the opposition threatened a nationwide strike. In 2013, Freedom House rated Cambodia as "not free," similar in rankings to Kazakhstan, Angola, and Qatar.[15] The peaceful campaign reflects a positive development given the recent history of bloody civil war in the country, a series of previous contests afflicted by violence, and the prosecution and exile of Sam Rainsy. Nevertheless, mass protests and the opposition boycott of parliament, in an atmosphere clouded by questions about the legitimacy of the close outcome, renewed challenges of political deadlock and instability in Cambodia.

Growing Concern about Problems of Electoral Integrity

The 2013 Cambodian election is far from an isolated case. Today, many contests around the world end in a flurry of claims and counterclaims about alleged stolen elections, fraud, and irregularities, which reduces trust in the legitimacy of the electoral process and elected authorities, and sometimes catalyzes violent clashes between the supporters of governing and opposition parties.[16] One factor driving this development has been an end of the era of absolute autocracies, governed by one-party states, personal dictatorships, monarchies, and military juntas, with leaders selected in many states by multiparty elections for the national legislature and direct elections for executive. Today, only a handful of states, mainly clustered in the Gulf, continue to be governed by traditional monarchies buttressed by appointed assemblies. With a few notable exceptions, regimes without the fig leaf of elections have dropped out of fashion. This process occurred following the third wave of democratization, which started in the early 1970s, the end of Communist Party dominance in the Soviet Union after the fall of the Berlin Wall in 1989, and the Arab uprisings since Tunisia in December 2010. The net impact has been dramatic; at the end of the Second World War, around 50 independent nation states had popularly elected national legislatures. Today, this number has quadrupled, so that 188 out of 199 national states worldwide hold such contests.[17]

Multiparty elections provide opportunities for significant advances in human rights and democratization.[18] Nevertheless, many challenges are raised by this development. During the early 1990s, the fall of the Berlin Wall and the collapse of the USSR generated a mood of heady optimism about the inevitable spread of democracy through elections, symbolizing the "end of history."[19] Countries that had experienced the demise of absolute autocracy but had not yet "consolidated" were widely regarded as "transitioning towards" eventually becoming liberal democracies. It was assumed that the rest would ultimately follow the West. Elections among competing candidates and parties, while insufficient by themselves, are central to the process of democratization.

A decade later, however, a more realistic and hardheaded perspective emerged, suggesting that earlier assessments were far too hopeful.[20] The spread of direct elections worldwide has been accompanied by growing concern about the unevenness of their quality, especially in more authoritarian states, generating a flood of new scholarship.[21] In far too many contests today, electoral laws, procedures, and district boundaries are skewed toward incumbents; voter and party registration procedures are overly restrictive, inaccurate, and flawed; campaign communications and financial resources are imbalanced; voting process and the ballot count lack transparency or honesty; announcements of results are unduly delayed; and electoral officials fail to prove impartial, effective, or independent.[22] Governing parties now face increased competition at the ballot box, but flawed contests lack a "level playing field."[23] This notion does not imply absolute equality, where all parties and candidates would have the same chance to succeed by gaining office. Rather, the concept emphasizes procedural fairness and equality of opportunity, where all contestants abide by the same rules of the game, for example through facing the same procedures for registering, campaigning, and seeking electoral support. In practice, the normative standards that achieve the broadest consensus around the world are drawn not from democratic theory but from international conventions, human rights treaties, and the practical guidelines promulgated by regional and international organizations.

One way to illustrate the growing concern about electoral malpractices can be shown from trends in media coverage in the world's major news outlets. Several search terms can be used, such as "electoral malpractices" or "vote-rigging," of which "electoral fraud" is probably the most popular and general in common language. The number of news stories about electoral fraud can be calculated from the online LexisNexis Academic database of major world publications.[24] This source contains 540 full-text news sources from around the world, including the world's major newspapers, magazines, and trade publications, which are relied upon for the accuracy and integrity of their reporting. Figure 1.1 shows that in 1990, there were approximately 200 stories

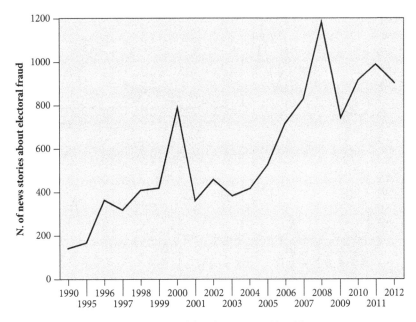

Figure 1.1: News stories about electoral fraud, major world publications, 1990–2012

Notes: Count of news stories about electoral fraud calculated from the online LexisNexis Academic Major World Publications group using a keyword search of [(elec*) and (fraud)] by the years 1990–2012. The Major World Publications group file, MWP, contains 540 full-text news sources from around the world that are held in high esteem for their content reliability. This includes the world's major newspapers, magazines, and trade publications that are relied upon for the accuracy and integrity of their reporting.

about electoral fraud, and attention rose gradually during this decade. Disputes during the Gore v. Bush 2000 US elections generated a sharp but short-lived spike of media attention. The following decade saw a long-term increase in news about electoral fraud, peaking with 1,200 stories around the globe in 2008, a six-fold increase since 1990. Concern about particular contests drive the rise in particular years, before attention falls back but remains at a relatively high level in recent years. How far can this be attributed simply to growing controversies and party polarization over electoral fraud in the United States? To examine this further, the results can be subdivided to trace trends in the world's global regions. Figure 1.2 reveals that the rise is evident in North America—which is largely due to stories about US elections. But the greatest growth in reporting about problems of electoral fraud during the early twenty-first century occurs in Africa, with some increase registered in Asia, Europe, and the Middle East. Thus, although many states have by now adopted multiparty elections, observed flaws and irregularities in electoral processes and procedures nevertheless drive concern about fraudulent, stolen, or rigged contests.

Electoral malpractices, whether arising from severe abuses of human rights or from more minor technical irregularities, are intrinsically important as the lynchpin

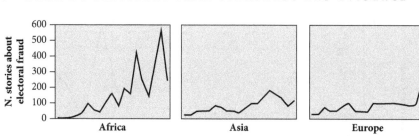

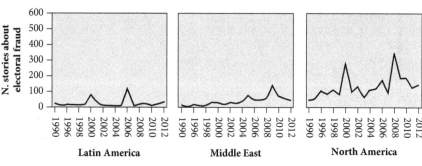

Figure 1.2: News stories about electoral fraud, major world publications by region, 1990–2012 Notes: Count calculated from the online LexisNexis Academic Major World Publications group using a keyword search of [(elec*) and (fraud)] by the years 1990–2012 and regional geographic classification. The Major World Publications group file, MWP, contains 540 full-text news sources from around the world that are held in high esteem for their content reliability. This includes the world's major newspapers, magazines, and trade publications that are relied upon for the accuracy and integrity of their reporting.

of liberal democracy. Failures can also have grave consequences, undermining feelings of political legitimacy and acceptance of the authority of the government, catalyzing protests, and sometimes spiraling into conflict and violence, which destabilizes fragile states.[25] The issue is often framed as though these problems are confined to the gray zone of "hybrid regimes," which are neither absolute autocracies nor stable democracies. In this context, a growing body of research has sought to explain why autocrats bow to domestic and international pressures by allowing elections to be held, at the risk of losing power, and how manipulated contests serve to legitimate their rule and deter challengers.[26] In fact, however, moderate and seriously flawed elections, through a failure of human rights or a failure of state capacity and governance, can arise in every country and type of regime, even within long-standing democracies such as the United States, Canada, and Britain.

The Core Concept of Electoral Integrity

To understand the contribution of this volume to the growing literature, it helps to clarify the core notion of "electoral integrity," a concept advanced in this book.[27]

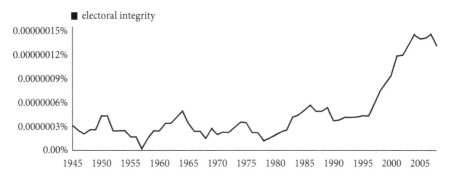

Figure 1.3: Books discussing electoral integrity, 1945 to 2008 Note: Search of Google books for the term "electoral integrity" (N-gram viewer). Source: http://books.google.com/ngrams/graph?content = electoral+integrity&year_start = 1945&year_end = 2008&corpus = 15&smoothing = 3&share =

Similar notions in the literature include related negative terms such as "electoral malpractice," "flawed elections," "manipulated contests," "rigged elections," and "electoral fraud." Positive terms are also commonly deployed that describe contests as "competitive," "credible," "acceptable," "genuine," "clean," "democratic," reflecting the "will of the people," or the standard diplomatic rhetoric of "free and fair."[28] Throughout this volume, the overarching concept of "electoral integrity" is understood broadly in terms of international commitments and global norms surrounding elections, endorsed in a series of authoritative conventions, treaties, protocols, and guidelines. These universal standards apply to all countries worldwide throughout the electoral cycle, including during the pre-electoral period, the campaign, on polling day, and its aftermath. Conversely, electoral "malpractice" refers to violations of electoral integrity. The electoral cycle is understood as a sequential process broken down into several components, ranging from the election laws, electoral procedures, and boundary delimitation to the voting process, vote count, and declaration of results. Like complex links in a chain, violating international standards in any one of the sequential steps undermines, and weakens, principles of electoral integrity. The concept of electoral integrity is gradually gaining in usage, as demonstrated by the surge in references in publications shown in Figure 1.3, attracting a rapidly growing body of pure and applied research drawn from diverse subfields in the social sciences and using multiple methods.[29]

The Plan of the Book

This book seeks to bring together some of the best of the emerging literature concerning three related themes about electoral integrity: (i) What normative standards and empirical evidence are available to determine when elections fail and to document the extent of problems of electoral malpractices, such as fraudulent and rigged contests? (ii) How can states administer these contests to international standards and strengthen the capacity of effective, impartial, and independent electoral management bodies? Finally, (iii) what are the consequences of lack of electoral integrity for feelings of political legitimacy among ordinary citizens?

Standards and Evidence

The first section of this volume considers the standards and evidence used to determine when elections fail—and succeed. What principles and criteria serve as the basis of normative judgments? As illustrated by the Cambodian case, evaluations can prove highly contentious, especially where losing parties and candidates claim that victory was denied them due to practices of malpractice, fraud, misuse of public resources, or vote-buying, but where systematic evidence is difficult to collect. Even in long-established democracies, many issues about the quality of elections can still prove controversial; for example, in the United States, heated court battles have become common over Republican claims that new regulations are needed to curb widespread voter fraud, and Democrat counterclaims that the new laws serve to disguise voter suppression. Not surprisingly, in recent contests elsewhere, such as in Russia, Nigeria, and Malaysia, domestic observer organizations, and also various international and regional monitoring missions, can and do differ from each other in their published assessment of the quality of elections. Election monitoring reports are an invaluable source of information about each contest, and the standards and principles of international monitoring organizations have become increasingly standardized over the years, generating more consistent assessments across countries and global regions. Nevertheless, confidence in the reports of monitoring agencies is strengthened if the evaluations coincide with each other and with alternative independent and authoritative sources of evidence.

Chapter 2 by Avery Davies-Roberts and David J. Carroll includes a conceptual framework for assessing election integrity based on international obligations. It provides a background and rationale for this framework, and illustrates how the approach is being applied by election observation missions, drawing upon the Carter Center's work during the 2012 Egyptian presidential election. The chapter concludes that objective assessments of electoral integrity require a broad consensus about its definition and components, and that a multitude of sources in international law exist upon which to build agreement.

Building upon this normative framework, chapter 3 tackles issues of measurement and evidence. Pippa Norris, Jørgen Elklit, and Andrew Reynolds seek to clarify the underlying concepts of electoral integrity and malpractice, and to consider what systematic, valid, and reliable evidence is available to allow scholars and practitioners to monitor the quality of elections. The chapter reviews the pros and cons of several methods and analytical techniques. Previous studies have usually relied upon one or several primary sources, including case studies, performance indices, and elite interviews, content analysis of observer mission reports, human rights reports, coding of news media coverage, forensic analysis of election results, randomized evaluations through natural or field experiments, and also public opinion surveys. It is argued that many of these approaches are useful, but they each suffer from important limitations, for example in terms of conceptual validity, cross-national coverage, and/or capacity to monitor all sequential stages throughout the electoral cycle. It is therefore useful to supplement this evidence through gathering evidence from a global survey of expert opinion. The new Perception of Electoral Integrity (PEI) Index, it is suggested, offers a comprehensive, systematic, and robust measure that can usefully supplement many other sources of empirical evidence, playing a valuable role for both the academic and the policymaking communities.

Chapter 4 by Ferran Martínez i Coma and Richard W. Frank goes on to describe the research design and the results of the pilot data from the Perceptions of Electoral Integrity, or PEI, that enables researchers and policy analysts to evaluate both specific disaggregated aspects of electoral integrity, as well as to construct an overall index of Perceptions of Electoral Integrity that meets the scientific criteria listed above. When completed, the PEI dataset will eventually evaluate all national elections—instead of the subset monitored by international or domestic organizations. It will also examine malpractices throughout the electoral cycle—instead of only on election day. In the PEI pilot stage, conducted in April and May of 2013, the survey instrument was implemented in 20 countries, after which coverage was then expanded to all presidential and parliamentary elections around the world. The initial results of the PEI pilot stage are encouraging. The mean response rate (30 percent) is consistent with existing expert surveys. Furthermore, the expert evaluations are strongly correlated with several independent existing sources (suggesting external validity). The PEI experts' evaluations coincide with mass perceptions of electoral integrity, as measured by the sixth round of the World Values Survey, suggesting reliable and legitimate estimates.

In addition, much information about the quality of elections comes from the reports published by election observer missions from international and regional organizations. But how reliable, consistent, and legitimate are the assessments contained in these reports? A growing body of research has sought to document the role of electoral observer missions conducted by international and regional organizations, and to determine whether the information provided by the observer reports has an impact on strengthening the quality of elections in countries through the international community's use of the "sticks and carrots" of aid conditionality, diplomatic engagement, or the provision of technical assistance and capacity-building programs.[30] In chapter 5, Ursula Daxecker and Gerald Schneider examine how regimes respond strategically to election monitoring. In particular, they argue that regimes facing high risks of being accused of election fraud and malpractice are likely to invite a range of monitoring observer organizations to evaluate the quality of their elections. If both negative and positive evaluation reports are published after the event, this mixed message helps to deflect international and domestic criticism. The tendency of trying to offset a possibly negative report through a more supportive one is expected to be particularly pronounced in institutionally weak, corrupt, and economically dependent countries. In addition, the authors predict that incumbents who invite the right combination of monitors are less likely to face post-election unrest at home. One implication arising from this study is that scholars should be cautious about overreliance on observer reports as a source of independent and trustworthy information about electoral integrity, since the diversity of monitoring organizations today means that evaluations differ systematically.

Election Management

While a burgeoning research literature has examined the deployment of electoral monitors, far less scholarship has looked at other common types of policies used by the international community to strengthen electoral integrity, including the technical assistance and development aid devoted to expanding the capacity of election management bodies (EMBs). The next section of the book goes on to consider the challenges arising from the effective administration of elections. Formerly obscure technical agencies, as well as controversies over electoral processes and outcomes, have thrust EMBs into the spotlight in recent decades.[31] In all contests, electoral officials are involved with every stage in the process, including the implementation of electoral laws and guidelines, the registration of parties and candidates, the design and printing of ballots, the selection and staffing of polling places, the training and management of local poll workers, the collection and counting of ballots, and the declaration of the results. For many countries transitioning from absolute autocracies and establishing competitive elections, it is important to develop the capacity of EMBs to run contests independently, impartially, efficiently, and legitimately. In states emerging from deep-rooted conflict, characterized by low-trust but high-stake contests, even minor flaws in electoral procedures may prove capable of reigniting violence. Problems such as undue delays in announcing the count, erroneous voter registers, or incompetent local poll workers can sow suspicion about the fairness and impartiality of the rules of the game. In addition, in several long-established democracies, the role and effectiveness of EMBs has become a topic of growing concern. This is exemplified by problems of balloting in Florida in the 2000 Gore v. Bush presidential contest, which led to increasing party polarization and litigation in the United States. But new challenges of regulating political finance and broadcasting in the age of social media confront even the best resources and most well-trained EMBs.

Electoral officials often face a series of logistical, administrative, and political hurdles. Elections are complex events requiring substantial capacity, financial and technical resources, strategic planning, and the organization, training, and manpower to deploy, coordinate, and manage a temporary army of staff dispersed throughout local polling stations. The majority of countries (125 nations) have established independent EMBs.[32] These agencies typically employ permanent officials and temporary staff, and they are accountable to legislative, executive, or judicial branches. A smaller number of countries (48) locate administrative responsibility for national elections within government ministries, while the remainder use a mixed model. Some electoral management bodies are highly decentralized, notably in the United States, where 13,000 local election agencies are responsible for voter registration, polling, and ballot counts, whilst elsewhere, control and regulation is more closely coordinated by regional or national agencies. Election management bodies require organizational capacity, regulatory procedures, and the human and technical resources, to manage elections effectively and efficiently.

To consider the role of these bodies, chapter 6 by Svitlana Chernykh, Zachary Elkins, James Melton, and Tom Ginsburg examines the constitutional requirements for electoral management bodies. One of the challenges of democratic governance is the enforcement of electoral results. Perversely, governing parties, who have powerful incentives to remain in power, typically control the legal framework, which administers elections and electoral disputes. A way to insulate electoral law from manipulation by incumbents is to entrench it in higher law. Constitutions increasingly speak to the administration, adjudication, and enforcement of elections. This chapter sets out to provide guidance to constitutional drafters about how far, if at all, constitutions have regulated elections, and then to see whether the "constitutionalization" of electoral management bodies is associated with greater electoral integrity.

The role of EMBs in newer democracies is a major challenge. In chapter 7, Antonio Ugues Jr. looks at the impact of politicization on EMB performance, in particular whether politicized EMBs function autonomously and in an impartial manner. This study analyzes these questions by examining de facto levels of autonomy and impartiality exhibited by the respective EMBs of El Salvador, Guatemala, Honduras, and Nicaragua. Ugues concludes that the autonomy and impartiality of the Central American EMBs largely depends on the degree of party politicization affecting each institution, notably the process of appointing members.

Chapter 8 by Toby S. James turns to examining electoral administration in the British case. Existing approaches to the study of electoral malpractice have focused primarily on how the strategic office-seeking behavior of incumbent rulers has led to defects in electoral practices. This chapter argues that problems can also occur through organizational failures in electoral management boards. James offers a new framework for assessing EMB performance and a typology for identifying failures. He then explores the environment in which policy makers and electoral officials run elections in the British case, using qualitative interviews. The study finds that new challenges and opportunities have emerged, requiring change and adaption.

Elections are now implemented in an era of post-industrial, digital-era governance, and this makes organizational performance more difficult to achieve.

The performance of EMBs is also thought to depend, in part, upon available capacities and resources. In chapter 9, Alistair Clark examines the common assumption that election quality suffers from lack of funding. This idea is widespread but it is seldom tested, and the relationship between electoral spending and electoral integrity remains unclear. This chapter draws upon an index of electoral administration derived from British election returning officers' performance standards data from the 2009 European elections. This index provides a considerably more nuanced overall picture of electoral integrity in Britain than previously available, adding a further tool for policy makers. The index is brought together with comprehensive data on the funding of election administration in Britain, compiled by the UK Electoral Commission, thereby testing the claim that resources matter for election quality.

Does Lack of Integrity Undermine Legitimacy?

There is no question that electoral malpractices are widely acknowledged as *intrinsically* important where they violate obligations, commitments, and principles of democratic elections in universal and regional human rights instruments. Article 21 in the 1948 Universal Declaration of Human Rights declares that "the will of the people shall be the basis of the authority of government; this will be expressed in periodic and genuine elections which shall be by universal and equal suffrage and shall be held by secret vote or by equivalent free voting procedures" guaranteeing everyone "the right to take part in the government of his country, directly or through freely chosen representatives."[33] But what are the other instrumental consequences of electoral malpractices for democratic cultures, including for citizens' confidence in electoral institutions, perceptions of electoral fraud, and support for democracy? And how do these consequences vary among global regions and countries?[34]

To consider these issues, in chapter 10 Nicholas Kerr analyzes the factors that influence citizens' perceptions of electoral integrity in terms of the performance of EMBs, the characteristics of the election environment, and citizens' individual attributes. The chapter evaluates these competing explanations using a multilevel analysis across 18 African countries from 1999 to 2008. Kerr concludes that EMB performance strengthens Africans' evaluations of integrity, while electoral violence significantly lowers these perceptions. Moreover, perceptions of integrity are consistently lower among electoral losers as well as those who are more educated.

In comparison, in chapter 11, Robert Mattes also examines whether elections change citizens' attitudes and behaviors toward democracy, and whether what matters in this process is repeated experience of elections over time, or whether the integrity of contests also matters. The chapter concludes that elections do matter by shaping how Africans see democracy working and that the quality of the contests shapes these attitudes, not just repeated experience of elections.

Are similar patterns evident elsewhere? In chapter 12, Arturo Maldonado and Mitchell Seligson examine the emergence of the third wave of democratization in Latin America and the Caribbean. In the region, elections have rapidly become more routinized and institutionalized, so that, with the sole exception of Cuba, regular competitive elections are now the norm. Citizens' trust in election, however, is a different matter; it shows a widespread lack of confidence but also sharp differences across Latin American countries. In this study, the authors examine individual- and contextual-level factors that explain differences in trust in elections across the Americas. In particular, they focus on contrasts among winners and losers, which is a strong predictor of trust in elections. Moreover, the winners-losers gap is contingent on the level of democracy, as measured by Freedom House. The gap is found to shrink in more democratic countries, suggesting that, as democracy deepens, this strengthens trust in electoral institutions. The chapter also tests whether the gap between winners and losers erodes over time, finding some evidence to support this expectation. Finally, the study analyzes whether the gap between winners and losers is smaller in countries where there is alternation in power, with the authors finding evidence to support this view.

In the United States, growing debate about voter fraud and voter suppression have become more polarized by party in recent years. Chapter 13 by Thad Hall and Charles Stewart examines how commonly election fraud, in its various forms, is thought to occur in American elections. Using data collected from surveys in all 50 states in the 2012 election, they test whether demographic, political, experiential, and state-level electoral attributes affect public evaluations of election fraud. They demonstrate that non-voters and supporters of losing candidates are more likely to think that voter fraud occurs in their community. A positive experience at the polls increases voter confidence in the process, but state laws requiring photo identification do not affect trust about in-person fraud activities, such as voter impersonation, voting twice, or non-citizens voting.

As a last point, what are the lessons from the ground? What have we learnt and what do we do next? Chapter 14 is a roundtable discussion held at the workshop meeting at the Weatherhead Center, Harvard University, presenting earlier drafts of these chapters, and engaging practitioners from many leading international organizations deeply engaged in strengthening electoral integrity. Roundtable participants included Staffan Darnolf (the International Foundation for Electoral Systems, IFES); Annette Fath-Lihic (International Institute for Democracy and Electoral Assistance, International IDEA); Eric Bjornlund (Democracy international); David Carroll (The Carter Center); Betilde Muñoz-Pogossian (Organization of American States, OAS); Aleida Ferreyra (United Nations Development Program, UNDP); and Chad Vickery (IFES). By reflecting upon the needs of the international community, this discussion seeks to identify the research agenda that would be most useful for practitioners, to build links between the practitioners and scholars.

Notes

1. Under the June 2006 electoral law, the 123 member National Assembly is elected with List Proportional Representation in provincial and municipal districts using the highest averages formula electoral quota.
2. http://www.aljazeera.com/indepth/features/2013/07/2013729101930837318.html.
3. http://www.voanews.com/content/as-cambodia-election-impasse-continues-opposition-pl ans-rally/1734644.html.
4. Robert Carmichael. July 27, 2013. "Cambodia Poll Monitors Report Problem With Indelible Ink." *Voice of America.*
5. *Phnom Penh Post,* August 1, 2013 http://www.phnompenhpost.com/national/extra-se ats-won-spread-across-country-cnrp.
6. http://www.necelect.org.kh/nec_english/index.php?option = com_content&view = article&id = 412&Itemid = 290.
7. http://www.comfrel.org/eng/components/com_mypublications/files/93595720130815_ Comfrel_Irregularity_Election_PR_Eng_Final.pdf.
8. National Election Commission. 2013. The 2013 general Election for the 5th Mandate of the National Assembly of the Kingdom of Cambodia. White paper (September 5, 2013). http:// www.necelect.org.kh/nec_english/index.php?option = com_content&view = article&id = 418&Itemid = 277.
9. Max Grömping. July 28, 2013. "Cambodian civil society keeps an eye on the election amidst widespread irregularities." http://electoralintegrity.blogspot.com.au/2013/07/cambodian-ci vil-society-keeps-eye-on.html.
10. http://www.cambodiadaily.com/elections/international-election-observers-proclaim- election-free-fair-37395/.
11. National Election Commission. 2013. The 2013 General Election for the 5th Mandate of the National Assembly of the Kingdom of Cambodia. White paper (September 5, 2013) p. IV. http://www.necelect.org.kh/nec_english/index.php?option = com_content&view = article&id = 418&Itemid = 277.
12. "The Secretary-General welcomes the peaceful conduct of the elections in Cambodia on 28 July. Amid reports of irregularities, the United Nations encourages the competent authorities to adjudicate complaints fairly and transparently, with the ultimate aim of ensuring the accu- rate determination of, and respect for, the will of the Cambodian people." http://www.un.org/ apps/news/story.asp?NewsID = 45558&Cr = cambodia&Cr1#.UkWTbIasim4.
13. http://www.hrw.org/news/2013/07/31/cambodia-ruling-party-orchestrated-vote-fraud.
14. National Election Commission. 2013. The 2013 general Election for the 5th Mandate of the National Assembly of the Kingdom of Cambodia. White paper (September 5, 2013) p. IV, http://www.necelect.org.kh/nec_english/index.php?option = com_content&view = article&id = 418&Itemid = 277.
15. Freedom House. *Freedom around the World 2013.* Using the Gastil index from 1 (high) to 7 (low), during 2012, Cambodia was rated 6 on political rights, and 5 on civil liberties. http://www.freedomhouse.org/sites/default/files/FIW%202013%20Charts%20and%20 Graphs%20for%20Web_0.pdf.
16. Pippa Norris. 2014. *Why Electoral Integrity Matters.* New York: Cambridge University Press.
17. Estimated from the Cross-National Time-Series data Archive, http://www.databanksinterna- tional.com/.
18. Staffan Lindberg. 2006. *Democracy and Elections in Africa.* Baltimore, MD: The Johns Hopkins University Press.

19. Francis Fukuyama. 1993. *The End of History and the Last Man Standing*. New York: Harper Perennial.
20. Thomas Carothers. 2002. "The End of the Transition Paradigm." *Journal of Democracy* 13: 5–21.
21. See, for example, Jennifer Gandhi and Ellen Lust-Okar. 2009. "Elections under authoritarianism." *Annual Review of Political Science* 12: 403–22; Susan D. Hyde. 2011. *The Pseudo-Democrat's Dilemma*. Ithaca: Cornell University Press; Sarah Birch. 2012. *Electoral Malpractice*. Oxford: Oxford University Press; Judith Kelley. 2012. *Monitoring Democracy: When International Election Observation Works and Why It Often Fails*. Princeton, NJ: Princeton University Press; Alberto Simpser. 2013. *Why Governments and Parties Manipulate Elections: Theory, Practice and Implications*. New York: Cambridge University Press; Daniella Donno. 2013. *Defending Democratic Norms*. New York: Oxford University Press. Pippa Norris. 2014. *Why Electoral Integrity Matters*. New York: Cambridge University Press.
22. Pippa Norris, Ferran Martinez i Coma and Richard W. Frank. 2014. "Assessing the quality of elections." *Journal of Democracy* (Forthcoming).
23. Steven Levitsky and Lucan Way. 2010. *Competitive Authoritarianism: Hybrid Regimes after the Cold War*, New York: Cambridge University Press.
24. This search was conducted using a keyword search of [(elec*) and (fraud)] by the years 1990–2012.
25. Pippa Norris. 2014. *Why Electoral Integrity Matters*. New York: Cambridge University Press.
26. Jennifer Gandhi and Ellen Lust-Okar. 2009. "Elections under authoritarianism." *Annual Review of Political Science* 12: 403–22; Alberto Simpser. 2013. *Why Governments and Parties Manipulate Elections: Theory, Practice and Implications*. New York: Cambridge University Press.
27. See, for example, The Global Commission on Elections, Democracy and Security. 2012. *Deepening Democracy: A Strategy for Improving the Integrity of Elections Worldwide*. Sweden: IDEA. The report was launched by the International Institute for Electoral Assistance (International IDEA) and the Kofi Annan Foundation in September 2012.
28. Jorgen Elklit and Palle Svensson. 1997. "What makes elections free and fair?" *Journal of Democracy* 8 (3): 32–46.
29. Pippa Norris. 2014. "Introduction: The new research agenda studying electoral integrity." Special issue of *Electoral Studies* 34(4) (Forthcoming).
30. Susan D. Hyde. 2011. *The Pseudo-Democrat's Dilemma*. Ithaca: Cornell University Press; Judith Kelley. 2012. *Monitoring Democracy: When International Election Observation Works and Why It Often Fails*. Princeton, NJ: Princeton University Press; Daniella Donno. 2013. *Defending Democratic Norms*. New York: Oxford University Press.
31. Rafael López-Pintor. 2000. *Electoral Management Bodies as Institutions of Governance*, New York: United Nations Development Programme; Shaheen Mozaffar and Andreas Schedler. 2002. "The comparative study of electoral governance: Introduction." *International Political Science Review* 23(1): 5–27; Alan Wall et al. 2006. *Electoral Management Design: The International IDEA Handbook*. Sweden: International IDEA.
32. Alan Wall. 2006. *Electoral Management Design: The International IDEA Handbook*. Sweden: International IDEA.
33. UN. 1948. Universal Declaration of Human Rights, http://www.un.org/en/documents/udhr/.
34. Pippa Norris. 2014. *Why Electoral Integrity Matters*. New York: Cambridge University Press.

2

Assessing Elections

AVERY DAVIS-ROBERTS AND DAVID J. CARROLL

This chapter provides an analytical framework for assessing elections based on obligations made in public international law.[1] We argue that international law offers a sound basis for understanding election integrity and assessing elections, since the obligations contained in international treaties and regional commitments have been freely accepted by the states that endorsed these documents. Assessment is therefore made against a mutually agreed benchmark recognized by the states themselves (and the international community at large) and is thus more likely to result in assessment reports seen as objective and credible. Furthermore, using international obligations in this way fosters greater transparency and accountability among observers by delivering a common set of criteria that can be shared with electoral stakeholders throughout the process. Finally, we argue that deepening a consensus formed around the principles within international legal obligations is an important means of promoting credible elections.

The chapter begins with a brief overview of the development of election observation and its role in international democracy development and aid. Part II provides a summary of the framework developed by The Carter Center and collaborating organizations, and the tools created to facilitate an assessment against international obligations—most importantly the Center's *Database of International Obligations for Democratic Elections*. We then outline our current efforts to develop a companion handbook to this database that explicitly links high-level obligations found in international treaties to election observers' data and analysis. In Part III, the 2012 Egyptian presidential election serves as a case study illustrating the use of our framework and analytical tools in a real-world setting. Next, we explore some of the challenges raised by an obligations-based approach, and why, despite these challenges, the use of international law remains the soundest basis for election assessment. Finally, we conclude by underscoring the important role that an obligations-based approach to election assessment can play in building a consensus definition for what constitutes democratic elections.

Part I: Democracy, Elections, and the Role of International Election Observers

The 1948 Universal Declaration of Human Rights codified the concept of genuine, periodic elections as the basis for the legitimate authority of government and secured the place of elections among the then emergent international human rights norms. Through the latter half of the twentieth century, and certainly since the end of the Cold War, an international consensus has emerged that periodic, genuine elections are an essential means of establishing the legitimate authority of governments and allowing citizens to hold their governments accountable. This consensus can be seen in the commitment of almost all countries to hold democratic multiparty elections. While it is widely agreed that elections are only one part of the larger and more complex process of democratic governance, elections provide a critically important snapshot of the health of democratic institutions and the status of key forces and conditions essential to democracy.

When they are recognized as credible and independent, election observation reports can shape perceptions about the quality and legitimacy of electoral processes (and hence the perceived legitimacy of the resulting government). In most cases, long-term observer missions that produce thorough, well-documented reports are trusted to provide relatively authoritative evaluations of an electoral process. In the end, the credibility and effectiveness of observers depends on the degree to which there is confidence and trust in their objectivity, professionalism, and comprehensiveness, which in turn rests in large part on quality of their methodology and its implementation.

In the past decade, criticism of observers has largely focused on questions of their professionalism and/or the use of different methodologies and standards either across groups or between countries. Observer missions are also criticized for having a limited impact on reducing fraud, improving elections, and encouraging more stable democracies over time.[2]

In many ways these critiques are flawed. While some organizations do deploy missions that lack professionalism and/or do not produce well-documented research and useful reports, many other organizations conduct election observation to higher standards. The *Declaration of Principles for International Election Observation* was an important development in this regard.[3] Initially commemorated at the United Nations in 2005 and now endorsed by more than 40 organizations, the *Declaration* established a consensus on how election observation is defined, and it provides guidance on the parameters of credible election observation. This guidance includes the appropriate scope and duration of missions and the key conditions required for effective missions, including host country guarantees to ensure access to key persons and electoral information, freedom of movement, and freedom to issue public reports on findings. The *Declaration* also serves as a foundational document for a global community of observer groups that meets regularly to reflect on experiences and common challenges. The leading international election observations organizations, particularly endorsers of the *Declaration of Principles* such as the European Union (EU), the Organization for Security and Cooperation in Europe (OSCE), the Electoral Institute for Sustainable Democracy in Africa (EISA), the Organization of American States, The Carter Center, the National Democratic Institute (NDI), and others, are committed to the continued improvement and harmonization of election observation methodologies in order to ensure more robust and consistent assessments of election processes.

In addition, some scholars' criticism of election observation's impact and its ability to prevent or deter fraud are misplaced and reflect a misunderstanding of the limited mandate and power of international election observation missions.[4] At its heart, election observation is a mechanism for providing a systematic third-party analysis and assessment of an electoral process. It is an evaluation. While observer missions hope that their presence and recommendations might help to reduce electoral malfeasance and improve elections in the long term, election observation missions have no control over the behavior of key national actors who are by far the most important drivers of electoral outcomes.

Election observation is best understood in the context of the broader field of democracy promotion, which encompasses a wide range of actors and activities, including the foreign aid and policy actions of governments and international organizations, technical assistance on elections and to a variety of democratic institutions (e.g., parties, legislatures, legal reform, etc.), and support to strengthen civil society organizations, among others. In this frame, the core objective of election observation is to provide a trusted and independent assessment of the quality of electoral processes—thus shaping *perceptions* of key actors and providing a potential road map for reform for both national actors and the broader community of democracy promotion actors.

As an outgrowth of the *Declaration of Principles,* The Carter Center developed its Democratic Election Standards project, a collaborative effort to design and implement an obligations-based methodological approach. The Center's applied work on election observation methodology also has drawn from other efforts to identify standards for democratic elections. These include academic research on the measurement of the quality of democracy, with elections as one component of that process[5]; academic writing with a more narrow focus on election assessment and observation[6]; and a variety of other analyses that have helped establish the connection between public international law and democratic elections.[7] Parallel to and reflective of these academic and analytic developments, election observation practitioners in the field have demonstrated a growing trend to reference public international law and/or international human rights in election assessments.[8]

Drawing theoretical insights from all of the above, the Center's obligations-based analytical framework represents an effort to develop a practical model for election observation, while also contributing to ongoing efforts to refine theory based on the collection and analysis of observation data from the field. The result is a framework that is robust, firmly rooted in public international law, implementable, and indicative of the evolving debate on these matters.

In the sections that follow, we outline the theoretical basis for the Carter Center's work, then demonstrate how this framework can be used to collect and analyze election data, employing the Center's observation of the 2012 presidential elections in Egypt as a case study.

Part II: Public International Law and Election Assessments

The use of public international law as the basis for understanding electoral integrity and assessing elections has several strengths.[9] First, states have voluntarily committed to the obligations contained therein through the signature and ratification of treaties, as well as through their own actions conforming to established state practice (customary law). On the one hand, these obligations are not externally developed standards, foreign to the state's relationship with its citizens, but have been developed by the community of states. On the other hand, the obligations found in treaties stand above the domestic law of the state and are grounded in broadly accepted international principles. Second, public international law is evolving and growing with the entry into force of new treaties and the endorsement of new political commitments. Third, while international human rights commitments create concrete obligations for state behavior, they are also aspirational in the sense that it is understood that state actions often fall short of obligations. They are legally binding but largely unenforceable, creating a global normative framework in which all states can improve on past practices as they strive to fulfill their international obligations. The unenforceable nature of these commitments poses many challenges for the international community, but it also provides a unique role for international civil society (including election observers) to help fill the enforcement gap by providing independent information needed to assess state behavior.[10] Fourth, assessments based on public international law and which take the entire electoral cycle into account allow observers to offer a more nuanced and comprehensive evaluation of elections. This in turn helps to move us away from the oversimplified "free and fair" sound bite that characterized many of the early election observation efforts. Finally, we argue that international obligations provide a sound foundation for fostering dialogue on the need for consistent understanding of the electoral process, not only among international observation organizations, but also among a broader range of actors such as election management bodies, parliamentarians, intergovernmental human rights bodies, election assistance providers, the international donor community, and academics.

As part of its Democratic Election Standards project, The Carter Center reviewed close to 200 sources of international law. These documents range from legally binding (though generally unenforceable) treaties such as the International Covenant on Civil and Political Rights (ICCPR), to interpretative documents, such as general comments of the United Nations Human Rights Committee, which provide general interpretation of the meaning of treaty obligations, to non-binding instruments and other documents that serve as evidence of emergent customary law and evolving norms based on the political commitments and/or practice of states over time. Reviewed as a whole, this body of documents provides a comprehensive set of 21 obligations for genuine elections. Figure 2.1 below shows these obligations arrayed in a two-level conceptual framework.

On the left is the macro-level obligation of states to hold genuine elections that express the will of the people. On the right are 20 obligations that are essential to

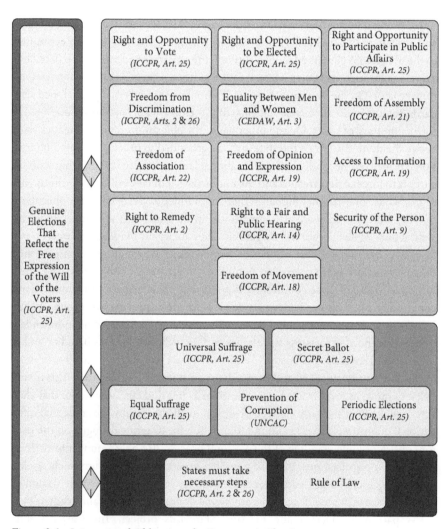

Figure 2.1: International Obligations for Democratic Elections

the fulfillment of that macro-level obligation. These include baseline obligations the state should implement—to ensure the rule of law, prevent corruption, and give effect to human rights, for example. Also included are individual and collective rights and freedoms. A short summary of these obligations is outlined in Table 2.1 below.

While these obligations are not always explicitly linked to democratic elections in the text of the treaties and other international instruments, it is clear that they are

Table 2.1: **Brief Summary of International Obligations for Democratic Elections**

The free expression of the will of the people through genuine elections—The popular will, freely expressed through genuine elections that offer voters real choice, must be the basis for legitimate political authority.

Periodic elections—Elections must be held at reasonable intervals, in a context that protects other fundamental rights.

The state must take necessary steps to ensure rights—States must take the steps necessary, in both law and practice, to give effect to fundamental rights.

The rule of law—The principle of the rule of law, implicit in international human rights law, is an essential condition for the fulfillment rights.

Universal suffrage—The state should ensure that the broadest pool of voters can cast ballots, only restricted on the basis of reasonable and objective criteria.

Equal suffrage—The weight or value of the votes of eligible voters should be equal.

Secret ballot—Voting by secret ballot is recognized as critical for protecting free expression.

Prevention of corruption—States should take steps to prevent corruption, including through the promotion of transparency measures.

Right and opportunity to participate in public affairs—Citizens have the right to participate in public affairs, including through civil society activities.

Right and opportunity to vote—Citizens have the right to vote, only restricted on the basis of objective and reasonable criteria.

Right and opportunity to be elected—Citizens have the right to be elected, only restricted on the basis of reasonable and objective criteria.

Freedom of assembly—Everyone has the right to assemble, including candidates and voters to assemble during campaigns. Restrictions must be prescribed by law and "necessary in a democratic society."

Freedom of association—Everyone has the right to free association including the establishment of political parties and other organizations. Restrictions must be prescribed by law.

(*Continued*)

Table 2.1: **Continued**

Freedom of movement—Everyone has the right to free movement, and any restrictions on that right must be proportionate to the interests it is intended to protect.
Equality before the law and freedom from discrimination—States are obligated to ensure equality before the law, and prevent discrimination in the exercise of rights and freedoms.
Equality between men and women—States must take steps to ensure de jure and de facto equality between men and women.
Freedom of opinion and expression—Everyone has the right to freedom of expression, including communication of information between voters and candidates and contribution to campaigns.
Access to information—Everyone has the right to seek and receive public information, helping to provide transparency in the electoral process.
Right to security of the person—Everyone has the right to security of the person, including protection from arbitrary arrest, detention, and exile. This includes protection of voters, candidates, poll workers, and observers from coercion or intimidation.
Right to an effective remedy—States are obligated to ensure an effective and timely remedy by a competent administrative, legislative, or judicial authority, including during an electoral process.
Right to a fair and public hearing—Everyone has the right to a fair and public hearing, with cases heard publicly and expeditiously by an impartial tribunal.

critical to the enjoyment of a participatory democratic process. These core obligations come into play in various parts of an electoral process, understood as cyclical in nature. Much more than a one-day event, elections involve ongoing political and institutional processes with critical steps taking place months (or years) in advance of (and after) voting. For the purposes of this analytical framework, emphasis is placed on those parts of the process that are most relevant to election observers, with greater emphasis on the eight to twelve months surrounding the election and less emphasis on those parts of the process that occur years before election day.

Practical Tools for Observation

The framework of 21 obligations tied to the electoral cycle creates the basic analytical framework that the Carter Center uses in its international election observation missions. Undergirding this framework is the Center's Database of Obligations for Democratic Elections, which was launched in August 2010.[11] The Database organizes excerpts from the nearly 200 sources of international law according to common theme, obligation, and part of the electoral process. Designed as a resource for election practitioners and researchers, the database is fully searchable by international obligation, part of the electoral process, treaty organization, and country, and also allows open text searches. Users can generate a summary report on the status of treaty ratification for any country in the world, as well as a variety of more focused reports depending on the interest of the analyst (e.g., focused on one or more specific obligations, part of the electoral process, or by obligations relevant to a specific country).

The database thus provides users with an invaluable resource on obligations-based benchmarks for assessing electoral integrity, based on international law and according to the parts of the electoral process. In addition to the database, the Center is developing several related tools, including reporting templates for long-term observers and core team analysts, observation forms for short-term observers, and, perhaps most importantly, a companion reference guide to the database.

This reference guide summarizes key information and central concepts in the database of obligations in a narrative format and provides a detailed list of checklist questions, which clarify the link between the higher-level obligations found in international law and the questions that election observer missions ask during the course of a mission. Intended as a ready reference tool for observer groups, researchers, academics, citizen observers and activists, and others, this handbook includes tables of assessment criteria and illustrative data collection questions reflecting two of the key functions of election observation—data collection and analysis. These tables can be used by observation missions to assess each part of the electoral process, as well as "cross-cutting" themes and topics, like campaign finance, or the ability of citizen observers to participate in the public affairs of their country.

In the Carter Center's work, a clear link is drawn between the relevant obligations found in international law and the associated key "assessment criteria," which guide observation mission members as they consider data collected in the field. The assessment criteria are, in turn, linked to a list of sample data collection questions that can guide data collection by observers deployed across the country. The list of questions is not comprehensive—it is impossible to foresee every important question that should be asked in the different contexts of electoral processes around the world. Instead, the questions are intended to give sufficient guidance to experienced observers and mission staff in developing specific reporting templates, tailored to the country being observed.

Part III: Using International Law to Assess Elections: A Case Study from Egypt

As mentioned above, the analytical framework outlined in this chapter is being used by The Carter Center in its election observation missions. In the following section, the runoff round of the 2012 Egyptian presidential elections is used to demonstrate our methodology in more detail, including the tools developed to assist in data collection, the analysis of information against obligations for democratic elections, and several difficult issues we encountered.

Some Background on Egypt's Presidential Elections

In February 2011, Egyptian President Hosni Mubarak stepped down after more than two weeks of ongoing public protest, bringing to an end his 30-year rule. In the weeks that followed, the Supreme Council of the Armed Forces (SCAF), which had interceded to serve as the interim transition authority, outlined a rough plan for an eventual transition to civilian rule. Central to the transition plan was the creation (and approval) of a new constitution, and the holding of parliamentary and presidential elections. However, the sequence of these events and the rules governing the elections and broader transition process remained unclear. In addition, a lack of genuine reform of the Egyptian government, the continuation of the emergency law, and the repression of political activities led to a deterioration of the relationship between the SCAF and the public. As a result, by late 2011, there was a growing rift between the military and civilians on the one hand and the Islamist and secular political forces on the other.

In the end, it was decided that parliamentary elections would be held first, between November 2011 and February 2012. The elected parliament would then appoint a committee charged with drafting the constitution. Succumbing to public pressure, the SCAF also agreed to hold presidential elections in parallel to these processes in May and June of 2012.

As the presidential elections approached, the electoral and political environment remained uncertain and confused. The increasingly unpopular SCAF continued to serve as the executive authority of the transition; the constitution drafting process that should have provided clarity on the role and function of the presidency remained stymied by political deadlock between the Islamists and secular forces; the legality of the parliament itself was being challenged in court; and the political atmosphere was increasingly polarized. It was in this context that The Carter Center deployed a mission to observe the 2012 presidential elections.

The Carter Center's Mission in Egypt

The Carter Center established a presence in Egypt in May 2011. Following formal accreditation from the Supreme Judicial Commission of Elections (SJCE), the Center deployed long-term observers to monitor the People's Assembly election in November 2011—the first international election observation mission to be formally accredited in Egypt's history. Following the parliamentary elections, the Center remained in Egypt to observe the presidential elections held in May and the runoff election in June 2012.[12]

The presidential election was overseen by a different authority—the Presidential Election Commission—which provided full accreditation to the Center only one week prior to the first day of voting for the election's first round. This severely hampered the ability of the Center to effectively observe pre-election processes in the weeks leading up to the first round of voting. In addition, the Commission issued a series of regulations that appeared initially to limit the ability of observers to release public statements, and which reduced observers' access to a polling station to only 30 minutes. While formally overly restrictive, in practice Carter Center observers reported that the time restrictions were not applied at most polling stations.

Given the Commission's restrictions, the Carter Center seriously considered withdrawing its observers, but ultimately decided to deploy a "limited mission" that focused on only those aspects of the process to which it was given access. The Center also made clear in its public statements released before the elections that these restrictions undermined meaningful observation and that the Center would not deploy observers if such restrictions were in force in future elections. In the end, the Center's observers were deployed for approximately two months, with the majority of their observations taking place in the 10 days immediately preceding the first round of the election and the weeks before and after the second round.

Observation and assessment therefore focused on the electoral institutions and legal framework for the elections, candidate registration, campaigning immediately before the first and second rounds of voting, voter education, the impact of voter registration issues during voting, election day voting processes, counting and aggregation, and electoral dispute resolution. The Carter Center could not comment on the longer-term pre-election campaign period, candidate nomination, voter registration process, and electoral complaints prior to the first round of voting.

The Carter Center released two statements on the presidential elections. The first was narrowly focused on the administration of the first round of voting. The second statement, released two days after the runoff, focused not only on election issues but, more importantly, on the worrisome trajectory of Egypt's imperiled democratic transition.

Data Gathered by Carter Center Observers: The Example of Voter Education

In this chapter we focus on reports by Carter Center observers regarding two sets of issues: the quality of voter education and the voting processes. Although voter education is not usually considered a critical issue in most elections, it took on added significance in the 2012 Egyptian presidential elections, which were characterized by high levels of uncertainty. The presidential elections were the fourth time in 18 months that Egyptians were voting—under frequently changing legal conditions. In addition, there was a lack of clarity about key issues, including the powers of the president to be elected. Carter Center observers reported on voter education using both qualitative long-term observation data and quantitative reports by short-term observers.

In Egypt, as in other Carter Center missions, long-term observers (LTOs) were deployed before election day and remained in the country after each of the two voting rounds to observe critical post-election processes. The principal responsibility of LTOs is collecting information about the electoral process and the political context in regions across the country and submitting weekly narrative reports on their findings in the weeks and months before and after election day. This information is gathered through interviews with election stakeholders such as election authorities, political party representatives, civil society representatives, voters, and others. In addition, LTOs conduct direct observation of campaign events, including rallies.

The LTOs' data collection and reporting is guided by international obligations in a number of ways. First, LTOs receive training not only on key aspects of the electoral process that they will be observing (on issues like the legal framework for the process, election procedures, etc.), but also on the obligations that underpin that aspect of the electoral process. Second, reporting templates and tools focus on the main obligations and principles pertinent to that part of the process, with guiding questions for LTOs' interviews and report drafting. All of this information is incorporated in the LTO reporting template.

The deployment of short-term observers (STOs) is a standard part of the observation methodology of most election observation organizations. STOs are typically deployed across the country for 7 to 10 days around the election, after a briefing on the electoral process, and instruction on how to perform their role as observers. The STOs' primary tasks are to collect information on the immediate pre-election environment, to hold last-minute meetings with local election stakeholders on electoral preparations, and to visit polling stations on election day, gathering information on the conduct of polling using a checklist observer form. The information collected in the checklist is then sent back to the mission's analysis center, where information from across the country is collated and patterns identified and assessed.

Like LTOs, the STOs' work is guided by international obligations for democratic elections. As part of the process of developing the analytical framework outlined here, the Carter Center has developed a number of questions in an election-day checklist form to assess how far pertinent obligations have been fulfilled. By making this link more explicit, the analysis of data against benchmarks based on obligations becomes a standardized process.

Understanding Observer Data

The combination of qualitative data from interviews conducted by LTOs, together with the largely quantitative data collected by STOs, provides a nuanced picture of an election as it unfolds. Data gathered by LTOs and STOs are reviewed throughout the electoral process by the mission's core team of election analysts, who assess the election against international obligations.

Over the course of their two-month deployment, LTOs in Egypt submitted a number of weekly reports. In each report, information regarding the voter education process in their area of responsibility was recorded and submitted to the mission's core team of analysts and experts, who assessed the data against obligations and indicators derived from those obligations.

The LTO teams from various areas of Egypt assess the degree to which key obligations appear to have been fulfilled each week using a three-point scale: "1" indicates that the obligations have not been adequately fulfilled, "2" indicates that they have been partially fulfilled, and "3" that they have been fulfilled to a reasonable extent. This information is then considered in conjunction with data collected by STOs, focusing on the impact of voter education on the implementation of procedures on election day.

The assessment suggested that while the Egyptian state did not take the steps necessary to provide voter education campaigns, the right to vote was not undermined (in the polling stations visited by Carter Center observers). Because multiple international obligations are related to each part of the electoral process, it is common for countries to partially fulfill their obligations, or to meet some obligations but not others. It is then the observation mission's task to assess what this means in the broader electoral context and provide recommendations for future improvement. In this case, the mission recommended that steps be taken to ensure adequate voter education in future elections.

While observer data can be used to analyze part of the electoral process, such as voter education, it can also be used to understand the degree to which specific obligations (like the right to vote or the secret ballot) have been fulfilled.

The data provide a generally positive assessment of Egypt's fulfillment of relevant obligations during the presidential runoff. However, it is important to remember that the overall assessment of the fulfillment of obligations also has to include information collected before and after the elections—similar to the process outlined above regarding voter education.

Discussion

At the end of the day, observation missions must reach an overall conclusion about the integrity of the electoral process and whether it fulfilled the state's obligations regarding democratic elections. In the case of the 2012 presidential elections in Egypt, the limitations placed on The Carter Center's mission prevented a full evaluation of the entire electoral process. Instead, the Center could only judge those parts to which it had access. For this reason the main conclusions in the Center's preliminary statement focused on only a few key issues, including: political parties' access to the voters list; the election's legal framework; the tone of electoral campaigns; voting and vote counting; and the poor provision of voter education.

Taking a systematic approach to data collection and analysis helps observers ensure consistency in their methods and in their overall conclusions. Nevertheless, given the complexity of electoral events and the reality that observers' reporting—no matter how thorough and well documented—will sometimes be imperfect, observer mission assessments necessarily include some subjective judgments about the process and the degree to which obligations are fulfilled.

However, the accuracy and balance of these assessments can be aided by the consideration of several key factors:

- *The frequency and significance of reported problems or irregularities*—Election observation missions should consider the number and relative importance of reported irregularities. Only one or two reports from observers of long lines due to polling station problems are likely to represent isolated issues and thus may end up a footnote in a preliminary statement. However, if observers report long lines due to procedural or other problems in many polling stations across the country, such that voters' ability to exercise their franchise is threatened, this would be a greater cause for concern. So might reports of long lines in particular areas of the country with marginalized populations or in areas recognized as strongholds of one political party or group (see section below on "patterns of discrimination").

- *Deliberate action vs. unintentional errors*—Observer missions should also consider whether reported irregularities are the result of intentional action on the part of the state, official actors, or others to manipulate the process, or whether observed patterns instead suggest that the state has made a good-faith attempt to meet obligations and that the irregularities appear to result from unintentional errors, perhaps due to lack of training, low skills, or other shortcomings. While unintentional irregularities tend to be a lesser concern, they can represent a serious problem if they are numerous or appear to have a systematic impact.

- *Emerging patterns of discrimination*—Relatedly, observers should also consider whether reported irregularities are systematic and appear as a pattern that may—intentionally or unintentionally—undermine the electoral rights of segments of the population (for example, specific geographic areas or areas that are strongholds of certain parties or that have large, marginalized populations).

- *The margin of victory*—Finally, election observation missions should consider whether the severity of an irregularity and failure to meet obligations is such that it could have a material effect on the final results, perhaps even changing who wins the election. In such cases, the margin of victory in the final results becomes an especially important factor in the evaluation process. That is, while failure to meet obligations is always of concern, it is even more so when data suggest that the failure could have changed the elections results. An obvious example is when observer reports indicate that the number of voters left off a voters list exceeds the margin of victory. Assessing the degree to which irregularities or failures to meet obligations affects election results can be particularly challenging, however, as it is often very difficult to quantify the impact of some irregularities or problems, and additional research and analysis in this area is warranted.

It is important to note that while international obligations apply equally to all states that commit themselves to these obligations, election observation missions take in account important "mitigating factors" (such as whether an election is the first after a conflict, or follows a difficult transition from authoritarian rule, etc.) where expectations regarding states' meeting of the obligations might reasonably be temporarily lower. In short, while the standard for the fulfillment of international obligations is the same for all elections in all countries, in some countries the context might make it impractical to expect a high degree of fulfillment—at least for an initial period. Even in such cases, however, observation missions should clearly underscore areas where important shortfalls in meeting obligations exist and stress that the immediate "mitigating factors" will not be an acceptable excuse for a continued failure to meet obligations in the future.

Conclusions

International election observation plays an important role in shaping public perceptions about the quality and integrity of an electoral process. The importance of this function merits a transparent and objective basis for making election assessments, and (given the standing of international law among states) we believe that the obligations found in international law provide such a foundation. Not only does international law provide high-level principles, but (as demonstrated above) it can be used to create assessment benchmarks and questions for data collection so that observer mission findings are firmly rooted in these principles.

The biggest challenges of any election assessment are analyzing the data collected, determining what they signify about the process as a whole, and reaching an overall conclusion. It is also a challenge to ensure that the recommendations are useful (and feasible) to the governmental agencies who will ultimately implement them. These challenges remain when using an obligations-based approach to election observation like the one we describe here.

Further, the analytical framework outlined in this chapter does not resolve a number of challenging questions. For example, how much weight or value should be assigned to the various parts of the electoral process and the relevant obligations when trying to arrive at an overall assessment of the process? Are certain obligations so fundamental to a democratic election that any significant shortfall in meeting these obligations necessarily means that the election fails to meet critical international standards (for example the right to an effective remedy, freedom from discrimination, or universal suffrage)? Are all obligations equally essential, or are some more important than others? Do obligations have equal importance and weight in all countries and in all political contexts? Does the relative importance of obligations fluctuate depending on the democratic development of the country? These are critically important questions that require significant investments of time and resources to even attempt to address them adequately.

Therefore, we believe that research should continue to consider the relative weights of obligations and electoral phases. In addition, we argue that observers and stakeholders must apply a consistent set of obligations and standards when evaluating electoral processes. At the same time, we believe that elections need to be understood and assessed in their political and cultural context, because the relative significance of obligations is linked to and can only be fully understood and assessed in the local context. While it is important to meet obligations during all stages of the electoral process, in some contexts, one or more obligations might be reasonably deviated from without fundamentally undermining the overall process.

Going forward, it will be critical that consensus-building efforts on these issues continue, not only among international election observation organizations but among a broader array of electoral stakeholders including election management bodies, parliamentarians, the media, election assistance providers, the academy, and others. Wider agreement on the components and principles of elections with integrity will, in the long run, promote better elections. The assessment method outlined in this chapter is one step in this process.

Notes

1. For purposes of brevity and clarity, for the rest of this chapter we use the term "international law" when referring to public international law.
2. See Ursula Daxecker and Gerald Schneider chapter (chapter 8, this volume); Alberto Simpser and Daniela Donno. 2012. "Can International Election Monitoring Harm Governance?" *The Journal of Politics* 74(2): 501–513; Judith G. Kelley. 2009. "The More the Merrier? The Effects of Having Multiple International Election Monitoring Organizations." *Perspectives on Politics* 7(1): 59–64.
3. Declaration of Principles for International Election Observation, http://www.carter-center.org/resources/pdfs/peace/democracy/des/declaration_code_english_revised.pdf (accessed August 20, 2013).
4. Susan D. Hyde and Judith G. Kelley. 2011. "The Limits of Election Monitoring: What Independent Observers Can (and Can't) Do." *Foreign Affairs*, June 28, 2011. http://www.foreignaffairs.com/articles/67968/susan-d-hyde-and-judith-g-kelley/the-limits-of-election-monitoring (accessed August 23, 2013); John Stremlau and David J. Carroll. 2011. "Monitoring the Monitors: What Everyone Gets Wrong About Election Observers." *Foreign Affairs*, September 14, 2011. http://www.cartercenter.org/news/publications/peace/democracy_publications/monitoring_the_monitors.html (accessed September 18, 2013).

5. Recent work in this regard includes: David Beetham. 2004. "Towards a Universal Framework for Democracy Assessment." *Democratization* 11(2): 1–17; Gerardo Munck. 2009. *Measuring Democracy: A Bridge Between Scholarship and Politics.* Baltimore: Johns Hopkins Press; Lise Storm. 2008. "An Elemental Definition of Democracy and Its Advantages for Comparing Political Regime Types." *Democratization* 15(2): 215–229; Thomas A. Koelble and Edward Lipuma. 2008. "Democratizing Democracy: A Postcolonial Critique of Conventional Approaches to the 'Measurement of Democracy'". *Democratization* 15(1): 1–28.

6. See, for example, Thomas Carothers. 1997. "The Observers Observed." *Journal of Democracy* 8(3): 17–31; Eric Bjornlund. 2004. *Beyond Free and Fair: Monitoring Elections and Building Democracy.* Washington D.C.: Woodrow Wilson Center Press; Jonathan Hartlyn and Jennifer McCoy. 2006. "Observer Paradoxes: How to Assess Electoral Manipulation." In *Electoral Authoritarianism: The Dynamics of Unfree Competition*, ed. Andreas Shchedler. Boulder, CO: Lynne Rienner; Jørgen Elklit and Palle Svensson. 1997. "What Makes Elections Free and Fair?" *Journal of Democracy*, 8(3): 32–46; Jørgen Elklit and Andrew Reynolds. 2005. "A Framework for the Systematic Study of Election Quality." *Democratization* 12(2): 147–162; Susan D. Hyde. 2008. "How International Observers Detect and Deter Fraud." In *Election Fraud: Detecting and Deterring Electoral Manipulation*, eds. R. Michael Alvarez, Thad E. Hall, and Susan D. Hyde. Washington, D.C.: Brooking Institution Press.

7. On public international law and elections, see, for example, Guy Goodwin-Gill. 2006. *Free and Fair Elections: New Expanded Edition.* Geneva: Inter-Parliamentary Union; Michael D. Boda. 2005. "Judging Elections by Public International Law: A Tentative Framework." In *Revisiting Free and Fair*, ed. Michael D. Boda. Geneva: Inter-parliamentary Union; Michael D. Boda. 2008. "Judging Free and Fair: International Law as a Norm for Electoral Practice." Oxford: Faculty of Law, University of Oxford; Veronika Hinz and Marku Suksi. 2003. *Election Elements: On International Standards of Electoral Participation.* Åbo, Finland: Institute for Human Rights; Larry Garber. 1984. *Guidelines for International Election Observing.* Washington D.C.: International Human Rights Law Group; Patrick Merloe. 2009. "Human rights—the Basis for Inclusiveness, Transparency, Accountability and Public Confidence in Elections." In *International Principles for Democratic Elections*, ed. John Hardin Young, Washington D.C.: American Bar Association; Gregory H. Fox. 1992. "The Right to Political Participation in International Law." *Yale Journal of International Law* 17(2): 539–607. Thomas M. Frank. 1992. "The Emerging Right to Democratic Governance." *The American Journal of International Law* 86(1): 46–49; Robert Pastor. 1998. "Mediating Elections." *Journal of Democracy* 9(1): 154–163; and Roland Rich. 2001. "Bringing Democracy into International Law." *Journal of Democracy* 12(3): 20–34.

8. See, for example, the work of the European Union, the Organization for Security and Cooperation in Europe, The Electoral Institute for Sustainable Democracy in Africa, and the National Democratic Institute for International Affairs.

9. See Avery Davis-Roberts and David J. Carroll. 2010. "Using International Law to Assess Elections." *Democratization*, 17:3: 416–441; David J. Carroll and Avery Davis-Roberts. 2013. "The Carter Center and Election Observation: An Obligations-Based Approach for Assessing Elections." *Election Law Journal*, 12(1): 87–93; and chapter 3 of this volume by Pippa Norris, Jørgen Elklit, and Andrew Reynolds.

10. Emilie M. Hafner-Burton and Kiyoteru Tsutsui. 2005. "Human Rights in a Globalizing World: The Paradox of Empty Promises." *American Journal of Sociology* 110(5): 1373–1411.

11. The Carter Center Database of Obligations for Democratic Elections, available at http://electionstandards.cartercenter.org

12. Statements from The Carter Center's Election Observation Mission to Egypt, http://www.cartercenter.org/news/publications/election_reports.html#egypt (accessed August 20, 2013).

3

Methods and Evidence

PIPPA NORRIS, JØRGEN ELKLIT, AND ANDREW REYNOLDS

Recent years have seen growing interest in conceptualizing and measuring notions of electoral integrity and malpractice. One reason is that these concepts are at the heart of contemporary scholarly debates about regime classifications. Following in the deep footprints of Joseph Schumpeter, minimalist notions have long focused on elections as the cornerstone of democracy.[1] Hence, Przeworski argues that "democracy is a system in which parties lose elections."[2] Przeworski et al. root their regime classification in a theory of "electoral contestation." In democratic regimes, those who govern are selected through contested elections, the opposition has some chance of winning, and elections have uncertainty, irreversibility of the results, and repeatability.[3] Yet the underlying notion of "electoral contestation" at the heart of this argument, which seems parsimonious and precise, is far from black and white in practice. In many democracies, opposition and government parties fight on a reasonably level playing field in gaining equitable access to the ballot, media, funds, and seats. In many other states, however, notably in "hybrid," "electoral autocracies," or "competitive authoritarian" regimes, multiparty competition is only allowed within strict boundaries and the odds are heavily stacked to favor the incumbent.[4] The accuracy of any regime classification based on minimalist notions therefore depends heavily upon the precision and reliability with which scholars can measure the underlying notions of electoral "contestation."

Notions of electoral integrity have also become central to discussions about how far, and under what conditions, events at the ballot box contribute toward regime transitions and the process of democratization.[5] These concepts are also believed to be important for emerging democracies and consolidated democracies, if lack of integrity weakens feelings of institutional trust, regime legitimacy, and support for democracy.[6] The consequences of vote rigging, bribery, fraud, and ballot stuffing are thought to be even more serious in transitional regimes and fragile states, if a backlash against such practices has the capacity to catalyze popular protests, opposition boycotts, and electoral violence.[7]

For practitioners as well, as elections have spread worldwide, organizations within the international community have played an increasingly active role in seeking to raise the quality of these contests so that they meet international standards and principles. This includes the work of regional and global agencies such as the United Nations, United Nations Development Programme (UNDP), Organization of American States (OAS), African Union (AU), European Union, Organization for Security and Cooperation in Europe (OSCE), International Foundation for Electoral Systems (IFES), Electoral Institute for Sustainable Democracy in Africa (EISA), International Institute for Democracy and Electoral Assistance (International IDEA), and the Carter Center. Popular interventions involve electoral monitoring by observer missions.[8] Domestic attempts at monitoring include the activities of election watch non-governmental organizations (NGOs), the use of social media, and the deployment of other innovative technologies like crowdsourcing. Other policies—probably even more important in the long term—include strengthening the capacity, independence, professional skills, and resources of Electoral Management Bodies (EMBs), exemplified by the ACE Electoral Knowledge Network and the Bridge training program.[9] Attention has also been given to the mechanisms available to mediate in cases of electoral disputes, strengthening the court systems' capacity to mediate impartially and in a timely fashion, thereby redressing grievances and preventing the spread of conflict.

Evaluations monitoring the effectiveness of any of these policies and programs require systematic evidence and careful measurement. The "indicator revolution" sweeping through other subfields of democratic governance, such as those concerning governance, corruption perceptions, media freedom, and human rights, means that the measurement of electoral integrity is in danger of lagging behind.[10]

For all these reasons—whether because of academic or political interest in the study of regime classification or transformation, interest in providing a baseline for what kinds of election complaints should be seen as reasonable, or fear of lagging behind other democratic governance subfields in methodological and conceptual development—it is important to clarify the underlying concepts of electoral integrity and malpractice, and to establish systematic, valid, and reliable operational indicators of these concepts, which could be used by scholars and practitioners to monitor election quality.

To consider these issues, the first part of this chapter unpacks electoral integrity as a concept, while the second part reviews the pros and cons of several approaches to gathering evidence. Previous studies have usually relied upon one or several primary sources, including case studies, performance indices, elite interviews, content analysis of observer mission reports, human rights reports, coding of news media coverage, forensic analysis of election results, randomized evaluations using natural or field experiments, and also public opinion surveys. It is argued that many of these approaches and analytical techniques are useful, but they commonly suffer from important limitations, such as in terms of conceptual validity, cross-national coverage, and/or capacity to monitor all stages of the electoral cycle. The third part argues that these methods would benefit by being supplemented by evidence from a global survey of expert opinion. The Perception of Electoral Integrity (PEI) Index is designed to offer a comprehensive, systematic, and robust measure, which can usefully complement many other sources of empirical evidence and play a valuable role for both the academic and the policymaking communities. The next chapter, by Martínez i Coma and Richard Frank, goes on to discuss the design and the results of the expert survey in more detail.

The Concept of Electoral Integrity

Any valid, systematic, and reliable measures have to be rooted in clear conceptual foundations. Many alternative notions are common, especially the description of contests as "free and fair."[11] In this chapter, building upon Davies-Roberts and Carroll in chapter 2, the core notion of "electoral integrity" is understood to refer to agreed international principles, values, and standards of elections, applying universally to all countries worldwide throughout the electoral cycle, including during the pre-electoral period, the campaign, and on polling day and its aftermath. Thus, we are conceptually quite close to the approach taken by the Carter Center. However, Davis-Roberts and Carroll develop a coherent conceptual baseline, building on the entire body of international law instruments against which results from international election observation missions can be assessed, while we admittedly have a less stringent—but maybe more realistic and more easily applicable—conceptual underpinning. Conversely, electoral malpractice refers to violations of electoral integrity. We are aware that "electoral malpractice" is sometimes conceptualized differently, but here it is to be understood either as violations of or a direct contrast to electoral integrity—primarily as a convenient shorthand.

This conceptualization has several distinct features that are worth highlighting.

First, it emphasizes the *universality* of the notion, which is applicable to long-established democracies as well as elsewhere. In this conceptualization, issues of integrity can arise concerning problems such as Floridian hanging chads and more restrictive registration process introduced in the United States, election management in the UK, as well as issues of party funding and media regulation in Western Europe. Electoral integrity is not simply a challenge facing electoral autocracies or newer democracies. As such, measurement needs to be applicable to all types of regimes, including long-established democracies, as well as manipulated contests held in the worst electoral autocracies.

Second, it emphasizes the role of *international principles, values, and standards* so that the concept goes beyond more restrictive notions, which focus purely upon domestic legal provisions.[12] The previous chapter established an analytical framework based on public international law. This framework is primarily intended to provide an objective baseline for analyzing international election observation reports, but it can also be very useful when attempting to conceptualize electoral integrity.

Problems of electoral malpractice may, and indeed often do, violate a country's laws. But domestic laws can also be used to impose undue restrictions upon the rights of opposition candidates and parties, to deny the right to vote for certain groups, to restrict fundamental freedoms of organization or speech, or to manipulate electoral competition so that these practices violate international standards, values, and principles. It remains the case that not all important aspects of electoral integrity are reflected in international agreements, including appropriate standards governing media coverage and regulating campaign finance. Nevertheless, widespread agreement has been reached, as reflected in text such as the "Declaration of principles for international election observation" endorsed at the United Nations in 2005, and in related codes of conduct, guidelines, treaties, and conventions published by multilateral associations engaged in electoral observation missions.[13]

Third, by escaping some of the common platitudes of "free and fair," the open-ended nature of the concept allows a range of normative values to be reflected and debated in assessments about the quality of elections. Thus, principles of effectiveness, efficiency, inclusiveness, transparency, equality, honesty, and accuracy can all be recognized as potentially important values underlying the overarching notion of electoral integrity, as well as the standard claims that elections should be free from undue constraints and fair to all parties. Poorly administered voter registers, unequal access to campaign media and funds, and laws limiting ballot access, from this perspective, can all undermine electoral integrity as much as fair vote counts or restrictions on freedom of speech.

Lastly, it also emphasizes the *cyclical* nature of electoral processes. Elections are often popularly understood to involve polling day and its aftermath. This view emphasizes problems arising through practices such as voter intimidation, carousel voting, ballot stuffing, fraud, and vote rigging at the count. Yet from the perspective of management bodies, and the multilateral agencies seeking to strengthen the capacity of these bodies, elections should be understood either as a continuous process or as an electoral cycle, as illustrated in Figure 3.1. The figure outlines the phases of an electoral cycle, which form the basis of our assessment instrument, presented in the next chapter.

The assessment of the electoral cycle requires all phases to be assessed, as they are all important in their own right and are intimately interwoven.[14] This perspective is close to the "menu of manipulation" that Schedler identified, where each link in the chain can be broken, undermining electoral integrity.[15]

Alternative Methods and Approaches

The concept of electoral integrity can be monitored through a range of comparative evidence and analytical techniques. Previous research has usually relied upon one or several primary sources, including case studies, performance indices, and elite

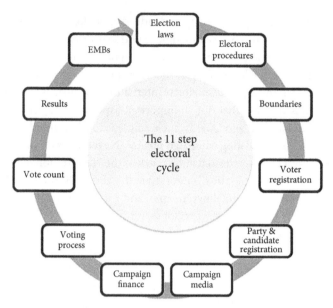

Figure 3.1: The electoral cycle

interviews, observer mission reports, human rights reports, coding of news media coverage, forensic analysis of election results, randomized evaluations using natural or field experiments, and also public opinion surveys. These approaches each involve certain well-known strengths and weaknesses. To supplement these existing techniques and sources of evidence, the Electoral Integrity Project has developed a systematic comparative method for assessing electoral integrity by implementing a global survey measuring expert perceptions of electoral integrity.

Case Studies, Performance Indices, and Elite Interviews

One common qualitative approach has been to examine problems of electoral maladministration and fraud within specific historical case studies, such as in Mexico and Costa Rica.[16] By tracing the impact of processes of democratization and reform, and examining performance indices from legal records, parallel vote tabulations, and official vote counts, single nation cases can provide detailed descriptive depth lacking in more abstract comparative studies. Complementing this approach, research seeking to evaluate the performance of electoral administrative bodies in established democracies, including in the United States and the United Kingdom, has drawn on several evaluation techniques derived from public sector management.[17] This includes surveys of citizens (see Hall and Stewart, chapter 13, this volume), local poll workers, and also in-depth personal interviews with more senior election officials in election management bodies (see James, chapter 8), as well as analysis of electoral expenditures (see Clark, chapter 9, this volume). Such studies provide insights into the organizational culture and structural constraints that officials confront when managing the process of registering, balloting, and polling. The concern is to establish metrics to audit how far elections meet public sector standards such as accuracy, transparency, efficiency, cost-effectiveness, and accountability. Nevertheless, the richness and depth of qualitative studies means that it is often difficult to generalize from these, even across organizational units within states and regions in the same country, let alone across diverse societal and political contexts. Although the comparative study of electoral management bodies is attracting a growing literature, we still know little about the structure and workings of these agencies.

Observer Mission Reports

Observer missions provide rich and detailed on-the-ground reports of procedures and practices in specific contests. The best-run missions by multilateral organizations provide an invaluable source of detailed information based on agreed international standards (see for example, chapter 2, this volume).[18] Observer reports from different agencies have been coded by scholars using content analysis to generate standardized cross-national datasets, some of which have subsequently also been used by other scholars (see, for example, chapter 5, this volume).[19]

Evidence derived from observer mission reports provides an invaluable source of information that can strengthen enforcement of global norms and help determine priorities for capacity building and technical aid provided by the international community. Nevertheless, reliance upon this source alone in cross-national research studies may generate a systematic bias in the sample of elections covered, as only certain countries allow and attract observer missions. Needs assessment exercises prior to deployment by international agencies often determine whether conditions are thought appropriate for ordinary observation missions. Hence, the OSCE guidelines recommend not sending observers to places with severe security threats. Moreover, not all countries allow international observers to visit, and powerful autocratic states with the most blatant disregard for human rights are most likely to prevent any mission. Daxecker and Schneider (chapter 5, this volume) also demonstrate how some governments—especially in Africa and the former Soviet Union—strategically invite different kinds of observer organizations, hoping for mixed assessments of the electoral exercise. In this manner, it might be easier to get away with various kinds of fraudulent behavior or it might even be not so necessary to commit fraud, as the reports from the more lenient election observation missions will probably not be very critical, no matter what. On the other hand, given limited budgets and personnel, observer missions are also not sent to countries where there are believed to be few or no major problems of electoral integrity.[20] Thus, both "floor" and "ceiling" effects determine the types of contests included in observer reports, and how far we can generalize from these cases. "Experts" employed as international observers—as well as US Department of State officials, diplomats or parliamentarians from other countries, and Western journalists—may also utilize evaluative standards, drawing primarily upon their own experiences but diverging sharply from the perceptions of ordinary citizens living within the observed countries.

Moreover, where international election observers are parachuted into a country for a short two- or three-week period, they may make snap judgments based on impressionistic and incomplete evidence, focused on the conduct of the vote and count on election day, rather than examining all the lengthy steps leading up to polling day during the whole electoral cycle. Observation missions (often from abroad and with their own government's or regional organization's lead) may also evaluate an election in a politicized way, detached from any relation to the integrity of the process on the ground. Another potential limit of relying upon election assessment mission statements has been the tendency of these reports to describe electoral integrity in bimodal terms. The overall election is often judged as either good or bad; or, when a fudge is required, it is labeled "substantially free and fair." The final assessment in reports is usually categorical rather than on a continuous graded scale. This tendency is reinforced by scholars developing binary regime typologies, who seek to create clear categories, thereby reducing or even eliminating the "fuzzy," "gray," or "hybrid" cases, even though many cases have exactly that character.

There has long been a debate about whether categorical or continuous measures of democracy are preferable, and each approach has certain strengths and weaknesses, depending upon the pragmatic needs of researchers.[21] But there is no doubt that electoral integrity varies across cases and across time on a continuum. Election management within a country can be strong in some areas and weak in others. The playing field that regulates the campaign can vary subtly in both de jure and de facto ways. Elections clearly can improve as well as decline on a number of dimensions over time. In essence, one needs to look at both process and outcome to gauge the full picture of electoral integrity.

Coding Media Reports

Content analysis of media reports, summarized in compilation sources such as *Keesing's World News Archives*, provides another common source for assessing the quality of electoral competition. For example, Susan Hyde and Nikolay Marinov's coding of National Elections Across Democracy and Autocracy (NELDA) uses an extensive list of secondary sources, including academic election handbooks, online resources, news media, and official reports. It thereby allows comprehensive analysis of countries worldwide, with the most recent version extending coverage to all national legislative and presidential election events in independent nation-states with populations over half a million during the period from 1945 to

2010.[22] Similarly, media reports have been used as an important information source to classify regimes.[23] More sophisticated machine coding is become more widely available for "event analysis," for example for incidence of protests, riots, or violence surrounding election campaigns and polling day.

Yet overreliance upon journalistic reporting, by itself, may also prove dangerously misleading. Estimates of the extent of electoral malpractices are likely to be exaggerated, as the media systematically skew coverage toward cases that are newsworthy, highlighting headline stories of electoral corruption, disputes, and conflict. Given the well-known predominance of the global media, the available journalistic coverage is also open to criticism that it is systematically biased toward the values and standards of (Western) reporters and broadcasters, and that it focuses most attention upon elections held in major world powers and in states of strategic or cultural interest to Western readers and viewers. For example, the Global Database of Events, Language, and Tone (GDELT), one major machine-coded events database with ambitious claims to cover "the entire planet," draws upon international news sources, such as those carried in *AfricaNews, Agence France Presse, Associated Press Online, Associated Press Worldstream, BBC Monitoring, Christian Science Monitor, Facts on File, Foreign Broadcast Information Service, New York Times, Google News, United Press International,* the *Washington Post,* and *Xinhua.*[24] Despite the scope, granularity, and thoroughness, this approach faces major challenges given the well-established, imbalanced international news flows available from these sources, in addition to disregarding the localized meanings that international journalists and broadcasters use to frame stories interpreting global events.[25]

Human Rights Reports

Human rights reports by official bodies are another source of data used by scholars. The indicators developed by Cingranelli and Richards (the CIRI dataset) exemplify this approach to measure human rights. Amongst other aspects, the project seeks to determine the concept of "rights to self-determination," based on information from US State Department annual country reports on human rights practices. This is classified and recoded into a three-point ordinal scale, based on the extent to which citizens are reported to enjoy "freedom of political choice" and "the right to change the laws and officials which govern them through free and fair elections." The CIRI dataset covers 195 countries from 1980 to 2011, allowing electoral self-determination rights to be compared with a broad range of human rights.[26] Similarly, Kelley also codes US State Department reports in her data on the quality of elections.[27]

It remains unclear, however, how "freedom of political choice" and "free and fair elections" are interpreted and coded in practice, given the multiple aspects of elections that can determine these outcomes. If a country is rated poorly by CIRI, is the problem one of legal restrictions of opposition party registration or ballot access, lack of freedom of the press, or vote rigging in polling stations? From the CIRI coding, it is not possible to determine the precise cause of any practices undermining electoral malpractice. Moreover, reliance upon the US State Department official reports as the source of evidence raises questions about the legitimacy of the dataset, as the estimates remain open to the charge of cultural or political bias. The US State Department is not an independent and impartial judge, and official assessments of human rights are likely to be colored by American foreign policy interests. There is, however, reason to believe that this problem may have lessened since the end of the Cold War.[28]

Electoral Forensics

Scholars have also sought to use several statistical techniques to determine anomalies in local election results.[29] Indeed, the study of "electoral forensics" has become increasingly popular during the last decade. Like medical autopsies conducted after death arising from suspicious circumstances, statistical techniques are used to analyze election returns reported in local wards, polling districts, or constituencies. The aim is to detect local outliers to the usual patterns of election results, such as in rates of voter registration, levels of voting turnout, vote shares cast for the incumbent, records of blank or invalid ballots cast, or other anomalies in the official results. Where outliers cannot be explained satisfactorily by other factors, such as localized levels of party support, these are interpreted as cases of irregularities arising from practices such as electoral fraud by local officials, ballot stuffing, or other types of vote tampering.

These techniques are most effective for capturing any problems occurring on (or just after) polling day. This can be a valuable way to detect the most obvious types of voting anomalies suggesting illegal practices, irregularities, and fraudulent manipulation of the outcome, particularly when statistical analysis is supplemented by other types of evidence, including the reports of observer missions, election watch NGOs, or journalists. The techniques are unable to detect various types of malpractice occurring earlier during the electoral cycle and prior to polling day, however, such as those arising from media bias in campaign coverage, electoral laws, partisan redistricting, or restrictions on party registration or ballot access for candidates.

Moreover, at present there is little agreement among statistical experts about the most appropriate mathematical techniques that can be used to identify overt fraud with any degree of reliability, such as the conditions under which it is appropriate to apply Benford's first digit or second digit "laws," or to analyze rounding of the final digit in local polling district returns. Debate about the use of these techniques continues among statisticians and analysts.[30]

Natural or Randomized Field Experiments

An increasingly popular approach is the use of natural or randomized field experiments.[31] One difficulty facing analysis of observational data taken at a single point of time concerns serious problems of endogeneity. For example, public disaffection with electoral procedures may be expected to stoke pressures for regimes to respond. But on the other hand, the way that regimes react to electoral malpractices in any particular contest (at t_1) can be expected to shape subsequent patterns of public opinion (as t_2). Thus, if the regime introduces widespread reforms that clean up malpractices such as corruption, irregularities, and intimidation in an election, this should strengthen public confidence in the electoral process. On the other hand, if the regime responds by using further repression, such as by passing new laws regulating public expressions of dissent and limiting opposition rallies, this could be expected to heighten public disaffection.

Demonstrating such interactive effects using cross-national time-series observational data remains difficult, however, even with the use of rigorous lagged time-series models. Observed evidence based on mass cross-national surveys is conducted among the same respondents at only one point in time, rather than through panel surveys of the same respondents over time. Randomized treatments in natural or field experimental research designs have the capacity to help rule out problems of endogeneity. This approach can thereby help to determine causal effects with more confidence. Traditional experiments hold constant several conditions and manipulate the treatment variables. Natural experimental designs take advantage of randomized or "as-if" randomized treatments within countries to allow analysts to draw plausible inferences about the effect of policy interventions (such as the deployment of international observers) within specific contexts.

Illustrations include studies of the effects of international election monitoring on electoral fraud in as-if randomized polling stations in Armenia, Indonesia, and Ghana. For example, Hyde examined whether the presence of international observers during the 2003 Armenian presidential elections reduced the share of the vote for incumbent candidates (suggesting election-day fraud), where observers were assigned to polling stations using a method that approximates to randomization.[32] The study concluded that the effect of international observers cut election-day fraud by around 6 percent in the first-round elections.

It remains hazardous, however, to generalize from randomized design natural experiments in single cases where the analyst has limited control over the treatment and conditions. Florida in 2000, for example, was not Minnesota, Georgia, or Oregon. Kenya is not the DRC. Afghanistan is not Iraq. India is not Pakistan. And so on. The effects of the deployment of electoral observers in the context of Armenian polling districts may well be expected to differ from, say, their impacts in Ukraine, Moldova, or Russia. Indeed, a three-nation experimental study comparing observer effects in polling places in Azerbaijan, Georgia, and Kyrgyzstan suggests that the effects of domestic monitoring on blatant forms of vote miscounting differed in these three cases.[33] The contrasts were attributed to the type of regime, with minimal effects on curbing fraud in the most autocratic regime under comparison (Azerbaijan).

Experiments hold constant a certain set of conditions. Yet in natural or field experiments about observer effects, other differences from one context to another may be expected to arise from multiple factors, such as the capacity and resources of different domestic and international monitoring organizations, the specific type, transparency, severity, and timing of the fraudulent practices that undermine electoral integrity (vote-buying during the campaign, for example, differs from voter intimidation or ballot-box stuffing on polling day), the training and capacity of electoral officials and security forces manning polling places, the culture tolerating electoral malpractices, and so on.

Thus, experiments help to determine whether a treatment in one particular context (the as-if random allocation of observers) has the effect of reducing ballot-box fraud, compared with polling places where observers were not present in the same society. But this does not mean that the results are necessarily generalizable to other contexts and countries. In addition, to date randomized evaluations have focused largely on the effects of the randomized impact of the deployment of observers across polling places and vote counts in several elections, such as in Ghana, Armenia, and Afghanistan, but this method has not yet been applied systematically to many other types of common interventions, such as voter education and capacity building among local electoral officials.

Public Opinion Surveys

In addition, as shown by the third section of this book, public opinion surveys provide direct insights into how the general electorate feels about elections and democracy. Typically, survey respondents are asked about their perceptions of violations of electoral integrity, or their reported experiences, as well as their broader attitudes toward political institutions and democratic governance, such as trust in electoral authorities and confidence in the responsiveness of elected officials. Social surveys use a standardized questionnaire to gather data from a representative sample of the adult population within each nation. Inferences are then drawn about the general population within each country. For example, campaign tracking and post-election national surveys of public opinion have been used by the International Foundation for Electoral Systems (IFES) to monitor citizens' perceptions of democracy, opinions about elections, and assessments of the overall situation in their country, such as in Indonesia, Kosovo, and Ukraine. These are invaluable for within country assessments, although the lack of a standardized questionnaire in the IFES surveys hinders their use for cross-national analysis. Surveys vary when measuring how people see the quality of elections, with most using one or two simple proxy or summary measures, such as asking respondents about their perceptions of the honesty or fairness of the contests. Studies such as the World Values Survey, the Afrobarometer, and the Latinobarometer provide a wide range of data about public attitudes toward electoral processes and cultural values, as well as capturing some direct experiences.

Nevertheless, the public may be poorly informed about more technical and legal aspects of electoral integrity, such as the exclusion of parties or candidates from the ballot, or the manipulation of constituency boundaries, which can occur well away from the media spotlight.

Developing the New Perception of Electoral Integrity Index

To summarize, each of these techniques have certain strengths and weaknesses. The ideal research design for studying electoral integrity, like other complex social and political phenomena, involves multi-method approaches that triangulate more than one technique and data source, counterbalancing and complimenting the advantages and disadvantages of stand-alone methods. If alternative approaches, data, and techniques arrive at similar findings, this boosts confidence in the reliability of these findings.

To supplement and enrich all these approaches, therefore, the Electoral Integrity Project launched a new Perception of Electoral Integrity (PEI) Index based upon an expert survey. The next chapter describes the methods and results in more detail. This chapter is limited to discussing the rationale and overall thinking behind the research design. The use of expert surveys is an increasingly common approach developed to gauge many aspects of democratic governance where direct observational evidence is lacking or problematic, such as monitoring human rights, perceptions of corruption, the left-right ideological position of political parties, press freedom, and media bias.[34] Data gathered from the PEI expert survey is designed to be consistent across case and time. The instrument has been pilot tested (see the next chapter) and is in the process of being extended worldwide.

Expert Perceptions

The PEI survey instrument is designed to monitor expert perceptions and evaluations. This approach is similar to expert surveys used to assess levels of human rights, corruption, and press freedom, such as by Freedom House and Transparency International, although the project design seeks a higher level of methodological robustness. Perceptions of electoral integrity provide only a proxy indicator of the actual practices followed in many countries, for many reasons. For example, expert evaluations may be colored by media reports and party cues as much as by direct experience. Three safeguards are built into the design.

First, for independent robustness checks, the project collects (or is in the process of collecting) several alternative types of evidence—derived, for example, from legal frameworks, aggregate election results, and surveys of public opinion. Thus, this expert survey is only one component, supplemented by many others. As seen in the next chapter, where independent indices are consistently correlated with the expert survey, this increases confidence in the robustness and validity of that survey.[35] Where there are major discrepancies, however, this suggests the need for more in-depth analysis to determine the causes.

Second, anchoring vignettes are also used (see below) to strengthen the comparability of responses.

Last, to evaluate each case, the project draws on the experience of both locally based and international experts. As discussed in the next chapter, the selected experts are political scientists knowledgeable about elections in the specific country being surveyed. For instance, the strategy used in Huber and Inglehart's widely cited classic study of party positions was to contact 20 expert respondents in each country.[36] PEI increased the sample size and reliability by contacting at least 40 experts for each election (see next chapter). Differences among experts can reflect varying perceptions of the actual situation. The questionnaire monitors the familiarity of respondents with the election.

Item Design

One of the chief questions when trying to gauge electoral integrity is where to draw the boundary when it comes to deciding which items are most relevant to electoral integrity. The lines are unclear. From an electoral cycle approach, however, it is important to go beyond polling day and the vote count, to include the broad determinants of political competition in the funnel of causality. Hence, many PEI items are included that unduly limit electoral competition well before or immediately after polling day. Close attention is paid to each step in the electoral cycle. Disaggregating the components of broad concepts is more worthwhile than attempting to define and catch all relevant measures of complex and essentially contested political concepts.

The PEI items are designed to capture expert judgments of the common values that underpin the internationally recognized principles and standards of elections. Thus, expert respondents are not asked to report their own direct experience of elections or factual matters—such as the level of the vote threshold for a party to qualify for seats or the proportion of the eligible electorate registered to vote—which can usually be gathered more accurately from alternative sources. Instead, expert respondents are asked to judge the quality of electoral integrity and malpractice in a specific national election in each country against a series of common and universally agreed upon normative values, such as the fairness, honesty, and efficiency of the sequential steps in the electoral cycle.

The electoral cycle in Figure 3.1 highlights many issues used to gauge these values. One is the levelness of the playing field for electoral district boundary delimitation, party finance regulations, or media access, to mention just a few of the sub-elements of that key concept. Likewise, perception of EMB administrative capacity and quality can be based on a multitude of elements, such as voter registration quality and completeness, operational training of electoral staff at all levels, or the way special or external voting—if applicable—is carried out.

In addition, even if expert perceptions are more or less erroneous, biased, or factually inaccurate, they are still important in themselves. For example, if opposition parties believe that an election was stolen, they could well decide to engage in protests or boycotts, irrespective of the truth of these claims.

As with all survey work, experts are not cued by the survey about the meaning of these values; instead, they can make their own judgments based on their own values and beliefs. One issue raised by this process is how to gauge values if respondents from different cultures, countries, or groups employ standards or understand questions in completely different ways. For example, it may be that experts living in long-established democracies are more critical of electoral fraud and inaccuracy in voter registers than are experts living in newer democracies. The use of anchoring vignettes is one way to overcoming these issues.[37] Thus, respondents are asked to evaluate brief descriptions of hypothetical problems of electoral integrity. The responses to the vignettes can be used to strengthen the comparability of responses to the other survey questions.[38]

Index Construction

Survey items are consistently scored on a five-point scale, with 1 the most negative evaluation ("strongly disagree") and 5 the most positive evaluation ("strongly agree"). Individual scores can then be averaged for the country as a whole. If the standard deviation to the mean in any country proves higher than average, the individual scores are further examined.

The availability of the raw scores allows secondary users of the dataset to experiment with different aggregation and multiplicative systems. An index constructed in this way is more robust, as individual panelists' biases have been averaged out and possible problems or misunderstanding with specific indicators have been evened out in the standardization processes. The end result is a robust overall index; the PEI index of electoral integrity is strongly correlated with independent measures of the quality of elections from other sources of evidence, including NELDA and QED.[39]

Conclusions: The Utility of Expert Surveys

As discussed, several methods and techniques are used in the rapidly growing research literature on electoral integrity. Expert surveys represent another valuable tool in monitoring complex political phenomena that are difficult to gauge satisfactorily through other methods. Building upon this approach, the new PEI Index is designed to serve multiple users, both scholars and policy makers.

The collected data provides new evidence for scholars seeking to study institutional design, democratization, electoral autocracies, regime transitions, and election management, amongst many other issues. In this regard, the dataset can serve similar functions to the Freedom in the World Political Rights/Civil Liberties scores, Polity IV, Transparency International's Perception of Corruption, and the Minority Rights Group International "Peoples under Threat" indexes. The data can be used in large-scale analyses aiming at testing general propositions and in small-scale, in-depth regional or country-specific studies, studying particular over-time processes. As with the Corruption Perceptions Index, scholars can use the PEI dataset to analyze the causes and consequences of electoral integrity. The development community can also employ the index to identify strategic priorities, to encourage reforms among poorly performing nations, and to evaluate change over time.

The dataset assists international organizations in prioritizing and diagnosing where help is needed, identifying where interventions are failing (or succeeding), and determining where democratic governance can be promoted. This can be valuable for organizations such as the UN Electoral Assistance Division (UNEAD), UN Development Program (UNDP), International Foundation for Election Systems (IFES), International IDEA, the Inter-Parliamentary Union (IPU), and the Carter Center, as well as for national stakeholders and electoral commissions, especially in transitional and post-conflict countries.

The disaggregated results help to determine more precisely which component of the electoral cycle provides the most fragile link in the chain—for example, whether problems are most common in the impartiality of electoral management bodies, the distribution of campaign resources, or fraudulent practices at polling stations and the vote count. For analysts, this generates more precise understandings into the nature of electoral flaws—for instance, distinguishing the problems in different types of regimes. For policy makers, it helps to identify the source of any weakness in elections and thereby determine the most appropriate types and stages of programmatic interventions. Thus, the PEI Index provides a comprehensive measure and new source of reliable data, which can usefully supplement many other sources of empirical evidence in this field, playing a valuable role for both the academic and the policymaking communities.

Notes

1. Joseph Schumpeter. 1942. *Capitalism, Socialism and Democracy.* London: George Allen & Unwin.
2. Adam Przeworski. 1999. "Minimalist conception of democracy: A defense." In Ian Shapiro and Casiano Hacker-Cordon (Eds.), *Democracy's Value.* Cambridge: Cambridge University Press. p. 10.
3. Adam Przeworski, Michael E. Alvarez, Jose Antonio Cheibub, and Fernando Limongi. 2000. *Democracy and Development: Political Institutions and Well-Being in the World, 1950–1990.* New York: Cambridge University Press. pp. 15–16.

4. Steven Levitsky and Lucan Way. 2010. *Competitive Authoritarianism: Hybrid Regimes after the Cold War*, New York: Cambridge University Press.
5. Staffan I. Lindberg. 2006. *Democracy and Elections in Africa*. Baltimore, MD: The Johns Hopkins University Press; Staffan I. Lindberg Ed. 2009. *Democratization by Elections: A New Mode of Transition*. Baltimore, MD: The Johns Hopkins University Press.
6. Sarah Birch. 2008. "Electoral institutions and popular confidence in electoral processes: a cross-national analysis." *Electoral Studies* 27 (2): 305–20.
7. Kristine Hoglund. 2009. "Electoral violence in conflict-ridden societies: concepts, causes, and consequences." *Terrorism and Political Violence* 21 (3): 412–27.
8. Judith G. Kelley. 2012. *Monitoring Democracy: When International Election Observation Works and Why It Often Fails*. Princeton, NJ: Princeton University Press; Susan. D. Hyde. 2011. *The Pseudo-Democrat's Dilemma*. Ithaca: Cornell University Press.
9. ACE Electoral Knowledge Network http://aceproject.org/; *Building Resources in Democracy, Governance and Elections* (BRIDGE). http://bridge-project.org/
10. Geraldo L. Munck. 2009. *Measuring Democracy: A Bridge between Scholarship and Politics*. Baltimore: The Johns Hopkins Press; Todd Landman and Edzia Carvalho. 2010. *Measuring Human Rights*. London: Routledge.
11. Jørgen Elklit and Palle Svensson. 1997. "What makes elections free and fair?" *Journal of Democracy* 8 (3): 32–46.
12. Chad Vickery and Erica Shein. 2012. "Assessing electoral fraud in new democracies." IFES: Washington D.C. http://www.ifes.org/~/media/Files/Publications/White%20 PaperReport/2012/Assessing_Electoral_Fraud_Series_Vickery_Shein.pdf
13. http://aceproject.org/electoral-advice/election-observation/declaration-of-principles-for-international
14. Jørgen Elklit and Andrew Reynolds. 2002. "The Impact of Election Administration on the Legitimacy of Emerging Democracies: A New Comparative Politics Research Agenda." *Commonwealth and Comparative Studies* 40 (2): 86–119; Jørgen Elklit and Andrew Reynolds. 2005. "A Framework for the Systematic Study of Election Quality." *Democratization* 12(2): 147–162.
15. Andreas Schedler. 2002. "The menu of manipulation." *Journal of Democracy* 13(2): 36–50.
16. See, for example, Fabrice Edouard Lehoucq, and Iván Molina Jiménez. 2002. *Stuffing the Ballot Box: Fraud, Electoral Reform, and Democratization in Costa Rica*. New York: Cambridge University Press; Beatriz Magaloni. 2006. *Voting for Autocracy: Hegemonic Party Survival and Its Demise in Mexico*. Cambridge: Cambridge University Press.
17. R. Michael Alvarez, Lonna Rae Atkeson and Thad Hall. 2012. *Evaluating Elections: A Handbook of Methods and Standards*. New York: Cambridge University Press.
18. Eric C. Bjornlund. 2004. *Beyond Free and Fair: Monitoring Elections and Building Democracy*. Washington D.C.: Woodrow Wilson Center Press.
19. Judith Kelley. 2010. *Quality of Elections Data Codebook*. http://sites.duke.edu/kelley/data/; Sarah Birch. 2011. *Electoral Malpractice*. Oxford: Oxford University Press; Susan. D. Hyde. 2011. *The Pseudo-Democrat's Dilemma*. Ithaca: Cornell University Press; Daniela Donno. 2013. *Defending Democratic Norms*. New York: Cambridge University Press.
20. Judith Kelley. 2010. "Election observers and their biases." *Journal of Democracy* 21: 158–172.
21. David Collier and Robert Adcock. 1999. "Democracy and dichotomies: A pragmatic approach to choices about concepts." *Annual Review of Political Science* 2: 537–565.
22. Susan. D. Hyde. 2011. *The Pseudo-Democrat's Dilemma*. Ithaca: Cornell University Press.
23. Andreas Schedler. (ed.). 2006. *Electoral Authoritarianism: The Dynamics of Unfree Competition*. Boulder and London: Lynne Rienner.
24. Kalev Leetaru and Philip A. Schrodt. 2013. "*GDELT: Global Data on Events, Location and Tone, 1979–2012.*" Paper presented at the International Studies Association meetings, San Francisco, April 2013. See also http://gdelt.utdallas.edu/about.html#datasources.

25. Pippa Norris and Ronald Inglehart. 2010. *Cosmopolitan Communications*. New York: Cambridge University Press; Alexa Robertson. 2010. *Mediated Cosmopolitanism: The World of Television News*. Oxford: Polity.

26. CIRI Human Rights Data Project. http://ciri.binghamton.edu/.

27. Judith. G. Kelley. 2012. *Monitoring Democracy: When International Election Observation Works and Why It Often Fails*. Princeton, NJ: Princeton University Press.

28. Steven C. Poe, C. Neal Tate, and Linda Camp Keith. 1999. "Repression of the human right to personal integrity revisited: A global cross-national study covering the years 1976–1993."*International Studies Quarterly* 43: 291–313.

29. See, for example, Joseph Deckert, Mikhail Myagkov and Peter C. Ordeshook. 2011. "Benford's Law and the detection of election fraud." *Political Analysis* 19(3): 245–268; Walter R. Mebane, Jr. 2011. "Comment on Benford's Law and the detection of election fraud." *Political Analysis* 19(3): 269–272.

30. Bernd Beber and Alexandra Scacco. 2012. "What the numbers say: A digit-based test for election fraud." *Political Analysis* 20(2): 211–234.

31. See, for example, Daniella Donno. 2010. "Who is punished? Regional intergovernmental organizations and the enforcement of democratic norms." *International Organization* 64(4): 593–625; Nahomi Ichino and Matthias Schuendeln. 2012. "Deterring or displacing electoral irregularities? Spillover effects of observers in a randomized field experiment in Ghana." *Journal of Politics* 74(1): 292–307; Daniella Donno. 2013. *Defending Democratic Norms*. New York: Oxford University Press.

32. Susan D. Hyde. 2007. "Experimenting in democracy promotion: international observers and the 2004 presidential elections in Indonesia." *Perspectives on Politics* 8(2): 511–27; Susan. D. Hyde. 2007. "The observer effect in international politics: evidence from a natural experiment." *World Politics* 60(1): 37–63.

33. Fredrik M. Sjoberg. 2012. *Making Votes Count: Evidence from Field Experiments about the Efficacy of Domestic Election Observation*. Harriman Institute Working Paper #1. Columbia University.

34. M. Meyer and J. Booker. 1991. *Eliciting and analyzing expert judgment: A practical guide*. London: Academic Press.

35. Marco R. Steenbergen and Gary Marks. 2007. "Evaluating expert judgments." *European Journal of Political Research* 46: 347–366.

36. John Huber and Ronald Inglehart. 1995. "Expert interpretations of party space and party locations in 42 societies." *Party Politics* 1(1): 73–111.

37. http://gking.harvard.edu/vign/.

38. Jonathan Wand, Gary King, and Olivia Lau. 2011. "Anchors: Software for Anchoring Vignettes Data." *Journal of Statistical Software* 42 (3): 1–25.

39. Pippa Norris. 2014. "Does the world agree about standards of electoral integrity? Evidence for the diffusion of global norms." *Electoral Studies* 34(4) (Forthcoming).

4

Expert Judgments

FERRAN MARTÍNEZ I COMA AND RICHARD W. FRANK

National elections have become virtually ubiquitous. While the conduct of these contests clearly varies widely around the world, there is surprisingly little agreement in either research or policy circles about why some elections have integrity while others do not. This is, in part, because these contests are complex multidimensional phenomena involving myriad actors interacting over extended periods of time and include many areas of potential manipulation. One part of the electoral process might be considered as free and fair while others are corrupted by institutional failure or an extralegal search for personal advantage. This lack of agreement about whether elections are free and fair is also partly attributable to the data that analysts use. Scholars also often rely on aggregated indices like Freedom House's index of political rights and civil liberties.[1] As discussed in the previous chapter, these measures do not allow a precise diagnosis of which parts of the electoral process succeed or fail. This chapter presents a new dataset that provides a more nuanced and comprehensive portrait of electoral integrity than previously possible.

Recent decades have also witnessed a profusion of new indices monitoring other complex political phenomena, building on the usefulness and popularity of indicators like Marshall and Jagger's[2] Polity IV index and Freedom House's political and civil liberties indices.[3] They include measures of perceptions of corruption,[4] human rights,[5] the representation of women,[6] and a human development index.[7] The Quality of Governance (QOG) Institute compiles a number of these indices into an integrated dataset containing more than 620 variables.[8]

The subfield focused on electoral integrity has lagged behind, although the last decade has witnessed several new datasets constructed from electoral observer, human rights, and election-related media reports. These include the National Elections Across Democracy and Autocracy (NELDA) dataset,[9] the Quality of Elections (QED) database,[10] and Birch's Index of Electoral Malpractice (IEM).[11] Each, however, has certain limitations—notably, the conceptualization and depth of the classification of election dimensions in NELDA and the restricted range of countries covered by electoral observer reports in QED and IEM. Moreover, as with other social science measures—especially expert surveys based on non-probability samples—any index monitoring election quality should be systematically evaluated using explicit criteria built on establishing their reliability, validity (both internal and external), and legitimacy.[12]

This chapter describes a new expert survey, the Perceptions of Electoral Integrity, or PEI, that enables researchers and policy analysts to evaluate specific disaggregated aspects of electoral integrity as well as to construct an overall index of PEI that meets the scientific criteria listed above.[13] When completed, the PEI dataset will eventually evaluate all national elections—instead of the subset monitored by international or domestic organizations. It will also examine malpractices throughout the electoral cycle—instead of only on election day.

In the PEI pilot stage, conducted in April and May of 2013, the survey instrument was implemented in 20 countries. Coverage was then expanded to all presidential and parliamentary elections around the world. The resulting dataset will be of interest for political scientists in many subfields of comparative politics (from electoral studies and voting behavior to regime comparisons and political instability) as well as for domestic and international policy makers interested in systematically evaluating, comparing, and improving election quality. Methodologically, it has a number of advantages over existing expert surveys. For instance, it includes both domestic and international experts as well as a larger number of experts per country than do many other surveys (e.g., Varieties of Democracy).[14]

The initial results of the PEI pilot stage are encouraging. The mean response rate (30 percent) is consistent with existing expert surveys. Furthermore, our experts' election evaluations are strongly correlated with several independent existing sources (suggesting external validity) while having several important differences from existing datasets, explained in more detail below. Lastly, the PEI experts' evaluations coincide with mass perceptions of electoral integrity, as measured by the sixth round of the World Values Survey.[15]

This chapter begins by providing a brief outline of our theoretical motivations for examining perceptions of electoral integrity. The second section describes the survey's research design, including its core concept, questionnaire development, and expert selection process. It also follows chapter 3 in highlighting several advantages that expert surveys have over other means of gauging electoral integrity. The third section outlines our initial empirical results and our tests of the survey instrument's validity, reliability, and legitimacy. It also shows how individual responses can be aggregated into a summary index comparable to existing Freedom House and Polity indices—while being more transparent and (arguably) robust than either index. The PEI index has the capacity to highlight specific reasons why elections might (and do) fail. The concluding section argues that, when fully implemented, the PEI dataset will complement existing data sources and deepen our ability to analyze and monitor election quality.

Theoretical Motivation for Studying Perceptions of Electoral Integrity

The practice of holding periodic national elections has spread to almost every country in the world, including many non-democracies. As this has occurred, concerns about electoral integrity have grown, catalyzing research by both the academic and policymaking communities.

To grasp the scope of the problem of electoral malpractice (and therefore what interventions are most likely to be successful), the various stages of the electoral process must be examined. After all, even in developed democracies, the electoral process can be marred by serious problems—for example, fall 2012 balloting in the US witnessed difficulties ranging from pre–election-day ballot access issues in Pennsylvania to lengthy election-day voting lines in Florida. These problems are exacerbated in other types of regimes that may possess both a lower institutional capacity to hold elections and higher incentives for manipulation. Other issues can also arise over the electoral cycle, from a lack of equal ballot access for opposition parties and a pro-government media bias to maladministration in electoral registers and vote rigging. New challenges also surround quickly changing landscapes of campaign finance, the political broadcast regulation, online voting, and voter registration. In short, studies that focus only on election-day issues like ballot stuffing or voter fraud miss crucial aspects of electoral manipulation that occur prior to, during, and after election day. Recent research has started to measure and monitor election quality in some detail and across a number of countries.[16]

The Electoral Integrity Project (EIP) takes the next step by using a multi-method approach—including a battery of questions added to the sixth round of the World Values Survey, a global database on elections' legal framework, in-depth case studies, and program evaluations of multilateral efforts at enhancing electoral integrity. This chapter focuses on one important part of the EIP's multi-method approach— the PEI survey of expert perceptions of electoral integrity.

The survey aims to provide a comprehensive, impartial, consistent, and reliable resource examining whether a national election meets internationally recognized standards. Its expert survey follows a methodology used for similar projects, including the Chapel Hill Expert Survey (CHES) of political party ideologies and policy positions, Transparency International's expert survey of perceptions of corruption, and the Varieties of Democracy project. Expert surveys are an increasingly common technique for evaluating many dimensions of democratic governance that cannot be monitored by other means—including the observation of the rule of law, bureaucratic quality, media freedom, political party ideologies, and policy positions. In the research design section below, we go into more detail about the strengths and weaknesses of expert surveys.

There are several reasons why a survey of experts is preferable as well as complimentary to using election monitor reports. Elklit and Reynolds provide two such reasons.[17] First, election observers judge an election's quality "on the basis of largely impressionistic and incomplete evidence centred on the conduct of the vote and count on election day," although many observation missions now have both long-term and short-term observers. Second, observations missions "'call' the result an election in a politicized way, detached from the reality of the process itself." Accordingly, monitors' assessments consider election quality largely in bimodal terms—the election is either *good* or *bad*. We believe, however, that election quality is multidimensional, and dichotomizing it misses crucial variation across cases.

Several additional arguments exist for adding experts' judgments to other means of electoral evaluation. First, international observers' involvement often consists of a week-to-10-day visit around election day. As a result, the likelihood of overlooking important election issues is quite high. Election quality includes concerns about the content of electoral laws, campaign finance regulation, media access, district boundaries, and voter registration well before polling day. Second, domestic perceptions matter because people make decisions based on how they view the world. If there is a difference between domestic and international evaluations, arguably the former is more informed due to potentially greater access to (and incentive to collect) information about election quality. Third, for many issues of electoral integrity (e.g., corruption and other illegal activities), few methodological alternatives to measuring people's perceptions are available. Fourth, because incumbent governments decide to either allow or ban international and domestic monitors, those countries preventing election monitoring (or not inviting it) would be excluded from any analysis based on monitoring reports. This has implications both academically and politically. Academically, existing research like that by Birch or Kelley often depends on election monitors deciding (or being able) to observe elections.[18] The quality of elections without monitors is uncertain—and these elections are precisely the ones most likely to be manipulated. Politically, reliance on observer reports could lead to biased foreign policy conclusions due to a lack of on-the-ground information about electoral misconduct.

Elections (and their concomitant institutional processes) are essential for liberal democracy, although no consensus exists on exactly what combination of electoral aspects are essential to defining democracy, due to problems with definitions, source choices, measurement precision and validity, coding decisions, and aggregation.[19] The PEI project strives to overcome a number of the shortcomings of existing data efforts in two ways: first, by creating new indicators of detailed aspects of the electoral process, and second, by encompassing more dimensions of the process throughout the electoral cycle. This survey allows experts with knowledge of specific elections to evaluate a number of relevant facets of this most important phenomenon.

Research Design: Operationalizing the Concept of Electoral Integrity

The Concept of Electoral Integrity

We turn now from the PEI's theoretical motivations to its research design. What concept are we seeking to measure? Alternative definitions of electoral integrity are common in the research literature. Hence, lawyers commonly emphasize violations of domestic electoral laws—especially fraudulent manipulation of polling and tabulation.[20] Scholars of public sector management draw upon the language of electoral maladministration, emphasizing electoral processes.[21] Democratic theorists, drawing upon ideas of liberal democracy, usually focus upon the failure of electoral procedures to meet certain normative values, such as accountability, inclusiveness, and transparency.[22] Each of these approaches provides important insights into this complex phenomenon, but they each also suffer from serious limitations.

Following the conceptual understanding discussed in earlier chapters of this volume, the overarching notion of *electoral integrity* is defined to refer to agreed international conventions and global norms, applying universally to all countries worldwide throughout the electoral cycle, including during the pre-electoral period, the campaign, on polling day, and its aftermath. [23]

The first part of this definition sees electoral integrity as contests reflecting *global norms*, where contests are evaluated as legitimate if they respect agreed upon international conventions and standards of elections. As discussed in chapter 2, the foundation for global norms of electoral integrity rests upon Article 21(3) in the Universal Declaration of Human Rights (1948), which constitutes the legal basis and the core principles legitimating international support to elections and electoral assistance. Agreements about the global norms that should govern the conduct of elections were further specified in Article 25 of the UN International Covenant for Civil and Political Rights (ICCPR of 1966). The most succinct statement of these norms is provided in the UN General Assembly resolution 64/155 (March 8, 2010): "Strengthening the role of the United Nations in enhancing periodic and genuine elections and the promotion of democratization." This version reflects and extends similar statements of principle endorsed regularly by the United Nations since 1991. In subsequent decades, global norms have been hammered out by the international community and endorsed in a series of human rights instruments, conventions, legal tools, and more detailed working standards, documented by the Carter Center database. Some of the most authoritative and detailed international standards to evaluate electoral integrity have been operationalized in the practical guidelines issued to electoral observers by regional intergovernmental organizations, exemplified by the OSCE *Election Observation Handbook*.[24]

The second part of our definition of electoral integrity sees its global norms as universally applicable, where violations of shared principles and standards have the capacity to undermine the quality of elections in *every* society, including in long-established democracies. The most egregious violators of electoral rights in places such as Belarus, Afghanistan, and Zimbabwe are commonly highlighted by dramatic news headlines. Yet our understanding is too narrow and partial if scholars simply focus upon the worst "first-order" cases of overt malpractices involving repression in electoral autocracies. While first-order malpractices in autocratic states generate widespread international concern, second-order challenges of electoral integrity reflect universal problems that may damage the legitimacy of electoral contests in *any* country—including in Anglo-American democracies like the United States, Britain, and Canada.[25] Malpractices, from this perspective, may be manipulated or accidental, legally sanctioned or illicit, arising from violations of democratic rights or from lack of technical capacity, or indeed all of the above.

Lastly, much attention in the news media and in the research literature has focused upon the problem of fraudulent ballots and vote count malpractices— acts at the end of the electoral process. But the international community understands that electoral assistance and electoral observation should not be focused purely upon election day, or even on the short-term period of the official campaign. Instead, elections should be seen as a sequential process or cycle involving a long series of steps.[26] As the ACE project suggests, the cycle involves all stages in the process of elections:

> from the design and drafting of legislation, the recruitment and training of electoral staff, electoral planning, voter registration, the registration of political parties, the nomination of parties and candidates, the electoral campaign, polling, counting, the tabulation of results, the declaration of results, the resolution of electoral disputes, reporting, auditing and archiving. After the end of one electoral process, it is desirable for work on the next to begin: the whole process can be described as the electoral cycle.[27]

Measurement

To operationalize the concept, the PEI database includes 49 variables measuring 11 dimensions of electoral integrity over the electoral cycle. The first three sections of the survey begin by looking at perceptions of the electoral laws, procedures, and boundary selection. The next two discuss the registration of voters, candidates, and parties. Sections six and seven focus on the election campaign—specifically the media coverage and how the campaigns are financed. Sections eight and nine discuss the balloting process and what happens after the polls closed. The last section discusses how the official results are promulgated. Table 4.1 summarizes the questionnaire. The survey instrument seeks to be conceptually valid by reflecting

Table 4.1: **Dimensions of the Electoral Cycle**

Period	Sections	Questions
Pre-election	1. Electoral laws	1. Electoral laws were unfair to smaller parties
		2. Electoral laws favored the governing party or parties
		3. Election laws restricted citizens' rights
	2. Electoral procedures	4. Elections were well managed
		5. Information about voting procedures was widely available
		6. Election officials were fair
		7. Elections were conducted in accordance with the law
	3. Boundaries	8. Boundaries discriminated against some parties
		9. Boundaries favored incumbents
		10. Boundaries were impartial
	4. Voter registration	11. Some citizens were not listed in the register
		12. The electoral register was inaccurate
		13. Some ineligible electors were registered
	5. Party registration	14. Some opposition candidates were prevented from running
		15. Women had equal opportunities to run for office
		16. Ethnic and national minorities had equal opportunities to run for office
		17. Only top party leaders selected candidates
		18. Some parties/candidates were restricted from holding campaign rallies
Campaign	6. Campaign media	19. Newspapers provided balanced election news
		20. TV news favored the governing party
		21. Parties/candidates had fair access to political broadcasts and advertising
		22. Journalists provided fair coverage of the elections
		23. Social media were used to expose electoral fraud
	7. Campaign finance	24. Parties/candidates had equitable access to public subsidies
		25. Parties/candidates had equitable access to political donations
		26. Parties/candidates publish transparent financial accounts
		27. Rich people buy elections
		28. Some state resources were improperly used for campaigning

(Continued)

Table 4.1: **Continued**

Period	Sections	Questions
Election day	8. Voting process	29. Some voters were threatened with violence at the polls
		30. Some fraudulent votes were cast
		31. The process of voting was easy
		32. Voters were offered a genuine choice at the ballot box
		33. Postal ballots were available
		34. Special voting facilities were available for the disabled
		35. National citizens living abroad could vote
		36. Some form of internet voting was available
	9. Vote count	37. Ballot boxes were secure
		38. The results were announced without undue delay
		39. Votes were counted fairly
		40. International election monitors were restricted
		41. Domestic election monitors were restricted
Post-election	10. Post-election	42. Parties/candidates challenged the results
		43. The election led to peaceful protests
		44. The election triggered violent protests
		45. Any disputes were resolved through legal channels
	11. Electoral authorities	46. The election authorities were impartial
		47. The authorities distributed information to citizens
		48. The authorities allowed public scrutiny of their performance
		49. The election authorities performed well

Source: Pippa Norris, Ferran Martínez i Coma, and Richard W. Frank. *The Expert Survey of Perceptions of Electoral Integrity, Pilot Study May 2013.* www.electoralintegrityproject.com.

international norms and standards, by applying to all countries universally, and by capturing all stages in the electoral cycle. The series of items monitoring integrity were also framed both positively and negatively, to avoid a systematic skew to the questionnaire's wording.

The PEI's pilot stage sought experts on every nationwide election in a selected group of 20 elections occurring during 2012. Table 4.2 lists the background questions that were also gathered from the experts.

Defining an Expert

A number of existing definitions are possible for who could be considered an election expert.[28] In this project, we define an *expert* as a political scientist (or social

Table 4.2: **Additional PEI Survey Background Questions**

• Are you currently in full or part-time employment?
• Do you work or have you worked, in…
• What is (or was) your most recent employment?
• What is your year of birth?
• What is your sex?
• What is your highest level of educational qualification?
• Were you born in this country?
• How long have you lived in this country, if at all?
• Did you participate in the last national election of this country in any of the following roles?
• Are you a citizen of this country?
• Which political party, if any, did you support in the last national election?
• Below is a 10 scale on which the political views are arranged from very left to very right. Where would you place your views on the scale?

Source: Pippa Norris, Ferran Martínez i Coma, and Richard W. Frank. *The Expert Survey of Perceptions of Electoral Integrity, Pilot Study May 2013.* www.electoralintegrityproject.com.

scientist in a related discipline) who has published on (or who has other demonstrated knowledge of) the electoral process in a particular country. Specifically, we define *demonstrated knowledge* by the following criteria: (1) membership of a relevant research group, professional network, or organized section of such a group; (2) existing publications on electoral or other country-specific topics in books, academic journals, or conference papers; and (3) employment at a university or college as a teacher. Occasionally, other social scientists were also used—from law, sociology, or, to a lesser degree, economics, anthropology, mathematics, or statistics. During the pilot phase, at least 40 experts per country were sought, including both domestic and international experts. The domestic/international distinction was made based on institutional affiliation, citizenship, and country of residence.

Expert Selection

For the pilot phase, the survey sought to identify and contact 40 experts per election. This number was difficult to reach in microstates and in countries without a strong community of political scientists. Furthermore, we sought to contact as many domestic experts as possible—with the view that the existing literature had focused on international monitors and perceptions and largely ignored domestic perceptions of electoral integrity. In some cases (e.g., Japan and the United States), all 40 experts were domestic. When this was not possible, we sought a balance between domestic and international experts. Nevertheless, for some countries in developing regions, we relied more on international than domestic experts, because it was difficult to find contact details for domestic experts. The first columns of Table 4.3 provide information about the country, the election, the date of the election, and the number of experts contacted.

How did we find the experts? A number of resources were used. First, to find local experts, we started with domestic universities. We focused on political science departments and looked for professors with publications relating to electoral issues. Broadening the topics on which academics conducted research beyond electoral politics arguably reduced the possibility of biasing our sample. Unfortunately, in a number of instances, university websites did not provide sufficient contact information about particular faculty members. In these cases, we moved to the second phase of the search, using other Internet and personal data sources. The Web of Science and Google Scholar were used to locate experts on a particular country's elections. The membership lists from professional academic associations including the American Political Science Association, the International Political Science Association, and the European Consortium for Political Research were also utilized. Lastly, we employed a snowballing procedure by inviting those experts we contacted to suggest others in their field with relevant country and election-specific knowledge. This technique for expert referral was useful for two reasons. First, the numerous referrals we received bolstered our confidence in the experts we had on file because there was a substantial overlap with the experts we already had. Second, experts referred by other experts are arguably more desirable as respondents because people on the ground recognize them as having relevant electoral knowledge. Once contact details were collected, experts were sent an email invitation to complete the online survey. Two reminder emails were sent to non-responders one and two weeks after the initial invitation.

The Pilot Stage

The pilot data for PEI include 20 national elections occurring from July to December 2012, listed in Table 4.3.[29] The ongoing survey project will include all national elections in all countries with more than 50,000 inhabitants.[30] An *election* is defined here as a national contest either for the executive or the legislature where citizens directly vote for the person (or group) on the ballot, and there is general voting (excluding voting by committee or institutions). This definition excludes referenda and plebiscites, as well as subnational and supra-national contests. Indirect elections are also excluded. Thus, for example, while we will include elections for the National Assembly of Madagascar, we will exclude its senate, since it is indirectly elected. By national election, we mean that the election is conducted across a country's entire territory at the same time.

Table 4.3: **Elections Included in the PEI Pilot Study**

Country	Election	Date	Number of experts	Response rate (%)	Rejection rate (%)
Angola	Legislative	Aug-31-12	40	32	16
Belarus	Parliamentary	Sep-23-12	42	15	12
Burkina Faso	Parliamentary	Dec-2-12	41	10	8
Congo, Republic of	Legislative	Jul-15-12	35	18	6
Czech Republic	Legislative	Oct-12-12	40	46	20
Georgia	Parliamentary	Oct-1-12	55	17	6
Ghana	Legislative	Dec-7-12	42	37	13
Japan	Parliamentary	Dec-16-12	40	35	5
Kuwait	Parliamentary	Dec-1-12	38	27	11
Lithuania	Parliamentary	Oct-14-12	41	31	17
Mexico	Legislative	Jul-1-12	40	38	3
Montenegro	Parliamentary	Oct-14-12	39	15	9
Netherlands, The	Parliamentary	Sep-12-12	45	53	9
Romania	Parliamentary	Dec-9-12	40	36	3
Sierra Leone	Legislative	Nov-17-12	40	9	11
Slovenia	Presidential	Nov-11-12	42	24	11
South Korea	Presidential	Dec-19-12	40	23	3
Ukraine	Parliamentary	Oct-28-12	36	42	3
United States	Legislative	Nov-6-12	40	38	8
Venezuela	Presidential	Oct-7-12	43	42	8
Total				**30**	**9**

Pippa Norris, Ferran Martínez i Coma, and Richard W. Frank. *The Expert Survey of Perceptions of Electoral Integrity, Pilot Study May 2013*. www.electoralintegrityproject.com.

Response Rates

Internet surveys have been critiqued for their low response rates. Shih and Fan estimate that web survey response rates are on average 10 to 11 percentage points lower than the response rates of other survey methods.[31] There are a number of different factors affecting response rates, but the most important here is the number of experts we need to invite. Studies suggest that (1) the fact that a survey is academically based, (2) a topic is salient, and (3) the survey is of reasonable length (below 13 minutes) lead to higher response rates than commercial surveys with less salient topics and longer lengths.[32]

We define our *response rate* as the number of complete surveys divided by the number of experts invited. This means that we include in our denominator those experts who decide to not take part in the survey.

We seek to maximize our response rate by carefully crafting the questionnaire's content and presentation and by personalizing the contact emails. We follow a logical sequence of questions, avoiding long and complicated sentence structure. We personalize contact emails with the expert's name, institution, and other characteristics to avoid spam filters and encourage a personal touch. We also send invitation emails in different languages (English, Spanish, French, German, and Russian), although for the pilot stage, emails and the questionnaire were only in English. In future iterations, experts will receive the invitation in English and/or in the dominant language of the country, and they will be able to respond to the questionnaire in a number of different languages.

Table 4.3 summarizes the response rates by country. The response rates were less than ideal in Belarus, Burkina Faso, the Republic of Congo, Georgia, Montenegro, and Sierra Leone.[33] In the pilot phase, we contacted 819 experts in 20 countries. The overall response rate was 30 percent. What explains the varying response rates? Some country-specific political factors, like the election's competitiveness or its media attention, may be important. Additionally, technical issues like the time since the election, Internet availability, and email or spam filters could also have had an influence. It may also be the case that domestic respondents are more motivated to answer a survey than are international experts.

Empirical Results

The variables included in the pilot questionnaire show wide variation in expert assessments of the quality of elections. Standardized 100-point summary scales were constructed, based on the variables in Table 4.1. Overall, comparing countries across their mean values in Table 4.4 indicates how they rank across different election characteristics. Comparison across the table suggests that many of the problems highlighted by our expert survey in each country reflected the main issues noted in published observer reports.

External Validity

It is important for our measures' external validity to explore whether the expert survey is divergent to other evidence. To do so, we aggregate our responses into a summary Electoral Integrity Index that can be compared to other measures. Once we had summed the substantive variables into the Electoral Integrity Index (after reversing the score of negatively worded questions), we then normalized the PEI Index to range from 0 to 100, in order to aid with interpretation.

Table 4.4: **Summary of Results**

	N	Electoral laws	Electoral procedures	Boundaries	Electoral register	Party registration	Campaign media	Campaign finance	Voting process	Ballot count	Post-election	EMBs	PEI index
Lithuania	11	88	75	87	84	88	70	62	75	87	76	78	80
Netherlands,The	26	92	92	83	83	82	67	67	82	89	91	90	80
Czech Republic	19	82	96	76	91	83	68	80	71	95	90	90	80
South Korea	8	65	90	66	94	78	61	69	74	97	82	81	77
Slovenia	11	73	90	66	93	83	56	66	85	100	65	89	77
United States	15	50	76	33	51	81	72	55	73	86	87	80	74
Mexico	14	66	80	77	81	68	65	53	64	88	59	74	73
Japan	15	62	86	60	79	70	62	66	74	83	75	78	72
Montenegro	5	75	72	71	46	74	53	41	63	76	68	60	64
Ghana	14	83	73	67	58	80	62	41	53	84	56	70	64
Romania	13	56	67	47	42	66	46	47	59	74	74	60	61
Venezuela	17	58	64	55	60	74	46	37	47	67	72	55	60
Sierra Leone	2	73	80			76	44	44	63	76	70	78	59

(Continued)

Table 4.4: **Continued**

	N	Electoral laws	Electoral procedures	Boundaries	Electoral register	Party registration	Campaign media	Campaign finance	Voting process	Ballot count	Post-election	EMBs	PEI index
Georgia	7	70	73	66	66	65	50	41	59	81	72	68	58
Burkina Faso	3	62	65	35	55	61	80	27		68	52	58	52
Congo, Rep. of	2	46	45	59	33	50	36	30	56	42	68	40	51
Ukraine	14	50	54	51	44	53	51	39	58	51	52	51	51
Kuwait	8	59	74	51	74	63	54	37	65	96	44	71	47
Angola	11	40	49	45	37	57	46	39	51	49	52	48	45
Belarus	6	29	44	42	59	40	37	32	54	39	63	31	40
Total	**221**	**67**	**76**	**60**	**69**	**73**	**58**	**53**	**68**	**78**	**69**	**71**	**67**

Note: Mean responses per country on standardized 100-point indices for all dimensions of the electoral cycle. See Table 4.1 for the items contained in each dimension.

Source: Pippa Norris, Ferran Martínez i Coma, and Richard W. Frank. *The Expert Survey of Perceptions of Electoral Integrity, Pilot Study May 2013.* www.electoralintegrityproject.com.

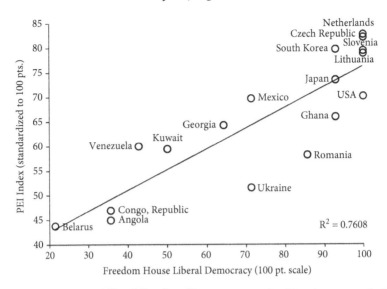

Figure 4.1: Comparing PEI and Freedom House. Note: Freedom House's estimates of political rights and civil liberties are summed, then standardized to a 100-point scale. Sources: Pippa Norris, Ferran Martínez i Coma, and Richard W. Frank. The Expert Survey of Perceptions of Electoral Integrity, Pilot Study May 2013. www.electoralintegrityproject.com; Freedom House. Freedom around the World 2013. www.freedomhouse.org

Figure 4.1 plots the PEI index against the 2013 Freedom House's index of liberal democracy (normalized to a scale of 0 to 100). Overall, these measures largely agree—58 percent of the variance of our index can be explained by the 2013 Freedom House index. There are a few outliers, however. For instance, Angola is ranked substantially higher in the PEI index than in the Freedom House one. Others, like Ukraine, do substantially worse. Clearly, Freedom House's index includes many aspects of political rights and civil liberties that extend beyond elections (e.g., freedom of the press, freedom of association, and the rule of law), so a perfect correlation with electoral integrity would not be expected.[34] There is a similar agreement with Kelley's Quality of Elections scale, in Figure 4.2, although these data are substantially older than the 2013 Freedom House data.

Whether the general public and elites have similar opinions of electoral integrity is also of theoretical importance. Previous studies note a high level of congruence between elite indices of electoral integrity, as well as between mass and elite measures.[35] Will our data reflect this congruence? Fortunately, the Electoral Integrity Project was able to add a battery of questions to the sixth round of the World Values Survey (WVS) that are identical to a number of questions in our expert survey, enabling us to directly compare opinions. The WVS survey is currently still collecting data in many countries at time of writing, so we only have a subset of the countries contained in the latest wave, and only a few overlap with countries included in the PEI pilot study. Nevertheless, where there is overlap,

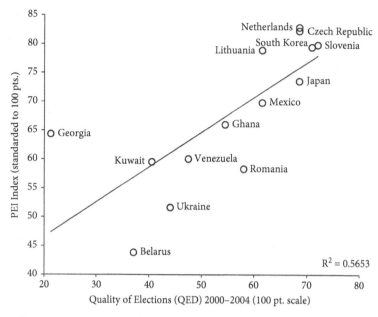

Figure 4.2: Comparing PEI and the Quality of Elections Data. Source: Pippa Norris, Ferran Martínez i Coma, and Richard W. Frank. The Expert Survey of Perceptions of Electoral Integrity, Pilot Study May 2013. www.electoralintegrityproject.com; Judith Kelley Quality of Elections Data. https://web.duke.edu/diem/docs/CodebookQEDlinked.pdf

Figures 4.3 and 4.4 present the most direct tests of mass and elite perceptions across both these datasets. Each figure's x-axis and y-axis are additive indices of four identical questions in both surveys regarding overall election integrity and electoral malpractice. The results are encouraging. The PEI experts and the general public in these few countries overwhelmingly agree on these aspects of electoral integrity, although there is slightly more divergence in mass and elite assessments of malpractices. In short, we believe that the pilot study's expert responses demonstrate substantial external validity when compared to other datasets and mass opinions.

Conclusions and Discussion

This chapter presents a brief overview of an ongoing data project focused on empirically measuring expert perceptions of electoral integrity. It discusses the theoretical motivations behind its creation and formation and it describes the research process from gathering election experts, inviting them to fill out the survey, and analyzing preliminary results. We also address potential concerns about using an expert survey to measure electoral integrity. Our data give a refined portrait of the election

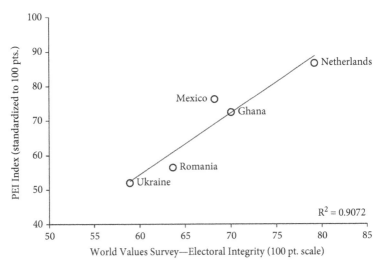

Figure 4.3: Comparing expert and mass perceptions of electoral integrity. Note: Strongly disagree (1) to strongly agree (5) questions asked in both surveys were: "Election officials were fair," "Journalists provided fair coverage of the election," "Voters were offered a genuine choice at the ballot box," and "Votes were counted fairly." The scores were added together and turned into a 100-point scale. Source: Pippa Norris, Ferran Martínez i Coma, and Richard W. Frank. The Expert Survey of Perceptions of Electoral Integrity, Pilot Study May 2013. www.electoralintegrityproject.com; The 6th wave of the World Values Survey 2012–2014, www.worldvaluessurvey.org

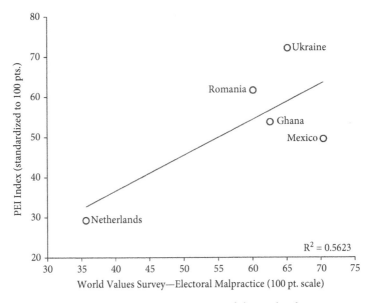

Figure 4.4: Comparing expert and mass perceptions of electoral malpractice. Note: Strongly disagree (1) to strongly agree (5) questions asked in both surveys were: "Rich people buy elections," "TV news favored the governing party," "Some opposition candidates were prevented from running," and "Some voters were threatened with violence at the polls." The scores were added and turned into a 100-point scale. Source: Pippa Norris, Ferran Martínez i Coma, and Richard W. Frank. The Expert Survey of Perceptions of Electoral Integrity, Pilot Study May 2013. www.electoralintegrityproject.com; The 6th wave of the World Values Survey 2012–2014, www.worldvaluessurvey.org

process, but they also map well overall to existing indicators measured by other researchers using media, international monitors, and individual-level data sources.

The chapter also describes the PEI's methodology rather than analyzing the preliminary empirical results in depth. This is done for both space and clarity reasons. In future research (with a more globally representative sample of countries), factor analysis will allow us to see whether our questions capture a few underlying conceptual indicators of electoral integrity. Additionally, it would be both theoretically and methodologically interesting to see whether experts respond consistently across elections, or whether their answers vary across either time or country. Having responses from the same experts over time will allow us to analyze how far the responses are contingent upon a particular election's dynamics. Furthermore, our survey data will also allow the multilevel modeling of variations in perceptions of electoral integrity at several tiers: the expert, the election, and the country.

In conclusion, this chapter has focused on a survey of experts' perceptions of electoral integrity, but the Electoral Integrity Project involves a number of other research components as well. Electoral integrity is understood as a multidimensional concept, and as a team of researchers we have a clear appreciation of the need to use different and complementary approaches to more accurately and completely represent the causes and effects of electoral integrity. This is why during the course of the project we will also employ other means of gathering evidence, using public opinion responses from the World Values Survey, generating an original database on electoral laws, employing in-depth case studies illustrating selected problems, and engaging in on-the-ground field experimental research with partners in the international community to evaluate the effectiveness of selected policy interventions.

Notes

1. Freedom House. 2013. *Freedom in the World 2013: Democratic Breakthroughs in the Balance.* Washington D.C.: Freedom House.
2. Monty Marshall and Keith Jaggers. 2001. *Polity IV Project: Political Regime Characteristics and Transitions, 1800–1999.* Dataset users' manual. Retrieved from: http://www.systemicpeace.org/polity/polity4.htm
    Polity IV Project. 2012. *Political Regime Characteristics and Transitions, 1800–2011.* Dataset. Vienna, VA: Center for Systemic Peace.
3. Ibid.
4. Transparency International. 2012. *Corruption Perceptions Index 2012.* Berlin: Transparency International.
5. David Cingranelli, and David Richards. 2010. "The Cingranelli and Richards (CIRI) Human Rights Data Project." *Human Rights Quarterly* 32: 395–418; Reed Wood, and Mark Gibney. 2010. "The Political Terror Scale (PTS): A Re-introduction and a Comparison to CIRI." *Human Rights Quarterly* 32(2): 367–400.
6. Inter-parliamentary Union. *The Proportion of Women in National Legislatures.* www.ipu.org.
7. United Nations Development Program. 2013. *Human Development Report 2013: The Rise of the South: Human Progress in a Diverse World.* New York: The United Nations Development Program.

8. Jan Teorell, Nicholas Charron, Stefan Dahlberg, Sören Holmberg, Bo Rothstein, Petrus Sundin, and Richard Svensson. 2013. *The Quality of Government Dataset, version 30Apr13*. University of Gothenburg: The Quality of Government Institute, http://www.qog.pol.gu.se. See also Geraldo L. Munck. 2009. *Measuring Democracy: A Bridge between Scholarship and Politics*. Baltimore: The Johns Hopkins Press; Michael Coppedge. 2012. *Democratization and Research Methods*. New York: Cambridge University Press.

9. Susan Hyde and Nikolay Marinov. 2012. "Which elections can be lost?" *Political Analysis* 20(2): 191–210.

10. Judith G. Kelley. 2012. *Monitoring Democracy: When International Election Observation Works, and Why It Often Fails*. Princeton, NJ: Princeton University Press.

11. Sarah Birch. 2011. *Electoral Malpractice*. New York: Oxford University Press.

12. Gerardo L. Munck and Jay Verkuilen. 2002. "Conceptualizing and Measuring Democracy" *Comparative Political Studies* 35(1): 5–34; Gerardo L. Munck. 2009. *Measuring Democracy: A Bridge between Scholarship and Politics*. Baltimore: The Johns Hopkins Press.

13. The PEI data are available for download at http://electoralintegrityproject.com.

14. Michael Coppedge, and John Gerring, with David Altman, Michael Bernhard, Steven Fish, Allen Hicken, Matthew Kroenig, Staffan I. Lindberg, Kelly McMann, Pamela Paxton, Holli A. Semetko, Svend-Erik Skaaning, Jeffrey Staton, and Jan Teorell. 2012. "Conceptualizing and Measuring Democracy: A New Approach." *Perspectives on Politics* 9(2): 247–267.

15. World Values Survey Association. www.worldvaluessurvey.org.

16. Birch (2011), Hyde and Marinov (2012), Kelley (2012).

17. Jorgen Elklit and Andrew Reynolds. 2005. "A Framework for the Systematic Study of Election Quality." *Democratization* 12(2): 147–162. The two quotes in this paragraph are from page 149 of this article.

18. Birch (2011) covers 161 elections in 61 countries from 1995 to 2007, and Kelley (2012) codes 1,324 elections (of which 442 were monitored) in 182 countries from 1975 to 2004.

19. Coppedge and Gerring, ibid.

20. John Young. 2009. *International Election Principles: Democracy and the Rule of Law*. Chicago: American Bar Association; Chad Vickery and Erica Shein. 2012. "Assessing electoral fraud in new democracies." IFES: Washington D.C. http://www.ifes.org/~/media/Files/Publications/White%20PaperReport/2012/Assessing_Electoral_Fraud_Series_Vickery_Shein.pdf; Michael Alvarez, Michael, Thad E. Hall and Susan Hyde. 2008. *Election Fraud: Detecting and Preventing Electoral Manipulation*. 2008. Washington, D.C.: Brookings Institution Press.

21. Michael Alvarez and Thad E. Hall. 2006. "Controlling Democracy: The Principle-Agent Problems in Election Administration." *Policy Studies Journal*, 34, 4: 491–510; Michael Alvarez, Lonna Rae Atkeson and Thad E. Hall (Editors). 2012. *Confirming Elections: Creating Confidence and Integrity through Election Auditing*. New York: Palgrave/Macmillan.

22. Birch. 2011.

23. Pippa Norris. 2014a. Forthcoming. "The Concept of Electoral Integrity." *Electoral Studies*.

24. Organization for Security and Cooperation in Europe (OSCE). 2010. *Election Observation Handbook*. Warsaw: OSCE/ODIHR. 6th Ed.

25. For example, *Elections Canada* reported receiving tens of thousands of complaints concerning fraudulent phone calls made during the campaign for the May 2011 federal election, where voters were directed away from their correct polling station.

26. Organization for Security and Cooperation in Europe (OSCE). 2007. *Handbook for Long-Term Election Observers: Beyond Election Day Observation*. Warsaw: OSCE/ODIHR.

27. See The Ace Project. 2013. *Electoral Cycle*. Available from: http://aceproject.org/ero-en/topics/electoral-management/electoral%20cycle.JPG/view (accessed May 13, 2013).

28. Marco Steenbergen and Gary Marks. 2007. "Evaluating expert judgments." *European Journal of Political Research* 46: 347–366.

29. Elections in Libya, Senegal, and Timor-Leste were not included due to time constraints.

30. Namely, Vatican City, Nauru, Tuvalu, Palau, San Marino, Monaco, and Liechtenstein. We define a state by United Nations' membership. Thus, territories like Palestine are excluded.

The reason for excluding extremely small micro-states is largely the lack of availability of enough election experts regarding each country.

31. Tse-Hua Shih and Xitao Fan. 2008. "Comparing Response Rates from Web and Mail Surveys: A Meta-Analysis." *Field Methods* 20(3): 249–271.

32. Weimiao Fan and Zheng Yan. 2010. "Factors Affecting Response Rates of the Web Survey: A Systematic Review." *Computers in Human Behavior* 26: 132–139.

33. We sent 819 contact emails. 83 people declined to take the survey, providing a variety of different reasons for doing so: 24 did not consider themselves an expert on a particular country; 23 said they were too busy and/or did not have time; 19 offered another reason, and 13 asserted that they were not experts on elections and politics. Finally, four said they were just not interested.

34. Angola promulgated a new constitution in 2010, doing away with an elected president. Nevertheless, Freedom House has not changed their Angola scores (six for political rights and five for civil liberties) since 2002. Our survey covered the August 2012 legislative election.

35. Pippa Norris. 2014a. Forthcoming. "Are There Global Norms of Electoral Integrity?" *Electoral Studies*.

DO INSTITUTIONS MATTER?
MANAGING ELECTIONS

5

Election Monitoring

The Implications of Multiple Monitors for Electoral Integrity

URSULA DAXECKER AND GERALD SCHNEIDER

The 2004 legislative elections in Kazakhstan were monitored by three international organizations engaged in election observation. One might expect that the supervision of electoral processes by multiple organizations would increase the amount of information on election quality available to voters, but the three participating organizations came to quite different conclusions regarding the credibility of the elections. The Council of Europe (COE) and the Organization for Security and Cooperation in Europe (OSCE) criticized the election, alleging that serious irregularities occurred and condemning the electoral process. Yet in contrast, the Commonwealth of Independent States (CIS) delegation concluded that minor shortcomings in the electoral process did not affect either voters' free choice or the election results, coming to an overall positive assessment.[1] Clearly, additional reports did not necessarily improve the quality of available information about this election's regularity, and Kazakhstan is not an isolated case. On the contrary, incumbents concerned about negative observer reports can often expect a beneficial cacophony of friendly and critical observer opinions if they invite more than one observer group.[2] Inviting organizations of varied quality would in this perspective be strategically advantageous by allowing governments under domestic pressure to highlight more positive assessments and selectively cite more critical ones—even if some observer organizations find serious irregularities. For instance, the Kazakh Electoral Commission's website for the 2004 elections includes a lengthy quote by the head of the CIS delegation endorsing the election and cites more favorable portions from the OSCE and COE statements and reports, but it omits the more critical elements from these reports.[3] In these elections, inviting a mix of observer organizations appears to have worked in favor of the government. Despite allegations of major fraud and irregularities by opposition parties and some monitoring organizations, election results giving President Nazarbayev's party more than 60 percent of the votes were left unchanged, and popular protests failed to materialize.

The 2000 presidential elections in Peru, conversely, show that the incumbent's gamble with the invitation of additional observers can also backfire. This case demonstrates how agreements on fraud between international election monitors bolster the legitimacy of their reports, thereby increasing the pressure on incumbents to rerun elections or even step down. All three observation missions invited to monitor the Peruvian elections were unanimous in condemning the elections as flawed and falling short of international standards.[4] Widespread protests over blatant election fraud followed, ultimately resulting in President Fujimori's resignation and his escape to Japan.[5] While admittedly anecdotal, these cases illustrate how incumbents can benefit from inviting the right mix of friendly and critical organizations, but they also illustrate how multilateral monitoring by reputable organizations can reinforce the credibility of their assessments, help bring about democratic reforms, or support the consolidation of democracy.

Election observation of the kind conducted in Kazakhstan and Peru is a key new norm in international politics that has altered the strategic calculus of governments and opposition groups alike. Two encompassing monographs have recently focused on the diffusion of this practice, arguing that norms of democracy promotion have rendered an increasing number of leaders interested in inviting observers regardless of whether they are truly interested in establishing democracy.[6] A growing number of formal models look through the lenses of decision or game theory for how potentially fraudulent incumbents can profit from election monitoring even when they risk being caught cheating.[7] These studies focus on how election monitoring provides information to domestic actors. However, they do not treat the observers as strategic actors whose reputation depends on the accuracy of the reports and the outcome of the election monitoring process. Combining the supply and the demand-side analysis of election monitoring, we examine the conditions under which asking for additional monitoring reports possibly offsets the informational gains that election observers provide to the domestic actors.

The formal literature on election monitoring suggests that voters and the opposition may perceive the invitation or acceptance of a less reputable monitoring mission as a sign of weakness.[8] Our argument draws on this reasoning and implies that desperate leaders who face a high risk to be accused of election fraud might nevertheless accept the stigma of electoral manipulation. The tendency of trying to offset a possibly negative report through a more supportive one should, in our view, be particularly pronounced in institutionally weak, corrupt, and economically dependent countries. We expect that incumbents who invite the "right" combination of monitors are less likely to face post-election unrest.

We test these complementary claims about the causes of complex monitoring and its consequences using a new dataset for international election monitoring missions from 1980–2004 described by Judith Kelley and Kirik Kolev.[9] We first model the causes of multilateral monitoring with models that distinguish the number and quality of invited monitoring organizations. The statistical evidence shows that leaders with a history of flawed elections and countries that are highly dependent on foreign aid are more likely to invite or accept a combination of low and high-quality monitors. Using evidence from these models in a matching procedure that helps account for endogeneity concerns, we proceed to examining the consequences of multilateral monitoring invitations. We find that incumbents who invite a mix of lenient and critical organizations can successfully avoid the costly consequences of cheating documented in existing research.

Regime Complexity in International Election Monitoring

Election monitoring is a growing international practice that has received ample theoretical and empirical scrutiny in recent years. International organizations have become increasingly involved in the supervision of electoral processes, and this growing interest in elections documents itself both in the number of monitored elections and the number of organizations present at elections. Susan Hyde[10] and Judith Kelley[11] show that the rate of internationally observed elections has increased markedly, from less than 10 percent of elections being monitored before the late 1980s to approximately 80 percent of elections today. However, not all elections are monitored. As Pippa Norris, Jørgen Elklit, and Andrew Reynolds point out in chapter 3 of this volume, the selection mechanisms at work result in "floor" and "ceiling" effects. Hence, monitoring organizations do not tend to send observers to countries in which they expect to encounter few problems, and they also avoid elections in which security threats are high. Finally, it is unlikely that the most authoritarian states invite them to monitor the vote.

Yet in addition to a higher rate of monitored elections, a growing number of elections are also observed by more than one organization. As Judith Kelley notes,[12] efforts by Western states to give primary responsibilities in election monitoring to the UN after the end of the Cold War failed, and more than 20 non-governmental and intergovernmental organizations are or have been active in international election monitoring as a result.[13] Since 1975, approximately half of all observed elections were monitored by more than one international organization.[14] Similar to the rate of monitored elections, this pattern has become more pronounced over time. Before 1990, less than 20 percent of elections were observed by more than one monitoring mission; now, over 60 percent of observed elections are monitored by two or more organizations.[15]

Importantly, these organizations differ significantly in their willingness and ability to criticize election quality. The election monitoring arms of the African Union (AU), the South African Development Community (SADC), or the CIS, for example, have a reputation for (almost) never criticizing elections.[16] Some argue that the CIS monitoring organization, for example, was created by regional governments specifically interested in counteracting the frequently critical reports by the OSCE for post-Soviet elections.[17] Arguably, even reputable organizations may at times fail to assess the quality of elections negatively. For example, as chapter 2 illustrates, the Carter Center mission observing the 2012 presidential elections in Egypt was hampered by substantial restrictions imposed by the electoral commission. Presumably, the emergence of this "shadow market" could benefit incumbents who face pressure to invite monitors but at the same time want to avoid the punishments that can follow critical reports.[18] The foreign aid literature suggests, along these lines, that donor fragmentation decreases the effectiveness of development assistance and the administrative capacity of the receiving state.[19]

The implications of multilateral election monitoring have received relatively little attention. While recent research has improved our understanding of the intended and unintended consequences of election observation, researchers have primarily compared situations in which observers were present to those in which they were not.[20] With regard to the benefits of election monitoring, studies have shown that international election observation, in particular observation by reputable organizations, can deter fraud and raise the costs of cheating for incumbents because of post-election punishment. For example, Susan Hyde and Judith Kelley find that the presence of reputable international observers can help reduce fraud and thus improve election quality.[21] Regarding the increased costs of cheating, Donno argues that the presence of high-quality observers in fraudulent elections mobilizes opposition and citizens and therefore increases the chance of punishment by regional organizations, which she supports with evidence from Latin American elections.[22] Similarly, Susan Hyde and Nikolay Marinov expect that information on fraud provided by credible observers increases the probability of post-election protests, which could lead to costly consequences such as the ousting of incumbents, or require the use of violence to contain anti-regime protests.[23] Also drawing on an informational logic, fraudulent elections monitored by reputable international observers have a greater likelihood of post-election violence.[24]

With regard to the unintended consequences of monitoring, Judith Kelley documents that international monitors at times legitimize flawed elections.[25] Other research has shown that the growing international attention to electoral processes can induce shifts in the manipulative strategies used by incumbents, leading to increasing pre-electoral fiscal manipulation, lower quality of governance, or a higher rate of boycotts in elections where monitors were present.[26]

Yet while these studies have produced valuable information on the domestic and international implications of the presence of (reputable) monitors compared to their absence, they do not examine whether or how the growing number and differing quality of organizations engaged in monitoring could affect these findings, nor do they evaluate whether some incumbent governments might strategically invite more than one observer organization or a mix of observers. One notable exception is Judith Kelley,[27] who argues that the density of international election monitors has potential costs, such as coordination problems or competition between monitoring organizations, but also benefits, such as the mutual reinforcement of democratic norms or the availability of multiple institutional channels to "help avoid deadlock and paralysis."[28] Although Judith Kelley[29] does not examine these scenarios with statistical analysis or case studies, she presents several illustrative examples that support the presence of costs and benefits in the international election monitoring regime. In our argument, developed in more detail below, we will outline the conditions under which the invitations of multiple organizations, particularly a mix of low- and high-quality organizations, could be exploited by incumbent governments and thus undermine the benefits provided by the international regime on election monitoring. Conversely, our argument implies that multilateral monitoring by credible organizations can help improve electoral integrity by either deterring cheating in the first place, or by punishing incumbents for cheating through the incidence of post-election unrest.

The Selection and Impact of Second Election Monitors

Formal theoretical work has analyzed how incumbent governments might profit from the reliance on election monitors or similar mechanisms like the appointment of an electoral commission. Beatriz Magaloni analyzed the credibility dilemma an autocrat faces vis-à-vis an opposition that might challenge any election regardless of whether it was clean or fraudulent.[30] However, delegating the organization of an election solves the dilemma that announcing orderly elections is not credible. Andrew Little shows, along these lines, that inviting election monitors and cheating in front of them is not paradoxical because it lowers citizens´ expectation about the level of fraud that will accompany an election.[31] Modeling the interactions between the incumbent and the citizens as a "global game" and thus a specific type of limited information model, Little argues that incentives to cheat linger on as long as the monitoring is imperfect, but that beliefs of a massive fraud occurring increase the risk of mass protests. Milan Svolik and Svitlana Chernykh similarly examine election observation as an information-gathering device, focusing on the observer's concern, labeled the "monitor's restraint," of falsely rejecting a claim by the incumbent that she has won the election.[32] More particularly, their model demonstrates that a rejection of the incumbent's claim of an election victory by highly restrained monitors is much more informative for the opposition than the equivalent opinion of less constrained observers.[33]

Susan Hyde and Nikolay Marinov support the contention advanced by these recent game-theoretic models that election monitoring is an information device that helps dissatisfied citizens to coordinate their protests.[34] However, governments have largely had a free hand in the selection and appointment of monitors, and they might have incentives to accept one or more additional observer missions in case they fear a particularly negative assessment by an international monitor. As

Judith Kelley shows, appointing multiple election observers has become more frequent. In her view, "the ability of governments to manipulate the election monitoring experience increases as the number of organizations available for monitoring grows."[35] Nevertheless, appointing a second or third monitor—or portraying these appointments as an act by the international community—creates the risk that these reports reinforce each other and that an accumulation of negative election assessments will force the incumbent out of office. However, contradicting evaluations by the international community will be beneficial and help the incumbent to avoid post-election protest and unrest.

Election observers should theoretically only be concerned with the regularity of the election process. However, they might also have previously formed contacts with either the government or the opposition, which may bias them favorably toward one of the candidates or parties. Election observers are therefore strategic actors who have to carefully evaluate whether it is worth taking the risk of agreeing with the wrong side. Whatever the bias and personal interest of an election observer in the outcome of an election might be, she faces the double risk of committing Type I (accusing an honest incumbent of cheating) or Type II errors (supporting a cheating incumbent). Whitewashing a stained incumbent through a rosy election observer report diminishes the monitor's reputation. However, some election observers might not care about such a loss very much, as they might want to continue to have close contact with the incumbent after the elections. The Kazakh example introduced above where the CIS provided a supportive statement of Nazarbayev's party is a telling example that not only the *demand* for electoral monitoring need be considered, but also its *supply*. In other words, electoral observation should be analyzed like general international conflict management, by jointly examining those who ask for the service and those who provide it.[36]

To this, "complex" monitoring missions add the chance that a contradicting view will inevitably face accusations from either the government or the opposition. While an assignment improves an organization's reputation, delivering a dissenting vote carries the risk of destroying—or at least undermining—it. This danger is especially large for Type II errors, so non-reputational benefits must exist for producing an assessment that contradicts a negative report. Unsurprisingly, such positive assessment often comes from organizations in which the incumbent is itself a major player and which are therefore most likely to provide biased assessments. We believe that incumbent governments will rely most often on observers who have not build up a reputation of delivering high-quality reports in the past and who are politically close, and therefore likely to team up with, another monitor. Specifically, we maintain that observer missions that depend on the incumbent government are much more likely to provide a positive assessment of an election. Hence, interest collusion between the observer and the observed might hinder the effective monitoring of suspicious elections. Liisa Laakso provides evidence for these shady tendencies for the 2000 election in Zimbabwe, noting that "some observers from the neighboring countries were astonishingly pro-government in their statements."[37]

In sum, there are strategic reasons for why we see multiple observers in some elections but not in others. This means, by extension, that multilateral monitoring efforts are not a random sample of all monitoring cases and that the average quality of unilateral and multilateral election observer mission reports should differ. The theoretical argument that we will develop below takes this stepwise decision-making process into account.

Selection of multilateral monitoring: Like other conflict resolution mechanisms, election monitoring is, by and large, a voluntary process on which governments and one or several outside parties have to agree. This implies that incumbent leaders have an almost free hand in asking additional observers to provide their monitoring services. The formal models summarized above suggest that asking for a second opinion might decrease the benefits that an incumbent government receives from its willingness to expose its election organization to independent scrutiny, especially if the additional observer is not highly reputable and is likely to produce a rosy election assessment. Hence, asking for a second opinion reduces the likelihood that an independent monitor's report will be taken seriously, whatever the evaluation's outcome will be. Some governments, however, might accept the risk of losing face if they believe that the danger of being stigmatized as an election fixer is too large. As Bruce Bueno de Mesquita, Alastair Smith, Randolph M. Siverson, and James D. Morrow and others have shown, the risk of losing office affects the present-day behavior of political leaders and forces them to use carrot-and-stick policies toward their "selectorates" to survive an imminent election or revolutionary challenge.[38] Asking for a second report therefore comes close to what George Downs and David Rocke have called "gambling for resurrection."[39]

The danger of a negative report looms particularly large in two contexts. First, the incumbent government might fear the shadow of past election fraud. If it or a predecessor had given the orders in the last election to manipulate the results, it might therefore believe that election observers will be especially careful in their evaluations. Second, incumbent governments in anocracies might fear that the international community does not trust that the elections for which they are responsible will be sufficiently free and fair compared to those of established democracies. Anocracies might also bear a disadvantage compared to autocracies because they do not necessarily have sufficient means to quell public protests after the publication of a negative assessment of the elections.

> *H1:* Incumbent governments that face a higher chance of negative reports because their countries lack a tradition of free and fair elections will have a more pronounced tendency to invite a mix of observers. This tendency manifests itself either (a) through a recent history of rigged elections, or (b) through the anocratic state of the political institutions.

A second reason for inviting an additional election observer might be international pressure. This is particularly the case for smaller developing countries in whose economies foreign aid plays an important role. Leaders in such countries might try to counteract a possibly negative report by inviting or accepting a second election observer team. Note, however, that international leaders whose countries depend on foreign aid do not necessarily have to fear single observer missions. Judith Kelley reports, for instance, that observers are more likely to endorse elections in such countries.[40] Case studies furthermore suggest that the strategic interest of donors has occasionally prolonged the tenure of leaders such as Kenyan President Daniel arap Moi.[41] However, aid donors frequently consider election observation as a precondition of further assistance. The call for monitors will, according to this reasoning, be most pronounced in countries in which the international community can make such demands quite credibly.

> H2: The more that an incumbent government profits from the international community's support, the higher the chance that a government invites a mix of observers.

How multilateral monitoring affects post-election unrest: Incumbent governments invite a mix of critical and friendly observers to avoid outcomes undesirable to them, such as being faced with post-election protests and rioting or having to use repression to contain these anti-regime protests. This gamble, however, only pays off if observers disagree or if, against all odds, all reports agree that the elections were free and fair. The principal-agent literature strongly suggests that multiple principals (and the disagreements associated with them) increase the power of the agent.[42] Observer disagreement mainly benefits those leaders who believe that fixing election results is the only thing that might help them stay in power. Conversely, more settled or self-confident leaders who do not see a need to cheat might prefer to stick to a unilateral mission because they do not want to signal their pre-election desperation to the voters and the opposition through the invitation of a team of monitors.

Technically, increasing potential conflict among observers increases the size of the core and thus the stability of the decision-making process. A growing literature in international political economy supports the conjecture that growing disagreement among principals increases the slack of the agent.[43] Although in their relationship with the outside world incumbent governments are not agents in the strict sense, they are nevertheless considerably weakened through negative reports. Hence, their "gamble for resurrection" will only be successful if they can count on at least some disagreement between the international monitors or an overall positive assessment by this team.

> H3: Inviting a mix of low- and high-quality observers reduces the risk of
> (a) post-election unrest and (b) post-election repression.

Research Design
Data and Methodology

We start by creating a dataset of all election rounds held from 1980 to 2004.[44] Elections data come from the National Elections Across Democracy and Autocracy (NELDA) dataset.[45] NELDA includes all countries that held competitive elections since 1945. The unit of analysis in our data is the election-round, meaning that runoff elections and multiple-round legislative elections are coded as separate cases.[46] The dataset includes 1,638 elections rounds for the time period under analysis.

Our empirical analysis consists of two parts. First, we model incumbents' decision to invite international election observer organizations to examine whether our hypotheses regarding the invitation of a mix of observers is supported. Since incumbents can decide whether to invite one or more organizations, or low or high-quality organizations, we use a multinomial logit model that can distinguish among different types of invitations.[47] Second, we examine the consequences of these different types of observer invitations for a variety of post-election outcomes. We use logit models to assess the effect of different types of observer invitations on post-election leadership protests and repression. Since our models of observer invitations show that certain elections are more likely to be observed, we use matching to preprocess the data and reduce concerns on endogeneity bias.

Dependent Variables

Observer Invitation: For the first two hypotheses, our dependent variable is a categorical measure of the number and quality of international election observer organizations present at each election. Recall that Hypotheses 1 and 2 focus on observer invitations and expect that incumbent governments with a history of cheating, those with questionable commitments to democracy, and those facing international pressure are more likely to invite a mix of low- and high-quality observer organizations. We use the Data on International Election Monitoring (DIEM) to indicate the number and quality of observer organizations.[48] The DIEM data are based on information from 592 reports by 19 organizations that monitored elections from 1980 to 2004 and are the most detailed available account of the activities of international monitors. The data include information on the number, names, and assessments of monitoring organizations present for each election, which we use to create a categorical variable indicating whether an election was observed by one or more organizations and the quality of the organization involved.

We create five categories for observed elections that seem most theoretically relevant: elections observed by one low-quality organization, elections observed by two or more low-quality organizations, elections observed by a combination of low and high-quality organizations, elections observed by one high-quality organization, and elections observed by two or more high-quality observers. Establishing the number of organizations is uncontroversial, but the categorization of organizations as low or high-quality merits explanation. Following Alberto Simpser and Daniela Donno,[49] as well as Susan Hyde and Nikolay Marinov,[50] we define high-quality organizations as those that have been willing to criticize fraudulent elections in the past. The following organizations were coded as high-quality: Asian Network for Free Elections (ANFREL), the Carter Center, Commonwealth, Council of Europe, Electoral Institute of Southern Africa (EISA), European Parliament (EP), European Union (EU), International Republican Institute (IRI), National Democratic Institute (NDI), Organization of American States (OAS), Organization for Security and Cooperation in Europe, and the United Nations (UN). Four organizations in DIEM remain and were then defined as low-quality: The African Union (AU), the Commonwealth of Independent States (CIS), the International Human Rights Law Group (IHRLG), and the South African Development Community (SADC).[51] Of the four low-quality organizations, the CIS, SADC, and IHRLG have never criticized a problematic election, and the AU has criticized highly fraudulent elections less than 15 percent of the time.[52] One might object that our definition of high-quality organizations is rather lenient, but we are most interested in cases where incumbents try to counteract the risk of a negative report by inviting organizations that are almost certain to provide an endorsement.[53] As we argued in our theoretical section, combining an invitation to friendly observers with those the international community deems reputable maximizes incumbents' chance to avoid the costly consequences of inviting observers. Table 5.1 presents the regional distribution of observer invitations with respect to the number and quality of organizations invited.

Table 5.1 shows that 388 of 1,638 elections in the data were monitored by international observers, leaving 1,250 election rounds without monitors. Since no election-rounds were monitored by two low-quality organizations, we do not show them in the table and exclude this category from our analyses.[54] Globally, we observe 36 elections that were monitored by a single low-quality organization. Elections observed by a mix are more common (16 percent), although the most frequent missions consist of one single high-quality organization (36 percent) and two or more high-quality organizations (39 percent). Table 5.1 also presents the regional distribution of observer organizations. We see the highest percentage of mixed monitoring missions in Africa (30 percent), followed by the Middle East and North Africa (25 percent), and Asia (18 percent).

The dependent variable in the statistical analysis contains five categories and is coded 0 for elections without observers, 1 for those with one low-quality organization, 2 for mixed observer groups, 3 for one high-quality observer, and 4 for two or more high-quality organizations.

Post-Election Unrest: We examine two dependent variables for our analysis of post-election unrest. The third hypothesis anticipates that inviting a mix of

Table 5.1: **Regional Distribution of Number and Quality of Observer Organizations Across Elections, 1980–2004**

Variable	Americas	Europe	Africa	Middle East & North Africa	Asia	Total (%)
One Low-Quality	5 (6.4)	0 (0.0)	27 (29.7)	3 (37.5)	1 (1.35)	36 (9.3)
Mix of Low- and High-Quality	2 (2.6)	18 (13.1)	27 (29.7)	2 (25.0)	13 (17.6)	62 (16.0)
One High-Quality	33 (42.3)	43 (31.4)	26 (28.6)	3 (37.5)	34 (46.0)	139 (35.8)
Two or More High-Quality	38 (48.7)	76 (55.5)	11 (12.1)	0 (0.0)	26 (35.1)	151 (38.9)
Total	78	137	91	8	74	386

Note: No elections were monitored by two or more low-quality organizations.

Source: Data on International Election Monitoring (DIEM) collected by Judith Kelley, available at http://sites.duke.edu/kelley/

observers, particularly in elections where incumbents cheated, will lower the risk of post-election protests and post-election repression, outcomes incumbents would prefer to avoid. Data for post-election protests and riots, and post-election repression by the government, respectively, come from NELDA. The first measure is a dichotomous variable indicating whether riots and protests related to the handling or outcome of elections occurred in elections' aftermath. The data set contains 150 election rounds (14 percent) that experienced post-election protests and riots. The second variable measures whether the government responded to such riots and protests with the use of violence. The repression variable is dichotomous, and governmental violence occurred in 70 election rounds (or 6 percent).

Independent Variables

Observer Invitation: In hypotheses 1 and 2, we argued that inviting a mix of friendly and critical observers would be particularly attractive to incumbents who worry about a negative report but are under international pressure to invite monitors. Incumbents fearing a critical report should be those who are inclined to manipulating elections. While we cannot empirically measure incumbents' intent to cheat, past fraudulent behavior should be a reasonable proxy for capturing this concept. We use the Quality of Elections Data (QED) to create this variable. QED utilizes information from US State Department Human Rights Reports and codes whether an election was acceptable, ambiguous, or unacceptable. We transform this measure into a dichotomous variable coded 1 for cases in which previous elections were considered unacceptable, 0 otherwise.[55] We also argued that uncertainty over whether a government is institutionally able to commit itself to democracy should lead to more observer invitations.[56] This risk should be particularly high in semi-democracies. To test for the possible curvilinear impact of democracy, we include the Polity IV democracy measure in its simple and its squared version.[57] The coefficient for the squared polity measure is expected to be significant and negative, indicating a curvilinear and n-shaped relationship between democracy and observer invitations.

Our second hypothesis regarding the invitation of multiple monitors focused on international pressure, and we expected that incumbents receiving large amounts of official development assistance should be particularly inclined to invite a mix of lenient and reputable observer organizations. We use data on official development assistance (ODA) from the AidData project to create this variable, which measures each country's net ODA flows in constant US dollars.[58] In addition, we take the natural log of ODA flows because the values are right-skewed, and we also lag values by one year to account for possible endogeneity.

We also include several control variables. First, Judith Kelley and Susan Hyde[59] expect that multiparty elections and initial elections after suspension are more likely to attract monitors. NELDA includes a variable that indicates whether elections were the first with multiple parties or after suspension. We then create a dummy variable coded 1 for such elections, 0 otherwise. Second, we control for the effect of economic development by including logged GDP per capita values and also lag values by one year. Third, we include dummy variables for the Americas, Europe, Africa, the Middle East and North Africa, and Asia to account for regional differences. Coefficients for dummy variables (with the Middle East and North Africa as the excluded category) are not reported to preserve space. Finally, following recommendations by Nathaniel Beck, Jonathan Katz, and Richard Tucker[60] we create a measure that counts the number of years since a government last invited multiple election observer organizations and three cubic splines to account for temporal dependence. We present results for the observer year variable but exclude splines to preserve space.

Post-Election Unrest: The third hypothesis examines the effect of different types of observer invitations on the probability of post-election protests and governmental violence against protesters. Our main expectation contends that a mix of friendly and critical monitoring organizations makes it easier for incumbents— particularly those who cheated—to avoid anti-regime rioting or the use of repression. As highlighted in the example of the 2004 Kazakh elections, incumbents can exploit contradictions between organizations of differing quality by highlighting the endorsements of friendly monitors and omitting more critical ones. We use the dependent variable in the invitations model to operationalize different types of observer organizations and disaggregate it into four dummies: a dichotomous variable for elections monitored by a single low-quality organization, a second variable for elections monitored by one low-quality and one high-quality organization, a third variable for elections observed by one high-quality organization, and a fourth variable for elections monitored by two or more high-quality organizations. Each of these variables is coded 1 if the respective configuration was present, 0 otherwise.

We argue that the benefits of inviting a mix of observers materialize especially when incumbents resort to cheating. While an invitation to a friendly monitoring organization likely undermines the credibility of an incumbent, he or she is unlikely to be punished for inviting such organizations if the elections are assessed as acceptable by all monitoring organizations present. For that reason, we expect that the advantages of strategic monitoring invitations are especially pronounced in fraudulent elections. To examine the combined effect of mixed monitoring missions and fraud in elections, we create an interaction between the dummy variable for elections observed by low- and high-quality monitors and a variable indicating the presence of serious fraud in elections. We use the QED data to measure fraud. The variable is coded 1 if elections were considered unacceptable, 0 otherwise. We also create interactions between fraud and the remaining types of monitoring missions (one low-quality observer, one high-quality observer, and two or more high-quality observers).

We include several control variables in the post-election models. First, we create a dummy variable that indicates whether opposition parties experienced gains in their vote shares. The NELDA data include this variable, and we expect that an increase in the number of votes for opposition parties would reduce the probability of anti-regime unrest. Second, we retain the development assistance variable from the selection equation to examine whether incumbents receiving aid are more likely to be removed or experience protests as a result of greater international pressure. Third, we again include regional dummy variables. Finally, we control for temporal dependence by creating variables that indicate the number of years since the protest and repression, together with three cubic splines. We use standard errors clustered by country in all models.

In the post-election models, we use matching methods to address threats to causal inference. In particular, international election monitoring could be the result of anticipating protests or violence after elections rather than having an effect on them. Observers may be more likely to monitor elections that have a high risk of leading to unrest and an empirical relationship could thus be driven by observers' anticipation of these outcomes rather than the presence of observers. We use coarsened exact matching to reduce the risk of such bias and match on variables that are likely to influence observer anticipation of election fraud, expecting that fraud in the preceding election-round, level of democracy, GDP per capita, first elections, and development assistance affect the likelihood of observation.[61] Matching preprocesses the data on these variables and excludes observations from the treatment group (i.e., observed elections) and control group (i.e., unobserved elections) that differ fundamentally on covariate values and thus might be driven by the absence or presence of observers.[62]

Results

Observer Invitations

The models in Table 5.2 present findings for our hypotheses on the likelihood of inviting observer organizations.

Our main theoretical focus is on incumbents who invite a combination of low- and high-quality observers (model 2). We find that incumbents who cheated in the past or whose commitment to democracy is uncertain (Hypothesis 1) and those who are dependent on international development assistance (Hypothesis 2) are

Table 5.2: **Explaining Observer Invitations, 1980–2004**

Variables	One Low Quality	Mixed Quality	One High Quality	Two High Quality
Fraud$_{t-1}$	−0.459	1.306**	0.244	0.063
	(0.499)	(0.433)	(0.346)	(0.411)
First Election	−0.100	0.013	0.249	0.715*
	(0.415)	(0.428)	(0.353)	(0.348)
ODA logged$_{t-1}$	−0.211	0.406**	0.302**	0.310**
	(0.151)	(0.098)	(0.077)	(0.075)
Polity$_{t-1}$	−0.069	0.092*	0.023*	0.038**
	(0.058)	(0.044)	(0.030)	(0.034)
Polity Squared$_{t-1}$	−0.031**	−0.027**	−0.012*	−0.036**
	(0.008)	(0.007)	(0.005)	(0.005)
GDP logged$_{t-1}$	−0.173	0.046	0.132	0.295
	(0.291)	(0.302)	(0.214)	(0.209)
Observer Years	0.014	−0.115**	−0.057**	−0.070*
	(0.030)	(0.044)	(0.022)	(0.030)
Constant	0.095	−5.525+	−5.605**	−15.909**
	(3.051)	(2.840)	(2.556)	(2.039)
Observations	1,332	1,332	1,332	1,332
Number of Countries	145	145	145	145
Log pseudo likelihood=−973.49				

Note: The table presents multinomial logit models beta coefficients with standard errors in parentheses and clustered by country. Models present coefficients for the different numbers and quality of observer organizations, using 'no observers' as the baseline category.

** $p < 0.01$, * $p < 0.05$, + $p < 0.1$ (two-tailed tests).

Source: Data on International Election Monitoring (DIEM) collected by Judith Kelley, available at http://sites.duke.edu/kelley/

more likely to invite a mix of observer organizations. The coefficients for all three variables are in the expected direction and significant at the 95-percent confidence level, thus supporting the first two hypotheses. While uncertain commitment to democracy and international assistance are significant for all observer invitations (model 1) and remain significant for high-quality observer invitations (models 3 and 4), the coefficient for fraud in previous elections is significant only in model 3. The findings therefore confirm that incumbents considering manipulation but simultaneously facing international pressure to invite observers are most inclined to ensure at least some positive reports by inviting a combination of lenient and reputable observers.

While less important for our argument, we also note that the determinants of observer invitations are quite different for varying types and numbers of observers. The coefficient for first elections is significant only for elections monitored by two or more high-quality organizations, suggesting that they are particularly likely to receive multiple high-quality observers, which could be due to greater international pressure or the need of incumbents to strongly signal their commitment to democracy. Table 5.3 presents the marginal effects for significant variables in Table 5.2.

Post-Election Unrest

The third hypothesis argues that inviting a mix of monitoring organizations—particularly if incumbents manipulated election outcomes—reduces the likelihood of post-election unrest and repression after elections.

Findings for post-election protests and repression are presented in Table 5.4. The first two models show coefficients without interactions between fraud and observer

Table 5.3: **Marginal Effects for Significant Variables in Table 5.2**

Variables	*One Low-Quality*	*Mixed Quality*	*One High-Quality*	*Two High-Quality*
Fraud$_{t-1}$	–	+0.063	–	–
First Election	–	–	–	+0.051
ODA logged $_{t-1}$	–	+0.012	+0.019	+0.014
Polity[a]	−0.039	−0.054	−0.018	−0.190
Observer Years	–	−0.004	−0.003	−0.003

Note: Marginal effects calculated by varying continuous variables ±1SD from the mean and 0 to 1 for dichotomous variables. [a] Polity and Polity squared are varied jointly from the mean to +1SD above the mean.

Source: Data on International Election Monitoring (DIEM) collected by Judith Kelley, available at http://sites.duke.edu/kelley/

Table 5.4: **Explaining Protests and Repression after Elections, 1980–2004**

Variables	Protest 1	Protest 2	Repression 1	Repression 2
One Low-Quality	0.234	−0.240	0.659	0.370
	(0.430)	(0.563)	(0.655)	(0.829)
Mixed Quality	0.906*	0.429	0.884+	0.324
	(0.454)	(0.528)	(0.481)	(0.668)
Two High-Quality	0.951**	0.474	0.785	0.258
	(0.361)	(0.439)	(0.512)	(0.563)
One High-Quality	0.101	−0.331	−0.042	−1.360
	(0.392)	(0.502)	(0.535)	(1.109)
One Low*Fraud	–	1.240	–	0.702
		(0.887)		(1.248)
Mixed*Fraud	–	1.281	–	1.444
		(1.000)		(1.130)
One High*Fraud	–	1.298	–	2.568+
		(0.791)		(1.314)
Two High*Fraud	–	2.171*	–	1.746*
		(0.866)		(0.872)
Fraud	−0.183	−0.729	−0.172	−0.707
	(0.300)	(0.380)	(0.403)	(0.486)
Opposition Gain	−0.689*	−0.686*	−1.013**	−1.029**
	(0.320)	(0.320)	(0.374)	(0.372)
ODA logged $_{t-1}$	−0.074	−0.071	−0.142	−0.156
	(0.087)	(0.088)	(0.139)	(0.146)
Protest Years	−0.267**	−0.275**	–	–
	(0.085)	(0.085)		
Repression Years	–	–	−0.130	−0.124
			(0.184)	(0.190)
Constant	−0.031	−0.393	−0.228	−0.269
	(0.811)	(0.826)	(1.139)	(1.199)
Observations	1,083	1,083	1,087	1,087
Number of Countries	145	145	145	145
Log pseudo likelihood	−434.28	−426.03	−254.75	−249.94

Note: Logit Models with standard errors in parentheses and clustered by country. ** $p < 0.01$, * $p < 0.05$, + $p < 0.1$ (two-tailed tests).

types, but since we would anticipate that only cheating incumbents have to worry about punishment, we are most interested in models including interactions (models 2 and 4). Findings confirm that the combination of inviting a mix of observers together with fraud in elections somewhat reduces the risk of protests and the need to use repression. The coefficient for the interaction between mixed observation missions and fraud is insignificant in both the protest and the repression model, but coefficients for interactions between fraud and one high-quality observer group (model 4), and two or more high-quality observer groups, respectively (models 2 and 4), are positive and significant. Hence, the punishment for cheating resulting from the judgments of high-quality observers does not occur in mixed observation missions. While our findings for the punishment imposed for cheating documented by high-quality monitors are thus somewhat inconsistent, we should consider collapsing these two categories, since the determinants of high-quality observer invitations were similar regardless of their number.

Taken together, while findings for post-election unrest do not support our expectations as strongly as expected, incumbents extending these invitations do not seem to incur punishments for manipulating elections despite the presence of some high-quality observers. Our findings thus imply that invitations of a combination of friendly and critical observers can help counteract the costly consequences of negative observer assessments for incumbents.[63]

Conclusions

Election monitoring has turned into a global norm almost no government can escape. However, incumbent governments have considerable possibilities to undermine the credibility of the international observers. One particularly frequent means is the appointment of a mix of low- and high-quality observers. As governments and the international community agree on "complex" monitoring missions, they are not representative of all elections to which monitors are assigned. In this chapter we contend that we can only understand the effect of these election monitors on political outcomes if we jointly examine these results with the origins of mixed monitoring missions. In our view, governments will invite a mix of friendly and critical observers if they face a relatively high risk of being confronted with a negative observer report but simultaneously face international pressure to invite reputable observers. This argument suggests that incumbents with a history of cheating as well as those under the close scrutiny of the international community will call for a second report by friendly monitors in the hope that these observers will offset a possibly negative report through a more positive assessment.

The empirical analysis lends qualified support to this double conjecture. We show that incumbents who cheated in the past and face international pressure to extend invitations are more likely to invite a combination of low- and high-quality observer organizations. As we have argued, these governments are more likely to face a critical report and therefore try to counteract this risk by inviting at least one friendly organization. While we do not find that a mix of observers in fraudulent elections significantly lowers the risk of post-election unrest, we argue that the absence of a positive relationship still marks an improvement from the perspective of incumbents. Since our findings show that elections certified as fraudulent by high-quality international monitors face a greater risk of anti-regime protests and repression, a mix of observers successfully undermines the costly consequences of electoral manipulation.

We should note that the supply of low-quality monitors is concentrated in Africa and the post-Soviet region and thus not equally available to all incumbents, implying that our findings are particularly important for reputable organizations active in those regions. Yet a potentially concerning development is the recent involvement in election monitoring by the Union of South American States (UNASUR), an organization that has not endorsed the Declaration of Principles for International Election Monitoring and sent its first mission to "accompany" the 2012 presidential elections in Venezuela.

More generally, our argument demonstrates how the growing norm of international election monitoring has led to strategic adaptation by both governments and international organizations. Absent a central organization in charge of coordinating election monitoring, a "shadow market" of lenient monitoring organizations has emerged, and this chapter helps clarify the conditions under which governments are particularly inclined to use this increasing supply of monitoring organizations to their advantage.

Acknowledgments: Previous versions of this chapter have been presented at the annual convention of the International Studies Association, San Francisco, April 2-5, 2013, the ENCoRe meeting in Amsterdam, April 24–26, 2013, and the Harvard Workshop of the Electoral Integrity Project in Cambridge, MA, June 3–4, 2013. The authors would like to thank the Leibniz Foundation and European Commission for travel support and workshop participants, as well as Nikolay Marinov, Andrea Ruggeri, and Brian Burgoon for helpful comments.

Notes

1. Information on observer assessments comes from the Data on International Election Monitoring (DIEM) collected by Judith Kelley, available at http://sites.duke.edu/kelley/.
2. Judith Kelley. 2009. "The More the Merrier? The Effects of Having Multiple International Election Organizations." *Perspectives on Politics* 7(1): 59–64.
3. http://www.kazelection2004.org/observers.htm.
4. The organizations present were the Organization of American States, the OSCE/Helsinki Center, and a joint mission by the Carter Center and the National Democratic Institute. For an example of their assessments, see chapter 2 and also the Carter Center/NDI report at http://www.cartercenter.org/documents/292.pdf.
5. The negative repercussions for Fujimori raise the question of why he invited high-quality monitors and then cheated in front of them. However, the Fujimori regime had strong control over the media and he may have hoped to suppress negative reports.

6. Susan D. Hyde. 2011. "Catch Us if You Can: Election Monitoring and International Norm Diffusion." *American Journal of Political Science* 55(2): 356–369; Judith Kelley. 2012. *Monitoring Democracy: When International Election Observation Works, and Why It Often Fails.* Princeton, NJ: Princeton University Press.

7. Beatriz Magaloni. 2010. "The Game of Electoral Fraud and the Ousting of Authoritarian Rule." *American Journal of Political Science* 54(3): 751–765. Little, Andrew T. 2012. "Elections, Fraud, and Election Monitoring in the Shadow of Revolution." *Quarterly Journal of Political Science* 7(3): 249–283; Svolik, Milan W. and Svitlana Chernykh. 2012. "Third-Party Actors and the Success of Democracy: How Electoral Commissions, Courts and Observers Shape Incentives for Election Manipulation and Post-Election Protest." *Unpublished Working Paper,* University of Illinois/Oxford University.

8. Magaloni 2010.

9. Judith Kelley and Kiril Kolev. 2010. "Election Quality and International Observation: Two New Datasets." Working paper, *Duke University.*

10. Hyde 2011: 356.

11. Kelley 2012: 16–17.

12. Kelley 2009a.

13. Kelley and Kolev 2010: 6.

14. Kelley 2009a: 59.

15. Kelley 2009a.

16. Kelley 2012: 53.

17. Jakob Tolstrup. 2009. "Studying a Negative External Actor: Russia's Management of Stability and Instability in the 'Near Abroad.'" *Democratization* 16(5): 922–944.

18. Kelley 2012.

19. See, for example, Stephen Knack and Aminur Rahman. 2007. "Donor Fragmentation and Bureaucratic Quality in Aid Recipients." *Journal of Development Economics* 83(1): 176–197.

20. Susan D. Hyde. 2007. "The Observer Effect in International Politics: Evidence from a Natural Experiment." *World Politics* 60(1): 37–63; Daniela Donno. 2010. "Who Is Punished? Regional Intergovernmental Organizations and the Enforcement of Democratic Norms." *International Organization* 64(4): 593–625; Ursula E. Daxecker, 2012. "The Cost of Exposing Cheating: International Election Monitoring, Fraud, and Post-Election Violence in Africa." *Journal of Peace Research* 49(4), 503–516; Hyde, Susan D. and Nikolay Marinov. 2013. "Information and Self-Enforcing Democracy: The Role of International Election Observation." *International Organization* (in press); Kelley 2012.

21. Hyde 2007; Kelley 2012.

22. Donno 2010.

23. Hyde and Marinov 2013.

24. Daxecker 2012.

25. Judith Kelley. 2009b. "D-Minus Elections: The Politics and Norms of International Election Observation." *International Organization* 63(4): 765–787.

26. Susan D. Hyde and Angela O'Mahony. 2010. "International Scrutiny and Pre-Electoral Fiscal Manipulation in Developing Countries." *Journal of Politics* 72(2): 690–704; Simpser, Alberto and Daniela Donno. 2012. "Can International Election Monitoring Harm Governance?" *Journal of Politics* 74(2): 501–513; Beaulieu, Emily and Susan D. Hyde. 2009. "In the Shadow of Democracy Promotion: Strategic Manipulation, International Observers, and Election Boycotts." *Comparative Political Studies* 42 (3): 392–415.

27. Kelley 2009a.

28. Kelley 2009a: 61.

29. Kelley 2009a. Kelley's (2012, 56) cross-tabulation of the number of monitoring organizations and the assessment of elections shows additionally that assessments are more critical when more than one organization is present.

30. Magaloni 2010.

31. Andrew T. Little. 2012. "Elections, Fraud, and Election Monitoring in the Shadow of Revolution." *Quarterly Journal of Political Science* 7(3): 249–283.

32. Milan W. Svolik and Svitlana Chernykh. 2012. "Third-Party Actors and the Success of Democracy: How Electoral Commissions, Courts and Observers Shape Incentives for Election Manipulation and Post-Election Protest." *Unpublished Working Paper*, University of Illinois/Oxford University.

33. The analogous relationship holds for a highly informative endorsement of the incumbent by unrestrained observers and for support with little informative value by highly restrained monitors.

34. Hyde and Marinov 2013.

35. Kelley 2009a: 63.

36. Jacob Bercovitch and Gerald Schneider. 2000. "Who Mediates? The Political Economy of International Conflict Management." *Journal of Peace Research* 37(2): 145–165.

37. Liisa Laakso. 2002. "The Politics of International Election Observation: The Case of Zimbabwe in 2000." *Journal of Modern African Studies* 40(3): 437–464.

38. Bruce Bueno De Mesquita, Alastair Smith, Randolph M. Siverson and James D. Morrow. 2003. *The Logic of Political Survival*. Cambridge, MA: MIT Press. Catherine M. Conaghan, 2002. "Cashing in on Authoritarianism: Media Collusion in Fujimori's Peru." *The Harvard International Journal of Press/Politics* 7(1): 115–125.

39. George W. Downs and David M. Rocke. 1994. "Conflict, Agency, and Gambling for Resurrection: The Principal-Agent Problem Goes to War." *American Journal of Political Science* 38 (2): 362–380.

40. Kelley 2009b.

41. Stephen Brown. 2001. "Authoritarian Leaders and Multiparty Elections in Africa: How Foreign Donors Help to Keep Kenya's Daniel Arap Moi in Power." *Third World Quarterly* 22(5): 725–739.

42. Ellen Mastenbroek, Heike Klüver, Gerald Schneider and Dietrich Drüner. 2013. "The Core or the Winset? Predicting Policy Change and Decision-Making Efficiency in the European Union." *Unpublished Manuscript*, Radbout Universiteit/Universtität Konstanz.

43. e.g., Mark Copelovitch. 2010. "Master or Servant? Common Agency and the Political Economy of IMF Lending." *International Studies Quarterly* 54(1): 49–77; Nielson, Daniel L. and Michael J. Tierney. 2003. "Delegation to International Organizations: Agency Theory and World Bank Environmental Reform." *International Organization* 57(2): 241–276.

44. Election monitoring data described in Kelley and Kolev (2010) are available for this time frame.

45. Susan D. Hyde and Nikolay Marinov. 2012. "Which Elections Can Be Lost?" *Political Analysis* 20(2): 191–210.

46. Concurrent elections (legislative and executive elections held on the same day) are coded as a single event.

47. Hausman and Small-Hsiao tests conducted for multinomial logit models showed that the assumption of IIA is not violated.

48. (Kelley and Kolev 2010). For most multiple-round elections, the organizations present in one round also observe subsequent rounds. Data are available at: http://www.icpsr.umich.edu/icpsrweb/ICPSR/studies/31461/version/1.

49. Simpser and Donno 2012.

50. Hyde and Marinov 2013.

51. While DIEM includes data on 19 organizations, reports were not available for three organizations and we can therefore not assess whether they criticized elections.

52. Kelley 2012: 53. A concern with this definition of low quality is that organizations becoming engaged in election monitoring only recently have fewer opportunities to criticize problematic elections. Yet several high-quality organizations have been active for similar or shorter time frames than low-quality ones. For example, ANFREL and EISA have been active since 1998, whereas the AU has started to monitor elections in 1992 and the SADC in 1999.

53. Kelley (2012) defines low-quality organizations as those criticizing problematic elections less than 50 percent of the time, yet we believe that a more restrictive definition of low-quality is appropriate for our argument since we focus on incumbents who attempt to ensure at least one supportive report. In addition, a lenient definition avoids accidentally labeling an organization as low quality for sometimes failing to criticize fraudulent elections. As discussed earlier, even credible organizations are sometimes limited in their ability to provide systematic assessments, or may refrain from providing them because of political concerns (see Davis-Roberts and Carroll chapter in this volume and Kelley 2012: 57).
54. This absence is unsurprising given the small number of low-quality organizations and the lack of legitimacy to be gained from the invitation of two organizations of questionable quality as opposed to just one.
55. While we would like to examine whether alternative measures of fraud would produce similar results, few other systematic sources are available. NELDA includes a variable that indicates the presence of pre-election concerns over fraud, but the variable does not measure the actual incidence of fraud, nor does it specify how serious these concerns were.
56. Kelley 2012; Hyde 2011.
57. Marshall and Jaggers 2011. We lag the Polity variables by one year to reduce concerns regarding endogeneity bias.
58. Available at http://www.aiddata.org/content/index.
59. Kelley 2012; Hyde 2011.
60. Nathaniel Beck, Jonathan N. Katz and Richard Tucker. 1998. "Taking Time Seriously: Time-Series-Cross-Section Analysis with a Binary Dependent Variable." *American Journal of Political Science* 42(4): 1260–1288.
61. Stefano M. Iacus, Gary King and Giuseppe Porro. 2012. "Causal Inference Without Balance Checking: Coarsened Exact Matching." *Political Analysis* 20(1):1–24.
62. Pre-processing of the data removes 335 observations from the data.
63. Hyde and Marinov 2013; Daxecker 2012.

6

Constitutions and Election Management

SVITLANA CHERNYKH, ZACHARY ELKINS, JAMES MELTON, AND TOM GINSBURG

In early 2013, Kenyans went to the polls in the first election after the adoption of a new constitution. Memories were fresh from post-election violence in 2007, in which more than a thousand people had been killed and thousands of others had been displaced after the Electoral Commission declared the incumbent, Mwai Kibaki, the victor. Kibaki had been losing to Raila Odinga for most of the vote-counting process, and so the Commission's decision lacked credibility. A major international effort to clean up Kenya's politics followed, brokered by Kofi Annan, an effort that included creation of a new constitution. Perhaps not surprisingly (given that constitutions are often written to solve recent problems), the charter featured a well-specified recipe of electoral management and adjudication. Odinga was again declared the loser in 2013 by the electoral commission, but this time no violence followed. Instead, the disputes were adjudicated in the courts, which by most accounts acquitted themselves well. One can speculate about the reasons for the more peaceful sequel in 2013. Our own proclivity – as constitutional scholars – is to wonder whether institutional reform played some restorative role. That is, did the newly constitutionalized electoral management plan help ensure that the story of the 2007–2008 election crisis was not repeated?[1]

For constitutional designers, this story (and question) provide the backdrop for real decision problems. What, if anything, should framers write down about how elections are administered and adjudicated? Silence is a common response, which is not surprising. Election mechanics are, after all, largely administrative matters and, historically, framers have left their design to bureaucrats. However, there are good reasons for framers to act more deliberately. Most importantly, governments have strong incentives to perpetuate their rule and, as such, it seems illogical to invest incumbents with the power to run the selection method that would decide their fate. But it is hard to devise methods to keep incumbents' thumbs off the scales.

Constitutions—because they can entrench administrative institutions and rules for staffing them—are one of the few ways to do so. Of course, the virtues of commitment often trade off against those of flexibility, and the balance of these two is the holy grail of constitutional design. The way to facilitate such balancing is to paint a clear picture of the choices available to designers, think carefully about the consequences of these choices, and evaluate any evidence—however circumstantial—that speaks to these consequences. These three objectives constitute our agenda in this chapter.

Conceptualizing Electoral Management

A basic division of labor in election management is that between administration and adjudication, a distinction that corresponds roughly to the election itself and its aftermath. Depending upon the electoral system, *administration* can involve the registration of candidates, the design and printing of ballots, the selection and staffing of polling places, and the collection and counting of ballots (see International IDEA guidelines). *Adjudication* refers to the hearing and resolution of disputes about the outcome, or about irregularities that may have affected the outcome. A critical decision, which we turn to at the end of this section, has to do with what—exactly—to put into the constitution.

Administration

Theoretically, institutional designers have considerable flexibility in deciding whom to charge with the management of elections. This diversity is reflected in the use of the general, if infelicitous, term, Electoral Management Bodies (EMB), which refers to any office or organization responsible for either administration or adjudication. Quite often—and *increasingly* often—countries adopt a model in which responsibility for election management is lodged in an independent electoral tribunal or commission.[2] These bodies are typically intended to be institutionally independent from the governments, meaning mostly that they are not accountable to any government ministry or department and manage their own budgets.[3] The main alternative to an independent model of electoral management is a governmental model, in which responsibility for the organization of elections lies with local authorities or the federal bureaucracy (typically the Ministry of Interior). Wall et al. also identify a mixed model, which combines the features of the independent-management and government-management models.[4] The mixed model usually includes an independent body responsible for policy, monitoring and supervision, and an implementation body that is part of a government department. However, the two bodies usually vary in functions and strength, making classification of countries within the mixed model very difficult. Wall et al. find that only 15 percent of countries in the world followed the mixed model, as of circa 2006. These days, the independent model is the modal form of electoral governance; an estimated 55 percent of countries have independent electoral commissions or tribunals, which are granted the power (either alone or in conjuncture with other bodies) to organize elections. Much of the recent scholarly work on election management has concerned the circumstances under which an incumbent would adopt an independent electoral management body.[5] The decision with respect to electoral administration, therefore, is largely one between a commission and the executive branch.

Adjudication

With regard to dispute resolution, a more complex choice presents itself. Authority to adjudicate disputes can reside either with the relevant entity tasked with administration (again, typically either commission or an agency within the bureaucracy), or with the courts. An example of a dual-tasked commission is the Electoral Commission of Thailand, which is granted broad authority to investigate and adjudicate electoral conflicts. In other countries, electoral commissions serve only as a first instance for election complaints, with their decisions appealable to the courts, thus establishing a two-tier system (i.e., Ghana, where between April and August 2013 the Supreme Court held a hearing on a challenge to the 2012 presidential election). This two-tier system has the theoretical advantage of being able to cope with complaints that might be directed at the actions of the electoral commission itself. In Ukraine, for example, complaints about the composition of the electoral commission resulted in a change in commission membership after the annulment of the disputed November 2004 contest but before its rerun shortly thereafter.

Thus, there is a basic institutional design question as to whether to consolidate management and adjudication functions in a single institution or to separate them. As the Ukrainian case illustrates, there is some reason to think that a dedicated adjudication body would be preferable to a dual-tasked agency. A standard argument in administrative design is that two institutions are better than one in terms of ensuring accountability, though there are corresponding increases in costs and uncertainty that might be undesirable in the electoral context.

Once one makes the decision to separate dispute resolution from administration, the next decision is what kind of adjudicative body should be given the task. In some cases, a constitutional or supreme court will have original jurisdiction in electoral matters. These courts are, of course, bodies that have a diverse set of matters before them, and lack experience in the technical aspects of elections. Therefore, courts will typically apply a standard set of procedures concerning evidence, presumptions, and standards of proof—standards that have been devised for a wide array of disputes.

An administrative process, by contrast, might be more flexible but less rigorous. There are also familiar trade-offs having to do with specialization and capture. Electoral commissions may have more expertise in elections than do courts, but because commissions are dealing only with electoral matters, such commissions may be relatively more attractive as targets of efforts to capture the process. Similarly, consolidating both management and adjudication in the same body might tempt politicians to try to capture the body. (One variation is to have a specialized electoral court, which ameliorates some of the concerns about generalist judges but also generates potential pressures for capture.)

Of course, in any particular context, the decision about whether to use extant courts may have much to do with their quality and reputation. Where courts are independent and high quality, it will be desirable to give them jurisdiction over the sensitive matter of electoral disputes. Electoral commissions are newer bodies but may also be able to develop a reputation for independence and quality over time.

Legal Framework

Our focus in this chapter is mostly about *where* in the fabric of the law these institutional decisions are stitched. Constitutional designers face a potentially large set of choices about electoral systems and administration. For each decision, they can choose to specify the details in the constitution, or leave them to be decided by ordinary law or executive order. Within these latter categories, of course, finer distinctions arise. For example, provisions about electoral oversight bodies could be a part of a single comprehensive electoral code, such as in Albania, Argentina, Armenia, and the Philippines. Alternatively, countries can define the structure, composition, and powers of their EMBs in a separate law (e.g., Azerbaijan, Latvia, Nigeria, South Africa, Uzbekistan, and Zambia).[6]

With respect to the use of the constitution, most designers choose a mixed strategy, constitutionalizing some issues but not others. For example, on the choice of the electoral system, constitutions might broadly specify the principle of proportional representation, without giving the details of the remainder calculation. With regard to electoral administration, designers might choose to set up an independent electoral commission or leave it to ordinary authorities in the legislative or executive branch. Clearly, the trend is toward the former, likely to avoid the problem of the fox guarding the henhouse.

A Theory of Constitutionalization
What Should Be Included in a Constitution?

We often think of constitutions as highly standardized pieces of statecraft—documents that take a very similar form across countries. But the simple fact remains that constitutional drafters are free to write anything and everything into their written charter. Our evidence suggests that many do have a mind of their own. Some constitutions stop at a few hundred words and some go on for 150,000. Some deal with reindeer husbandry (Sweden) and some with sports (Brazil). Of course, there are some subjects (e.g., rights) that are so essential (or, at least, so *constitutional*) that nearly every constitution has them.

On which topics are constitutions silent and on which are they vocal? And, more prescriptively, when *should* they be silent and when vocal? Constitutions, of course, serve a number of different functions. At a basic level, constitutions provide an important accounting and organizational function by defining the basic patterns of authority. Most constitutions set up branches of government and specify how they are to be formed.

But a very central function of constitutions, one that some think is the most important, is the critical task of limiting government power in domains and situations in which the incentives of government officials are not aligned with the common good; or, relatedly, situations in which the short-term interest of government is not aligned with its long-term interest—that is, a problem of *dynamic inconsistency*, in the vocabulary of economics. Constitutions solve this problem by committing officials to laws that trump ordinary law and that are difficult to change.

Constitutional rights are a paradigmatic example of this sort of solution. Governments, at times, have immediate incentives to infringe upon rights—infringements that may be highly undesirable in the long term. Not surprisingly, then, nearly every constitution enumerates at least a small set of rights. Of the 188 constitutions in our data in 2013, only three do not contain any rights provisions in their constitutions. Of those constitutions with rights, we estimate that, on average, 16 percent of the document is dedicated to the specification and elaboration of these rights. Of course, constitutions vary with respect to which rights they enshrine. Certain rights—the classic negative liberties such as freedom of religion and speech—are so ubiquitous as to be nearly universal. Most rights, however, are much less prevalent.

Another example is defining states of emergency. If executives can invoke emergency to escape constitutional restrictions, they may be tempted to put their short-term political interest over the long-term collective health of the polity. For this reason, more than 90% of constitutions in force have some provisions specifying rules about a state of emergency, such as when it can be invoked and by whom. A further example is executive selection. The majority of constitutions with elected heads of state include some kind of limit on the number of terms that the executive can serve. The rationale, it is commonly thought, is that the advantages of incumbency are so great that the people cannot be expected to throw executives out after they serve a long time. Constitutions therefore remove this decision from popular control, providing a maximum number of years any individual can serve.

By entrenching rights and certain institutions, constitutions put them beyond the reach of short-term political calculations. As a general matter, then, it makes sense to constitutionalize those domains that seem particularly vulnerable to dynamic inconsistency problems. Or, to put it differently, domains characterized by dynamic inconsistency will exhibit better outcomes when law in those domains is constitutionalized.

Enter Election Management

Under these criteria, election management would seem to be an obvious candidate for constitutionalization. Incumbent governments have a number of interests, some of which may have something to do with the public good. However, one motivation for incumbents is that they or their party remain in power. Indeed, the image of the incumbent clinging relentlessly to power is at the heart of any discussion of democratic deepening and consolidation. It is no surprise that some scholars even define democracy by the act of an incumbent government turning over the reins of power by elections peacefully to the opposition.[7] The electoral motive fuels a well-known tension in representative democracy: while we entrust elected representatives to generate long-term public goods, we incentivize their activity through a relatively short-term mechanism (elections) that often compromises public good provision. So, for example, representatives may strongly believe in fiscal austerity and structural reform but may be unwilling to inflict such costs on voters in the short term, lest they lose elections. This problem of dynamic inconsistency argues for shielding some functions of government (such as central banking) from the purview of elected representatives.

From this vantage point, it would seem perverse to expect incumbents to organize and administer the very elections that may oust them from power. The temptation for governments to intervene is simply too great. Or, perhaps more to the point, the *perception* that they would or do intervene is palpable. Of course, perception is often more meaningful than reality, and in this case, perceived electoral improprieties can have some deleterious effects on citizens' attachment and support of the democratic process.

The perception of electoral malfeasance leads to another important aspect of constitutionalization. It may matter less about *how* exactly electoral management is organized, and more about *whether* it is institutionalized. An election commission staffed in an independent fashion, along with independent courts that offer some redundancy and oversight, may well be an ideal recipe. However, regardless of the recipe, what may be most consequential is that these procedures are equitable, predictable, and resistant to change. Put differently, as long as the rules of the game remain more or less intact, it may not matter that they are suboptimal as long as all parties suffer or benefit equally from them—or at least appear to. It is at this more measured recommendation that the Venice Commission rested in its Code of Good Practice for electoral matters: the commission recommends stability or constitutionalization of electoral management, but beyond that, it does not make any particular recommendation about the form of management.[8]

A recent study of Eastern Europe and the former Soviet Union by Svitlana Chernykh provides reason to embrace stability. Chernykh finds that incumbents frequently change the rules guiding the composition of electoral management bodies before elections in order to increase their chances of victory—moves that, understandably, are vigorously contested by opposition parties.[9] Furthermore, political parties in the region have rejected every election preceded by a change in rules governing the electoral commission. Changes in the rules governing electoral commissions constitute a sufficient condition for electoral rejection by the losing party. It seems likely, then, that the stability of electoral management feeds the perception of electoral fairness by elites. Wall et al. make an argument along these lines and suggest that public trust in election management depends in part on whether the processes are constitutionalized.[10] This raises a question about not only *whether* the electoral management body is constitutionalized but also *how detailed* the provisions guiding its composition and powers are.

We know, of course, that commitment and stability often come at the cost of flexibility. Once constitutionalized, it will be very difficult to change the rules in light of experience, rendering the system rigid and unable to adapt to changing political realities. Despite the clear importance of EMBs, we still know very little about the constitutionalization of electoral oversight bodies over time and across countries, as well as the effects the inclusion of these provisions in the constitution has on different aspects of the electoral process. Which countries are more likely to constitutionalize electoral management? Does constitutionalization lead to comparably higher election quality? Are political parties more likely to accept electoral outcomes or follow legal route of conflict resolution if constitutions provide for an independent electoral management body? We use data from the Comparative Constitutions Project to address these and other questions below.

What Do Constitutions Say about Election Management?

We appeal here to data from the Comparative Constitutions Project (CCP). The CCP records the content of written constitutions for all independent countries since 1789.[11] The CCP survey instrument (see Appendix) includes a basic set of variables regarding election management, though perhaps without the granular detail an EMB scholar might crave.

As we describe above, one can think of election management in terms of administration and adjudication. Regarding administration, the question is whether to establish a commission or defer the matter to the bureaucracy. Regarding adjudication, the question is whether to vest power in the management agency or a court (and within the court system, whether to establish a special electoral court). The CCP allows us to identify the various bodies that are vested with any sort of election

Table 6.1: **Distribution of EMBs in Constitutions Promulgated Between 1946 and 2010**

Court	Electoral Commission	No Commission	Total
Electoral Court	6 (1.3%)	31 (6.6%)	37 (7.9%)
Constitutional Court	13 (2.8%)	50 (10.6%)	63 (13.4%)
Supreme Court	16 (3.4%)	45 (9.6%)	61 (13.0%)
No Court	124 (26.3%)	186 (39.5%)	310 (65.8%)
Total	159 (33.8%)	312 (66.2%)	471 (100%)

Note: Cell frequencies with percentage of total observations in parentheses, n = 471 constitutions.

management authority. Effectively, the three principal players are the electoral commission, a special court, or the supreme or constitutional court. Table 6.1 provides the distribution of drafter's choices about electoral management since World War II, before which the constitutionalization of election management was rare. The majority (60 percent) of modern (post-WWII) constitutions adopt one or more of the aforementioned solutions. 34 percent of constitutions written since World War II establish an electoral commission, 26 percent vest the power to supervise elections with an actor in the judiciary, and 8 percent establish an electoral court.[12]

One interesting pattern that emerges from Table 6.1 is that constitutional drafters seem to view commissions and courts as substitutes. Only 8 percent of constitutions specify both an electoral commission and provide a court (either an electoral court or one of the high courts) with the power to supervise elections.[13] This decision appears to run against the conventional wisdom of separating the administration and adjudication functions played by EMBs. Note, that these and other statements should be qualified by "as designated by the constitution." Of course, a number of countries have electoral commissions that are *not* stipulated in the constitution. The 8 percent that split these functions is, therefore, likely an underestimate.

The widespread inclusion of EMBs in national constitutions is a fairly recent phenomenon. Only a handful of countries included detailed provisions about electoral oversight bodies prior to 1945. Among the early bodies is Uruguay's Electoral Court, which was created in 1924 (in an electoral law) and was included in the 1934 constitution, making it one of the oldest constitutionally entrenched EMBs.[14] It was not until after World War II that EMBs became a common feature in national

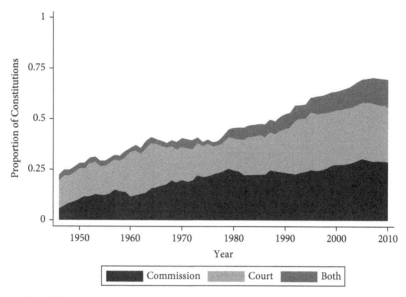

Figure 6.1: The proportion of constitutions with an EMB, 1946 to 2010. Note: N = 8,705 Country-Years. Source: The Comparative Constitutions Project (CCP).

constitutions. The post-war constitutional era has witnessed a steady increase in the number of countries that incorporate fundamental provisions about EMBs in their constitutions.

This trend is illustrated in Figure 6.1, which tracks the proportion of constitutions in force since World War II that include either an electoral commission (black), a court charged with supervising elections (light grey), or both (medium grey). The number of constitutions with electoral commissions has exhibited the most growth over the last 60 years. In 1946, only 6 percent (4) of the world's constitutions speci-fied an electoral commission. By 2010, that percentage had increased to 29 percent (56), nearly a five-fold increase. There have also been increases in the percentage of constitutions that give electoral oversight powers to a court or provide for both types of EMBs. The prevalence of the courts with electoral oversight powers nearly doubled in prevalence—from 14 percent of constitutions to 27 percent—and the percentage of constitutions with both EMBs shot up 10 percentage points, from a measly 3 percent of constitutions to 13 percent.

In addition to the temporal variance illustrated in Figure 6.1, there is also some notable geographic variance in the distribution of EMBs in national constitutions. The constitutions of Western Europe and North America, perhaps because of their relative age, say very little about election management. This finding stands in stark contrast to the pattern in Latin America, South Asia, and Sub-Saharan Africa, the large majority of which have constitutions with constitutionalized EMBs. The other regions fall somewhere between these two extremes.

There is also variance in the *type* of EMB most likely to be found in different regions. Virtually all constitutions in South Asia have an electoral commission and some also give supervision powers to a court. Conversely, constitutions in force in Eastern Europe, the Middle East, and North Africa tend to rely more on courts, with only a few countries opting for electoral commissions.

One distinctive pattern is the unique distribution of electoral courts. Table 6.1 demonstrates that electoral courts are the rarest form of constitutionally entrenched EMB. Not only are they not as common as electoral commissions, but there has been no increase in their use since 1946. If anything, there has been a slight decrease in the use of electoral courts over the last 60 years. Furthermore, the vast majority of electoral courts appear in Latin America. The sole exceptions are Nepal, the Philippines, and Turkey, which are the only countries outside of Latin America to have a constitutionally entrenched electoral court in 2010.

Even though EMBs are entrenched in constitutions, this does not mean that they are wholly autonomous from actors in the executive and legislative branches. In fact, quite often constitutions simply provide for the creation of an EMB and leave it to the legislature to fill in the details. Some constitutions even make EMBs entirely dependent on the executive by allowing the executive to have sole control over the selection and removal of members. There are other constitutions, however, that not only establish the presence of an EMB but also provide a selection procedure that involves multiple actors and fully specify its powers. For instance, the 1998 Constitution of Albania specifies that the central election commission is composed of seven members who are elected for seven years. Two members of the commission are elected by the assembly, two by the president, and three by the High Council of Justice. The constitution also grants to the commission the powers to prepare, supervise, direct, and verify all aspects related to conduct of elections and referenda in the country as well as to declare their results.[15] The constitution of Indonesia, on the other hand, only states that "the general elections shall be organized by a general election commission that shall be national, permanent and independent in nature" but does not provide details about its powers and appointment procedure.[16]

One of the recent debates in the literature has focused on which type of institutional organization of EMBs leads to higher credibility of elections. In particular, the distinction has been made in terms of different levels of professional and partisan autonomy of EMBs.[17] Unfortunately, we have only a limited ability to understand the details provided about EMBs in the constitution. This is particularly true of electoral commissions (the most prevalent EMB) because the CCP's survey instrument only asks two open-ended response questions about electoral commissions, which we have not yet systematized. Thus, our primary goal in this chapter is not to determine the type of institutional organization of EMBs that is constitutionalized but rather *whether* it is constitutionalized or not. Although an imperfect proxy, we operationalize the detail provided about EMBs as the number of characters contained in the responses to those two questions.[18] Longer responses to those questions suggest that

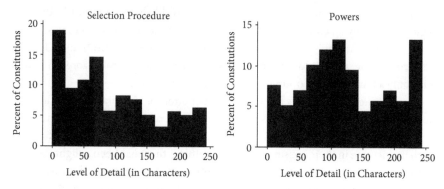

Figure 6.2: Detail about Electoral Commissions in constitutions, 1946 to 2010. Note: N = 159 Constitutions. Source: The Comparative Constitutions Project (CCP)

a constitution provided more information about the selection procedure and pow- ers of the electoral commission. The distribution of these variables is illustrated in Figure 6.2. The panel on the left is a histogram of the number of characters in responses to the selection procedure question, and the panel on the right is a histogram of those for the powers question. Notably, there are peaks in the distribution near 0 in both panels, indicating that numerous constitutions specify very few details about elec- toral commissions. The other interesting result in Figure 6.2 is that constitutions tend to provide more detail about the powers of the electoral commission than the selec- tion procedure for its members, as demonstrated by the fact that more of the mass of the distribution in the panel on the right is near 0 than the panel on the left.

Factors Affecting Entrenchment

The previous section described a significant amount of variance across time and space in the constitutional entrenchment of EMBs, but what factors are driving these trends? We estimate a series of multivariate models to answer this question. In each, the unit of analysis is the constitution (as interpreted in the year of its prom- ulgation). Our choice of estimator is based on two observations: 1) constitutional drafters make related decisions about both the administration and adjudication of elections and 2) they seem to view the choice between an electoral commission and a court as substitutes. Thus, we use a bivariate probit estimator to understand the factors that affect the likelihood each institution is entrenched in the constitution. The dependent variables are binary and indicate whether the constitution provides for either an electoral commission or a court.

We view this analysis as a preliminary look at a few intuitive predictors of EMB choices. The predictors that we investigate are the same for each dependent vari- able and include a spatial lag (to pick up geographic clustering), the strength and autonomy of the court (specifically, judicial independence and judicial review), and legal tradition (common or civil law). We also expect new democracies to be more likely to include EMBs in their constitutions than established democracies.[19] Finally, countries with a recent history of electoral disputes will be more likely to include EMB provisions in their constitutions either in order to avoid election disputes in the future or as a result of an agreement reached during resolution of the dispute. (See the Appendix for detail on the construction and source of these variables.)

The results from the aforementioned regression models are reported in Table 6.2. The table reports the change in probability associated with a shift in each independent variable from its minimum to its maximum value, while holding all of the other variables at their means. The estimates reported in table 6.2 are based on the models reported in the appendix. Recall that we are simultaneously estimating the effect of each covariate on the probability of entrenching each an electoral commission or providing a court with the electoral oversight powers. As a result, one can calculate the effect of each covariate on the probability that no EMB is entrenched, an electoral commission is entrenched, a court with electoral oversight power is entrenched, or both an electoral commission and a court with electoral oversight power is entrenched; we report marginal change in each of these probabilities in Table 6.2. Furthermore, since we expect that drafters in authoritarian and democratic settings might entrench EMBs for different reasons, we report estimates for both democratic and authoritarian constitutions, as measured by the level of democracy immediately subsequent to the writing of the constitution.

There is much to digest in Table 6.2. We will start by looking at the top of the table, which analyzes the factors associated with the entrenchment of EMBs in authoritarian constitutions. The single most important factor is legal heritage. Common-law countries have a a much higher probability (an increase of 0.76) of having an electoral commission than non-common law countries. Common-law countries are unlikely to entrench a court with electoral oversight power. This result is probably at least partially driven by the lack of electoral commissions and presence of electoral courts in Latin America.

Another result that stands out is the relationship between the autonomy and power of the courts and the entrenchment of EMBs. Both countries with high levels of de facto judicial independence and countries with constitutions that grant the judiciary the power of judicial review are significantly more likely to entrench EMBs. Each of these attributes increases the probability that authoritarian drafters will give the power of electoral oversight to a court. Note that the results regarding judicial autonomy and power are unlikely to be driven by the fact that the power of the courts in many countries around the world has increased over time because we are controlling for the year when the constitution is written.

Yet another interesting finding is the effect of past electoral disputes. In authoritarian constitutions, a history of electoral disputes decreases the likelihood that an EMB will be entrenched in the constitution. This effect seems to be driven by the

Table 6.2: **Effect of Covariates on the Probability of Constitutionally Entrenching EMBs, 1946 to 2008**

Variable	Δ Pr (Neither)	Δ Pr (Commission Only)	Δ Pr (Court Only)	Δ Pr (Both)
Authoritarian Constitutions (N = 236)				
D.F. Judicial I Independence	−0.53***	−0.02	0.32	0.22
D.J. Judicial Independence	−0.11	0.17	−0.08	0.02
D.J. Judicial Review	−0.34***	−0.01	0.30***	0.05
Common Law	−0.43***	0.76***	−0.37***	0.03
Electoral Disputes	0.23*	−0.15**	−0.05	−0.03
D.J. Elections	−0.33***	0.15***	0.14*	0.03**
Year	−0.72***	0.48***	0.02	0.22***
Democratic Constitutions (N = 83)				
D.F. Judicial Independence	−0.04	−0.19	0.17	0.06
D.J. Judicial Independence	0.08	0.08	−0.10	−0.06
D.J. Judicial Review	−	−	−	−
Common Law	−0.37***	0.77***	−0.39***	−0.01
Electoral Disputes	−0.35***	0.24	−0.15**	0.26
D.J. Elections	−	−	−	−
Year	−0.52	0.34	−0.02	0.20
Young Democracies	0.16	−0.20	0.09	−0.05

Notes: The estimated effects are based on the estimates presented in Table 5.4. The estimates for authoritarian constitutions are from model 4, and the estimates for democratic constitutions are from model 5.5. All estimated effects are calculated using the minimum and maximum values of the specified variable while holding all covariates at their sample means. Statistical significance is denoted as follows: * = $p < 0.10$; ** = $p < 0.05$; *** = $p < 0.01$.

Source: The Comparative Constitutions Project (CCP).

electoral commission equation. The probability that an electoral commission will be entrenched in the constitution decreases by 0.15 if the country experienced one (or more) electoral disputes under the previous constitution. This is an interesting, and potentially counter-intuitive finding. One reading is that that, even in authoritarian regimes, these institutions improve the integrity of elections. Otherwise, why would authoritarian regimes that are the most at risk of experiencing an electoral dispute, where an EMB would be most beneficial, avoid entrenching one? An alternative, of course, is that the factors that plague elections in these countries also thwart the creation of instiutions that would make any improvements.

We now turn to the rows in the bottom of table 6.2 that assess the factors affecting EMB entrenchment in democratic regimes. There are two main findings about democratic constitutions. First, as with authoritarian constitutions, those written in common law countries are significantly more likely to have electoral commissions and significantly less likely to have courts with electoral oversight authority. Second, electoral disputes have the opposite effect on drafters of democratic constitutions. Democratic constitutions written in contexts with a history of electoral disputes are significantly more likely to have some form of EMB entrenched in them. These constitutions seem particularly likely to entrench an electoral commission, but we cannot be certain of the precise arrangement of EMBs because none of the changes in probability in rows 2-4 is statistically significant.

To our knowledge, this is the first analysis of the factors that affect the constitutional entrenchment of EMBs. A number of factors increase the likelihood that authoritarian drafters will entrench EMBs, but few of these factors are significant predictors of entrenchment in democratic constitutions. We emphasize two findings here. First, at least in authoritarian regimes, the autonomy and power of the judiciary are powerful predictors of EMB entrenchment. It seems that if the courts are respected then they are much more likely to be given the power to adjudicate electoral disputes. Second, past electoral disputes decrease the likelihood of EMB entrenchment in authoritarian constitutions and increases the likelihood of EMB entrenchment in democratic constitutions. This is an interesting and intuitive finding: democracies are inclined to clean up their electoral house, while authoritarians seem to take a sweep-under-the rug approach.

The Effect of EMBs on Election Quality

Is there greater electoral integrity when election management is constitutionalized? We are not in a position to offer an authoritative answer yet. Not only does such a question pose great analytical difficulties (e.g. the possibility of endogeneity), but we also lack data on appropriate outcomes for many elections. Fortunately, we can draw upon data monitoring the quality or integrity of elections from projects directed by Susan Hyde and Nikolay Marinov, and Judith Kelley.[20] Given the data on election attributes, the question becomes, which outcomes are likely to be associated with constitutionalization? We begin with an aggregate set of outcomes associated with the administration (if not adjudication) of elections. Here, we draw on two indicators from the Hyde and Marinov NELDA dataset: whether the opposition accepts the outcome (accept) and whether monitoring officials deem the election to be fair (fair). We draw a third from the Kelley dataset: whether the overall

Table 6.3: **Constitutionally Entrenched EMBs and Election Quality, 1946 to 2008**

EMBs	Authoritarian Elections			Democratic Elections		
	Fair	Accepted	Quality	Fair	Accepted	Quality
None	65%	86%	21%	91%	97%	98%
	(28)	(310)	(27)	(67)	(489)	(256)
Commission	61%	82%	32%	91%	86%	98%
Only	(52)	(178)	(33)	(72)	(147)	(154)
Electoral Court	79%	69%	83%	98%	97%	100%
Only	(11)	(31)	(15)	(55)	(144)	(73)
High Court Only	61%	81%	22%	92%	92%	95%
	(53)	(191)	(29)	(67)	(137)	(98)
Multiple EMBs	50%	60%	50%	84%	89%	98%
	(1)	(3)	(1)	(21)	(70)	(42)
Total	63%	82%	27%	92%	94%	98%
	(145)	(713)	(105)	(282)	(987)	(623)

Note: N = 2,039 Elections.

Source: The Comparative Constitutions Project (CCP).

quality of the election is "acceptable" (quality). Each of these indicators is measured as a thumbs-up/thumbs-down (binary) score.

Table 6.3 reports the percentage of elections reaching these three thresholds, according to what part of the electoral management, if any, is constitutionalized. By these measures, constitutionalization does not seem to have much of an effect on election integrity. The set of elections within democracies shows very little variance across these indicators, perhaps unsurprisingly in a tautological sense. By contrast, elections within authoritarian settings seem to vary quite a bit across these measures. *Some* of this variance seems to be associated with how election management is constitutionalized, but no clear pattern emerges.

Table 6.4 further analyzes the patterns (or lack thereof) represented in table 6.3 The table reports the results from several random-effects probit models. In each, the dependent variable is one of the binary measures reported in table 6.3. Columns 1, 2, and 7 use "fair" as the dependent variable; columns 3, 4, and 8 use "accept" as the dependent variable; and columns 5, 6, and 9 use "quality" as the dependent variable. A number of covariates are included in the models, but for our purposes, the focus is on the 6 measures of EMB reported in the top rows of the table.

The effects of only two EMB measures are statistically different from zero: the presence of an electoral court in model 5 and the details of the selection procedure for members of the electoral commission in model 4. The magnitude of these

Table 6.4: **Constitutionally Entrenched EMBs and Election Quality, 1946 to 2008**

	Authoritarian Elections						Democratic Elections		
Variables	*(1)*	*(2)*	*(3)*	*(4)*	*(5)*	*(16)*	*(7)*	*(8)*	*(9)*
Electoral Comm.	0.11		−0.03		0.16		−0.49	−0.64***	−0.19
	(0.39)		(0.18)		(0.27)		(0.39)	(0.21)	(0.81)
EMB Selection		−0.05		0.33*		0.36			
		(0.39)		(0.19)		(0.27)			
EMB Powers		0.19		−0.15		0.18			
		(0.59)		(0.19)		(0.33)			
Electoral Court	1.01		0.51		1.27**		−0.14	0.41	0.61
	(0.91)		(0.34)		(0.63)		(0.51)	(0.34)	(1.29)
High Court	0.15		0.02		−0.11		0.01	−0.11	0.51
	(0.42)		(0.20)		(0.29)		(0.34)	(0.23)	(1.06)
Courts		−0.71		0.52		−0.59			
		(0.65)		(0.34)		(0.52)			
D.F. Judicial Ind.	1.14	3.03	−1.53***	−1.33	2.57***	5.81***	2.95***	2.48***	6.95*
	(1.44)	(1.96)	(0.53)	(0.91)	(0.83)	(2.00)	(1.08)	(0.60)	(3.81)
D.J. Judicial Ind.	−0.25	0.73	0.09	0.01	−0.57	−0.21	−0.68*	0.00	−0.51
	(0.57)	(0.63)	(0.29)	(0.48)	(0.47)	(0.67)	(0.36)	(0.27)	(0.86)
D.J. Judicial Rev.	−0.61	−0.95	−0.54***	−0.46	0.80***	0.56	−5.19	0.82***	1.42
	(0.52)	(0.75)	(0.20)	(0.32)	(0.31)	(0.49)	(1,618.52)	(0.31)	(0.94)

(Continued)

Table 6.4: **Continued**

Variables	Authoritarian Elections						Democratic Elections		
	(1)	(2)	(3)	(4)	(5)	(16)	(7)	(8)	(9)
Domestic Conflict$_{(t-1)}$	-0.18	-1.26***	-0.23	-0.52**	0.34*	-0.52	0.22	0.38*	0.12
	(0.28)	(0.48)	(0.14)	(0.25)	(0.20)	(0.39)	(0.30)	(0.20)	(0.57)
Young Democracy							0.72**	0.32	1.90*
							(0.34)	(0.22)	(1.07)
Year	-0.03	-0.04	-0.01	-0.01	0.01	0.01	0.04**	-0.01	0.02
	(0.02)	(0.03)	(0.01)	(0.01)	(0.01)	(0.02)	(0.02)	(0.01)	(0.04)
ρ	0.52***	0.10	0.19***	0.00	0.33***	0.00	0.16*	0.11	0.65***
	(0.14)	(028)	(0.08)	(0.00)	(0.10)	(0.00)	(0.15)	(0.10)	(0.26)
D.V.	Fair	Fair	Accept	Accept	Quality	Quality	Fair	Accept	Quality
Number of cowcode	77	28	116	44	100	32	79	106	107
Observations	225	78	731	196	369	100	294	877	617

Notes: The table includes coefficient estimates from nine random-effects, probit regression models. Robust standard errors clustered on country are in parentheses. The dependent variable in each model is one of the three measures of election quality. The constant and region fixed-effects are omitted from the table. Statistical significance is denoted as follows: * = p < 0.10; ** = p < 0.05; *** = p < 0.01

Source: The Comparative Constitutions Project (CCP).

Table 6.5: **Explaining the Constitutional Entrenchment of EMBs, 1946 to 2008**

Variables	(1)		(2)		(3)		Authoritarian Constitutions (4)		Democratic Constitutions (5)	
	Comm.	Court	Comm.	Court	Comm.	Court	Comm.	Court	Comm.	Court
Regional Spatial Lag	-0.01	0.15	-0.28	-0.63	-0.29	-0.65	-0.12	-0.49	-1.00	-0.79
	(0.22)	(0.44)	(0.29)	(0.55)	(0.31)	(0.57)	(0.36)	(0.71)	(0.72)	(1.24)
Judicial Independence (de facto)			-0.07	1.13**	0.33	1.39***	0.66	1.70**	-0.37	0.80
			(0.58)	(0.48)	(0.69)	(0.50)	(1.07)	(0.73)	(1.05)	(0.88)
Judicial Independence (de jure)			0.61**	-0.16	0.54*	-0.27	0.53	-0.19	0.04	-0.55
			(0.29)	(0.29)	(0.32)	(0.30)	(0.43)	(0.37)	(0.54)	(0.54)
Judicial Review (de jure)			0.31	1.11***	0.40	1.30***	0.13	1.27***		
			(0.26)	(0.25)	(0.28)	(0.28)	(0.30)	(0.29)		
Common Law			1.96***	-1.17***	2.28***	-1.28***	2.53***	-1.29***	2.70***	-1.46**
			(0.26)	(0.25)	(0.28)	(0.28)	(0.32)	(0.32)	(0.69)	(0.60)
Young Democracies			-0.62**	-0.24	-0.92***	-0.22			-0.66	0.13
			(0.31)	(0.26)	(0.36)	(0.28)			(0.60)	(0.48)
Old Democracies			-0.22	-0.27	-0.25	-0.45				
			(0.37)	(0.35)	(0.39)	(0.35)				

(*Continued*)

Table 6.5: **Continued**

Variables	All Constitutions						Authoritarian Constitutions		Democratic Constitutions	
	(1)		(2)		(3)		(4)		(5)	
	Comm.	Court	Comm.	Court	Comm.	Court	Comm.	Court	Comm.	Court
Electoral Disputes					0.25	-0.07	-0.72*	-0.25	1.64*	0.32
					(0.36)	(0.38)	(0.42)	(0.46)	(0.85)	(0.61)
Elections (de jure)	0.55***	0.74***	0.51**	0.73**	0.81***	0.60*	0.74***	0.60*		
	(0.18)	(0.24)	(0.26)	(0.30)	(0.27)	(0.32)	(0.29)	(0.32)		
Year	0.02***	0.02***	0.02***	0.01*	0.03***	0.01*	0.04***	0.01	0.02	0.01
	(0.00)	(0.00)	(0.01)	(0.01)	(0.01)	(0.01)	(0.01)	(0.01)	(0.02)	(0.01)
ρ	-0.48***		-0.36***		-0.44***		-0.46***		-0.34*	
	(0.09)		(0.12)		(0.12)		(0.15)		0.19	
Countries	181		145		127		103		57	
Observations	470		356		319		236		83	

Notes: The table includes coefficient estimates from bivariate probit regression models. Robust standard errors clustered on country are in parentheses. The dependent variables are binary variables indicating the presence of a constitutionally entrenched electoral commission or court with the power to supervise elections. The constant and region fixed-effects are omitted from the table. Statistical significance is denoted as follows: * = p < 0.10; ** = p < 0.05; *** = p < 0.01.

Source: The Comparative Constitutions Project (CCP).

effects is actually quite large. Electoral courts increase the likelihood of "acceptable" elections by 30 percentage points and an increase from 22 to 244 characters in the description of the selection procedure for members of the electoral commission increases the likelihood of acceptability by 20 points. One could, maybe should, see these as mixed results. Constitutionalization of electoral administration, when it matters, seems to have a strong effect, but it does not seem to matter very often.

Conclusions

One of the challenges of democratic governance is the administration of fair elections and the enforcement of their results. Scholars seem to have recognized this challenge as a serious one. According to Diamond and Morlino, an independent and authoritative electoral commission is "the single most important institutional guarantee of freedom and fairness... in elections."[21] Scholars are not alone in taking notice; unlike electoral formula, which have a technical and remote quality that mostly scholars appreciate, the administration and adjudication of elections seem to motivate citizens and politicos as well. For example, in a reaction to an election law that changed the composition of the electoral commission prior to the 1996 election in Albania, opposition party leaders charged that the structure of electoral commissions amounted to a "coup d'etat." Similarly, opposition parties in Georgia expressed their concern with the composition of the electoral commission and fairness of the upcoming election prior to the events of the Rose revolution. These incidents represent serious threats to democracy and political stability.

Our point of departure has to do with the legal fabric of election management. In particular, our sympathies are with those framers in the five to ten countries that are expected to replace their constitution each year. These writers face a real conundrum. What, exactly, should they put in their constitution, as opposed to ordinary law? This is not an easy question. We tackle it in a general sense and with an application to election management. Our answer is a simple one: topics that lead to serious problems of dynamic inconsistency, in which a government faces strong incentives to act counter to the public good, are ones that require commitment in the form of constitutionalization. Election management certainly seems to be a case in point. It seems almost preposterous to allow sitting governments to administer and adjudicate elections that decide their fate. So, we postulate, election management regimes that are constitutionalized should exhibit better outcomes. But do they?

Our empirical strategy is to leverage a set of original data in order to document, first, what constitutions do say about election management. We show that constitutionalization of election management is on the rise over the last half century. We also show a trend toward the creation of independent election commissions together with an explicit role for the courts in adjudication. We note that it is fairly uncommon for constitutions to establish separate administrative and adjudicative

Table 6.6: **Technical Appendix—Description of Variables**

Variable	Description	Source
Election Commission	Binary variable coded 1 if the constitution specifies an electoral commission (based on CCP variable OVERSGHT)	CCP
EMB Selection	Number of characters used to describe the selection procedure for the electoral commission (based on CCP variable ECOMSEL)	CCP
EMB Powers	Number of characters used to describe the powers of the electoral commission (based on CCP variable ECOMSEL)	CCP
Electoral Court	Binary variable coded 1 if the constitution specifies an electoral court (based on CCP variable OVERSGHT)	CCP
High Court	Binary variable coded 1 if the constitution specifies that either the Supreme Court or Constitutional Court has the power to "supervise elections" (based on CCP variables SUPPOW_1 and CONPOW_1)	CCP
Courts	Binary variable coded 1 if either Electoral Court or High Court is coded 1	CCP
Fair	Binary variable coded 1 if there were no allegations of vote fraud by Western election monitors (based on Nelda variable 47)	Nelda
Accept	Binary variable coded 1 if there were no protests or riots after the election (based on Nelda variable 29)	Nelda
Quality	Binary variable coded 1 if the overall election quality is "acceptable" (based on variable SA1)	Kelley (2012)
Regional Spatial Lag	Proportion of countries in a given country's region that had either an electoral commission or a court responsible for supervising elections, depending on the model, in the year prior to the promulgation of that country's constitution	CCP
D.F. Judicial Ind.	Level of de facto judicial independence (based on a multi-rater measurement model that averages several extant measures of de facto judicial independence based on their reliabilities)	Linzer and Staton (2013)

(*Continued*)

Table 6.6: **Continued**

Variable	Description	Source
D.J. Judicial Ind.	Binary variable coded 1 if the constitution specifies both a selection and removal procedure for the highest court (i.e., the Supreme Court or the Constitutional Court, depending on the country) that enhances the judicial independence of that court	CCP
D.J. Judicial Rev.	Binary variable coded 1 if the constitution gives a court the power to interpret the constitution	CCP
Common Law	Binary variable coded 1 if the country has a common law legal system	Juriglobe
Young Democracies	Binary variable coded 1 if the country has been a democracy for 10 years or less; democracies are those countries that fall below 0.16 on the UDS	Pemstein et al (2010)
Old Democracies	Binary variable coded 1 if the country has been a democracy for more than 10 years; democracies are those countries that fall below 0.16 on the UDS	Pemstein et al (2010)
Electoral Disputes	Number of electoral disputes observed since the promulgation of a country's previous constitution (based on Nelda variable 29)	Nelda
Domestic Conflict	Binary variable coded one if Bank's conflict index is greater than 0; the variable is lagged one year so as not to correlated with the Electoral Disputes and Accept variables	Banks (2010)
D.J. Elections	Binary variable coded 1 if a country's constitution states that the head of state, head of government, first chamber of the legislature, or second chamber of the legislature is elected by its citizens	CCP
Year	Year	CCP
Region	Region to which the country belongs: Latin America; Western Europe, the United States, and Canada; Eastern Europe; Sub-Saharan Africa; Northern Africa and the Middle East; South Asia; East Asia; Oceania	CCP

bodies, something that would seem to be an optimal strategy. Whatever the established structure, it is not clear that its specification in the constitution gives rise to cleaner elections. In an investigation of successful and not successful elections, we find that constitutionalization exhibits a mixed effect. Electoral courts and detailed instructions for election commissions seems to be associated with improved results, but these are a handful of positive results within a larger set of null findings. Surely more investigation of this question is warranted, both for scholars and policymakers concerned with electoral integrity.

Notes

1. While pacts among the top candidates played a role, sound electoral management helps make such pacts more credible. A neutral third party can provide information about factual matters in dispute among parties to a pact, and can generate common knowledge to facilitate coordination in parties' responses to disputes that arise under a pact.

2. International IDEA. *International Electoral Standards: Guidelines for Reviewing the Legal Framework for Elections.* Stockholm: International IDEA, 2002.

3. Alan Wall, Andrew Ellis, Ayman Ayoub, Carl W. Dundas, Joram Rukambe and Sara Staino. 2006. *Electoral Management Design: The International IDEA Handbook. International Institute for Democracy and Electoral Assistance.* Stockholm: IDEA.

4. Ibid.

5. Beatriz Magaloni. 2010. "The Game of Electoral Fraud and the Ousting of Authoritarian Rule." *American Journal of Political Science* 54(3): 751–765; Andrew Little. 2012. "Elections, Fraud, and Election Monitoring in the Shadow of Revolution." *Quarterly Journal of Political Science* 7: 249–283.

6. Other sources may include international documents, provincial or state laws, ordinances and regulations made by national or lower-level authorities, customary law and conventions (Wall et al. 2006).

7. Adam Przeworski, Michael Alvarez, José Antonio Cheibub and Fernando Limongi. 2000. *Democracy and Development: Political Institutions and Well-Being in the World, 1950–1990.* New York: Cambridge University Press.

8. "The fundamental elements of electoral law, in particular the electoral system proper, membership of electoral commissions and the drawing of constituency boundaries, should not be open to amendment less than one year before an election, or should be written in the constitution or at a level higher than ordinary law." Venice Commission, Code of Good Practice in Electoral Matters, Opinion No. 190/2002, CDL-AD (2002) 23 rev, at p. 10.

9. Svitlana Chernykh. "When Do Political Parties Protest Election Results?" Forthcoming in *Comparative Political Studies.*

10. Alan Wall, Andrew Ellis, Ayman Ayoub, Carl W. Dundas, Joram Rukambe, and Sara Staino. 2006. *Electoral Management Design: The International IDEA Handbook. International Institute for Democracy and Electoral Assistance.* Stockholm: IDEA.

11. http://www.comparativeconstitutionsproject.org/.

12. Note that the sample here includes all "constitutional systems." The CCP makes a conceptual distinction between amended and replaced constitutions: those that are replaced are considered "new" constitutional systems and denote a separate case in this analysis.

13. There are no constitutions in our sample that entrench an electoral court and vest the power to supervise election in a member of the judiciary.

14. See art. 278 of the 1934 Constitution of Uruguay. Alan Wall, Andrew Ellis, Ayman Ayoub, Carl W. Dundas, Joram Rukambe, and Sara Staino. 2006. *Electoral Management Design: The International IDEA Handbook. International Institute for Democracy and Electoral Assistance.* Stockholm: IDEA.

15. 1998 Constitution of Albania, art. 153–154.

16. Constitution of the Republic of Indonesia of 1945 as amended in 2002, art. 22E.5.

17. Guillermo Rosas. 2010. "Trust in elections and the institutional design of electoral authorities: Evidence from Latin America." *Electoral Studies* 29 (1): 74–90.

18. Future iterations will build more refined measures of the selection and removal procedures for members of electoral commissions, electoral courts, and actors in the judiciary with the power to supervise elections as well as of the powers of these actors.

19. Sarah Birch. 2011. *Electoral Malpractice*. Oxford: Oxford University Press.

20. Susan D. Hyde and Nikolay Marinov, 2012. "Which Elections Can Be Lost?' *Political Analysis,* 20(2), 191–210; Kelley, Judith. 2012. *Monitoring Democracy: When International Election Observation Works, and Why It Often Fails*. Princeton: Princeton University Press.

21. Larry Diamond and Leonardo Morlino. 2004. "Quality of Democracy: An Overview." *Journal of Democracy* 15(4): 20–31.

7

Electoral Management Bodies in Central America

ANTONIO UGUES JR.

In August 1999, the two major parties in Nicaragua, the FSLN (*Frente Sandinista de Liberación Nacional*) and the PLC (*Partido Liberal Constitucionalista*), announced that they had reached an inter-party agreement to modify the electoral system in Nicaragua. On the surface, the agreement between the Sandinistas and Liberals, known as *El Pacto*, was intended to improve democracy in Nicaragua by consolidating the two-party system. In reality, the agreement served to consolidate the power of the two dominant parties (the FSLN and PLC) by giving them more control over several features of the Nicaraguan political system.[1] Among other things, the agreement gave the PLC and FSLN the informal power to select and appoint magistrates to the Supreme Court and Supreme Electoral Council (CSE), both of which were expanded in size. The agreement also gave these two parties the formal authority to appoint the presidents and vice presidents of the Municipal Electoral Councils throughout the country.[2] Through *El Pacto*, the two parties consolidated their power over the political system and effectively politicized election management in Nicaragua. Since 2000, Nicaragua has struggled to hold free and fair elections.[3] These events exemplify the dangers of politicization for the performance of an electoral management body and, thus, electoral integrity.

While the specific features of this example are exclusive to Nicaragua, the overall dynamics of electoral manipulation exemplified in this case are ubiquitous throughout Central America. Indeed, the Nicaraguan case exemplifies the threats facing electoral management bodies across the region and the difficulties for positive performance by the Electoral Management Body (EMB). This example, moreover, gives rise to an important set of questions: What impact does politicization have on EMB performance? Can politicized EMBs function autonomously? Can they function in an impartial manner?

This study analyzes these questions by examining de facto levels of autonomy and impartiality exhibited by the respective EMBs of El Salvador, Guatemala, Honduras, and Nicaragua. [4] This work finds that the performance of the Central American EMBs—both institutional autonomy and impartiality—largely depends on the degree of politicization affecting each institution. As such, this study contributes to the larger discussion on the ideal type of electoral management body and measures actual EMB performance, rather than relying on classifying institutional structures.

The rest of this chapter is organized as follows. The first section discusses theoretical arguments seeking to explain the performance of electoral management bodies. The second delineates the scope of this study and provides a descriptive analysis of EMB performance in El Salvador, Guatemala, Honduras, and Nicaragua. The third section presents the key findings of this study, along with an analysis of each case. The study concludes with a summary of the key findings, a discussion of the implications of these findings for scholarship on electoral integrity, and avenues for future research.

Competing Explanations for EMB Performance

There are three competing arguments seeking to explain the performance of EMBs. The first concerns the establishment of each institution, the second considers the role of electoral assistance organizations, and the final explanation focuses on the politicization of each electoral management body.

The Nature of EMB Introduction and EMB Performance

According to this perspective, the way in which each EMB was established should have an important effect on its subsequent performance. The underlying logic is that political institutions help to solve collective action problems, but, more importantly, they are typically created to serve the interests of those who established them. [5] Hence, it is expected that the nature of this process, and in particular *whether the institution was imposed by the governing party* or else *negotiated among multiple parties*, should have an impact on the development of EMB autonomy and impartiality.

Electoral management bodies introduced as a result of a process of negotiation are thought more likely to function autonomously and impartially, because the political debate regarding the design and subsequent establishment of the EMB involved multiple parties that were roughly equal in terms of political power and influence. As such, no single group possessed the power to impose their interests on this process. In contrast, electoral management bodies established by one dominant political party, coalition, or even the military, are more likely to be hindered, at least initially, in their ability to function autonomously and impartially, since they would be established with the intent of restricting or managing the degree of competition in future elections.

Electoral Assistance Organizations and EMB Performance

In many developing democracies, electoral assistance organizations have become increasingly involved in election technical assistance—for example, the United Nations Development Programme, OAS, the United States Agency for International Development (USAID), the International Foundation for Election Systems (IFES), the International Institute for Democracy and Electoral Assistance (IDEA), and many others. Electoral assistance organizations are defined as those organizations, both domestic and international, that seek to "improve the fairness and credibility of the electoral process" within the country in which they operate.[6]

The importance of electoral assistance organizations has been noted by various scholars.[7] These types of organizations have had a positive impact on electoral processes around the world by, among other things, providing financial assistance to EMBs, assisting with core EMB tasks, and shedding light on irregularities.[8] What is more, these types of organizations have had a significant presence throughout South and Central America during the "third wave of democratization."[9] The main expectation, then, is that the technical assistance provided by international organizations should have a positive and significant effect on whether an EMB functions autonomously and impartially.

Politicization and EMB Performance

This explanation looks at how EMB magistrates with the most influence within each institution are appointed to their posts. In some cases, EMB magistrates are recruited because of their experience in, and knowledge of, election administration, public management, or law. These appointments are based on expertise and typically result in low levels of politicization.[10] In other cases, however, EMB magistrates are selected based on their partisan affiliations, party activism, or previous positions in the government. These appointments typically result in high levels of politicization. Finally, there are also cases in which the appointment process is formally based on expertise but informally based on partisan affiliations. These instances also typically result in higher levels of politicization.

International IDEA's handbook on electoral management bodies suggests that the "ideal model" of election management for developing democracies is one that is legally independent from other branches of government and that features members who are "politically" independent.[11] The selection and presence of politically independent EMB members has been shown to be strongly correlated with free and fair elections in Latin America.[12] Nevertheless, it is not entirely clear whether the type of appointment would contribute to institutional autonomy and impartiality. Lehoucq and Molina suggest that the selection and appointment of politically independent EMB members is more likely to contribute to better EMB performance, because this structure of election management removes many opportunities for political manipulation.[13] The most thorough comparative study by Birch found that whether EMB members were appointed on partisan or expert grounds did appear to influence the independence of EMBs, although she was unable to detect any significant effects on electoral integrity arising from the formal independence of EMB institutions.[14]

Scope of this Study

Case Selection and Time Frame

Throughout the 1980s and 1990s, the regimes of El Salvador, Guatemala, Honduras, and Nicaragua underwent significant political changes. During this period, each country experienced the transition to civilian rule as well as the introduction of new political institutions and processes. One important element in this process of change was the introduction of multiparty elections and electoral institutions. This was part of the regional shift toward electoral democracy, where the struggle for power shifted from armed violence to competition at the ballot box.

This study examines the electoral processes and electoral management bodies in the Central American cases from the point at which each country allowed full-fledged multiparty competition—including the incorporation of leftist and center-of-left parties that had previously been outlawed—through the cessation of armed conflict, the signing and implementation of peace accords, or the end of excessive military influence in the political arena. Although each of these cases held elections throughout the 1980s, these elections were not inclusive of certain segments of the political spectrum. For instance, in El Salvador, Guatemala, and Honduras, it was very common for leftist and center-of-left parties to be excluded from electoral contests. Moreover, in Nicaragua, various political groups chose not to participate in the 1984 elections—for instance, due to their opposition to the Sandinista regime (and external pressure from the United States). Hence, this study examines El Salvador from 1994 to 2009, Guatemala from 1995 to 2007, Honduras from 1993 to 2009, and Nicaragua from 1990 to 2006. This chapter reviews the performance of the respective Central American EMBs in national elections (executive and legislative) for a period of approximately 15 years (on average).

Measuring EMB Performance

Scholars have put forth several ideas on what features are ideal for EMBs in developing democracies, such as the role of efficiency, transparency, fairness, diversity, equity, effectiveness, impartiality, and so on.[15] Research has also examined how these institutions influence democracy and elections.[16] The current work draws on the International Institute for Democracy and Electoral Assistance handbook as a basis for measuring EMB performance, because this provides an accessible approach to understanding some of the most important and fundamental features of election management.[17]

Performance, in this respect, is measured as institutional autonomy and impartiality. These are not the only values and standards available for evaluating the performance of EMBs, by any means, but they are arguably some of the most important.

Autonomy

Electoral management body *autonomy* is defined as the ability to operate free from the interference of any outside pressure, including government officials, political parties, the military, or other groups with an interest in influencing the electoral process. EMB autonomy is assessed in the following areas:

(1) *The appointment of EMB members;*
(2) *The operation of EMB members;*
(3) *The term of office of EMB members* (and ease at which they can be removed from their posts); and,
(4) *The EMB budget* (e.g., control of the budget and its size).

Violations (or discrepancies) of the formal procedures in any of these four areas are noted. EMB autonomy is coded by election year for each country. The technical appendix provides details about the coding scheme and measurement (see Table 7.2).

Impartiality

Electoral management body *impartiality* is defined as the ability to operate without any political favoritism or bias, including preferential treatment toward government officials, political parties, or other groups with an interest in influencing the electoral process. EMB impartiality can be assessed in the following areas:

(1) *The registration of parties and candidates;*
(2) *The financing of parties and candidates;*
(3) *The reporting of election results;* and,
(4) *Electoral rulings* (made by the EMB).

As with EMB autonomy, violations (or discrepancies) of the formal procedures in any of these four areas are coded by election year for each country. Data for both autonomy and impartiality are collected from relevant news reports, government

Table 7.1: **Key Propositions and Findings by Case**

	Guatemala	*Nicaragua*	*El Salvador*	*Honduras*
Variables				
EMB establishment by ruling party	Yes (Imposition)	No (Negotiation)	No (Negotiation)	Yes (Imposition)
International electoral assistance	Yes	Yes	Yes	Yes
Non-partisan EMB magistrates	Yes	No (informal politicization)	No (formal politicization)	No (formal politicization)
Outcomes				
Overall Autonomy	Most autonomy	Mixed	Mixed	Least autonomy
Overall Impartiality	Most impartiality	Mixed	Least impartiality	Mixed

Source: Author's own analysis of primary and secondary materials.

documents, and election observation reports. The technical appendix provides details about the coding scheme and measurement (see Table 7.2).

EMB Performance over Time

Based on the coding scheme, this study uses primary and secondary data to identify violations of EMB autonomy and impartiality during the period under scrutiny for each case. The most common violation of EMB autonomy had to do with the operation of EMB members, the EMB budget, and finally, the appointment of EMB members and the term of office of EMB members. Overall, the Salvadoran Supreme Electoral Tribunal had the highest total number of violations, followed by the Honduran Supreme Electoral Tribunal. The Nicaraguan Supreme Electoral Council was third in number of violations, while the Guatemalan Supreme Electoral Tribunal had the fewest problems. These data suggest that the Guatemalan agency demonstrated the most autonomous performance, whereas the Honduran had the least autonomous.

In regard to EMB impartiality, the most common violations were the electoral rulings made by the respective EMBs, then the reporting of election results, and the registration of political parties and candidates. The least common violation had to do with the financing of political parties and candidates. These data suggest that the Guatemalan agency also had the most impartial performance, whereas the Salvadoran TSE had the least impartial (see Table 7.1).

Table 7.2: **Technical Appendix: Coding Scheme**

Autonomy

I. **Appointment.** EMB member appointment should strictly follow the codified procedures for the nomination and appointment of these individuals. A violation of EMB member appointment occurs if:

---

   a. EMB members are appointed in a way that is contrary to the codified procedures for the nomination and appointment of these individuals, or

---

   b. The legislature (the appointment body for EMB members) is (concerning the nomination and appointment of new EMB members) subject to

---

      i. Legal action

---

      ii. Physical coercion, or

---

   c. EMB appointees who have been appointed following codified procedures are prevented from assuming their posts due to

---

      i. Legal action

---

      ii. Physical coercion

II. **Operation.** EMB members should strictly follow the codified procedures for managing the conduct of national, regional, and local elections and elections to the Central American Parliament. A violation of EMB member operations occurs if:

---

   a. EMB members are prevented from

---

      i.   Registering voters,

---

      ii. Counting ballots,

---

      iii. Tabulating and aggregating votes

III. **Tenure.** The term of office of EMB members should strictly follow codified procedures. A violation of EMB member tenure occurs if:

---

   a. The tenure of members is altered contrary to the codified procedures for the term of office and removal of EMB members.

IV. **Budget.** The EMB budget should strictly follow the codified procedures for the proposal, presentation, approval, and allocation of the EMB budget. A violation of EMB autonomy with respect to the budget occurs if:

---

   a. The budget proposal, presentation, approval, or allocation is altered contrary to the codified procedures for the EMB budget.

(Continued)

Impartiality

I. **Registration of political parties and candidates.** The registration of political parties and candidates by each EMB should strictly follow the codified procedures for the registration of political parties and candidates. A violation of EMB impartiality with respect to the registration of political parties and candidates occurs if:

    a. The EMB registers a political party or political candidate in a way that is contrary to the codified procedures for the registration of political parties and political candidates or

    b. If the EMB rejects the registration of political parties or political candidates without communicating a rationale for doing so (that accords with codified procedure).

II. **Financing of political parties and candidates.** The oversight of public financing for political parties and candidates by each EMB should strictly follow the codified procedures for the financing of parties and candidates. A violation of EMB impartiality with respect to the financing of political parties and candidates occurs if:

    a. The financing of political parties and candidates is conducted in a manner that is contrary to the codified procedures for the distribution of public finance or

    b. The EMB incorrectly reports certified election results to the government body responsible for determining the distribution of public finance for parties/candidates).

III. **Reporting of election results**. The reporting of election results by each EMB should strictly follow the codified procedures for the reporting of election results. A violation of EMB impartiality with respect to the reporting of election results occurs if:

    a. The EMB reports election results in a manner that is contrary to the codified procedures for the reporting of election results or

    b. The EMB reports election results to a particular party or candidate before it does so for other parties or candidates or

    c. The EMB prematurely announces the victory of an election in favor of one party or candidate.

IV. **Electoral rulings.** Electoral rulings made by each EMB should strictly follow the codified procedures for electoral rulings. A violation of EMB impartiality with respect to the EMB's electoral rulings occurs if:

    a. The EMB makes an electoral ruling in a manner that is contrary to the codified procedures.

    b. The EMB makes an electoral ruling without disclosing the justification for a particular ruling.

Analysis

Evidence for the Nature of EMB Introduction and EMB Performance Explanation

According to this first explanation, the way each new electoral authority was established should, at least initially, significantly impact subsequent performance of each institution. Hence, in regard to the autonomy and impartiality of each institution, the expectation is quite simple. Those EMBs introduced with the input of multiple parties and interests should perform better, at least initially, than those introduced under military-authoritarian regimes. The four cases of this study provide an excellent opportunity to assess this proposition, since two of these cases—Nicaragua and El Salvador—were introduced through a process of multiparty negotiation and the other two—Guatemala and Honduras—were introduced through a process of governing party imposition.

In Nicaragua, the Sandinistas, although they had firm control of the political apparatus within the country, negotiated the Law of Political Parties and the new Electoral Law with an array of different political factions after they had sought advice regarding the design of new political institutions from the international community.[18] The empirical evidence suggests that these negotiations among multiple political interests and the resulting introduction of the body had a positive impact, at least initially, on the performance of the *Consejo Supremo Electoral* (CSE) in regard to both autonomy and impartiality.[19] However, in subsequent electoral contests, the impact of this process was negligible.

In El Salvador, the *Tribunal Supremo Electoral* was introduced following the reforms to the electoral system put forth in the National Commission for the Consolidation of Peace (COPAZ) with the signing of the Chapultepec Peace Accords between the Salvadoran government and the FMLN in 1992.[20] Based on the empirical evidence, it is difficult to identify a clear impact of the nature of the introduction of the Supreme Electoral Tribunal on its performance, in regard to either autonomy or impartiality.[21] Overall, the inconsistent performance of the Supreme Electoral Tribunal following the introduction of the body suggests that other factors may be at work in this process.

In contrast to Nicaragua and El Salvador, both Honduras and Guatemala introduced their respective EMBs through a process of imposition. In Honduras, the government of General Juán Alberto Melgar Castro introduced the *Tribunal Nacional de Elecciones* (TNE) following the decree of the electoral law of 1977 (*La Ley Electoral y de las Organizaciones Politica de 1977*).[22] As expected, according to the *nature of introduction hypothesis*, the Tribunal generally demonstrated inconsistent performance, especially with respect to autonomy during the period under scrutiny.

Guatemala, however, provides the strongest counterevidence to the *nature of introduction hypothesis*. The Guatemalan *Tribunal Supremo Electoral* was introduced under the leadership of Efraín Ríos Montt through the execution of decree law

30-83, the Organic Law of the Supreme Electoral Tribunal.[23] However, contrary to the nature of introduction hypothesis, the Tribunal has consistently outperformed its counterparts in the region. Moreover, compared to its counterparts, the Tribunal has had the lowest average number of violations of EMB autonomy (1.5 violations/ election cycle) and impartiality (1.25 violations/election cycle) throughout the period under scrutiny, respectively.

Evidence for the Electoral Assistance Organizations and EMB Performance Explanation

This explanation considers the role that electoral assistance organizations have on the performance of each EMB. Given the fact that throughout the period under scrutiny electoral assistance organizations have been active in the region, in areas such as election observation and technical assistance, it is expected that these organizations would have a positive impact on whether an EMB functions autonomously and impartially. According to this explanation, then, EMBs with extensive backing from electoral assistance organizations should perform better than those without these types of backing due to the financial and technical support provided by these organizations. In each of the four countries, electoral assistance organizations have operated with different intensities and scope.

In Nicaragua, electoral assistance organizations had a significant presence and impact in 1990; in this contest, more than half a dozen major international organizations were present in addition to the myriad domestic and grassroots organizations associated with the FSLN, UNO (*Unión Nacional Opositora*), and other political parties.[24] The presence of so many highly organized and well-financed electoral assistance organizations complemented the professional work of the CSE and contributed positively to the transparency and cleanliness of this contest. However, the presence of these organizations in subsequent elections did not seem to have the same impact as in the initial contest.

In El Salvador, another country with a high level of activity by electoral assistance organizations, the presence and activity of these organizations seems to have produced mixed results. The evidence suggests that the respective electoral assistance organizations were successful at promoting transparency and highlighting the shortcomings of the tribunal but limited in its ability to assist in overcoming these issues. The successive electoral contests demonstrated a similar trend, especially with regard to EMB impartiality.

In Honduras and Guatemala, the presence and level of activity of electoral assistance organizations has been slightly lower than in Nicaragua and El Salvador. In Honduras, the presence of these organizations has, as in El Salvador, helped shed light on the various shortcomings of election management, both technical as well as political.[25] Contrary to the *electoral assistance organization* hypothesis, however, the empirical evidence suggests that the assistance provided by these organizations has not contributed to positive performance in relation to EMB autonomy and impartiality.

In contrast, the evidence suggests that electoral assistance organizations have had a positive impact in Guatemala. In spite of the high levels of violence associated with electoral contests in Guatemala, the presence of electoral assistance organizations, as expected according to the electoral assistance organization hypothesis, have served to enhance the transparency of the electoral process in Guatemala.

Evidence for the Politicization and EMB Performance Explanation

According to this perspective, it is important to examine how EMB magistrates—those with the most influence within each institution—are appointed to their posts. In effect, the issue is whether EMB magistrates are selected because of their partisan affiliations (formally or informally) or whether they are selected because of their expertise in the administration of elections. The expectation is that those EMBs that provide for the selection and appointment of politically independent EMB members are more likely to perform better with respect to EMB autonomy and impartiality than those that select EMB members based on their political affiliations. The four cases of this study offer an excellent opportunity to assess this proposition, given that two of these cases—Honduras and El Salvador—provide for the selection of EMB magistrates based on a combination of partisanship and expertise, while the other two cases—Nicaragua and Guatemala—provide for the selection of EMB magistrates based solely on expertise.

In El Salvador, the five magistrates of the Supreme Electoral Tribunal are nominated based on a combination of partisanship and expertise. Selecting magistrates based on partisanship is one of the most serious issues facing the Tribunal, since this nomination process has resulted in a high level of politicization within the institution. A common theme that has emerged in El Salvador is the tendency of the members of the Tribunal to deadlock on matters such as the electoral registry, the system of identification cards, and routine questions of personnel, among other issues, because of political infighting.[26] The performance of the Supreme Electoral Tribunal has, thus, been adversely affected by the politicization stemming from the nomination and appointment of magistrates based on partisanship.

A similar trend has emerged in Honduras. From its foundation, one of the fundamental problems of the Tribunal has been its politicization.[27] This feature of the Tribunal has adversely affected areas such as the registration of voters,[28] the production and distribution of voter identification cards,[29] the registration of candidates for office,[30] and the announcement of election results.[31] In spite of the reforms in 2005, in which magistrates are now nominated and appointed based on expertise rather than partisanship, the Tribunal has continued to experience a number of violations of EMB autonomy and impartiality due to the persistent influence of politics within the institution.

In Nicaragua and Guatemala, the magistrates of the respective electoral management bodies are selected based on their expertise in electoral matters. The seven members of the Nicaraguan Supreme Electoral Council (and three substitutes) are nominated by the president of the republic and members of the National Assembly, in consultation with civil society organizations, and elected by at least 60 percent of the deputies of the National Assembly. Unfortunately, the Council, which performed exceptionally well during the 1990 general elections, has become highly politicized through various formal and informal measures undertaken by the prevailing political powers in Nicaragua, thus limiting the overall effectiveness of the institution.

In contrast to Nicaragua, the case of the Guatemalan Supreme Electoral Tribunal represents an example of an electoral authority that has exhibited a positive record of electoral management. One of the principal reasons for this is the low level of politicization within the institution, especially among the magistrates of the Tribunal. The five magistrates (and substitutes) of the Guatemalan Supreme Electoral Tribunal are nominated by a special nominating commission and confirmed by the national legislature with a two-thirds vote. The non-partisan nature of the Tribunal has significantly contributed to a positive record of electoral management in Guatemala.[32]

Discussion and Future Research

The main findings of this study are as follows. *First, the evidence suggests that the way that EMBs were established by a multiparty coalition or by one party had an important impact* in Nicaragua during the 1990 elections and in Honduras during the 1993 elections. *This impact is modest, however, and it does not last beyond these initial contests.* In El Salvador and Guatemala, the analyses suggest that there is no identifiable impact arising from the way that EMBs were established. (See Figures 7.1 and 7.2.)

Second, the analyses lend modest support to the electoral assistance organization hypothesis in Guatemala and, to a lesser extent, in Nicaragua. In both countries, electoral assistance organizations provided critical assistance to the respective electoral authorities during important transitional elections. Electoral assistance organizations also played an important role in facilitating political participation in Guatemala, in spite of the crime and violence afflicting the electoral process. Electoral assistance organizations were also present and active in El Salvador and Honduras, but in these cases these organizations were much more adept at publicizing the technical and political shortcomings of the respective tribunals rather than providing significant assistance in the administration of elections in those cases.

Finally, the empirical evidence and forgoing analyses lend strong support to the politicization hypothesis across all four cases. In Guatemala, the selection of magistrates based

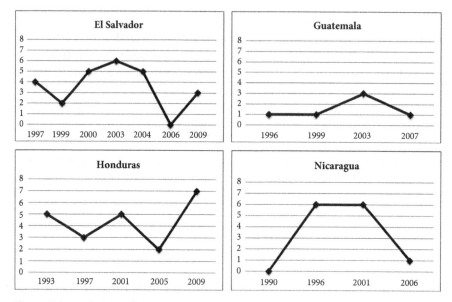

Figure 7.1: Violations of EMB autonomy

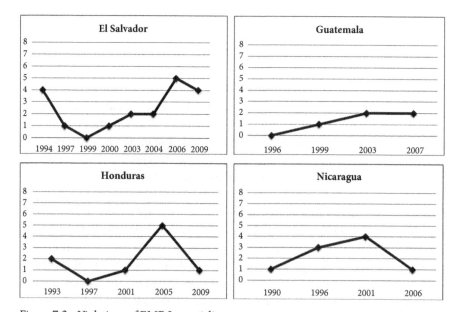

Figure 7.2: Violations of EMB Impartiality

on expertise and from academic and legal backgrounds seems to have strengthened the Supreme Electoral Tribunal by providing a safeguard against extreme politicization. The Nicaraguan case, in contrast, suggests that the influence of political parties and other important political interests can have a demonstrable impact on the performance of an electoral management body in spite of formal safeguards against politicization; hence, this case demonstrates the impact of informal politicization on the performance of the Supreme Electoral Council. The Honduran and Salvadoran cases also cohere with the *politicization hypothesis* in that each case has experienced a relatively high number of violations of EMB autonomy and impartiality largely due to the high level of politicization that has resulted from the formal representation of political parties within each institution.[33] *In sum, the evidence suggests that higher levels of politicization, both formal and informal, has had adverse effects on the performance of the respective electoral authorities of Central America, whereas lower levels of politicization has tended to result in more positive outcomes* (see Table 7.1).

This study has set out to accomplish two tasks. First, this work has tracked the performance of four Central American EMBs over 15 years from the point at which each country allowed multiparty competition at the ballot box. Overall, the findings of this study indicate that there are significant differences in the performance of each Central American EMB. Indeed, the results indicate that the Salvadoran Supreme Electoral Tribunal and the Honduran National Election Tribunal/ Supreme Electoral Tribunal had the most violations of EMB autonomy and impartiality, while the Guatemalan Supreme Electoral Tribunal had the fewest violations on both dimensions.

Second, this work has sought to explain the performance of these electoral authorities by assessing the relationship between the nature of the introduction of each institution, the presence and activities of electoral assistance organizations, and the politicization of each EMB. While this work cannot provide a definitive answer as to the causes of EMB performance, the data and analyses suggest that *the performance of these institutions largely depends on the degree of politicization affecting each institution.* The nomination, appointment, and tenure of EMB magistrates and their staff matters a great deal to the performance of each institution. By the same token, the analyses suggest that informal politicization is important as well. Overall, the empirical evidence suggests that higher levels of formal or informal politicization have adverse effects on the performance of the respective electoral authorities, while lower levels of politicization tend to produce better performance.

The findings suggest an important relationship between the role of politics and EMB performance moving beyond static conceptions of EMB independence (autonomy) and impartiality. Further research should examine this relationship, applying the insights of this study to cases outside of Central America. Future studies should also note that institutions like EMBs operate within a larger political environment that can affect the conduct of elections in numerous, sometimes unintended, ways; this is true as well in cases that have exhibited positive performance, such as the Guatemalan Supreme Electoral Tribunal. Thus, further research into the additional factors that impact EMB performance, such as budgetary constraints, technical capacity, efficiency, and transparency, is warranted.

Ultimately, understanding how EMBs develop into autonomous and impartial institutions is important from a scholarly perspective, since this aids our understanding of the process of democratization and the development of democratic institutions. This is also important from a policy perspective because it helps policy makers, intergovernmental organizations, and non-governmental organizations identify concrete steps to facilitate democratic elections.

Notes

1. Katherine Hoyt. 2004. "Parties and pacts in contemporary Nicaragua." In *Undoing Democracy: The Politics of Electoral Caudillismo*, ed. David Close and Kalowatie Deonandan. Lanham, MD: Lexington Books.

2. Katherine Hoyt. 2004. "Parties and pacts in contemporary Nicaragua." In *Undoing Democracy: The Politics of Electoral Caudillismo*, ed. David Close and Kalowatie Deonandan. Lanham, MD: Lexington Books.

3. Samuel Greene. 2010. "Learning the wrong Lessons about Nicaraguan democracy: A response to Anderson and Dodd." *Journal of Democracy*, http://www.journalofdemocracy.org/exchange-nicaragua, (accessed August 12, 2013); Maureen Meyer. 2011. "Elections in Nicaragua: Concerns about the electoral process and the state of democracy." Washington Office on Latin America, http://wola.org/country/nicaragua, (accessed August 11, 2013).

4. It is important to note the difference between formal (legal) independence and autonomy. Formal independence refers to the de jure independence of the EMB; that is, whether the institution is legally independent from other branches of government such as the executive or legislature. Autonomy, on the other hand, refers to the de facto independence of each EMB; in other words, whether the institution has the ability to function independently and not just the legal right to do so.

5. Terry Moe. 2005. "Power and political institutions." *Perspectives on Politics* 3: 215–233. Terry Moe. 1990. "Political Institutions: The neglected side of the story." *Journal of Law, Economics, and Organization* 6: 213–253; Jack Knight. 1992. *Institutions and Social Choice*. Cambridge: Cambridge University Press.

6. Kevin J. Middlebrook. 1998. *Electoral Observation and Democratic Transitions in Latin America*. San Diego: Center for U.S.-Mexican Studies, University of California, San Diego.

7. Anne Van Aaken. 2009. "Independent Electoral Management Bodies and international election observer missions: Any Impact on the observed level of democracy? A conceptual framework." *Constitutional Political Economy* 20: 296–322; Robert Pastor A. 1999. "The third dimension of accountability: The international community in national elections." In *The Self-Restraining State: Power and Accountability in New Democracies*, ed. Andreas Schedler, Larry Diamond, and Marc F. Plattner. Boulder, CO: Lynne Rienner; Margaret E. Scranton. 1998. "Electoral observation and Panama's democratic transition." In *Electoral Observation and Democratic Transitions in Latin America*, ed. Kevin J. Middlebrook. San Diego: Center for U.S.-Mexican Studies, University of California, San Diego.

8. Patricia Bayer Richard and John A. Booth. 1995. "Election observation and democratization: Reflections on the Nicaraguan case." In *Elections and Democracy in Central America Revisited*, ed. Mitchell A. Seligson and John A. Booth. Chapel Hill and London: The University of North Carolina Press. Scranton, 1998.

9. John A. Booth, Christine J. Wade, and Thomas W. Walker. 2010. *Understanding Central America: Global Forces, Rebellion, and Change*, 5th ed. Boulder, CO: Westview Press; Tommie S. Montgomery. 1998. "International missions, observing elections, and the democratic transition in El Salvador." In *Electoral Observation and Democratic Transitions in Latin America*, ed. Kevin J. Middlebrook. San Diego: Center for U.S.-Mexican Studies, University of California, San Diego; Jennifer McCoy. 1998. "Monitoring and mediating elections during

Latin American democratization." In *Electoral Observation and Democratic Transitions in Latin America*, ed. Kevin J. Middlebrook. San Diego: Center for U.S.-Mexican Studies, University of California, San Diego.

10. Alan Wall, Andrew Ellis, Ayman Ayoub, Carl W. Dundas, Joram Rukambe and Sara Staino. 2006. *Electoral Management Design: The International IDEA Handbook*. Stockholm: International IDEA; International Institute for Democracy and Electoral Assistance. 2002. *International Electoral Standards: Guidelines for Reviewing the Legal Framework of Elections*. Stockholm: International IDEA.

11. Alan Wall, Andrew Ellis, Ayman Ayoub, Carl W. Dundas, Joram Rukambe, and Sara Staino. 2006. *Electoral Management Design: The International IDEA Handbook*. Stockholm: International IDEA.

12. Jonathan Hartlyn, Jennifer McCoy and Thomas Mustillo. 2008. "Electoral governance matters: Explaining the quality of elections in contemporary Latin America." *Comparative Political Studies* 41: 73–98.

13. Fabrice Lehoucq and Ivan Molina. 2002. *Stuffing the Ballot Box: Fraud, Election Reform, and Democratization in Costa Rica*. Cambridge: Cambridge University Press.

14. Sarah Birch. 2006. *Electoral Malpractice*. New York: Oxford University Press. pp. 131.

15. Alan Wall, Andrew Ellis, Ayman Ayoub, Carl W. Dundas, Joram Rukambe and Sara Staino. 2006. *Electoral Management Design: The International IDEA Handbook*. Stockholm: International IDEA; Rafael López-Pintor. 2000. *Electoral Management Bodies as Institutions of Governance*. New York: United Nations Development Programme; Shaheen Mozaffar and Andreas Schedler. 2002. "The comparative study of electoral governance: Introduction." *International Political Science Review* 23: 5–27; Louis Massicotte, André Blais and Antoine Yoshinaka. 2004. *Establishing the Rules of the Game: Election Laws in Democracies*. Toronto: Toronto University Press.

16. Guillermo Rosas. 2010. "Trust in elections and the institutional design of electoral authorities: Evidence from Latin America." *Electoral Studies* 29: 74–90; Nicholas Kerr. "Popular perceptions of free and fair elections in Sub-Saharan Africa" (chapter 10, this volume); Sarah Birch. 2008. "Electoral institutions and popular confidence in electoral processes." *Electoral Studies* 27: 305–320.

17. Alan Wall, Andrew Ellis, Ayman Ayoub, Carl W. Dundas, Joram Rukambe and Sara Staino. 2006. *Electoral Management Design: The International IDEA Handbook*. Stockholm: International IDEA.

18. Susanne Jonas. 1989. "Elections and Transitions: The Guatemalan and Nicaraguan Cases." In *Elections and Democracy in Central America*, ed. John A. Booth and Mitchell A. Seligson. Chapel Hill and London: The University of North Carolina; Jules Lobel. 1987. "The new Nicaraguan Constitution: Uniting participatory and representative democracy." *Monthly Review* (December); Envío. 1985. *Monográfico: The Final Stretch of the Electoral Process. Analysis of Electoral Results (I-II), and Interview: An Inside View of the Elections*. Managua: Instituto Histórico Centroamericano.

19. Latin American Studies Association. 1990. "Electoral Democracy under International Pressure." *The Report of the Latin American Studies Association Commission to Observe the 1990 Nicaraguan Election*. Latin American Studies Association (LASA); The Carter Center. 1990. *"Observing Nicaragua's Elections, 1989–1990."* Atlanta: The Carter Center.

20. See http://www.elsalvador.com/noticias/especiales/acuerdosdepaz2002/index.html (accessed March 30, 2010).

21. Jack Spence and George Vickers. 1994. *Toward a Level Playing Field? A Report on the Post-War Salvadoran Electoral Process*. Cambridge, MA: Hemisphere Initiatives; Fabrice Lehoucq. 1995. "The Election of 1994 in El Salvador." *Electoral Studies* 14: 179–240.

22. Rachel Sieder. 1996. "Elections and democratization in Honduras since 1980." *Democratization* 3: 17–40; Caroline Boussard. 2003. *Crafting Democracy: Civil Society in Post-Transition Honduras*. Lund, Sweden: Department of Political Science, Lund University.

23. Dinorah Azpuru. 2006. *Building Democracy in Post-Conflict Societies: Guatemala and El Salvador in Comparative Perspective—Executive Summary*. Guatemala, Guatemala: ASIES, IDRC, FUNDAUNGO. Also, see http://www.cidh.oas.org/countryrep/Guatemala83eng/TOC.htm (accessed March 28, 2011).

24. Richard and Booth 1995. Booth et al. 2010.

25. Tim Merrill. 1995. *Honduras: A Country Study*. Washington: GPO for the Library of Congress; Michelle M. Taylor-Robinson. 2011. "The Honduran General Elections of 2009." *Electoral Studies* 30: 366–383.

26. European Union. 2009. *European Union Election Observation Mission, El Salvador 2009: Final Report on the General Elections*. Brussels, Belgium. European Commission, Election Observation; Shawn L. Bird and Philip J. Williams. 2000. "El Salvador: Revolt and Negotiated Transition." In *Repression, Resistance, and Democratic Transition in Central America*, ed. Thomas W. Walker and Ariel C. Armony. Wilmington, DE: Scholarly Resources, Inc.; United Nations "Observer Mission in El Salvador. 1995." *Report of the Secretary-General on the United Nations Observer Mission in El Salvador*. New York: United Nations, Security Council. Lehoucq, 1995. Montgomery, 1998.

27. Michelle M. Taylor-Robinson. 2011. "The Honduran General Elections of 2009." *Electoral Studies* 30: 366–383.

28. Michelle M. Taylor-Robinson. 2009. "Honduras: Una Mezcla de Cambio y Continuidad. Honduras: A Mix of Change and Continuity." *Revista de Ciencia Política* 29: 471–489.

29. International Foundation for Electoral Systems. 2001. *Election Observation Mission: Honduras General Elections, November 25, 2001, Final Report*. Washington: International Foundation for Electoral System (IFES).

30. Michelle M. Taylor-Robinson. 2003. "The elections in Honduras, November 2001." *Electoral Studies* 22: 503–559.

31. Michelle M. Taylor-Robinson. 2007. "Presidential and Congressional elections in Honduras, November 2005." *Electoral Studies* 26: 507–533; Michelle M. Taylor-Robinson. 2006. "La Política Hondureña y Las Elecciones de 2005." *Revista de Ciencia Política* 26: 114–124.

32. Dinorah Azpuru. 2008. "The 2007 Presidential and Legislative elections in Guatemala." *Electoral Studies* 27: 547–577; Dinorah Azpuru. 2005. "The General Election in Guatemala, November-December 2003." *Electoral Studies* 24: 123–160; European Union. 2003. *European Union Election Observation Mission, Guatemala 2003: Final Report on the General Elections*. Brussels, Belgium: European Commission, Election Observation; Daniel Montalvo. 2009. "Trust in Electoral Commissions." *AmericasBarometer Insights* 23: 1–4.

33. Indeed, the Honduran Supreme Electoral Tribunal has the highest average number of violations of EMB autonomy, while the Salvadoran Supreme Electoral Tribunal has the highest average number of violations of EMB impartiality.

8

Electoral Management in Britain

TOBY S. JAMES

Understanding the causes, consequences, and remedies for defects in the practice of elections is being subjected to renewed scrutiny. Considerable attention has focused on how elections are subverted by elites seeking to maintain power. Scholars have established a comprehensive menu of manipulation including electoral violence, vote buying, and maintaining favorable electoral laws.[1] This has been conceptualized as electoral malpractice[2] or as undermining international standards of electoral integrity.[3] Not all flaws in elections are the direct result of the partisan activity of elites and their agents, however. In *Electoral Malpractice*, Birch notes that systems of electoral administration can be prone to 'electoral mispractice'—"incompetence, lack of resources, unforeseen disturbances, and simple human error"[4]—but then focuses on the deliberate "manipulation of electoral processes and outcomes."[5] Elsewhere, Norris notes that elections can be plagued by 'electoral maladministration': "routine flaws and unintended mishaps by election officials...due to managerial failures, inefficiency and incompetence."[6] These problems can affect voter confidence and threaten democratic consolidation. However, previous accounts have not offered sufficient conceptual disaggregation or empirical research to help establish the types, causes, and potential remedies for such problems.

This study makes two contributions to the literature. First, it develops a new conceptual terminology for understanding a different type of electoral malpractice. Electoral integrity can be compromised through failures of rowing and steering in electoral management boards (EMBs), which can cause suboptimal levels of organizational performance. Second, the study contributes toward knowledge of the causes of poor organizational performance in the case of Britain by using semi-structured interviews to identify the contemporary challenges facing electoral administrators. Proponents of "bottom-up" policymaking have long suggested mining the knowledge of "street-level bureaucrats" when developing policies, because of their unique insights into elections on the ground, but few studies have adopted this methodology. This chapter argues that many challenges are new in a historical perspective to long-established democracies such as Britain. Elections in post-industrial, digital-era governance make organizational performance more difficult to achieve without appropriate managerial responses. This environment is likely to be typical of that faced by many of the older post-industrial democracies.

The chapter begins by defining and conceptualizing the study of organizational performance in electoral management as a variety of electoral malpractice. A framework for evaluating organizational performance is proposed and applied to Britain. The chapter then identifies the challenges that policy makers and implementers face in organizing elections.

Standards of Electoral Management Board Performance

Democratic theory requires elections to provide fairness amongst parties, candidates, and citizens. For example, Beetham defines democracy as a system of rule that "embraces the concepts of popular control and political equality."[7] Studying electoral systems and boundaries has identified how they might generate bias, disproportionality, or "wasted votes." Electoral finance laws can provide candidates and parties with (dis)advantages. Restrictive voting and registration technologies, such as elector identification, are thought to depress turnout amongst particular groups. The *management and implementation* of election administration provides a further opportunity for citizens to have unequal influence and for parties or candidates to be (dis)advantaged. Consecutive US presidential elections have seen long lines for voters, poor ballot paper design, and faulty equipment.[8] The 2010 UK general election saw lines at polling stations because of understaffing. Significant technical and operational difficulties in the 2013 Kenyan elections caused a delayed count. An evaluation of the Canadian 2011 federal elections found that election officers, on average, made more than 500 serious administrative errors per electoral district on election day.[9] In the 2013 Malaysia contest, election officials were criticized for not shaking the bottles of indelible ink, meaning that some citizens could wash off the ink and double vote.[10] In each of these cases, individual citizens experienced unequal levels of service. These problems may disadvantage candidates and parties and undermine public confidence in the electoral process.[11] In emerging democracies, such events can threaten democratic consolidation and may cause electoral violence.[12]

An emerging subfield in electoral studies addressing these problems is the study of the public administration of elections. Work has considered how performance management tools, auditing, funding, and election observation can affect the quality of elections.[13] But what constitutes "good" quality elections in the first instance?

The discipline of public sector management promises much given the dense literature on the topic.[14] Organizational performance has always been a concern for governments but it became increasingly prominent since the 1980s under the banner of "good governance" when Western states implemented management reforms and development aid was made conditional on public sector reforms. Today, it remains central for organizations such as the UNDP.[15] For scholars, organizational performance has been described as the "ultimate dependent variable of interest for researchers concerned with just about any area of management."[16]

Performance is also a contested concept dividing those who seek objective or subjective measures.[17] The former are sometimes treated as the "gold standard" because of the allure of scientific objectivity. However, the case that performance is socially constructed is strong. For example, assuming that there is a trade-off, should policy makers prioritize voter security or participation? According to Andrews et al., if there is any disagreement about what is to be measured, how it is to be measured, or the weighting attached to each measure, then performance is subjective.[18] To deal with these issues, a multiple-indicator or mixed approach is increasingly preferred to capture the multifaceted nature of organizations.[19] Boyne, for example, has forged a comprehensive list of performance criteria for evaluating public sector organizations by merging previous competing approaches.[20] Public organizations can be evaluated, he suggests, on the basis of the quantity and quality of the outputs that they produce, the efficiency with which these outputs are produced, and the degree to which those outputs are effective at producing the desired outcomes. Going beyond a simple inputs-outputs-outcomes model, however, organizations should also be responsive to the demands of citizens and staff within the organization and their evaluations should be taken into account. Public organizations, Boyne argues, should also be evaluated by whether they achieve democratic outcomes such as ensuring probity, participation, and accountability.

Boyne's framework is adapted here to assess EMB performance as it identifies what the core aims of these bodies should be according to democratic theory (Table 8.1). The *outputs* produced by EMBs, although varying by country, usually include canvasses of citizens, polling cards, staff training, and voter education. It is important that these are of high quality, because they can affect whether citizens vote and their confidence in the electoral process. Economic efficiency is also important because, whatever the context, resources will be finite, and outcomes need to be maximized. In terms of *service outcomes*, outcome effectiveness such as registration rates, turnout rates, cases of fraud, and levels of voter education remain central to the proper functioning of elections. For example, low turnout can undermine the legitimacy of government and democratic rule, and also reduces inclusiveness. A significant variation in outcomes by gender, ethnicity, or other social cleavage also generates political inequality. The impact of the EMBs' work on other government services should be considered. A focus on *responsiveness* means that

Table 8.1: **A Framework for Evaluating Electoral Management Board Performance**

Dimension of performance		Example for EMBs
Outputs	Quantity	The number of invalid votes, doors knocked, registration enquiries processed, polling cards sent, advertisement, outreach activities organized.
	Quality	The speed of the count, the clarity of election materials, ballot paper design, the accessibility of registration procedures, polling line wait times
	Cost per unit of production	Cost per unit of production
Service Outcomes	Formal effectiveness	Registration rates Voter turnout Cases of electoral fraud Levels of voter education
	Impact	The positive and negative side-effects. For example, the effects the creation of databases for electoral registration which are useful for other government services
	Equity	The distribution of registration and turnout rates by gender, age, race, income, and geographical area
	Cost per unit of service production	Cost per registration and vote cast
Responsiveness	Citizen satisfaction	Citizen satisfaction with the services provided and confidence in the electoral process
	Staff satisfaction	Levels of staff satisfaction
	Cost per unit of responsiveness	Cost per unit of responsiveness
Democratic Outcomes	Probity	The proper use of public funds and the absence of fraud by electoral administrators
	Accountability	Redress for errors such as miscounting, rejection of paper, or long polling lines

EMBs should be assessed by their levels of staff satisfaction, in addition to citizen satisfaction, because EMBs have a duty of care to their employees; and, more importantly, higher staff satisfaction can increase the quality of service to citizens. A focus on *democratic outcomes* means that probity and accountability are also important. Electoral officials should discharge their functions without resort to personal gain and there should be the opportunity for redress for voters. These two criteria have been the main standards through which EMBs have been assessed.[21]

It follows that a further type of electoral malpractice is poor organizational performance based on the above criteria. The framework provides a heuristic matrix for identifying deficiencies in the quality of electoral management through a mixed-methods approach combining both quantitative and qualitative information.

Failures of Steering and Rowing

Why do organizational failures occur? There are two core types or pathways. First, a *failure of steering in electoral management* is defined as *the adoption of practices and strategies that have generated suboptimal organizational performance in EMBs*. These types of problems are system level and exist in the management of organizations. Andrews et al. suggest that common management failures in the public sector are the absence or poor use of indicators, unrealistic aims and goals, weak relations between managers, inadequate relations with external stakeholders, and ineffective leadership.[22] Importantly, what constitutes a failure of steering might depend on context, since good practice in one might not be so in another.

Problems can also be found in the implementation or "rowing" of centrally defined strategies. For example, EMBs might set clear guidelines for processing postal vote application forms, but an individual administrator or team of administrators might not follow these appropriately. A second type of failure, a *failure of rowing in electoral management,* is therefore defined as an *error in the implementation of practices and strategies that results in suboptimal organizational performance in the management of elections*. These types of problems are limited to particular units of organizations. Examples are provided in Table 8.2.

It is important, however, to understand the context in which actors operate when identifying the type and cause of poor performance. Walshe et al. suggest that in the private sector, some symptoms or causes of failure are "primarily internal to the organization, such as poor leadership," however, "others are primarily external and concerned with its environment, such as increased competition, product or service innovation or changes in consumer expectations."[23] Andrews et al. claim that the same is true of the public sector.[24] Shifting demographic trends, for example, place new pressures on health care systems. Poor organizational performance can therefore be partly determined by the *environment*, or organizational responses to the environment. The political, economic, and social context combines to create conditions under which

Table 8.2: **Types of Organizational Failure in Electoral Management**

Failures of steering	Failures of rowing
Poor strategic leadership—e.g., response to external changes	Errors in implementing of centrally defined rules—e.g., mistabulating ballots
Poor learning from other organizations—e.g., other EMBs locally, nationally, or internationally	Failures to follow instructions, such as shaking bottles of indelible ink
Under resourcing—e.g., of polling stations	Failures to enforce penalties and fines to citizens and candidates in elections
Inadequate provision of guidelines to staff—e.g., guidance on when a voter's signature is "legitimate"	
Adoption of inappropriate managerial policy instruments—e.g., absence of use of performance information	
Adoption of inefficient procedures for outputs—e.g., canvassing citizens if this is not the most effective use of resources	
Poor planning and contingency mechanisms—e.g., problems on polling day	
Failure to test appropriate technologies—e.g., vote counting machines	
Inadequate staff training	
Failures to develop procedures to enforce penalties and fines to citizens and candidates	

it may be easier or more difficult for administrators and managers to achieve high performance.

The Context of the British Case Study

The British case illustrates the challenges facing electoral administrators in long-established democracies. British electoral law is defined by Parliament in Westminster and guidance is issued by the Cabinet Office. A UK-wide Electoral Commission has a statutory duty to evaluate elections, keep electoral practices under review, and provide advice and guidance. At the local level, Returning Officers (RO) and Electoral Registration Officers (ERO) have ultimate legal responsibility for implementing the poll and the compilation of the electoral register subject to these laws. They are local government employees but they are independent of government with respect to their electoral functions.

In Scotland, Joint Valuation Boards (JVBs) are responsible for compiling the electoral register. A Scottish Electoral Management Board was established in 2011 to coordinate the work of officials for Scottish local elections. Steering therefore takes place across a range of organizations, but rowing is undertaken by staff employed in local government (see Figure 8.1).

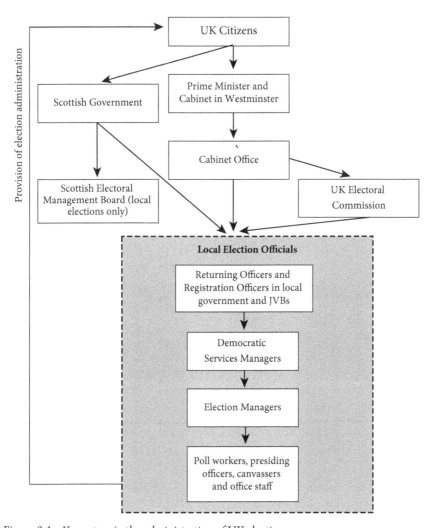

Figure 8.1: Key actors in the administration of UK elections

Systems of electoral management have often been categorized into those where the government runs elections, a body independent of government runs elections, or there is a mixed approach.[25] The UK was originally categorized by Wall et al. as a government model similar to the US, France, and Italy.[26] The growth of the de facto powers of the UK Electoral Commission has meant that the system has moved toward the mixed model, alongside states such as Argentina, Japan, the Netherlands, and Portugal.[27]

What has been the quality of organizational performance in Britain? There is evidence of some contemporary problems. Historical data is limited, but there are good grounds to think that there has been a recent decline in performance, long after the problems of nineteenth-century elections were thought to have been eradicated.

In terms of *output quantity and quality*, the results of the Electoral Commission's performance standards show significant variation in the range of activities undertaken by local authorities. Some are proactive at undertaking public awareness activities, for example, whereas others undertake little or none.

There is also evidence of significant variations in *cost per unit of service production*. For example, the cost of printing ballot papers varied in the 2012 referendum: they were 2.44 times higher in Northern Ireland than in London.[28] In terms of the key *service outcomes*, there has been a significant decline in formal effectiveness measured by voter turnout and registration levels. Figure 8.2 demonstrates how registration levels are estimated to have fallen dramatically, especially in the last decade. They

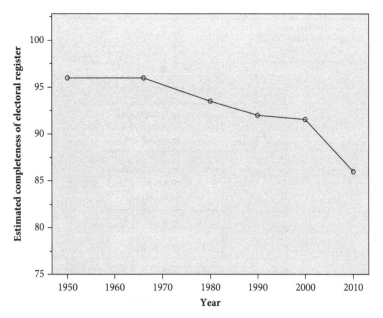

Figure 8.2: The estimated completeness of the electoral register in Great Britain, 1950–2010. Source: Based on estimates in Gemma Rosenblatt, Phil Thompson and Davide Tiberti. 2012. "The quality of the electoral registers in Great Britain and the future of electoral registration." *Parliamentary Affairs*, p. 4.

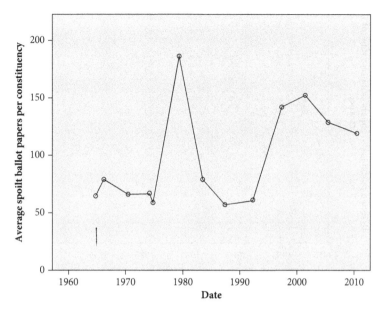

Figure 8.3: Average number of spoilt ballot papers per constituency. Source: Collin Rallings and Michael Thrasher. 2006. *British Electoral Facts*. London: Ashgate. p. 115; Colin Rallings and Michael Thrasher. 2010. *The 2010 General Election: aspects of participation and administration.* Plymouth: LGC Elections Centre report, p.12

are also lower amongst the young, those renting property, black and minority ethnic communities, and eligible non-UK citizens.[29] Voter turnout has also witnessed a general decline but it is generally lower amongst the young, less educated, and less affluent.[30] The average number of spoilt ballot papers per constituency and the number of rejected postal ballot papers remains low, but both have seen slight upward trends (see Figures 8.3 and 8.4). The case has been made that electoral fraud, which was thought to have been eradicated by the end of the nineteenth century, has returned to haunt British elections since 2000.[31] However, election petitions, which were very common in the nineteenth century, still remain very rare (see Figure 8.5). The cost effectiveness of temporary pilot schemes to increase turnout 2000-2007, however, were often evaluated as poor.[32] Early voting schemes in 2006, for example, were estimated to have cost between £3.00 and £115.00 per vote.[33]

In addition, there have been concerns about service *responsiveness*. Surveys undertaken between 2003 and 2012 found that anywhere from 75 to 85 percent of respondents were satisfied with the process of registering to vote. Many dissatisfied citizens claimed that the registration process was too confusing or inconvenient.[34] Figure 8.6, reporting satisfaction with the voting process amongst respondents, demonstrates that satisfaction with the process of voting has also remained high, but the number of respondents that were "fairly unsatisfied" or "very unsatisfied" has grown since 2005. The proportion of people confident that elections were well run stood at less than

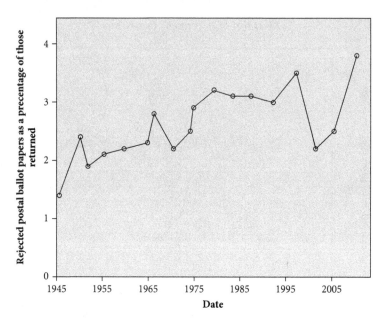

Figure 8.4: Rejected postal ballot papers as a percentage of those returned, 1945–2010.

Source: Collin Rallings and Michael Thrasher. 2006. *British Electoral Facts*. London: Ashgate, p. 112; Colin Rallings and Michael Thrasher. 2010. *The 2010 General Election: aspects of participation and administration*. Plymouth: LGC Elections Centre report, p.10

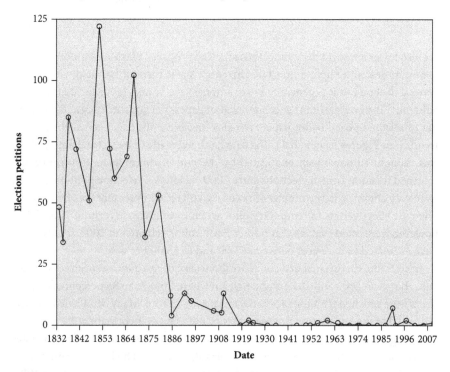

Figure 8.5: Election petitions at British general elections, 1832–2010. Source: Collin Rallings and Michael Thrasher. 2006. *British Electoral Facts*. London: Ashgate, p. 245.

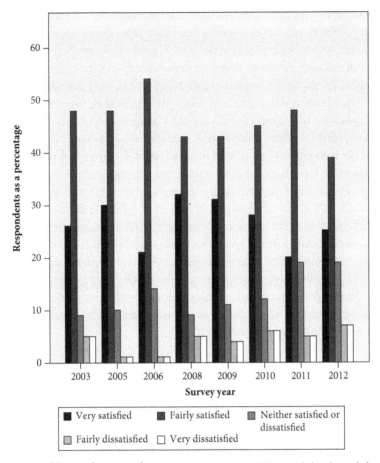

Figure 8.6: Public satisfaction with voting process Note: Q. *"How satisfied or dissatisfied are you with the actual process of voting at elections in Great Britain/Northern Ireland?"*. Source: TNS. 2013. p. 7.

two-thirds (61 percent) in 2012. Just over a third (36 percent) thought that electoral fraud was a problem and one in ten (9 percent) claimed that it was a very big problem.[35] Although there are no specific evaluations of staff satisfaction within electoral service departments, satisfaction levels amongst public sector workers in general are often reported as being behind those of private and third-sector employers.[36] Despite concerns about voter fraud, there have been few questions raised about the probity of electoral officials themselves. Problems regarding the lack of opportunity for redress were raised in 2010, after 1,200 citizens were thought to have been unable to cast their ballot and some miscounts occurred, such as in Birmingham in 2006.[37]

There are plenty of examples of *failures of steering in electoral management* that have contributed toward suboptimal performance. The Electoral Commission review found some election officials culpable for inadequate planning, risk management, and contingency planning in the 2010 general election, with the resulting problems affecting 1,200 citizens.[38] Poor planning and ballot paper design were blamed for the rejection of 140,000 ballot papers in the 2007 Scottish Parliamentary and Local government elections.[39] Problems were also experienced with the design of electronic counting machines, which had to be abandoned. It has been claimed that the considerable fraud that was found to have taken place in local elections in Birmingham in 2004 (amongst others) was a result of poorly designed postal voting procedures.[40] Other long-established procedures such as household registration have been criticized for not being robust enough to detect and deter electoral fraud, even by international observers.[41] For instance, many authorities have not undertaken door-to-door canvasses, even though they are under a statutory responsibility to do so.[42]

There are also plenty of examples of *failures of rowing in electoral management*. Miscounts have led to the wrong candidate being declared the winner in cases such as the local elections in Birmingham's Kingstanding ward in 2006, Waltham Forest in 2010, and Denbighshire County Council's Prestatyn North in 2011. In addition, ballot boxes were lost, resulting in delayed counts in the 2012 London mayoral elections.[43] There have been uneven rejection rates of postal vote applications around the country and variations in how far waivers were granted by authorities, suggesting inconsistent application of the rules.[44]

The New Context for Managing Elections in Britain

What is the nature of the environment in which elections are organized in Britain? What challenges do electoral administrators face in the implementation of elections today? Has electoral management become more difficult? Might this partially explain concerns about performance and cases of failures of steering and rowing? Concepts from historical institutionalism help us understand how a changing context can cause change in organizational performance. One key feature of historical institutionalism is the interest in the temporal development of political institutions. As contexts change over time, the effects of different institutions may alter.[45] The concept of institutional drift refers to how "rules remain formally the same but their impact changes as a result of shifts in external conditions."[46] The sources of change are not necessarily a result of active policy changes, but of exogenous dynamics. Institutional drift therefore occurs because "institutions require active maintenance; to remain what they are they need to be reset and refocused, or sometimes fundamentally recalibrated or renegotiated."[47]

This concept is useful because the institutions, policy instruments, and methods that electoral administrators employ to implement elections have not regularly changed. British election administration has its roots in the 1872 Municipal Elections Act, which established the secret ballot, and the 1918 Representation of the People Act, which set out the framework for the annual canvass and compilation of the electoral register. During what could be considered a *pre-modern period* (c.1832–1918) in Britain, electoral administrators faced particular challenges for which these initial voting technologies and systems of management might have been well suited. Elections were conducted with a limited franchise, the population was relatively stable, and the legal framework was simple. There was a relatively low take-up of mass media, but knowledge of electoral fraud was widespread, especially in elections such as the 1868 general election.[48] Elections were initially via a show of hands and no electoral registration was required prior to 1832. Parish officers, who oversaw the Poor Law, were given responsibility for compiling the register. The Secret Ballot Act led to paper ballots being introduced.

New challenges were, however, brought by the *modern period* (c.1918–1990). The dramatic extensions to the franchise in 1918, and 1928 meant that expanded administrative machinery was required to deal with the enormous growth in registrations and ballot papers cast. This posed logistical challenges, especially because World War I created significant population displacements and drained resources.[49] Electoral administrative functions were consolidated into local government, and the significant growth in the size of the state and bureaucracy enabled local government to achieve high levels of organizational performance. High levels of registration were maintained, and the integrity of Britain's electoral machinery was rarely questioned.

More recently, a new *post-industrial, digital age* era (c.1990s–present) has emerged, characterized by demographic, technological, legal, economic, and political complexity and fluidity (Table 8.3). Significant changes in Britain pose new challenges for electoral administrators. In terms of demographic change, recent decades have seen more internal migration across Britain,[50] and an increasingly linguistically and culturally diverse population, because of rising immigration, especially from the EU.[51] Socioeconomic, cultural, and legal changes have also occurred. In addition, there may have been a rise in political apathy and "anti-politics," with the electorate less likely to vote.[52] Rising economic inequality and the "ghettoization" of parts of urban Britain pose problems for conducting the electoral canvass. A more complex legal framework has developed as a result of the layering of legislation.

There have also been major changes in the management of the British state. Resource and financial austerity have been core concerns since the "crisis of the state" in the 1970s, but also since the financial crisis of 2008. This, combined with the rising costs of elections, pose cost pressures and tough choices about which areas to maximize performance in. New public management reforms, introduced to many advanced capitalist democracies such as Britain, have led to the fragmentation of the state. The process of disaggregating public sector hierarchies has led to the state being "hollowed out," reduced the capacity of core actors to achieve policy outcomes, introduced new coordination problems, and caused complex delivery chains.[53] Meanwhile, constitutional devolution to Scotland and Wales has added further legal complexity to the rules for elections.

Technological change has opened up new opportunities and challenges for the state to provide public services. New ICT offers the prospect of increasing

Table 8.3: **Periods of Election Administration in Britain**

	Pre-modern	*Modern*	*Post-industrial*
Time	1832–1918	1918–1990s	2000–
Characteristics	Limited	Mass franchise	Demographic, technological, legal, economic, and political complexity and fluidity.
Main methods	Self-administered	House-to-house enquiries Annual canvass	Moves toward: Online registration individual registration, electronic registration, data matching
Political participation and civic trust	Limited franchise	Mass franchise-mass participation	Mass franchise depleted participation
Population dynamics	Stable	Stable	Fluid
Legal framework	Linear	Linear	Complex Multilevel
Media	Low take-up	Mass media	24/7 Internet age Web 2.0
Technology	Paper	Mass record systems	ICT and database driven
Expectations gap	Low resources required, low expectations	High resources, high expectations	Potential for under-resourced, high expectations
Governance	Locally led	Centrally led split	Networked governance
Partisanship	High	Low	High

productivity gains by consolidating existing "labyrinths of discrete mainframe facilities and associated administrative units."[54] The provision of "one-stop shops" offers the opportunity to remove the duplication of government services.[55] However, it has also changed citizens' expectations about how governments use ICT, which can make it more difficult to register electors. The development of 24/7 news and social media reports means that any errors that electoral administrators make are discovered more quickly and loudly.

Methods and Evidence

How do electoral officials respond to these developments? This study draws from semi-structured interviews with those involved in implementing elections. In total, 74 interviews were undertaken with local election officials (LEOs): returning officers, electoral registration officers, democratic services managers and elections mangers. These interviews were spread across 41 organizations in England, Scotland, and Wales during 2011. Respondents were asked to explain the key challenges that they faced in the organization of elections. Interviews lasted about an hour and were semi-structured to allow the interviewees to define the issues. The names of individuals and authorities included in the study were withheld so that the interviewees could speak freely. A quota sampling method was used to ensure that all different authority types were included in England, Scotland, and Wales.[56] A mix of urban and rural authorities was also included. A thematic analysis of the interviews was conducted to identify common challenges. Thematic analysis "involves the searching across a data set . . . to find repeated patterns of meaning" through an iterative movement between theory and data.[57] Interviews were transcribed and themes identified from the texts. The aim was to identify both semantic and latent meanings.

Interviewing local election officials holds much potential as a method for understanding the effects of different reforms to election administration because the academic literature from public administration suggests that "top-down" implementation of policies can often face implementation problems and unforeseen consequences.[58] Proponents of "bottom-up" policy making have therefore long suggested mining the knowledge of "street-level bureaucrats" when developing policies.[59] A disadvantage of the approach is that actors might overemphasize the problems that they face in order to make their performance look good. This can be overcome, however, by collaborating information with other sources when possible. Moreover, without "listening" to frontline perspectives, scholars and policy makers will not know *how* potential problems manifest themselves into the everyday experience of electoral administrations and elections on the frontline. Other methods, such as surveys and cross-national studies, can complement but not replace this.

Contemporary Implementation-Level Challenges

The interviews revealed 10 core challenges that staff face in implementing elections effectively.

1. Increased Apathy, Decreased Trust

Local election officials complain that increased citizen apathy causes them significant problems when compiling the electoral register. A core pool of citizens failed to be included on the register each year.

> There's a general apathy towards elections and politics... we'll never crack that final 5-10% of people who just have absolutely no desire to get onto the register.

Staff suggested that they needed to invest increasing resources on schemes such as performance pay for canvassers, employing former bailiffs, and extended local advertising to stop the register from falling further.

A minority of staff also claimed that citizens increasingly questioned the "anachronistic" security provisions that they had in place for voting. No electoral identification is required at either the polling or registration stage of the election. They claimed that this system was based on "trust" but that this no longer exists. There were changing expectations amongst citizens about the security procedures required when interacting with government services.

> [E]verybody needs to produce a PIN number or a signature for most things they do nowadays.

Achieving high levels of citizen satisfaction could therefore be more difficult.

2. Changing Urban Britain: Increased Crime and Problems with Urban Geography

The main source of names for the electoral register has traditionally been the annual canvass, but this has become more difficult to conduct. Public abuse of canvassers is rather common, leading to concerns about their safety and a difficulty in recruiting new ones.

> If a person of authority is seen to be part of an institution goes in there they're just drummed out. I mean they're just not accepted...

Councils would ask canvassers whether there were areas where they did not feel safe and would not go resulting in disproportionate attempts to register citizens across neighborhoods. Furthermore, the process also works both ways, with an increasing number of the public refusing to answer the door due to fear of unsolicited callers.

> And then you get little old ladies who are on their own who just won't answer the door after 6pm because there have been bogus callers.

Urban architecture does not facilitate an annual canvass, either, with properties such as high-rise flats being rather difficult to access.

> [W]here you've got HMOs, where three or four storey property is—there are bedsits there, there's shared communal facilities, and there are 8 to 16 doorbells that don't work on the door, or at the side of the door. How do you get somebody to the door? Legislation doesn't cater for that.

Throughout rural areas, in contrast, the population can be so sparse that conducting a complete door-knock canvass becomes very expensive.

3. Legal Complexity and Diversity

There has been a considerable increase in the legal complexity of elections in Britain as a result of a rise in the *frequency* of elections and *types* of elections since 1997. In addition to Westminster, local government, parish council, and European parliamentary elections, there are now elections for the Greater London Council, Scottish government, Welsh government, mayor and police, and crime commissioner and more frequent referenda. Many of the contests are run under a different electoral system. This has added to the complexity of election administration and makes administrative errors and poor organizational performance more likely. One officer recalled how it was in a combined election that their authority "made an administrative error" that led to a BNP candidate being elected instead of a Labour one, because of the double counting of ballots.

> Poll management is different... One year is very different from the next year. A few years ago...a combination of elections was the rarity. Now it's completely tipped up on its head.

Devolution has also created different regulatory frameworks for elections. One local election official reported that one year had conflicting deadlines for the closing dates of postal vote applications. Legal complexity also makes it more difficult to convey information to the electorate and for them to be understood.

Legal fragmentation is a further problem. Election law is spread across a variety of acts and amendment acts—over 35 primary pieces of legislation and over 100 pieces of secondary legislation.[60] This poses particular problems for "newcomers" who are not aware of older legislation.

> One of the things that we all find quite difficult is the convoluted legislation. Different pieces of legislation have different timetables... Some of the legislation is UK, some of it is Scottish Government. And it's all amendment Act, amendment Act, amendment Act... It's just not understandable to the vast majority of people and most of the administrators as well.

Legislative changes have also become more frequent, and they are commonly made very close to the run-up to an election, leaving uncertainty in the planning. The Gould inquiry into the problems in the 2007 Scottish elections found that late legislation was a key problem and recommended that no changes be made less than six months before an election. However, this advice was not always heeded.

> Legislators don't account for the time it takes software houses to change systems, test them, implement them with all the customers and let customers confidently run with it. So again you get the impression that the legislators or the political classes seem to think that computers just sort themselves at the press of a button.

The challenge of rising complexity is heightened, LEOs report, by an exodus of staff from the profession. Many long-standing members are retiring early because of public sector cuts or pressures of the job. New staff is not being brought through the system, they suggest, and authorities have faced problems recruiting experienced staff.

4. New Technology

The wider availability of new technology has led to rising expectations amongst citizens about electoral services. Many citizens think that electoral registration is not necessary because they use other government services and they expect their data to be shared. Some citizens therefore turn up at the polls without registering.

> You know I'm registered for Council Tax is a huge misconception. They think because they're registered and paying Council Tax they're registered for electoral registration.

Citizens' expectations about data-sharing also cause many to not register. Some refuse to be included, LEOs reported, because they fear that their information will be made public, or used for other purposes such as calculating benefit entitlements or preventing tax avoidance.

> So many of our canvassers come to us and say "I'm sure there's somebody else living there but she says she's there on her own."

Some staff are proactive at data-matching databases within their local authority. However, such databases are often imperfect for the purposes of compiling or checking the accuracy of a register, as, unlike in some other countries, there is no single national identity record in Britain.

New technology offers opportunities for increased productivity. However, LEOs report that this requires increased investment in new skills for staff. Errors can easily be made in the process of adapting to them.

5. Population Movements

Increased population movements have made keeping the electoral register up-to-date more challenging. Inner-city areas were difficult to keep track of because of "huge population churns."

> [E]very couple of months and we get thousands of new names. So there's this constant pressure throughout the year for the updating of the register (sic).

Immigration from non-English speaking countries poses new challenges for staff because some communities may not engage with the registration process or it may require significant investment in multilingual materials.

> We have got quite a large black minority ethnic community, big chunks of which are not necessarily culturally attuned to the life in the UK. Many of [them] don't speak English as their first language; those are all a whole host of barriers that you need to get across.

Some authorities have been proactive at tackling under-registration by employing canvassers who speak the native language. Bilingual printed resources can also be costly and complex for the citizen.

> If you compare our [bi-lingual English & Welsh] forms to an English Authority, their forms are far more user-friendly (sic).

6. Resources and Financial Austerity

Staff commonly report that they are faced with high costs running elections and frequently experience difficulty obtaining sufficient money from the Council. This echoes comments from Electoral Commission officials (see Clarke, this volume). One authority explained that they commonly had to build up reserves in one election to pay for the next, and there would commonly be unexpected costs.

> [T]he national elections are funded generally from central Government but you can't, you don't recover all the costs, there are a lot of costs that are borne by the Council.... And that determines obviously how much you want to invest.

Difficult choices often have to be made about what services could be provided to the public. Services that were non-statutory, such as public awareness schemes, are therefore often cut. Because of costs, some local authorities did not canvass all houses that did not return an electoral registration form, even though this was a legal requirement, and also a requirement to meet the Electoral Commission performance standards.[61] There are also many other everyday examples where staff weigh the value of additional registered citizens or votes.

> Ultimately my goal is to get 100% registration. But I know that that is a bridge too far. But you should advertise more, you should be doing this. We're downsizing as a council. My resources, staff-wise, have gone down. So to maintain what we've got is a challenge.

The challenge of providing sufficient funding has heightened, staff suggest, because local government has to undertake budget cuts, yet simultaneously, election departments were required to undertake new work.

> I think that the electoral administration is in a world of its own, really, as if the credit crunch hadn't occurred as if we didn't have to take 20% out of our budgets (sic).

Staff very commonly stress the tight timetables involved in the delivery of elections. The period from the deadlines for completing the electoral register and nomination of candidates to election day are particularly tight. If they are under-resourced during these times, then errors become likely. Staff are consequently forced to work extremely long hours during the election period, which can result in burnout.

> [We made it] only by the skin of our teeth really, particularly with this year's election. We were working until 12 'o clock every night, we came in at weekends and you rely on the commitment of the staff, really, to see through that election because you've deadlines for everything.

Larger authorities are often more able to cope in the run-up to elections because of the additional capacity. Yet clearly, resource constraints and spiraling costs contribute to a situation in which names can be missed off registers, errors can appear on ballot papers, and polling stations can be underresourced.

7. Networked Governance

Staff often face increased problems coordinating the rising number of actors involved in the provision of electoral services. Some staff are often reliant on a small pool of private organizations such as printers, since councils do not have in-house facilities.

The outsourcing of this work has not always been successfully completed by private contractors. In England and Wales, coordination is also commonly required among authorities because there are different tiers of local government in the election. In Scotland, the functions of electoral registration and the conduct of the poll are split between organizations. Parliamentary districts commonly cross council boundaries, which means that organizations have to coordinate registers. These relationships may sometimes break down.

> Constituencies [are] always going to be beyond the Council area, so then we would have a working relationship with a neighbouring Local Authority. And again we have good relationships, so it works. But there are dangers where if that was to break down, then you have issues.

Whereas staff were once reliant on information provided to them by the Home Office, information now comes from a range of organizations, including the (national and regional) Electoral Commission, SOLACE, Scottish Electoral Management Board, the police, and the Association of Electoral Administrators. Some staff also report common coordination problems within authorities, because the formally appointed returning officer is a high-level official who has little interest in running the election.

8. Rising Partisanship?

In some authorities, staff claim that election administration has been increasingly politicized, with local candidates making accusations of fraud against other candidates, or malpractice against administrators. Local politicians complain about polling station adjustments if they feel that their interests are adversely affected. In some areas, they suggest, electoral challenges were becoming increasingly common.[62]

> It's become more divisive politics; whereas before it may have been done more on an amenable level, there are now real party political divides, for which administrators will get caught in the middle.

These claims were isolated to particular areas and were built on previous antagonisms, but they could be widely reported in the national media. This is significant because Vonnahme and Miller find that the public, knowing little about the quality of election administration, take "cues" from politicians. [63] Partisan criticism can therefore lower citizens' satisfaction with electoral services, whatever the quality of service provided.

9. Changing Lifestyles; Changing Expectations

Staff report that they face changing public expectations about the services that they should provide. Employment patterns have changed dramatically in Britain, with a rise in service-sector and part-time employment. This has meant that some citizens find it increasingly hard to vote on election days.[64] Some UK pilots of innovative systems, such as text-message voting and Internet voting, were trialed in 2000-2007 but most were not adopted.[65] One LEO explained that citizens could reregister via telephone, SMS, or the Internet, if there were no changes to their status.

> However, when it comes to an election, they can't vote that way and…they don't understand why they can't in this day and age, where everything is electronic.

10. The Development of 24/7 and Social Media

Staff suggest that the development of the 24/7 news media and social media have placed additional pressures on electoral administrators by amplifying any mistakes. On the night of the 2010 general election, the news media focused on problems in polling stations, which were then circulated by social media. These problems were, perhaps, not new or uncommon in the past, but they could now be more readily reported and circulated by citizens. According to one official who had worked in elections for over 30 years:

> [G]oing back 15 or 20 years there were far worse things that happened at elections but they never, ever got into the public eye because the public gaze wasn't on that aspect of elections. But now it highlights that we have to be extremely careful about every single aspect of the operation of an election that we undertake.

Many LEOs suggest that in a "post-Florida" environment, the media and politicians were more aware of the news-worthiness of electoral failures:

> Our local newspaper is very on-the-ball and would pick up any issue that we've not dealt with.
> Local politicians will even pick on the smallest wee thing they can find to get themselves in the newspaper, promote themselves and stuff.

Maintaining high levels of citizen satisfaction with electoral services can therefore be more difficult, even if the quality of electoral services is high.

Conclusions

Research on the integrity of elections has often focused on how rival elites have sought to subvert the democratic process for strategic advantage. Yet poor organizational performance by electoral management bodies constitutes another variety of electoral malpractice.

The chapter has evaluated organizational performance in Britain, noting some recent causes for concern. Theories from implementation studies suggest that we need to understand the challenges that street-level bureaucrats face when implementing elections. Evidence from qualitative interviews with staff demonstrates that, historically and qualitatively, new challenges have emerged that help to explain recent concerns about electoral management. The interviews provide support for the emergence of a more challenging environment for managing and implementing elections in Britain. Lack of resources, as well as financial austerity and networked governance, have manifested in additional challenges for electoral administrators. The development of 24/7 news and social media, new technology, and changing lifestyles and expectations reflect the importance of technological changes. Population movements concern the effects of demographic changes as Britain has become a linguistically and culturally more diverse nation. Increased apathy and decreased trust, and changing urban Britain, demonstrate the role of socioeconomic and cultural developments. A more complex legal framework exists, and the practices and tactics of local candidates have evolved over time.

A shifting environment does not mean that declining organizational performance and failures of steering and rowing are inevitable, however. Electoral officials stress the difficulties that they face, but their changing environment also poses opportunities. A flexible and disaggregated state may encourage innovation. The availability of new technology can offer opportunities to increase efficiency through the use of "big data" and Web 2.0 tools. Social media can be harnessed for encouraging electoral registration and voter registration, and perhaps should also be celebrated because it might make electoral officials more accountable and responsive to errors. The environment in which officials run elections evolves over time, and this may influence organizational performance. Importantly, electoral management bodies need to adapt to the new challenges, otherwise institutional drift can occur.

Future research needs to establish whether these are challenges that are found elsewhere. Are these typical? If so, for what type of state? Democracies that have similar forms of electoral governance, according to the International IDEA classifications? Or are other variables more important? We might expect some problems relating to networks to be more present in those systems with the mixed model, because the greater variety of actors is more likely to contribute toward coordination problems. However, it seems that other variables might be more important, since most of the challenges are not necessarily related to electoral governance type. In the UK, problems of coordination were not just caused by the mixed model used. The complex institutional environment owed more to the institutional structure of local government, historically divergent institutional arrangements across the UK for electoral management, a dynamic for devolution since 1998, and the new public management reforms that encouraged the contracting out of services to the private sector. Other trends, such as demographic shifts, economic develop-ments, technological transformations, a shifting political culture, and a fragmenting legal structure, are common to many established democracies. We might therefore expect many similar challenges to be confronting other post-industrial democracies as well. Further comparative research using mixed-methods is needed to test this argument in order to see whether the challenges are comparable or different.

Acknowledgments: An earlier version of this paper was presented at the American Political Science Association Annual Conference in New Orleans, August 2012, the Political Studies Association Annual International Conference in Cardiff, May 2013, and the Electoral Integrity Project annual workshop on "Concepts and Indices of Electoral Integrity," June 3–4 2013, Weatherhead Center for International Affairs, Harvard University, US. I am grateful to participants and the editors for their comments on earlier versions of the manuscript. The findings draw from research interviews funded by the Nuffield Foundation and McDougall Trust.

Notes

1. Sarah Birch. 2011. *Electoral Malpractice*. Oxford: Oxford University Press; Toby S. James. 2012. *Elite Statecraft and Election Administration: Bending the Rules of the Game*. Basingstoke: Palgrave Macmillan; Pippa Norris. 2013. "The new research agenda study-ing electoral integrity." *Electoral Studies* 32(4), 563–575; Alan Renwick. 2010. *The Politics of Electoral Reform: Changing the Rules of Democracy*. Cambridge: Cambridge University Press; Andreas Schedler. 2002. "The menu of manipulation." *Journal of Democracy* 13(2), 36–50.

2. Sarah Birch. 2011. *Electoral Malpractice*. Oxford: Oxford University Press.

3. Pippa Norris. 2013. "The new research agenda studying electoral integrity." *Electoral Studies* 32(4), 563–575.

4. Sarah Birch. 2011. *Electoral Malpractice*. Oxford: Oxford University Press. p. 26.

5. Sarah Birch. 2011. *Electoral Malpractice*. Oxford: Oxford University Press. p. 14.

6. Pippa Norris. 2013. "The new research agenda studying electoral integrity." *Electoral Studies* 32(4), 563–575.

7. David Beetham. 1994. "Key Principles and Indicies for a Democratic Audit" in David Beetham (Ed.), *Defining Democracy*. London: Sage, p. 28.

8. Richard L. Hasen. 2012. *The voting wars: From Florida 2000 to the next election meltdown*. Grand Rapids, MI: Yale University Press.

9. Harry Neufield. 2013. *Compliance Review: Final Report and Recommendations*. Ottawa: Elections Canada, p. 6.

10. Adrian Lai. 2013. "Staff may have failed to use indelible ink properly: EC." *New Straits Times*. http://www.nst.com.my/latest/staff-may-have-failed-to-use-indelible-ink-properl y-ec-1.268714 (accessed May 13, 2013).

11. Lonna Rae Atkeson and Kyle L. Saunders. 2007. "The effect of election administration on voter confidence: A local matter?" *PS: Political Science & Politics* 40(4): 655–660; Ryan Claassen, David Magleby, J. Monson and Kelly Patterson. 2012. "Voter Confidence and the Election-Day Voting Experience." *Political Behavior* 35(2): 215–235; Ryan L. Claassen, David B. Magleby, J. Quin Monson and Kelly D. Patterson. 2008. "'At Your Service' Voter Evaluations of Poll Worker Performance." *American Politics Research* 36(4), 612–634; Thad E. Hall, J. Quin Monson and Kelly D. Patterson. 2009. "The Human Dimension of Elections: How Poll Workers Shape Public Confidence in Elections." *Political Research Quarterly* 62(3): 507–522.

12. Jorgen Elklit and Andrew Reynolds. 2002. "The impact of election administration on the legitimacy of emerging democracies: A new comparative politics research agenda." *Commonwealth & Comparative Politics* 40(2), 86–119; Robert A. Pastor. 1999. "The role of electoral administration in democratic transitions: Implications for policy and research." *Democratization* 6(4): 1–27; Michael R. Snyder. 2013. "For want of a credible voter registry: Do problems in voter registration increase the likelihood of electoral violence?" *Josef Korbel Journal of Advanced International Studies.* Summer 2013.

13. Toby S. James. 2013. "Fixing failures of U.K. electoral management." *Electoral Studies,* 32(4): 597–608; R. Michael Alvarez, Lonna Rae Atkeson and Thad E. Hall. 2012. *Evaluating Elections: A Handbook of Methods and Standards.* New York: Cambridge University Press; R. Michael Alvarez, Lonna Rae Atkeson and Thad E. Hall (eds). 2012. *Confirming Elections.* New York: Palgrave Macmillan; Alistair Clark. 2014. "Investing in Electoral Management" in Pippa Norris et al. (eds). *Advancing Electoral Integrity.* New York: Oxford University Press.

14. Neil Carter, Rudolf Klein and Patricia Day. 1992. *How Organizations Measure Success: The Use of Performance Indicators in Government.* London: Routledge; Elinor Ostrom. 1973. "The need for multiple indicators of measuring the output of public agencies." *Policy Studies Journal* 2: 85–91; Roger B. Parks. 1984. "Linking objective and subjective measures of performance." *Public Administration Review of International Political Economy* 44: 118–127.

15. UNDP. 1997. *Governance for sustainable human development.* New York: United Nations.

16. Pierre J. Richard, Timothy M. Devinney, George S. Yip and Gerry Johnson. 2009. "Measuring organizational performance: Towards methodological best practice." *Journal of Management* 35(3): 718–804, p. 19.

17. Kenneth J. Meier, Jeffrey L. Brudney and John Bohte. 2002. *Applied statistics for public administration.* Orlando: Harcourt College; Gene A. Brewer. 2006. All measures of performance are subjective: more evidence on US federal agencies. In George A. Boyne et al. (Eds.), *Public Service Performance* (pp. 35–54). Cambridge: Cambridge University Press.

18. Rhys Andrews, George A. Boyne and Richard M Walker. 2006. Subjective and objective measures of organizational performance: An empirical exploration. In George A. Boyne et al. (Eds.), *Public Service Performance* (pp. 14–34). Cambridge: Cambridge University Press, p. 19.

19. Janet M. Kelly and David Swindell. 2002. "A multiple-indicator approach to municipal service evaluation: correlating performance measurement and citizen satisfaction across jurisdictions." Public Administration Review 62, 610–20; Parks. 1984; Richard et al. 2009.

20. George A. Boyne. 2002. "Theme: Local Government: Concepts and indicators of local authority performance: An evaluation of the statutory frameworks in England and Wales." *Public Money & Management* 22(2): 17–24.

21. For example, see: Antonio Ugues Jr. 2014. "Election Management Bodies in newer democracies: Nicaragua, Honduras and Guatemala" in Pippa Norris et al. (eds). *Advancing Electoral Integrity.* New York: Oxford University Press.

22. Rhys Andrews, George A. Boyne and Gareth Enticott. 2006. "Performance failure in the public sector." *Public Management Review* 8(2): 276–280.

23. Kieran Walshe, Gill Harvey, Paula Hyde and Naresh Pandit. 2004. "Organizational failure and turnaround: Lessons for public services from the for-profit sector." *Public Money & Management* 24(4): 201.

24. Rhys Andrews, George A. Boyne and Gareth Enticott. 2006. "Performance failure in the public sector." *Public Management Review* 8(2): 273–296.

25. Rafael Lopez-Pinter. 2000. *Electoral Management Bodies as Institutions of Governance.* Washington D.C.: United Nations Development Programme; Alan Wall, Andrew Ellis, Ayman Ayoub, Carl W. Dundas, Joram Rukambe and Sara Staino. 2006. *Electoral Management Design: The International IDEA Handbook.* Stockholm: International IDEA.

26. Alan Wall, Andrew Ellis, Ayman Ayoub, Carl W. Dundas, Joram Rukambe and Sara Staino. 2006. *Electoral Management Design: The International IDEA Handbook.* Stockholm: International IDEA.

27. Toby S. James. 2013.
28. Electoral Commission. 2012. *Costs of the May 2011 referendum on the UK Parliamentary voting system*. London: Electoral Commission, p. 19.
29. Gemma Rosenblatt, Phil Thompson and Davide Tiberti. 2012. "The Quality of the Electoral Registers in Great Britain and the Future of Electoral Registration." *Parliamentary Affairs*, http://dx.doi.org/10.1093/pa/gss032.
30. Harold D. Clarke, David Sanders, Marianne C. Stewart and Paul Whiteley. 2004. *Political Choice in Britain*. Oxford and New York: Oxford University Press.
31. Stuart Wilks-Heeg, Andrew Blick and Stephen Crone. 2012. *How Democratic Is the UK? The 2012 Audit*. Liverpool: Democratic Audit.
32. Toby S. James. 2011. "Fewer 'costs,' more votes? UK Innovations in Electoral Administration 2000–2007 and their effect on voter turnout." *Election Law Journal* 10(1), 37–52.
33. Electoral Commission. 2006. *May 2006 electoral pilot schemes: early voting*. London: Electoral Commission.
34. TNS. 2013. *Electoral Commission 2012 Winter Research: Mainstage Topline Findings*. London: Electoral Commission, p. 11–12.
35. Ibid, p. 4.
36. CIPD. 2012. Employee Outlook: Summer 2013. London: Chartered Institute of Personnel and Development.
37. Electoral Commission. 2012. *Challenging elections in the UK*. London: Electoral Commission.
38. Electoral Commission. 2010. *2010 UK Parliamentary general election interim report*. London: Electoral Commission.
39. Ron Gould. 2007. *Independent review of the Scottish Parliamentary and local government elections*. Edinburgh: Electoral Commission.
40. James. 2012. p. 149–150.
41. Council of Europe. 2008. *Opinion of the Bureau of the Assembly*. Strasbourg: Council of Europe.
42. Electoral Commission. 2012. *Electoral registration in Great Britain Report on performance of Electoral Registration Officers*. London: Electoral Commission, p. 1.
43. The Telegraph. 2012. "Mislaid ballot boxes delay mayoral election results." *The Telegraph*. 4 May 2012.
44. Colin Rallings and Michael Thrasher. 2009. *Postal vote verification and rejections in Great Britain: European and local elections 2009*. Plymouth: LGC Elections Centre.
45. Paul Pierson. 2004. *Politics in time: History, institutions, and social analysis*. Princeton, New Jersey: Princeton University Press.
46. James Mahoney and Kathleen Thelan. 2010. "A Theory of Gradual Institutional Change." In James Mahoney and Kathleen Thelan (Eds.), *Explaining Institutional Change: Abiguity, Agency and Power* (pp. 1–37). New York: Cambridge University Press, p. 17.
47. Wolfgang Streeck and Kathleen Thelan. 2005. "Introduction: Institutional Change in Advanced Political Economies." In Wolfgang Streeck and Kathleen Thelan (Eds.), *Beyond Continuity* (pp. 1–39). Oxford: Oxford University Press, p. 24.
48. Cornelius O'Leary. 1962. *Elimination of Corrupt Practices In British Elections,1868–1911*. London: Clarendon Press, p.58.
49. James. 2012. p. 129–133.
50. Tony Champion. 2005. "Population movement within the UK." *Focus on people and migration*, 91–113.
51. Office for National Statistics. 2011. *International Migration in England and Wales*. London: Office for National Statistics.
52. Colin Hay. 2007. *Why We Hate Politics*. Cambridge: Polity Press.
53. Patrick Dunleavy et al. 2006. "New Public Management Is Dead: Long Live Digital-Era Governance." *Journal of Public Administration Research and Theory*. 16:467–494; Rod Rhodes. 1997. *Understanding Governance*. Buckingham: Open University Press.
54. Dunleavy et al. 2006. p. 482.
55. Dunleavy et al. 2006. p. 484.

56. The sample included London boroughs (5), Unitary Authorities (4), Metropolitan district authorities (9), Two-tier "shire" counties (5), Welsh unitary authorities (6), Scottish councils (5) and Scottish VJBs (7).

57. Virginia Braun and Victoria Clarke. 2006. "Using thematic analysis in psychology." *Qualitative Research in Psychology* 3(2), p. 86.

58. Paul A. Sabatier. 1986. "Top-Down and Bottom-Up Approaches to Implementation Research: a Critical Analysis and Suggested Synthesis." *Journal of Public Policy* 6(01), 21–48.; Jeffrey L. Pressman and Aaron Wildavsky. 1973. *Implementation*. Berkeley: University of California Press.

59. Michael Lipsky. 1980. *Street Level Bureaucracy*. New York: Russell Sage Foundation; Catherine Durose. 2009. "Front-line workers and local knowledge: Neighbourhood stories in contemporary UK local governance." *Public Administration* 87(1), 35–49.

60. Electoral Commission. 2012. *Response of the Electoral Commission: Law Commission Review of Electoral Law—Consultation Scoping Paper*. London: Electoral Commission.

61. Electoral Commission. (2012). *Electoral registration in Great Britain Report on performance of Electoral Registration Officers*. London: Electoral Commission.

62. Many accusations made were informal. However, for historical data on petitions and convictions, see: Stuart Wilks-Heeg. 2008. *Purity of Elections in the UK: Causes for Concern*. York: Joseph Rowntree Trust. p. 71–84.

63. Greg Vonnahme and Beth Miller. 2012. "Candidate Cues and Voter Confidence in American Elections." *Journal of Elections, Public Opinion & Parties* 23(2): 223–239.

64. There is evidence of broad demand for e-government services across Europe. See: Dinand Tinholt et al. 2013. *Public Services Online: "Digital by Default or by Detour?"* European Commission.

65. James 2011.

DOES LACK OF INTEGRITY
UNDERMINE LEGITIMACY?

9

Investing in Electoral Management

ALISTAIR CLARK

One of the most prevalent implicit hypotheses in the electoral integrity literature, particularly but not exclusively in advanced democracies, is that electoral administration is underfunded and that, as a result, election quality suffers.[1] This is seldom tested, however, and the relationship between spending on elections and the quality and integrity of those elections remains unclear. Addressing this issue is important if analysts are to better understand the component parts of the broader concept and practice of electoral integrity. The key contribution of this chapter is to examine the relationship between election spending and election quality using extensive spending data in the context of a case study of the British elections to the 2009 European Parliament. The quality of elections is measured by an index of electoral administration derived from British election returning officers' performance standards data. This index provides a more nuanced overall picture of election integrity in Britain than previously available, adding a further tool for policymakers. The index is brought together with comprehensive data on the funding of election administration in Britain, compiled by the UK Electoral Commission, allowing the hypothesis that spending affects election quality to be tested. The lessons may well also apply to other established democracies.

The chapter proceeds in three sections. The first derives some hypotheses from a general discussion around issues of election integrity, administration, and spending. The second part outlines the data utilized in this study, while the third section presents an analysis. The results suggest that overall spending on electoral management has a positive relationship with electoral integrity, with spending on registration activities proving particularly important. While spending increases are likely to lead to incremental improvements, the findings enable a clearer picture of the relationship between spending and electoral integrity to inform academic and practitioner debates around election quality.

Election Integrity, Administration, and Spending

The integrity of elections has long been a concern of policymakers at both the national and international level. As demonstrated by this edited volume, this has also recently become an area of increasing concern to a diverse range of scholars. Such questions have been taken most seriously by those examining electoral autocracies and democratic transitions. In potentially high conflict situations, the integrity, fairness, and equitable arrangement of the electoral process is a key area where the legitimacy of election outcomes can be challenged, often by participants alleging electoral fraud or malpractice or failing to recognize the result.[2] Questions around integrity have also recently been raised in relation to the electoral process in a number of advanced democracies, particularly in the United States.[3] Other cases include, for example, the conduct of elections in the United Kingdom, where the electoral process had largely been taken for granted for a lengthy period of time.[4] Particularly in advanced democracies, it often requires some high-profile difficulty before questions of integrity are raised; examples include the disputed 2000 US presidential election and postal ballot fraud in local elections in England in 2004. Such work has involved scholars of electoral politics more generally, as well as analysts of public law, public policy, and administration.[5]

Debates about electoral integrity have often been framed negatively, examining issues around electoral fraud or malpractice where what would pass for integrity is left implicit.[6] Electoral integrity can nevertheless be thought of in both broad and narrow terms. Most broadly, it relates to a framework of promoting democracy, respect for fundamental freedoms, and human rights. Such freedoms are fundamental to declaring any election "free and fair."[7] To Birch, three aspects lead to democratic electoral outcomes: inclusiveness; policy-directed voting; and effective aggregation of votes.[8] More narrowly, this final point is crucial since it is often difficulties in electoral administration (the process through which votes are cast and aggregated) and implementation that give political actors the opportunity to allege fraud and challenge electoral outcomes' credibility.[9] Consequently, electoral administration has to be seen as "fair, transparent and equitable."[10] These issues clearly interact with questions of integrity. For both Frederic Schaffer and the UK Electoral Commission, integrity means an accurate, honest, and transparent tallying of the vote.[11]

Running elections effectively is a highly complex challenge, and the need for administrative efficiency could potentially conflict with questions of political neutrality and public accountability.[12] Administrative efficiency can be prone to errors and mistakes, something that Birch labels "mispractice."[13] A number of authors underline the sheer scale of organization and logistics needed to run a national election process to almost inevitably short timescales, with the vast majority of staff being non-specialists trained and employed only for the very short-term conduct of the election.[14] While this might appear to require national standards, central coordination, and planning, in reality voting is something that, of necessity, occurs in the voter's local area. This means that integrity also depends on how elections are locally implemented. Localized standards in electoral administration can vary considerably, rendering perceptions of the electoral process as, at best, not uniform, and, at worst, threatening the entire credibility or integrity of the process.[15] Alvarez and Hall highlight the difficulty:

> Elections are where the public makes primary decisions that affect all citizens...It is where public preferences manifest themselves in decisions about who will run all levels of government and...even how the government will be run. Yet the history of election administration is one where frequently ill-equipped, poorly-trained, part-time administrators have been trusted with managing this critical democratic function.[16]

In analyzing electoral administration, typically the electoral process is divided into four broad periods: pre-campaign, campaign, polling day, and post-election. Effective administration is crucial at all stages of the process. A number of checklists have been proposed to allow an overall assessment of the state of electoral administration within a country. Chapters 2 through 5 of this volume show how these debates have developed and highlight the current state of the art in indicators of election quality.

Implicit in most of these approaches is the idea that the administrative aspects of electoral integrity can be combined to provide an overall assessment of a set of elections.[17] The utility of such an overall assessment has been strongly advocated by Heather Gerken.[18] She argues that too little is known about the state of electoral administration, with much data either difficult to collect or simply unknown. She proposes a "democracy index" to provide a tool for both policymakers and voters to assess the performance and administration of their electoral process. Such an index would focus on the central issues of registration, balloting, and counting. It would potentially provide both a national level assessment, and one that highlights variation between states and localities. Similarly, Jørgen Elklit and Andrew Reynolds highlight the utility of such an approach for cross-national comparisons and for different types of democracies.[19] Such variation could be used to highlight best practice and to improve electoral processes in localities or countries showing substantial variation from best practice. As Gerken argues, such an index should:

> help election administrators make the case for change...By providing a professional touchstone and making successful policies visible to election administrators and policymakers, the index should help push in the direction of more professional management and better policies.[20]

This idea has appealed beyond scholarly debates to some policymakers. For example, presidential candidates Barack Obama and Hillary Clinton both put the idea into proposed legislation in 2007. Although the Voter Advocate and Democracy Index Act 2007 was not implemented, the US Congress still allocated $10 million to five states to improve data collection that year.[21]

Questions regarding the finance and resourcing of elections are often only implicit in debates about how to measure, index, and assess election administration and integrity.[22] Resources are not explicitly mentioned in two key comparative frameworks, while a third only cryptically mentions potential "material constraint(s)" as affecting electoral governance.[23] The idea of resourcing often appears to be used as shorthand for the funding of elections. However, technical and administrative capacity, human capital, and the accountability of election administrators are all also resources that contribute to electoral integrity. A failure or error in any of these aspects can harm perceptions of electoral integrity.

The relationship between spending on electoral administration and electoral integrity is therefore not immediately obvious. Broader developments in public administration have seen demands for greater efficiency go together with reductions in the public financing of services. In particular, "back-office" services have come under pressure to cut spending. In many policy areas, services are now delivered through networks of public, private, and third-sector organizations, thereby building capacity and achieving reduced financial demands on the state. Election administration is one such "back-office" service in advanced democracies. In this volume, Toby James shows how network governance has impacted upon electoral administration in Britain, while also indicating that funding elections is far from being a priority to council managers faced with budget pressures on many high-profile and seemingly more sensitive public services. Others note similar developments in the United States, while also highlighting the budgetary pressures that current austerity policies place on the effective delivery of elections.[24]

Yet money matters. The complex range of activities that contribute to running elections are expensive. Without adequate funding, election staff and experts could not be employed, ballot papers could not be distributed, or voting and counting technology purchased. Elections therefore require considerable, and increasing, levels of public expenditure.[25] For example, the 2010 Australian federal election cost upwards of $146 million (A$161 million) to administer, while the 2011 Canadian national contest cost around $280 million (C$291 million). Even elections other than those to the national parliament are costly. The 2011 UK-wide referendum on electoral reform, a single-question ballot, is reported to have cost around $116 million (£75 million), while just one American state, Wisconsin, spent $37 million to administer five elections in 2012, including presidential primaries, the general election, and a number associated with a recall contest.[26]

Where election funding is mentioned, it is often to suggest a negative relationship between spending on electoral administration and levels of electoral administrative performance. Thus, in her comparative study, Sarah Birch posits a relationship between a lack of resources and incidences of electoral mispractice.[27] Robert Pastor argues that in developing countries, there is a causal chain between weak spending on infrastructure and public administration and poor performance in electoral processes.[28]

Such a link has also been made in advanced democracies. Studies by Hall and Tokaji and Gerken both suggest that US electoral administration is inadequately financed.[29] Alvarez and Hall highlight the link between spending and capacity by showing how insufficient funding leads to difficulties in recruiting poll workers. Low pay and a demanding workload mean that many fail to turn up for work, leading to obvious unhelpful consequences for election quality.[30] Stuart Wilks-Heeg suggests that British electoral administration is almost at a breaking point because of a lack of resources.[31] The Chair of the UK Electoral Commission similarly notes inconsistencies throughout the UK within the amounts available to fund electoral administration, indicating that this inconsistency affects the service received by voters on polling day.[32] Increasing demands from new legislation, technology, and practices (such as the extension of on-demand postal voting in the UK) all stretch scarce electoral administration resources even further—as do current austerity policies across many advanced democracies.[33]

Such an argument is far from new in the field of public administration. Public bodies have an incentive to make claims of being under-resourced in an attempt to increase their share of public funding.[34] Following this line of argument, the corollary of complaints about the under-resourcing of electoral administration should therefore be that a positive relationship exists between higher levels of resources and financing and higher levels of performance. Robert Pastor draws a clear link between an adequately resourced Electoral Commission and "a far greater likelihood of conducting an election that is free and fair."[35] Hale and Slaton suggest that increased federal funding would improve local capacity in election administration.[36] And as Benjamin Highton concludes in his study of voting lines, "administering elections requires ample resources. Administering them well requires even more."[37] These debates echo others about the nature of the relationship between the capacity of public administration and its performance.[38] Similar themes can be found in political science, where a positive relationship between local party election spending and strength of campaign has been established.[39]

In these debates, the relationship between spending on elections and their quality is often either asserted or based on qualitative interview evidence.[40] It is, however, seldom tested with extensive empirical spending data. Montjoy explains this empirical gap by noting that "measuring the cost of elections across jurisdictions is exceedingly difficult because they tend to record expenses in different categories, even within the same state."[41] Beyond national headline figures, detailed costs of elections are rarely reported across localities, giving little sense of variation in spending practices. While a recent and extensive international project that looked into the issue did much to categorize election costs, it only reported these costs at the national, not local, level.[42] This chapter's major contribution is therefore to deploy extensive data on local electoral administration and a measure of electoral integrity to test hypotheses to provide data-driven insights to this debate. The key aim is to begin to establish the direction and nature of the relationship between spending on elections and election quality.

An important but untested hypothesis for the field of electoral administration can therefore be derived from the arguments outlined above.

> H1: Electoral management performance improves with more spending on electoral administration.

It may be that other factors besides overall spending levels affect electoral administration performance. A number of additional ideas can also be derived from the combined literature on electoral administration and public administration performance. One issue relates to different types of spending. Gerken underlines the centrality of electoral registration to judging election administration (in addition to the practical aspects of balloting voters and counting their votes), while Montjoy suggests that registration levels may drive overall costs.[43] Thus, it may be that it is not just the actual practical organization of elections but also the spending levels for electoral registration that is important.

> H2: Electoral management performance improves with more spending on electoral registration activities.

> H3: Electoral management performance improves with more spending on the practical aspects of election administration.

A number of additional factors may also affect performance. In many advanced democracies, different levels of local government are responsible for electoral administration. Although political control has not been found to affect the service performance of British local authorities, Clark observes institutional variation in electoral administration performance in the 2010 UK general election between different types of local public administrations.[44] Similarly, Andrews and Boyne point to a link between organizational aspects of public administration and performance and external factors such as socioeconomic structure and population density more generally.[45] Others, however, have proven more skeptical.[46] Electoral performance therefore ought to be examined, for example, in relation to its region and type of local administration, its socioeconomic structure, and the density of the electorate that councils serve.[47] The importance of spending will be underlined if the hypothesized positive relationships discussed above remain statistically significant even after such exogenous variables are controlled for.

The British Case Study

An insight into these broad theoretical issues can be provided by assessing the relationship between British election administration spending levels and electoral administrators' performance. Britain is an excellent case for examining these questions because (like a number of advanced democracies, most obviously the United States) British elections are run by local authorities who have discretion (within statutory requirements) when determining how elections are implemented. Consequently, considerable variation is evident to test the above ideas against. If Pastor's argument linking weak spending on public administration and poor electoral performance in developing countries is accepted, evidence from Britain can help inform debates on election quality more broadly than this immediate case study.[48] Indeed, it may be that increases in spending lead to relatively small improvements in electoral administration in an established democracy like Britain but could lead to much larger improvements in less established democracies.[49] Arguably, even small substantive effects in an established democracy like the United Kingdom provide confidence that the relationship is likely to be in the expected direction in less established settings.

While it must be said that British election administration has been largely taken for granted, two factors have gradually changed this. First, a number of high-profile difficulties in British electoral administration in recent years have highlighted the fragile nature of election quality. Examples include an extraordinarily large number of invalid ballots in the 2007 Scottish elections—the number grew from less than 10,000 (0.4 percent of all constituency votes cast) in 1999 to 85,644 (4 percent). Other incidents include voters being turned away from some polling stations in the 2010 general election, complaints about the speed and process of vote verification and counting in the 2011 Northern Irish Assembly elections, and, in 2005, an election court judge likening the conduct and administration of postal voting in local elections in Birmingham to that of "a Banana Republic."[50]

Second, since the *Political Parties, Elections and Referendums Act (PPERA) 2000*, an independent UK Electoral Commission has been responsible for overseeing numerous aspects of the electoral process. This commission reports to Parliament, but it essentially operates independently, which makes it something of a hybrid in the standard threefold classification of Electoral Management Bodies (EMBs).[51] As part of the Commission's work, increasing amounts of information about the conduct of electoral politics have become publicly available. The UK Electoral Commission was also given the role of overseeing both election process spending and setting performance standards in the *Electoral Administration Act (EAA) 2006*. Their data therefore now include information on both performance standards for returning officers (ROs)—council officers responsible for the conduct and administration of elections—and electoral registration officers (EROs)—those responsible for registration activities. Electoral Commission data also includes electoral administration spending. Third, the UK Electoral Commission notwithstanding, the delivery of electoral administration in Britain ultimately remains the responsibility of local government, and the Electoral Commission has no formal powers of direction over the local ROs and EROs that are ultimately responsible for delivering the elections. Consequently, there are inevitable variations in both practice and performance in delivering electoral administration, which need to be explained.[52]

Data and Evidence

Evidence for this study is drawn from the two separate sets of data collected by the Electoral Commission.[53] The first relates to the performance standards for returning officers across Britain in the 2009 European elections. These 2009 elections differ from those to the Westminster Parliament primarily because they are conducted using a closed-list proportional representation system in 12 electoral regions. As "second-order" elections, they also tend to experience lower turnout than a UK-general election. Since less is likely to be spent on such elections, they thus provide a tough test of the ideas discussed above. If a relationship can be found under such circumstances, then this relationship is also likely to be found under general election conditions. Nonetheless, European elections can still be argued to be broadly representative of British elections. Elections to the European Parliament are, alongside those to Westminster, one of only two UK-wide rounds of elections. Despite the regional nature of the electoral system, as with all other elections in Britain, they are administered locally using the same electoral infrastructure such as polling stations. As happened in 2009, they are occasionally held concurrently with some English local authority elections in an attempt to both maximize turnout and minimize costs.

The 2009 European Parliament elections were the first time that the Electoral Commission measured the performance of returning officers across Britain. The performance standards revolved around three broad areas from which seven measurable standards were derived. These are outlined in Table 9.1.[54]

Established frameworks of judging election quality tend to utilize ordinal scales on which particular aspects of the election can be rated. Thus, Elklit and Reynolds offer a four-point Likert scale to rank their variables. They argue that such a methodology has a long record in judging issues like comparative democracy and corruption.[55] A similar approach is taken in the Electoral Commission's performance standards. They adopt a three-point ordinal scale (not currently meeting the performance standard; meeting the standard; and above the standard). In each performance standard, a range of criteria is specified that the returning officer (RO) must meet. For example, under performance standard three, relating to training, to be

Table 9.1: **Performance Standards for UK Returning Officers in the 2009 European Election**

Subject	Performance standard
Planning & organization	1: Skills & knowledge of returning officer
	2: Planning processes in place for an election
	3: Training
Integrity	4: Maintaining the integrity of an election
Participation	5: Planning and delivering public awareness activity
	6: Accessibility of information to electors
	7: Communication of information to candidates & agents

Sources: Electoral Commission, 2009a; 2010a: 2.

classified as "not meeting the standard" ROs would either not provide training or do so only at a basic level for permanent members of electoral staff. To be classified as "meeting the standard," ROs must provide ongoing training to permanent and temporary staff about legislative requirements, ensure this includes information on access issues for polling station and count staff, and ensure that these training activities are evaluated. To be "above the standard," the RO must have a written plan for both permanent and temporary staff and guarantee that evaluation of this and training needs more broadly is carried out regularly.[56]

To provide variation and an overall assessment of election quality that can be utilized as the dependent variable, an index of election administration integrity derived from the Electoral Commission's RO performance standards data and inspired by the debates around indexing election quality mentioned earlier was created. This is an additive index, created by summing the scores achieved on each of the seven performance standards set by the Electoral Commission, with values of 1 given to not currently meeting the standard, 2 given to meeting the standard, and 3 to where ROs were above the standard. The resulting integrity index therefore varies between a minimum score of 7 and a potential maximum score of 21. The index is based on returns from a full population survey of almost all local council ROs in Britain (N = 379). Reliability analysis has achieved a Cronbach's Alpha score of.761, thereby demonstrating that these indicators are suitable for index construction.[57]

It is worth noting that the Electoral Commission declined the opportunity to create such an overall performance index, claiming that this would "maintain transparency and simplicity...aggregating the total number of standards not met, met or exceeded across all seven standards may not give an accurate picture of

performance."[58] Nevertheless, such an aggregate approach has been utilized in relation to performance standards data before in British local government, notably the
2002-09 Comprehensive Performance Assessment (CPA).[59] Such an approach is
therefore widely accepted in assessing public administration in Britain. The index
includes data from performance standards throughout the electoral cycle. While it
may not be able to address broad macro issues such as freedom of speech and the
potential for violence highlighted in earlier chapters on measuring integrity, it nevertheless answers Gerken's call for a comprehensive index focusing on fundamental issues of electoral administration.[60] The index therefore offers a complementary
and important advance on what is currently known about the performance of ROs
in three key ways. It provides more variation than permitted by the performance
standards as originally reported. It also permits an overall view of electoral administration to be obtained, while also enabling easier comparison of standards between
different types of local government and areas within Britain than hitherto possible.
Finally, it provides an indicator against which potential drivers of performance can
be assessed.

The second set of data are derived from the Electoral Commission's Financial
Information Survey, which was designed to collect information on the financing of
elections across Britain. As with the performance standards data, this was a full population survey with a high response rate (79 percent; N = 379). Such an extensive,
nationwide survey of financial data on election spending is rare in electoral administration analysis.[61] This survey was designed with leading UK experts on public
finance, the Chartered Institute of Public Finance and Accountancy (CIPFA).[62] The
survey provides data from 2008 to 2009. The data offer an overall assessment of
the total spent on various registration activities in this period for each local authority. This includes: core team staffing; design and printing; mail distribution; distribution of canvassing; processing of forms, queries, and appeals; publicity and
outreach; and management and compilation of the register and other registration
spending. The data also provide an overall figure for the amount spent on various
practical activities in holding elections. These include: core team staffing; design
and printing of polling cards and ballot papers; postal vote preparation and distribution, receipt, and processing; polling station premises and processing costs;
counting votes premises and processing; IT systems; publicity and outreach; and
a miscellaneous "other" category. Funding for local elections and for electoral registration comes from local government budgets in Britain, while national elections
are funded by central government.[63]

A number of independent variables are utilized. Three relate to spending. The
first is an additive composite measure of the total amount spent on both registration and holding elections. This will provide an overall assessment of the relationship between total spending and performance. The second variable is the total
amount spent on the various electoral registration activities in 2008–2009. The

third is a total of the amount spent on the various practicalities of holding elections detailed above. All three variables were originally measured in £ sterling, and based on figures reported in the survey as objective expenditure on these various items.[64] For the purposes of this analysis, all spending data has been converted to US$.[65]

Additional control variables are also utilized. Electorate density, expressed as the number of electors per hectare, provides a measure both of the size of the electorate the council has to deal with and the concentration of those electors in either urban or rural areas. The socioeconomic structure of the council area is also deployed, expressed as the proportion of people in various occupation categories, to assess the effect of the employment structure. Finally, dummy variables for region and authority type permit an assessment of the impact of spending vis-à-vis two additional exogenous variables.[66]

Two caveats about the data need to be acknowledged. First, there is a slight disjuncture in the two datasets deployed. The spending was incurred in the year immediately preceding those major nationwide elections. Given that IFES/UNDP argue "it is not always easy to split budgets and assign costs to different elections," such spending will inevitably have had an impact upon preparations for the 2009 elections.[67] The relatively constant nature of electoral cycles in Britain means that questions of performance in electoral administration in 2009 should be generally representative of performance in the years immediately preceding it. There is no a priori reason why standards of performance in 2009 should have been any different to those in either 2007 or 2008. Moreover, that the EAA 2006 had given powers to the Electoral Commission to assess performance standards should have been widely known among professional electoral administrators. Indeed, such legislative change can drive the focus of election administrators.[68] While further research will be necessary as further data become available, assessing these questions on a preliminary basis is therefore possible and appropriate with the data at hand.

Second, both the performance standards and financial information surveys rely on self-completed data. Performance standards have been claimed to be open to manipulation as public administrators attempt to "game" outcomes, to misdirecting administrators' activity toward targeted goals instead of other crucial, and unmeasured, ones, and to being constrained in their achievement by external circumstances.[69] Nevertheless, RO responses to these standards are audited, albeit on a sampled basis, and evaluated by the Electoral Commission. This has led to a number of self-assessments being regraded from the original assessment given by the RO.[70] Consequently, they can be considered relatively reliable assessments of the standard of electoral administration within councils. Similarly, the financial information survey was also extensively audited by CIPFA. The spending data can also therefore be taken as reliable for the analysis at hand.

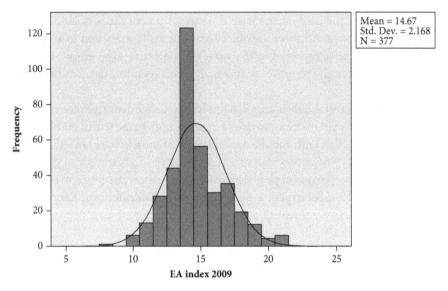

Figure 9.1: The distribution of the Index of Election Integrity, 2009

Table 9.2: **Spending by British Electoral Administration, 2008–09**

	Min	*Max*	*Mean*	*N*
Registration	159	2,029,038	338,120	278
Practicalities	−1885	1,181,743	220,511	279
Total spending	207	3,029,400	560,287	270
$ per elector	0	9.54	4.7	270

Note: Spending measured in US$

Source: Electoral Commission's Financial Information Survey.

Analysis

Figure 9.1 shows the distribution of the 2009 index of election integrity. Returning officer performance varied between a score of eight at the low end of the index to 21 at its high end. The mean score across all local authorities was 14.67, while the median and mode measures of central tendency were both 14. There is some regional variation, with London achieving a mean of 16.16 at the high end, and Eastern region recording a mean of 13.87 at the lower end. At the national level, despite a slight positive skew in the index, the results can nevertheless be effectively taken as a normal distribution and suitable for subsequent analysis.[71]

The Electoral Commission estimate that between 2007 and 2009, local authorities spent a gross total of around $478.5 (£307.1) million on various aspects of electoral administration in Britain.[72] For this analysis, what is most important is how

Table 9.3: **The Relationship Between Electoral Administration Spending and Performance**

Type of spending	Correlation
Registration	.314**
EA practicalities	.138*
Combined total spending	.276**

Note: ** Statistically significant at the .01 level; * statistically significant at the .05 level.

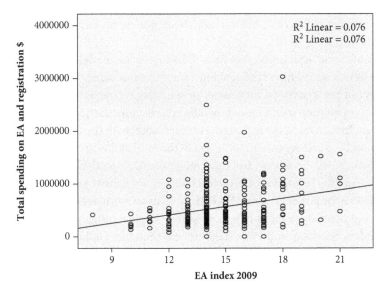

Figure 9.2: The relationship between total EA spending and the performance index

much individual councils spent on the aspects identified above in 2008–2009: registration activities, the practicalities of organizing elections, and the total combined spending. Considerable variation is evident on each of these aspects in Table 9.2. Based on the registered electorates for the local authorities at December 1, 2008, councils spent an average of approximately \$4.7 (£3) per voter on electoral administration activities, with some spending considerably more. This would seem to place Britain in 2009 outside estimates for other stable democracies, where the cost of elections has been estimated to be around \$1–3 per elector.[73]

How does this affect election quality? Table 9.3 reports bivariate Pearson correlations between different types of spending and performance on the electoral integrity index, while Figure 9.2 shows the relationship between overall spending levels and performance as a scatterplot. Table 9.2 in particular permits an initial testing of Hypotheses 1 to 3. In short, the bivariate analyses suggest that all three hypotheses can, at least initially, be confirmed. All three types of spending have, as expected, a positive relationship with election integrity. Moreover, all three correlations are statistically significant with spending on registration and overall levels of spending both being significant at the $p < 0.01$ level. Levels of spending on the practicalities of running elections are also statistically significant, albeit at the lower level of $p < 0.05$. The key finding of this bivariate analysis is therefore to observe that, on their own, levels of spending on election administration do appear to have a positive impact upon election quality in Britain and that this relationship does appear to be robust. On the other hand, however, these are not overly strong correlations. Rather than indicating that increasing spending will improve quality considerably, they instead appear to underline the idea that improving electoral integrity in Britain may be incremental and that it is not only about money, but also involves additional determinants.

Tables 9.4 and 9.5 each present three OLS regression models of various categories of election spending on the election administration index.[74] Table 9.4 analyzes the effect of the combined total levels of spending, while Table 9.5 assesses the impact of registration spending and spending on election practicalities broken down separately. In each table, the first model is a regression with spending, the electorate density, and the socioeconomic structure of the local authority area. Following the discussion above, the second and third models add, respectively, the type of local authority and the region to these socioeconomic and density variables.[75] There are good reasons for presenting both these latter analyses separately. London borough, Welsh, and Scottish councils have a virtually complete geographical overlap with the London, Scotland, and Wales regions, and therefore could not be considered together. Nevertheless, regional variation was evident in 2009 as noted above, and analysis of performance standards in 2010 has suggested that there may be differences in electoral administrative performance both in different council types and in different regions.[76] Finally, while Scottish and Welsh unitaries and London borough councils are geographically concentrated local authority types, the others are not and are found throughout England. Controlling for both council type and region are therefore necessary. Presenting two separate analyses provides an additional test of the election spending variables of interest.

Table 9.4 appears to partially confirm Hypothesis 1 and underlines the bivariate findings for two of the three models. Total spending is in the expected direction, having a positive and statistically significant ($p < .05$) relationship to performance on the electoral administration index in both the socioeconomic and the regional models. As anticipated, the relationship for spending is not particularly strong, suggesting that the effects may be relatively small in practice. Thus, based on the unstandardized coefficients, for total spending in the first socioeconomic model, $250,000 spent on election administration in 2009 could be expected to lead to an improvement on the index of around 0.23, $500,000 to an improvement of 0.47, and $1 million to 0.9. In other words, just over $1 million could be expected to

Table 9.4: **Explaining the Effects of Total Electoral Administration Spending on Performance**

Variables	Model 1			Model 2			Model 3		
	b	*(S.E.)*	*Beta*	*b*	*(S.E.)*	*Beta*	*b*	*(S.E.)*	*Beta*
Constant	16.181	2.117		15.945	2.265		17.224	2.382	
Total Spending	9.344E-7	.000	.147**	6.3388E-7	.000	.101	8.8080E-7	.000	.127**
Electorate density	0.12	.011	0.69	.004	.013	.025	.001	.013	.006
Managerial/Prof %	.014	.031	.045	.014	.033	.430	-.003	.034	-.009
Intermediate %	-.108	.051	-.127**	-.102	.053	-1.946*	-.126	.055	-.147**
Routine/lower	-.025	.037	-.069	-.019	.039	-.051	-.031	.041	-.085
London borough				.942	.578	.123			
Metropolitan districts				.679	.484	.092			
Non-met districts				.058	.334	.014			
Welsh Unitary				-.400	.554	-.043			
Scottish Unitary				.527	.479	.068			
Eastern							-.506	.471	-.077
London							.897	.672	.115

(*Continued*)

Table 9.4: **Continued**

Variables	Model 1			Model 2			Model 3		
	b	*(S.E.)*	*Beta*	*b*	*(S.E.)*	*Beta*	*b*	*(S.E.)*	*Beta*
North East							-.573	.738	-.045
North West							-.152	.490	-.021
Scotland							.315	.512	.041
South East							.264	.462	.047
South West							.171	.507	.023
Wales							-.677	.595	-.073
West Midlands							.279	.512	.035
Yorkshire and Humber							.172	.582	.018
R^2	.078			.096			.106		
N	379			379			379		

Notes: b = Unstandardized regression coefficients; Beta = standardized regression coefficients; *** Statistically significant at the .01 level; ** statistically significant at the .05 level; * statistically significant at the .1 level.

lead to an increase in performance of one step on the integrity index. For model three, which controlled for regional effects, $250,000 could be expected to lead to a 0.2 increase in the integrity scale, $500,000 to a 0.4 increase and $1 million to a 0.8 increase. The only other variable that is statistically significant is the proportion of people employed in intermediate-level occupations, which consistently demonstrates a negative relationship with electoral performance. Neither electorate density, nor the type of council or region, has any independent statistically significant relationship with electoral performance.

Table 9.5 disaggregates spending into the two separate independent variables of total spending on registration activities and total spending on the practicalities of running elections. This appears to confirm Hypothesis 2, that there will be a positive relationship between higher levels of registration spending and performance on the integrity index. This relationship is consistently in a positive direction and is statistically significant at the $p < .01$ level across all three models, although, as with total spending, the effect is relatively weak. The socioeconomic model's results suggest that spending $250,000 on registration activities is likely to lead to an increase of .5 on the integrity index, while $500,000 is likely to be associated with an increase of 1 on the index. The other two models return similar results. In the regional model, $250,000 is likely to lead to an increase of 0.47 on the index, while $500,000 spent on registration is associated with an increase of .9.

Table 9.5's results do not support Hypothesis 3. Spending on the practicalities of running elections did not have an independent or significant effect on the integrity index, and returns very weak negative correlations. This analysis therefore suggests that spending on registration in the run-up to the 2009 European elections in Britain therefore mattered more than spending on the practicalities of organizing elections in the run-up to 2009.

There is some evidence in Table 9.5 that other variables may also have an impact on election quality when spending is broken into its component elements. Consistent with the previous analyses, the proportion of people employed in intermediate occupations has a statistically significant ($p < .05$) negative relationship with performance on the index. In two cases, council type also appears to make a difference. London boroughs, which performed best in regional analysis of the index, demonstrate a positive and statistically significant ($p < 0.1$) relationship with electoral quality, as do metropolitan district councils. Although this differs from the results in Table 9.4, the reason for the London relationship may be that chief executives of London borough councils regularly met in London-wide forums where the planning of electoral issues was often discussed in advance of the 2009 European elections. They also benefited from extensive training and had experienced difficulties in previous London elections in 2000, thereby focusing minds on performance.[77] It is unclear if such circumstances are also applicable to metropolitan districts, although it is unlikely that this was a widespread effect in 2009. Scotland, which had also experienced major

Table 9.5: **Explaining the Effects of Types of Spending on Performance**

Variables	Model 1			Model 2			Model 3		
	b	(S.E.)	Beta	b	(S.E.)	Beta	b	(S.E.)	Beta
Constant	15.985	2.100		15.287	2.259		16.680	2.381	
Registration spending	2.051E-6	.000	.210***	1.906E-6	.000	.195***	1.897E-6	.000	.194***
Practicalities spending	-3.534E-7	.000	-.030	-1.010E-6	.000	-.086	-4.430E-7	.000	-.038
Electorate density	.009	.010	.056	.000	.012	.003	-.003	.013	-.015
Managerial/Prof %	.016	.030	.049	.022	.033	.070	.002	.034	.007
Intermediate %	-.110	.050	-.129**	-.103	.052	-.120**	-.128	.055	-.150**
Routine/lower	-.021	.037	-.058	-.007	.039	-.018	-.020	.041	-.055
London borough				1.086	.577	.142*			
Metropolitan districts				1.023	.501	.139**			
Non-met districts				.113	.331	.026			
Welsh Unitary				-.147	.558	-.016			
Scottish Unitary				.215	.489	.028			
Eastern							-.416	471	-.064
London							1.047	.674	.135
North East							-.392	.739	-.030

North West		.025	.495	.003
Scotland		.079	.521	.010
South East		.402	.464	.071
South West		.160	.505	.022
Wales		-.461	.600	-.050
West Midlands		.316	.510	.040
Yorkshire and Humber		.366	.589	.039
R²	.094	.113		
N	379	379		

Notes: Spending in (US$) b = Unstandardized regression coefficients; Beta = standardized regression coefficients; *** Statistically significant at the .01 level; ** statistically significant at the .05 level; * statistically significant at the .1 level.

electoral difficulties two years earlier, remains a weak and non-significant relationship to performance on the electoral integrity index.

These findings suggest that increases in spending are likely to buy incremental improvements in Britain. The magnitude of spending required means that large breakthroughs are probably unlikely, while major increases in funding are also unlikely given pressure on public budgets. This, however, is broadly consistent with what might be expected. As a stable democracy, electoral expertise and infrastructure in Britain has accumulated over time. As IFES/UNDP observe, institutionalization is itself a cost-reducing measure.[78] Consequently, increases in spending are likely to produce steady incremental increases in electoral quality. Yet in 2009, 84 percent of councils spent more than $250,000 in total on electoral administration, while 38 percent spent more than $500,000. For what are relatively small sums of public expenditure, gradual improvements in electoral quality can be made. Indeed, in Britain and elsewhere, many difficulties in electoral administration have been highly localized. These findings are not incompatible with the idea that relatively small sums of spending in such circumstances could help electoral integrity by, for example, buying extra capacity to deal with problematic issues, whether extra poll workers or expertise, additional training, or new technology.

Conclusions

This chapter has presented an analysis of the relationship between spending on election administration and election quality in Britain. The key aim was to begin to establish the nature and direction of that relationship, and to assess whether this relationship remained when different aspects of spending were disaggregated and additional control variables were introduced.

This chapter's key finding is that spending matters in this case, even when additional factors such as electorate density, socioeconomic structure, and type of local authority are held constant. This is important because it begins to confirm one of the most prevalent but implicit hypotheses in the literature on electoral administration—that higher levels of spending on elections will lead to higher levels of election quality. The findings suggest that in the British case, spending the relatively small additional sum of around $250,000 on electoral administration could lead to an increase of just under a quarter step in the integrity index. This indicates that in established democracies, incremental improvements from additional spending are likely to be the key outcome, not least in systems which have localized implementation and administration of elections. Establishing this directionality is important more broadly, however, adding confidence to what have mainly been assertions about the relationship between spending and electoral integrity. For example, given Pastor's point about weak spending on public administration and poor electoral performance in less established democracies, analysts can have some confidence that spending more on elections will lead to improvements in such settings.[79] Indeed, under such circumstances, the effects might be expected to be larger than demonstrated in this chapter.[80]

Nonetheless, key questions remain. While total levels of election spending in 2008–09 show a positive relationship with electoral integrity in Britain, the picture is still somewhat more complex than this suggests. Indeed, breaking total spending into two component parts, spending on registration activities, and spending on the practicalities of running elections, suggests that the key variable is not the amount spent on the practicalities, but the amount spent on registration activities. This requires further investigation. Montjoy provides one possible explanation by observing that "registration numbers drive election costs. Many expenses, such as ballot printing and pre-election mail-outs are based on the number of active registrants."[81] Nevertheless, the relationships are not overly strong, thereby underlining the complexities of determining election quality. Things such as staffing, training, how polling workers operate on the day, their supervision, the use of technology, and so on are all also likely to matter.[82] Further research is required on these aspects in Britain and elsewhere, including in less established democracies, as is examination of the relationship between spending and election quality in what might be considered the largest test for electoral administrators, that of a national general election. This notwithstanding, the key messages for policymakers and electoral administrators are that to maintain election quality requires resources and that any budgetary squeeze is likely to have a negative impact on both capacity and integrity.

Notes

1. See, for example, Heather K. Gerken, 2009. *The Democracy Index: Why Our Election System is Failing and How to Fix It*, Princeton: Princeton University Press; Robert S. Montjoy, 2010. "The Changing Nature…and Costs…of Electoral Administration," *Public Administration Review*, 70: 6, 867–875; Robert A. Pastor, 1999. "The Role of Electoral Administration in Democratic Transitions: Implications for Policy and Research," *Democratization*, 6:4, 1–27; Jenny Watson, 2011. "Public Confidence in Elections," in *Political Communication in Britain: The Leader Debates, The Campaign and the Media in the 2010 General Election*, eds. Dominic Wring, Roger Mortimore and Simon Atkinson. Basingstoke: Palgrave.

2. Jorgen Elklit and Andrew Reynolds. 2005. "A Framework for the Systematic Study of Election Quality," *Democratization*, 12: 2, 147–162; Shaheen Mozaffar and Andreas Schedler. 2002. "The Comparative Study of Electoral Governance: An Introduction," *International Political Science Review*, 23: 1, 5–27; Pastor, 1999. *Op. Cit.*

3. John Fund and Hans von Spakovsky. 2012. *Who's Counting? How Fraudsters and Bureaucrats Put Your Vote at Risk*, New York: Encounter Books; Gerken, 2009. *Op. Cit.*; Richard L. Hasen. 2012. *The Voting Wars: From Florida 2000 to the Next Election Meltdown*, New Haven: Yale University Press.

4. Toby S. James. 2012. *Elite Statecraft and Election Administration: Bending the Rules of the Game?* Basingstoke: Palgrave.

5. E.g., R. Michael Alvarez and Thad E. Hall. 2006. "Controlling Democracy: The Principal-Agent Problems in Election Administration," *Policy Studies Journal*, 34: 4, 491–510; Lonna Rae Atkeson and Kyle L. Saunders. 2007. "The Effect of Election Administration on

Voter Confidence: A Local Matter?, *PS: Political Science and Politics*, 40: 4, 655–660; Avery Davis-Roberts and David Carroll. 2010. "Using International Law to Assess Elections," *Democratization*, 17: 3, 416–441; David Denver, Rob Johns and Chris Carman. 2009. "Rejected Ballot Papers in the 2007 Scottish Parliament Election: The Voters' Perspective," *British Politics*, 4: 1, 3–21; Thad Hall, J. Quin Monson and Kelly D. Patterson. 2007. "Poll Workers and the Vitality of Democracy: An Early Assessment," *PS: Political Science and Politics*, 40: 4, 647–654; Pippa Norris. 2013a. "The New Research Agenda Studying Electoral Integrity," *Electoral Studies*, http://dx.doi.org/10.1016/j.electstud.2013.07.015; Pippa Norris. 2013b. "Does the World Agree About Standards of Electoral Integrity? Evidence for the Diffusion of Global Norms," *Electoral Studies*, http://dx.doi.org/10.1016/j.electstud.2013.07.016; John Stewart. 2006. "A Banana Republic? The Investigation into Electoral Fraud by the Birmingham Election Court," *Parliamentary Affairs*, 59: 4, 654–667.

6. Fund and Spakovsky. 2012. *Op. Cit*; Gerken, 2009. *Op. Cit.*; Hasen, 2012. *Op. Cit.*; Lorraine C. Minnite 2010. *The Myth of Voter Fraud*. Ithaca, NY: Cornell University Press.

7. Davis-Roberts and Carroll 2010. *Op. Cit*; Jorgen Elklit and Palle Svensson. 1997. "What Makes Elections Free and Fair?" *Journal of Democracy*, 8: 3, 32–46; Norris, 2013a. *Op. Cit.*

8. Sarah Birch. 2011. *Electoral Malpractice*, Oxford: Oxford University Press, p. 17.

9. Minnite, 2010. *Op. Cit.*

10. ACE Electoral Knowledge Network (n.d., a) "Overview of Electoral Integrity," http://aceproject.org/ace-en/topics/ei/ei10 (accessed March 16, 2012).

11. Frederic C. Schaffer. 2008. *The Hidden Costs of Clean Election Reform*. Ithaca, NY: Cornell University Press; Electoral Commission 2009a. *Performance Standards for Returning Officers in Great Britain*, London: Electoral Commission.

12. Mozaffar and Schedler, 2002. *Op. Cit.*, p.8–9.

13. Distinguishing it from "malpractice," which she defines as the "manipulation of electoral processes and outcomes so as to substitute personal or partisan benefit for the public interest." Birch, 2011. *Op. Cit.* p. 14 & 26.

14. Mozaffar and Schedler 2002. *Op. Cit.* Alvarez and Hall 2006. *Op. Cit.*

15. Atkeson and Saunders 2007. *Op. Cit*; Hall et al., 2007. *Op. Cit.*

16. Alvarez and Hall 2006. *Op. Cit.*, p.491.

17. Elklit and Reynolds 2005. *Op. Cit.*, p.156.

18. Gerken 2009. *Op. Cit.*

19. Elklit and Reynolds 2005. *Op. Cit*, pp.155–156.

20. Gerken 2009. *Op. Cit.* p. 92.

21. Ibid, p.110.

22. To the extent that questions relating to financing are addressed, they normally refer to regulating party and candidate campaign finance.

23. Elklit and Reynolds 2005. *Op. Cit*; Elklit and Svensson 1997. *Op. Cit*; Mozaffar and Schedler 2002. *Op. Cit.* p.10.

24. Kathleen Hale and Christa Daryl Slaton. 2008. "Building Capacity in Election Administration: Local Responses to Complexity and Interdependence," *Public Administration Review*, 68:5, 839–849; Montjoy, 2010. *Op. Cit.*

25. Ibid.

26. Pew Charitable Trusts. 2012. "The Cost of the 2012 General Election in Wisconsin," http://www.pewstates.org/research/analysis/the-cost-of-the-2012-general-election-in-wisconsin-85899460945 (accessed May 8, 2013).

27. Birch 2011. *Op. Cit.*, p.26.

28. Pastor 1999. *Op. Cit.*

29. Thad Hall and Daniel Tokaji 2007. "Money For Data: Funding the Oldest Unfunded Mandate," *Equal Vote Blog, Election Law at Moritz*, http://moritzlaw.osu.edu/blogs/tokaji/2007_06_01_equalvote_archive.html (May 8, 2013); Gerken 2009. *Op. Cit.* p.118.

30. Alvarez and Hall 2006. *Op. Cit*, p.496.

31. Stuart Wilks-Heeg. 2009. "Treating Voters as an Afterthought? The Legacies of a Decade of Electoral Modernisation in the United Kingdom," *Political Quarterly*, 80: 1, 101–110.

32. Watson, *Op. Cit.*, p.139.
33. Montjoy 2010. *Op. Cit.*
34. William Niskanen. 1971. *Bureaucracy and Representative Government.* Chicago: Aldine-Atherton.
35. Pastor 1999. *Op. Cit.*, p.17–18.
36. Hale and Slaton 2008. *Op. Cit.*, p.843.
37. Benjamin Highton. 2006. "Long Lines, Voting Machine Availability, and Turnout: The Case of Franklin County, Ohio in the 2004 Presidential Election," *PS: Political Science and Politics*, 39: 1, p.68.
38. Rhys Andrews and George Boyne. 2011. "Corporate Capacity and Public Service Performance," *Public Administration*, 89: 3, 894–908.
39. Ron Johnston and Charles Pattie. 1995. "The Impact of Spending on Party Constituency Campaigns at Recent British General Elections," *Party Politics*, 1: 2, 261–273.
40. Wilks-Heeg 2009. *Op. Cit.*; James, this volume.
41. Montjoy 2010. *Op. Cit.* p.870.
42. IFES/UNDP 2005. *Getting to the CORE: A Global Survey on the Cost of Registration and Elections*, New York: UNDP.
43. Gerken 2009. *Op. Cit*; Montjoy, 2010. *Op. Cit.* p.872.
44. Rhys Andrews, George Boyne, Jennifer Law and Richard Walker. 2005. "External Constraints on Local Service Standards: The Case of Comprehensive Performance Assessment in English Local Government," *Public Administration*, 83:3, 639–656; Peter Murphy, Kirsten Greenhalgh and Martin Jones. 2011. "Comprehensive Performance Assessment and Public Services Improvement in England? A Case Study of the Benefits Administration Service in Local Government," *Local Government Studies*, 37: 6, 579–599; Alistair Clark. 2012. "Still a Model Democracy? Electoral Administration and the Integrity of the Electoral Process in British Elections," Paper to the IPSA-ECP Workshop, Challenges of Electoral Integrity, IPSA Conference, Madrid July 7–12.
45. Andrews and Boyne 2011. *Op. Cit.*; Andrews et al., 2005. *Op. Cit.*
46. Murphy et al. 2011. *Op. Cit.*
47. David C. Kimball and Brady Baybeck. 2013. "Are All Jurisdictions Equal? Size Disparity in Election Administration," *Election Law Journal*, 12: 2, 130–145.
48. Pastor 1999. *Op. Cit.*
49. IFES/UNDP 2005. *Op. Cit.*, pp.21–24.
50. E.g. Clark 2012. *Op. Cit.*; Denver et al. 2009. *Op. Cit*; James 2012. *Op. Cit*; Richard Mawrey, 2005. *Fraud at the Elections.* Nottingham: Spokesman Books; Stewart, 2006. *Op. Cit.*
51. EMBs tend to be placed in one of three categories: as part of a government office or agency; as part of a government agency but under some sort of supervisory authority; or a fundamentally independent organization. Jorgen Elklit and Andrew Reynolds 2001. "Analysing the Impact of Election Administration on Democratic Politics," *Representation*, 38: 1, 3–10; International IDEA 2006. *Electoral Management Design: The International IDEA Handbook*, Stockholm: International IDEA, Ch. 1.
52. Clark 2012. *Op. Cit.*
53. The original data in Excel format can be downloaded from the following Electoral Commission websites: http://www.electoralcommission.org.uk/find-information-by-subject/performance-standards/performance-in-running-elections-and-referendums (accessed May 3, 2013); http://www.electoralcommission.org.uk/find-information-by-subject/performance-standards/financial-information (accessed May 3, 2013).
54. These performance standards were also in use at the 2010 general election. Clark 2012. *Op. Cit.*
55. Elklit and Reynolds 2005. *Op. Cit.*
56. For the full list of criteria for each performance standard, see Electoral Commission 2009a. *Op. Cit.* For discussion of the more general issues around performance standards, see Clark 2012. *Op. Cit.*
57. See Paul Pennings, Hans Keman and Jan Kleinnijenhuis. 1999. *Doing Research in Political Science*, London: Sage. 96–97 who note that a Cronbach's Alpha score of.7 or over means that the component indicators of such an index are suitable and that creating an index from such variables "adds to the discriminating power of the theoretical concept."

58. Electoral Commission. 2009b. *Report on Performance Standards for Returning Officers in Great Britain: European Parliamentary Elections 2009*, London: Electoral Commission.

59. Andrews et al. 2005. *Op. Cit*; Andrews and Boyne, 2011. *Op. Cit.*

60. Gerken 2009. *Op. Cit.*

61. Montjoy 2010. *Op. Cit.*

62. See Electoral Commission 2010b. *The Cost of Electoral Administration in Great Britain: Financial Information Survey 2007-08 and 2008–09*, London: Electoral Commission, pp.8–11.

63. Electoral Commission 2010b. *Op. cit.*, p.12.

64. The distinction between subjective and objective expenditure in the survey is based upon the difference between gross expenditure (subjective) and that net of income (objective). The latter is utilized, as it provides a more conservative measure upon which to base the findings. Electoral Commission, *Op. Cit.*, 2010b: p.6. All regressions were also run as gross (subjective) expenditure. Although not reported here because of space considerations, they confirm the chapter's findings.

65. Converted on an exchange rate of 1.558 on August 15, 2013.

66. There are different types of local authorities in Britain. Scotland, Wales, and some parts of England have unitary councils. England also has metropolitan district councils, non-metropolitan district councils, and London Borough councils.

67. IFES/UNDP 2005. *Op. Cit.*, p.15.

68. Montjoy, 2010. *Op. Cit.*

69. Andrews et al. 2005. *Op. Cit*; James Heckman, Carolyn Heinrich, Jeffrey Smith. 1997. "Assessing the Performance of Performance Standards in Public Bureaucracies," *American Economic Review*, 87: 2, 389–395; Carolyn J. Heinrich. 2002. "Outcomes-Based Performance Management in the Public Sector: Implications for Government Effectiveness," *Public Administration Review*, 62: 6, 712–725.

70. Electoral Commission 2009b. *Op. Cit.*

71. Robert Andersen 2004. "Regression Models for Ordinal Data" in *The Sage Encyclopedia of Social Science Research Vol. 3*, eds. Michael S. Lewis-Beck, Alan Bryman, and T. F. Liao, London: Sage, 941–942.

72. Electoral Commission 2009b. *Op. Cit.*

73. IFES/UNDP 2005. *Op. Cit.* Why some councils spent so little, even into negative amounts, is unclear at the time of writing but requires further investigation.

74. It is recognized that there are difficulties with treating the dependent variable as an interval variable for OLS regression when it is essentially an ordinal 15-point scale. Nevertheless, the practice of using OLS under such conditions is widespread and broadly accepted under certain conditions in the quantitative and research literature (Andersen, 2004; Andrews et al., 2005). For the preliminary analysis at hand it is therefore appropriate, not least since the aim is an exploratory determination of the nature of relationships between spending and election quality. In each regression, missing values are replaced by the mean on the spending independent variables of interest.

75. The reference category for the council type dummy variables is English unitary councils in both tables, while the reference category for region is the East Midlands.

76. Clark 2012. *Op. Cit.*

77. Electoral Commission 2009b.

78. IFES/UNDP 2005. *Op. Cit.*, p22.

79. Pastor 1999. *Op. Cit.*

80. IFES/UNDP 2005. *Op. Cit.*

81. Montjoy 2010. Op. Cit., p.872.

82. E.g., Alvarez and Hall, 2006. *Op. Cit.*; Atkeson and Saunders 2007. *Op. Cit.*; Hall et. Al 2007. *Op. Cit.*; Montjoy, 2010. *Op. Cit.*

10

EMB Performance and Perceptions of Electoral Integrity in Africa

NICHOLAS N. KERR

For many Nigerians, the 2011 national elections represented the most credible polls since the reintroduction of democratic rule in 1999. Approximately 70 percent of Nigerians surveyed in 2012 rated the elections as either free and fair or free and fair with minor problems, compared to 31 percent of citizens surveyed in 2007.[1]

How can we explain this drastic improvement in Nigerians' perceptions of electoral integrity? Most stakeholders, including international and domestic election observers, linked the historic 2011 elections to improvements in the autonomy and capacity of the Independent National Electoral Commission (INEC). In 2011, Nigerians also experienced fewer instances of electoral fraud compared with the 2007 elections that were characterized by widespread theft of ballot boxes, fabrication of election results, and intimidation of voters.[2] Nonetheless, relative to other elections in Nigeria (1999, 2003, and 2007), the 2011 contest witnessed more election-related violence, especially during the post-election period when close to 800 Nigerians lost their lives.[3]

Scholars and policy experts have begun to pay closer attention to the perspectives of citizens when making assessments about electoral integrity. This is important for a number of reasons. First, various studies emphasize the strong association between citizens' electoral integrity perceptions and democratic attitudes. When citizens consider elections as free and fair, they are more likely to espouse positive evaluations of democratic performance and to believe in the legitimacy of the regime.[4] Views of electoral integrity are also important predictors of citizens' electoral behavior. Instances of voter intimidation, violence, and ballot box stuffing, discourage voter turnout, drive citizens to protest, and enhance the likelihood of post-election violence.[5] Third, when compared to elite and expert opinions of electoral integrity, scholars suggest that the perspectives of citizens gathered through public opinion surveys (based on nationally representative samples) provide a more representative snapshot of electoral integrity within a country.[6]

Despite the importance of gauging citizens' views of electoral integrity, the existing literature has been relatively silent on how citizens develop these views. This is especially the case in Africa, where the quality of elections has important implications on regime legitimacy and where there are multiple threats to electoral integrity. If we return to the 2011 Nigerian elections, it is not clear if Nigerians based their electoral integrity perceptions on their personal experience during multiple stages of the election cycle or just on events surrounding election day. Furthermore, to what extent did Nigerians' electoral integrity perceptions reflect the performance of the election commission, the degree of election-related violence, or the success of their own parties at the polls?

This chapter seeks to advance the existing literature by examining the factors that shape citizens' perceptions of election integrity in African states. I argue that citizens are, for the most part, capable of making informed assessments of the integrity of elections in their country.[7] More specifically, I contend that citizens' electoral integrity perceptions are multidimensional, and I propose three main sources of their perceptions: (1) the performance of electoral administrative institutions, such as electoral management bodies (EMBs); (2) characteristics of the election environment, such as the incidence of electoral malpractice; and (3) citizens' individual attributes, including partisan affiliations and political awareness. However, of these main sources, I expect EMBs' performance to have the greatest influence on citizens' electoral integrity attitudes.

One reason for EMBs' strong influence is that citizens have become increasingly aware of the role that EMBs should play in promoting credible elections in African countries that hold periodic elections.[8] For many citizens, EMBs may influence electoral fairness by maintaining institutional autonomy and holding political elites accountable to the rules of electoral competition.[9] EMBs may also affect the quality of citizens' voting experience depending on the institution's effectiveness in managing various dimensions of the election process and minimizing administrative and logistical failures.[10]

Another reason is that EMBs have become publicly visible during the electoral cycle. Voters have direct experience with EMBs when registering to vote and when casting their ballots on election day. Meanwhile, political parties, news media, and election observers often disseminate information about the independence and preparedness of EMBs.[11]

I examine the sources of citizens' electoral integrity perceptions using cross-national data on elections in Africa. I rely on recent data from the Afrobarometer public opinion survey that gauges mass perspectives in 18 countries and 28 election periods between 1999 and 2008. I also incorporate election-level data from several sources, including on EMB performance from the Quality of Elections Data.[12] The results indicate that Africans' electoral integrity evaluations are boosted during elections where EMBs perform well and election violence is minimized. In fact, during election periods where EMBs perform well, citizens are 42 percent more likely to consider elections acceptable. Furthermore, I find that electoral integrity assessments are consistently lower among citizens affiliated with electoral losers, those who are more educated, and those less interested in politics.

The chapter makes the following contributions to the existing literature. First, it represents one of the first studies that attempt to model the individual and election-level correlates of citizens' electoral integrity perceptions across several African states.[13] Second, my research provides a rigorous examination of the relationship between EMBs and citizens' electoral integrity perceptions, by focusing on the impact of EMB performance. So far, very few cross-national studies have examined the influence of EMB performance and generated results that are consistent with the theoretical literature and single-country empirical analysis that underscore the democratic enhancing effects of independent and professional EMBs. Finally, the chapter highlights some of the challenges of using public perceptions as a measure of electoral integrity. Mainly, I show that Africans' electoral integrity perceptions are a function of their rational evaluations of the electoral environment and the performance of electoral administration. Citizens' partisan affiliations and their level of political awareness, however, also shape the reliability of these judgments.

The next section surveys the existing literature on the sources of citizens' electoral integrity perceptions. I then outline the empirical analyses and discuss the results. Finally, I explore the main implications of the results and provide a brief conclusion.

Public Perceptions of Electoral Integrity: Theory
Conceptualizing Electoral Integrity Perceptions

Democratic theorists have approached the conceptualization of electoral integrity in myriad ways.[14] I adopt the conceptualization proposed in this volume whereby electoral integrity reflects the "international conventions and global norms, applying universally to all countries worldwide throughout the electoral cycle, including during the pre-electoral period, the campaign, on polling day, and its aftermath."[15]

Following this, I assume that citizens are capable of developing summary judgments of the integrity of elections.[16] Such judgments are not limited to the activities on election day; instead, they span all the stages of the electoral cycle, from the designing of legislation related to election administration, to the adjudication of electoral disputes.[17]

To measure popular perceptions of electoral integrity, I rely on a question from the Afrobarometer survey that gauges citizens' evaluations of the freedom and fairness of the last election. From the citizens' perspective, freedom usually refers to candidates' ability to run for elected office and engage in campaigning, as well as voters' ability to choose a preferred outcome, all without constraint or coercion.

Meanwhile, fairness signifies the impartial and consistent application of rules (international and domestic) in ways that do not adversely bias some political competitors relative to others.

The "free and fair" measure is compatible with this volume's notion of electoral integrity. First, similar to electoral integrity, the free and fair conceptualization maintains some degree of universality and has been applied across different regime types. For instance, various studies have used the free and fair measure as a summary indicator to examine electoral integrity in electoral autocracies and electoral democracies.[18] Second, international laws and conventions specifically reference the free and fair terminology in ways that emphasize its international acceptability.[19] Third, and as will be highlighted below, first- and second-order violations of electoral integrity (electoral malpractices) have also been popularly identified as factors undermining the freeness and fairness of elections. Finally, despite criticisms that the free and fair terminology is conceptually ambiguous,[20] using it as a summary indicator provides one way of assessing citizens' views on electoral integrity.

Sources of Public Electoral Integrity Perceptions

The literature on mass perceptions of electoral integrity highlights numerous factors that shape citizens' views on the freeness and fairness of elections. I group these potential factors into three broad categories: the performance of institutions associated with election administration (e.g., electoral management bodies), characteristics of the electoral environment (e.g., incidence of electoral malpractice), and citizens' individual attributes (e.g., political party affiliation and political awareness).

Institutions of Election Administration

Scholars and policy practitioners have become increasingly interested in the role of electoral management bodies (EMBs) in shaping citizens' electoral integrity evaluations. For many, EMBs help to enhance the procedural legitimacy and substantive uncertainty of elections when they effectively manage various stages of the election process and hold political elites accountable to the rules of the electoral game.[21]

One group of empirical studies have examined the consequences of EMB design (formal rules that define the institution's powers and responsibilities), with the expectation that greater formal-legal and professional autonomy are more likely to foster popular confidence in the freeness and fairness of elections.[22] However, those findings have been largely inconsistent with the expectation that EMB formal autonomy will enhance electoral integrity perceptions. For instance, Birch examines citizens' confidence in electoral process across 28 elections in new and established democracies.[23] She finds that citizens living in countries with institutionally independent EMBs are less likely to have confidence in their electoral processes.

She attributes this counterintuitive finding to the possibility that formal-legal independence might not reflect the actual independence of the institution.

As the chapters in this section illustrate, another group of scholars have explored the link between the actual performance of EMBs and citizens' electoral integrity evaluations and generated promising findings. Some studies identify the performance of election administration—seen through evaluations of poll worker performance, the proper function of voting machines, and the length of time waiting to vote—as one of the most influential sources of citizens' electoral integrity judgments.[24] Scholars attribute this strong association to the critical role that EMBs play on election day and during other stages of the electoral cycle. As chapter 13 discusses, Hall and Stewart examine the perceived competence of election workers and find that poll workers' performance significantly influences citizens' confidence that their votes will be accurately counted.

Those studies also provide some indication on how citizens develop their evaluations of EMB performance. Citizens may formulate their opinions of election administration by directly interacting with the institution during different phases of the electoral cycle. By registering to vote or casting a ballot on election day, citizens can evaluate the impartiality, competence, and preparedness of the poll staff and assess the availability of election materials and proper functioning of voting machinery.[25]

Citizens may also gain knowledge about EMB performance through the media, political parties, and civil society organizations. In many African states, print and broadcast media entities play an important role in evaluating the independence and preparedness of EMBs and make this information available for public consumption.[26] In some instances, EMBs use state and independent media to publicize information about the voting process and the EMBs' commitment to promoting electoral integrity.[27] Political parties also disseminate valuable information on the performance of EMBs to their supporters and the public in general. This is especially the case when political parties unearth deficiencies in election administration and use the information to justify boycotting elections or challenging unfavorable election results.[28] Admittedly, information on EMBs accessed through the media and political parties is susceptible to bias; however, these sources provide alternative channels through which citizens can track EMB performance beyond their own experience.

I suggest that in many African states, citizens have become increasingly aware of the role that EMBs play in elections.[29] Furthermore, citizens also have various opportunities to evaluate EMB performance either through first-hand experience or through publicly available information. Following this, I assume that EMB performance may shape citizens' impressions of electoral integrity in Africa.

First, when citizens observe an EMB that equally engages all political parties, makes decisions that are transparent and insulated from political interference, and sanctions political parties for violating electoral rules, citizens are more inclined to believe that

EMB officials have not predetermined the outcome of the elections. In other words, citizens are more likely to think the electoral playing field is level. In turn, they may then use this information to positively evaluate the fairness of the election.

Second, EMB performance may also shape citizens' freedom to exercise their franchise. For example, this freedom may be impinged through deficiencies in election administration that (1) abrogate citizens' right to vote (such as a botched voter registration process and unreliable voters list); (2) undermine the quality of the voting experience (such as late arrival of voting materials and long lines at polling stations); and (3) weaken the reliability of results (such as faulty counting and tabulation process and delays in the announcement of results). As a consequence of one or a combination of these acts, citizens may be less likely to rate the elections as free. When taken together, I expect that:

H1: During election periods where EMBs perform well, citizens are *more likely* to perceive elections as free and fair.

Characteristics of the Electoral Environment

The prevailing conditions of the electoral environment may also shape popular attitudes toward electoral integrity. A number of scholars have examined the consequences of electoral malpractice on citizens' electoral integrity opinions.[30] I define electoral malpractices as the range of activities that political actors or election authorities employ intentionally to alter election outcomes and undermine the integrity of the electoral process. This definition distinguishes malpractice from other unintentional practices or maladministration that may influence electoral integrity.

Citizens' judgments of electoral freedom and equality, I argue, may also reflect the incidence of electoral malpractice. Widespread ballot stuffing, violent intimidation, misappropriation of government resources, and vote buying challenge popular notions of electoral equity because they offer an unfair advantage to the culprits at the expense of other competitors. In the same way, pervasive malpractice discourages voter participation and undermines the quality of the voting experience. Based on this, I expect that:

H2: During election periods with high levels of electoral malpractice, citizens are *less likely* to perceive elections as free and fair.

Citizens' Individual Attributes

A final source of citizens' understandings of the freeness and fairness of electoral contests are their own individual attributes. I focus specifically on the effect of partisan affiliations and political awareness. Within the literature, the importance of political affiliations as a source of electoral integrity perceptions cannot be over-stated. Citizens' partisan preferences often reflect an association with the winning or losing party in the most recent elections.[31] This association provides a perceptual frame for processing information regarding the integrity of elections. On the one hand, citizens who supported the winning party at the polls are more willing to accept the process that led to their party's (candidate's) electoral victory. On the other hand, those affiliated with the losing party (candidate) search for evidence to justify the electoral defeat. As a result,

> H3: Citizens affiliated with the party of the electoral winner are *more likely* to perceive elections as free and fair.

Another important individual attribute is citizens' level of political awareness, which is, often shaped by their educational background or consumption of news media. The conventional wisdom is that citizens who are more politically aware are more likely to have confidence in elections.[32] The main rationale is that informed citizens are more liable to participate in elections, and relatively higher degrees of participation increase citizens' familiarity with election processes, which in turn enhances confidence in elections. However, studies exploring electoral integrity in Africa find that political awareness is negatively associated with citizens' electoral integrity attitudes.[33] In particular, Moehler's study shows that Africans who rely frequently on radio, television, and newspapers for political information, as well as those with higher levels of education, were more critical of electoral integrity across 12 African countries.

I suggest an alternative approach. Namely, politically aware citizens should have greater insight on the principles that guide electoral integrity and are more likely to rely on a variety of informational sources, in addition to their personal experience, when assessing the integrity of elections. As a result, those who are politically aware may be more likely to recognize when elections adhere to, or deviate from, these democratic principles when compared to those with less awareness. Based on this perspective, it is difficult to propose any a priori hypotheses about the influence of citizens' level of awareness on their electoral integrity judgments.

Interdependence of the Sources of Public Electoral Integrity Perceptions

So far, I have modeled EMB performance, electoral malpractice, partisanship, and electoral awareness as separate, independent sources of citizens' perceptions of electoral integrity. In actuality, however, these sources are interdependent, and may jointly shape how citizens evaluate the freeness and fairness of elections. While it is beyond the scope of the study to examine potential interrelatedness empirically, it is still beneficial to consider how these sources interact and how they may shape citizens' views on electoral integrity. For instance, the performance of EMBs and the incidence of electoral malpractice may be interrelated. During elections where politicians attempt to manipulate the process by stealing ballot boxes and intimidating voters, these forms of electoral malpractice may directly undermine the ability of election administrative officials to manage the election process effectively and ensure that votes are accurately counted. When this occurs, citizens are more likely to think that EMB officials are complicit in electoral malpractice and more likely to castigate EMB officials for operational and administrative problems that occur.

Sources of Africans' Electoral Integrity Perceptions

I next see how well the main sources of perceptions of integrity—the performance of electoral management bodies, the incidence of electoral malpractice, and citizens' political party affiliations and political awareness—can explain the cross-country variation in Africans' electoral integrity perceptions.

Data and Methods

To explore the hypothesized determinants of Africans' electoral integrity evaluations, I incorporate various sources, including individual-level data from the Afrobarometer and election-level data from multiple cross-national datasets.[34] The scope of the analysis includes election periods from 1996 to 2004, based on a sample size of approximately 41,000 respondents nested in 28 election periods (in a total of 18 countries), with an average of 1,590 respondents per election period.

Because the sample includes data that are measured at two levels of analysis (individual-level and election-level), I utilize a multilevel regression model.[35] Furthermore, the main dependent variable, citizens' perceptions of free and fair elections, is measured dichotomously. As a consequence, I estimate a random-intercept logistic multilevel regression model.[36]

Dependent Variable: Africans' Perceptions of Free and Fair Elections

The main dependent variable captures respondents' perceptions of the freeness and fairness of the most recent elections. The Afrobarometer asked respondents, "On the whole, how would you rate the freeness and fairness of the last national election held in [YEAR]?" The response scale includes "Not free and fair," "Free and fair with major problems," "Free and fair with minor problems," and "Completely free and fair." For the regression analysis, I re-scale the original measure into a dichotomous indicator, with 1 indicating that citizens perceived the elections as "completely free and fair" or "free and fair with minor problems," and 0 denoting the elections as "free or fair with major problems" or "not free and fair."[37]

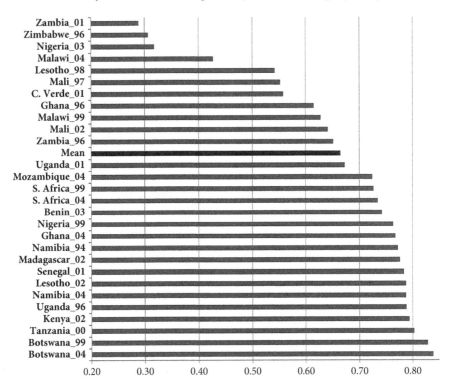

Figure 10.1: African Evaluations of Electoral Integrity. Note: Mean Electoral Integrity Perceptions: 1 = "completely free and fair" or "free and fair with minor problems"; 0 = "free or fair with major problems" or "not free and fair." Source: Afrobarometer Rounds 1,3 and 4, with Afrobarometer combined weights.

Figure 10.1 displays the mean perceptions of electoral integrity across the 28 elections in the sample. At one end of the spectrum, citizens in Zambia's 2003 election espouse the lowest levels of confidence (mean = 0.29), while citizens in Botswana's 2004 election reported having the highest levels of confidence (mean = 0.84). Figure 10.1 also reveals that in some countries, including Ghana (1996 and 2004), Nigeria (1999 and 2003), and Zambia (1996 and 2001), the mean electoral integrity evaluations changed significantly across election periods. In other countries, including Botswana and South Africa, mean electoral integrity perceptions remained relatively more consistent over time.

EMB Performance

First, I examine the hypothesized impact of election administration on citizens' electoral integrity perceptions. I use an election-level indicator of the performance of electoral management bodies constructed through an additive index of two variables that reflect various problems with election administration during the pre-election period and on election day. The variables are obtained from the Quality of Elections Data collected by Kelley.[38]

I consider the EMB performance index a valid indicator, as it incorporates experts' evaluations of the actual autonomy and capacity of electoral management bodies during various stages of the election cycle.[39] According to Kelley, both original indicators reflect key dimensions of EMB autonomy, including the impartiality of the appointment process in practice or how impartially the EMB has been enforcing the electoral law.[40] With respect to capacity-related attributes, the measure captures logistical problems at voting locations, problems associated with election-day workers, and deficiencies with the voter's register.

Like many cross-national measures of institutional characteristics, the EMB performance index does have its shortcomings. For instance, the index does not allow researchers to disaggregate the autonomy and capacity dimensions of the measure. Additionally, some may criticize the measure for focusing more on the capacity-related dimensions of the EMB performance at the expense of autonomy-related ones. Despite these shortcomings, however, the measure provides the most accurate and reliable gauge of EMB performance that allows for meaningful cross-time and cross-national comparisons. Most importantly, the performance index represents an advancement over measures that only reflect dimensions of EMB design, such as formal-legal autonomy used by some cross-national studies.[41] Meanwhile, the use of an aggregate-level, expert-based measure of EMB performance may provide further corroboration for studies that employ citizens' evaluation of EMB performance to explain their electoral integrity evaluations.[42]

EMB performance index is normalized on a 0–1 scale, with "1" indicating high levels of performance. The measure shows substantial variation across countries and within countries over time. For instance, Ghana's electoral commission received a performance score of 0.5 during the 1992 elections; this increased to 1.0 between 1996 and 2000 but fell to 0.668 in the 2004 elections. In Zimbabwe the performance of election administration falls from 1.0 in 1990 to 0.67 in 1995 to 0.17 in 2000 but up to 0.5 in 2002.

Election Malpractice

To capture characteristics of the electoral environment, I focus primarily on the consequences of electoral malpractice on perceived electoral integrity. In doing so, I distinguish between two types of electoral malpractice.[43] The first is election violence and the second is electoral fraud (including forms of ballot rigging, vote buying, the abuse of government resources, and political intimidation). Although I expect both electoral violence and electoral fraud to negatively affect citizens' electoral integrity judgments, recent studies have found that the effect of each type of malpractice may have different implications for citizens' electoral integrity attitudes.[44] To measure electoral violence, I use an indicator from Staffan Lindberg's *Elections in Africa*

Data, which gauges the extent of violence that occurs during the campaign period and on election day.[45] The indicator for electoral fraud is constructed through an additive index of two indicators from the QED that measures the incidence of electoral fraud (cheating) during the pre-election period and on election day. While the existing literature has clearly outlined the link between citizens' experience with electoral malpractice and their perceptions of electoral integrity, by using indicators of electoral malpractice measured at the election level, we are in a better position to understand how cross-national variation in levels of violence and fraud may explain differences in citizens' electoral integrity judgments.

Partisan Affiliation and Political Awareness

Citizens' individual attributes also have important implications on their electoral integrity evaluations. The first, and most theorized, is citizens' partisan affiliation. I operationalize this measure through a question from the Afrobarometer asking citizens to identify the party they feel closest to. I then construct three separate dichotomous variables: (1) Winning partisans—citizens who reported an affiliation with the winning party; (2) Losing partisans—citizens who indicated an affiliation with one of the losing parties; and, (3) Non-partisans—citizens who reported no partisan affiliation. I expect losing partisans and non-partisans to be more critical of the quality of elections, relative to winning partisans.

Second, I contend that the level of political awareness can mediate the formation of election quality perceptions. I account for citizens' level of political awareness through three indicators: media exposure, education, and interest in politics. The indicator for media exposure reflects citizens' frequency of obtaining news through the radio, TV, and newspapers. I construct an additive index based on a factor analysis of the three items, which I then normalize on a scale from 0 to 1, 1 indicating higher levels of media exposure. I also include a measure of the respondents' level of education, which ranges from no education (0) to post-graduate education (9). Finally, I incorporate a composite measure for citizens' level of political interest, based on two items that measure citizens' interest in public affairs and citizens' frequency of discussing politics.

Controls

I also include additional election-level and individual-level controls that the existing literature has associated with the integrity of elections. At the election level, I include controls for the proportionality of the electoral system, economic development (GDP per capita), level of democracy, competitiveness of elections, presence of international observers, and time between AB survey and the last election. At the individual level, I account for whether respondents voted in the last election, as well as various social and demographic factors including gender, and urban/rural residency.

Results

Results of the regression model are displayed in Table 10.1[46], while Table 10.2 illus-trates the change in predicted probabilities of a respondent perceiving the elections to be free and fair given a minimum to maximum change of a specific independent variable.[47] The results demonstrate that EMB performance has a positive and sig-nificant coefficient. Providing crucial support for the main hypothesis (H1), it shows that the actual performance of EMBs has a positive influence on citizens' views on the integrity of elections. A closer examination of the substantive results in Table 10.2 indicates that in election periods where EMBs display high levels of EMB performance (EMB performance index = 1), Africans are 42 percent more likely to consider election processes free and fair compared to election periods with low levels of actual EMB autonomy and capacity (EMB performance index = 0.33). Compared to the other sources of electoral integrity perceptions, EMB performance has the largest substantive effect. The relative predictive power of EMB performance highlighted in this study parallels the findings of other chapters in this volume that use micro-level indicators of EMB performance.[48]

The coefficient for electoral violence is negative, as anticipated, indicating that citizens have less confidence in elections characterized by widespread violence dur-ing the election period, all things being equal. In fact, when citizens experience high levels of violence during the campaign period or on election day (Election Violence = 2), the probability that they will consider elections free and fair is reduced by 10 percentage points, relative to election periods that are relatively peaceful (Election Violence = 0). However, the hypothesis regarding electoral malpractice (H2) is only partly confirmed, as the indicator for electoral fraud fails to attain sig-nificance. This finding is surprising given results from other studies emphasizing the deleterious impact of electoral fraud on citizens' electoral integrity perceptions.

Next, I consider the effect of individual-level factors on popular electoral integ-rity perceptions. The model indicates that losing partisans and non-partisans are less likely to consider elections acceptable when compared to winning partisans, once we control for other covariates. Citizens who report an affiliation with the losing party or those who report no affiliation are, respectively, 31 percent and 19 percent less likely to consider elections credible. These findings have crucial policy impli-cations because they indicate that a substantial proportion of African citizens are more likely to find elections unacceptable because of their status as election losers or non-partisans. These findings bear similarities with other studies in this section of the book, and provide some indication that Africans are no more or less likely to rely on partisan affiliation to sway their electoral integrity judgments.

Furthermore, to assess the potential mediating effect of citizens' level of political awareness, I included a composite index of citizens' media exposure and indicators for citizens' level of education and their interest in politics. While the coefficients

Table 10.1: **Explaining African Perceptions of Electoral Integrity**

Variables	Perceptions of Electoral Integrity
Election-level	
EMB Performance Index	2.219**
	(0.863)
Election Violence	−0.570***
	(0.215)
Electoral Fraud Index	0.663
	(0.611)
Individual-Level Controls	
Losing Partisans	−1.324***
	(0.035)
Non-Partisans	−0.769***
	(0.032)
Index of Political Interests	0.157***
	(0.044)
Index of Media Exposure	−0.029
	(0.058)
Education	−0.048***
	(0.008)
Voted in Last Elections	0.335***
	(0.030)
Urban Resident	−0.103***
	(0.030)
Female	0.015
	(0.030)
Random Intercept	−1.008***
	(0.272)
Individual Observations	40,371
Election Periods	28

Note: Dependent Variable: Perceptions of Electoral Integrity. The analysis is conducted using xtlogit in Stata 10. Cell entries indicate the logistic regression coefficient and the standard errors in parentheses. ***$p < 0.01$, **$p < 0.05$, *$p < 0.1$.

Source: Afrobarometer Round 1, 3 and 4.

Table 10.2: **Predicting Perceptions of Electoral Integrity**

	Change in Probability	5% Confidence Interval	95% Confidence Interval
Election-Level Variables			
EMB Performance Index	0.42	0.21	0.60
Election Violence	−0.1	−.028	−0.18
Individual-Level Variables			
Winning Partisans	0.434	0.492	0.35
Losing Partisans	−0.31	−0.34	−0.27
Non-Partisans	−0.19	−0.17	−0.20
Voted in Elections	0.08	0.06	0.09
Interest in Politics Index	0.03	0.02	0.05
Education	−0.09	−0.07	−0.12
Urban Resident	−0.02	−0.03	−0.01

Note: All non-binary variables are held at their mean, while losers and non-partisans are held at 0 and voters and urban residents are held at 1.

for media exposure and education are negative, only the latter variable achieves statistical significance. To put it plainly, highly educated citizens are 10 percentage points less likely to consider elections as free and fair compared to those with lowest levels of education. This finding corroborates existing studies conducted in Africa[49] and provides some support to the notion that educated citizens are more cynical about election quality in Africa, as they see elections as falling below acceptable democratic standards.

The negative effect of education on electoral integrity perceptions contrasts the positive influence of citizens' level of interest in politics. This reveals an intriguing dynamic where the electoral integrity opinions of highly educated respondents diverge from those who report high levels of political interest. A potential explanation for this finding is that citizens who report high levels of interest in politics are more likely to be affiliated with electoral winners. Finally, the results indicate that voters are more liable to have faith in the freeness and fairness of elections relative to non-voters when holding other variables constant. Substantively, voters are 8 percentage points more likely to report that elections are free and fair. This finding has important policy implications. On one hand, it could mean that familiarity with the electoral process inspires greater confidence in elections. On the other hand, it may mean that citizens who believe that elections will not be free and fair are more likely to stay away from the polls.

Robustness Checks and Alternative Model Specifications

To verify the robustness of the findings, I conducted additional robustness checks that included various election-level factors that may influence citizens' electoral integrity perceptions. As mentioned previously, I include controls for the proportionality of the electoral system, economic development (GDP per capita), level of democracy, competitiveness of elections, presence of international observers, and time between a survey and the last election. The results are shown in Table 10.3 (Models 1–6). What is important to note is that the inclusion of these controls has no substantial effect on the main findings reported above. For instance, in Model 1, I control for the proportionality of electoral system, as some studies have found that citizens' electoral integrity perceptions are boosted in countries with proportional electoral rules. However, the results demonstrate that across the sample of 28 election periods, proportional electoral rules do not have a significant effect on Africans' electoral integrity perceptions.

Conclusion and Discussion

In this chapter, I examined the individual-level and election-level sources of Africans' perceptions of electoral integrity. Guided by existing scholarship, I suggested that "ordinary" Africans form their electoral integrity opinions based on the performance of election management bodies, the incidence of election malpractices, their affiliation with the winning political party, and their level of political awareness. These conjectures were evaluated using a multilevel analysis based on survey data from the Afrobarometer that reflects the views of approximately 40,000 citizens in 18 countries between 1999 and 2008. Similar to my expectations, the results indicate that during election periods where EMBs performed effectively and election violence was not pervasive, Africans were more likely to consider elections free and fair. Furthermore, citizens affiliated with the winning political party and those least educated were more likely to consider election quality favorably.

These findings should resonate with scholars and policy experts. Generally speaking, the findings emphasize the enduring influence of electoral management bodies on public confidence in African elections. Throughout the countries included in the sample, there is evidence of an emerging norm among African citizens through which they equate credible elections with the effective functioning of EMBs. As a result, election legitimacy rises when electoral management bodies like those in Ghana or in South Africa organize elections effectively. But election legitimacy also falls when performance is substandard, like in Kenya and Nigeria in 2007, where EMBs botched various aspects of the electoral process.

Table 10.3: **Alternative Models Explaining African Perceptions of Electoral Integrity**

	Model 1	Model 2	Model 3	Model 4	Model 5	Model 6
Election-Level Variables						
EMB Performance Index	2.349***	2.025**	2.113**	2.230**	2.291***	2.214***
	(0.856)	(0.967)	(0.921)	(0.881)	(0.883)	(0.851)
Election Violence	−0.477**	−0.542***	−0.557***	−0.573***	−0.567***	−0.568***
	(0.211)	(0.205)	(0.199)	(0.199)	(0.195)	(0.192)
Election Fraud	0.970	0.585	0.721	0.654	0.692	0.535
	(0.669)	(0.635)	(0.635)	(0.628)	(0.615)	(0.619)
Election-Level Controls						
Proportional Electoral Systems	0.308	–	–	–	–	–
	(0.297)	–	–	–	–	–
GDP per capita (log)	–	0.169	–	–	–	–
	–	(0.386)	–	–	–	–
Democracy (FH Index)	–	–	0.271	–	–	–
	–	–	(0.842)	–	–	–

	(1)	(2)	(3)	(4)	(5)	(6)
Competitiveness of Elections	—	—	—	-0.007	—	—
	—	—	—	(0.106)	—	—
Time Since Elections	—	—	—	—	0.003	—
	—	—	—	—	(0.007)	—
International Observers	—	—	—	—	—	-0.178
	—	—	—	—	—	(0.121)
Random Intercept	-1.099***	-1.068***	-1.065***	-1.061***	-1.061***	-1.066***
	(0.272)	(0.272)	(0.272)	(0.272)	(0.272)	(0.272)
Individual Observations	40,371	40,371	40,371	40,371	40,371	38,359
Election Periods	28	28	28	28	28	28

Note: Dependent Variable: Perceptions of Electoral Integrity (Afrobarometer Round 1, 3, and 4). The analysis is conducted using xtlogit in Stata 10. Cell entries indicate the logistic regression coefficient and the standard errors in parentheses: ***$p < 0.01$, **$p < 0.05$, *$p < 0.1$. Individual variables have been excluded from the table.

Admittedly, these findings are intuitive and perhaps not surprising given the importance placed on electoral management bodies by policy-practitioners. However, I argue that these findings make significant contributions to the existing empirical literature on the consequences of electoral management bodies in two respects. First, by demonstrating the positive effect of EMB performance on public electoral integrity evaluations, this research advances existing cross-national scholarship that has relied on indicators of EMB design, including formal-legal autonomy and capacity. By using an indicator of EMB performance, my research more effectively accounts for various factors within electoral autocracies and electoral democracies (such as the influence of informal rules that substitute or compete with formal rules) that may mediate the relationship between EMBs and citizens' attitudes. For example, the Zimbabwe Electoral Commission (ZEC) is constitutionally independent, but in practice the incumbent has used a variety of mechanisms such as existing patronage networks to manipulate the ZEC and secure favorable electoral results.[50]

A second contribution is that it addresses the problem of endogeneity that may affect studies examining the link between citizens' evaluations of EMB performance and citizens' electoral integrity perceptions. Most of the existing literature that probes the effect of EMB performance utilizes citizens' evaluations of EMB performance captured from survey data collected after elections. One problem is that it is difficult to distinguish whether citizens use their evaluations of EMB performance to develop their assessments of electoral integrity or vice versa. To put it another way, there is little independence between the measures of perceived EMB performance and perceived electoral integrity. By using an expert indicator of EMB performance that is independently measured from citizens' electoral integrity views, we have greater leverage to assert that EMB performance shapes citizens' electoral integrity views and not vice versa. While this study provides substantial evidence for the importance of EMB performance, future research could shed light on the ways citizens obtain information about the performance of EMBs during the course of an election cycle.

Another important finding is that Africans' affiliation with electoral winners has a positive influence on citizens' evaluations of election credibility. Even more interesting is the large gap in electoral integrity perceptions between Africans who report an affiliation with the losing and winning parties. These findings are consistent with ones of other research in this volume for the United States and Latin America, proving that although the "winner effect" is important in Africa, Africans are no more likely than citizens in other regions to be swayed by their political affiliations.

When taken together, the study provides clear evidence that Africans' electoral integrity perceptions are multidimensional. Similar to citizens in other regions of the world, Africans' judgments on electoral integrity are driven by rational considerations linked to the performance of electoral management bodies and incidence of electoral malpractice, along with more affective influences, such as citizens' status as a political winner or loser.

Appendix A: Variables and Coding

EMB Performance Index (Quality of Elections Data: Kelley 2011): Additive index of two variables that measure the problems with the *pre-election administration* and *election-day administration*. The index has been normalized on a 0–1 scale and reverse-coded, with 1 indicating high EMB performance. According to Kelley, *pre-election administration* measures "problems with voter registration process, appointment of election commissioners; enforcement of election law by commission; level of commission's transparency; voter/candidate information and education; technical/procedural problems with ballot design and printing." *Election-day administration* measures "logistical problems at voting locations— large crowds, long wait, confusion, inadequate information on voting procedures, inadequate facilities for voting. Human resource deficiencies—voting locations opening late, poll officials' unfamiliarity with election laws or inconsistent application of voting procedures, and complaints about the conduct of election officials. Voter–list problems—missing names, fictitious names and names of deceased on list, list not at polling station of time."

Election Violence (Elections in Africa Data: Lindberg 2006): Did election campaign/day violence occur? 2 = yes to a significant extent; 1 = yes, but only isolated incidents; 0 = no, peaceful.

Election Fraud (Quality of Elections): Additive index of two variables that measure various *pre-election cheating* and *election-day cheating*; the index has been normalized on a 0–1 scale, with 1 indicating high fraud.

Proportional Electoral System (Elections in Africa): 0 = Plurality/Majoritarian; 1 = Proportional Electoral System/Mixed Electoral System.

Freedom House Index (Quality of Governance): Weighted index of Freedom House civil liberties and political rights sub-scores. 0–1, 1 indicating more democratic states.

Log GDP PPP (World Bank Indicators): Log of gross domestic product per capita.

Competitiveness of Elections (Elections in Africa): Presidential elections: difference in the percentage of votes between the winning presidential candidate and runner-up candidate. Legislative elections: difference in the largest party's share of seats and the seats of the second-largest party in the legislature.

Time since Elections (Original): Number of months between the date of the last election and the corresponding date of the Afrobarometer survey.

Free and Fair Elections (Afrobarometer): On the whole, how would you rate the freeness and fairness of the last national election?: 0 = Not free and fair, and Free and fair, with major problems; 1 = Free and fair, but with minor problems, and Completely free and fair; Missing = Do not understand question, Don't know, Refused.

Partisan Affiliation (Afrobarometer): Do you feel close to any political party? Used three dummy variables. Winning Partisans: 1 = Affiliation with winning party; 0 = Losing Partisans and Non-partisans. Losing Partisans: 1 = Affiliation with losing party; 0 = Winning Partisans and Non-partisans. *Non-Partisans*: 1 = Affiliation with no political party; 0 = Winning Partisans and Losing Partisans.

Political Interest Index (Afrobarometer): How interested would you say you are in public affairs? When you get together with your friends or family, would you say you discuss political matters? Two item additive index normalized on a 0–1 scale: 0 = low interest; 1 = high interest.

Index of Media Exposure (Afrobarometer): How often do you get news from the following sources? Radio, TV, Newspaper (Three item additive index normalized on a 0–1 scale: 0 = low exposure; 1 = high exposure).

Education (Afrobarometer): Level of education of respondent (0 = no education to 9 = post graduate).

Voted in Last Elections (Afrobarometer): With regard to the most recent, [last] national elections, which statement is true for you? 1 = Voted in elections; 0 = Did not vote in elections.

Social Structure: Gender: 0 = Male, 1 = Female. Location of Respondent: 0 = Rural, 1 = Urban.

Notes

1. These results are based on a question from the Afrobarometer Rounds 4 and 5 surveys conducted in Nigeria in 2008 and 2012: "*On the whole, how would you rate the freeness and fairness of the last national election held in 2007/2011?*"
2. Peter M. Lewis. "Nigeria Votes: More Openness, More Conflict" *Journal of Democracy* 22(4): 60–74.
3. Human Rights Watch. 2011. "Nigeria: Post-Election Violence Killed 800." www.hrw.org.
4. See Mattes, chapter 11 in this volume.
5. Philipp Kuntz and Mark R Thompson. 2009. "More than Just the Final Straw: Stolen Elections as Revolutionary Triggers" *Comparative Politics* 41(3): 253–272.
6. Pippa Norris. 2014. "Are there Global Norms of Electoral Integrity? *Electoral Studies* 32(4): 576–588.
7. Michael Bratton, ed. 2013. *Voting and Democratic Citizenship in Africa.* Boulder: Lynne Rienner Publishers.
8. Ismaila M. Fall, Mathias Hounkpe, Adele L. Jinadu and Pascal Kambale, eds. 2011. *Election Management Bodies in West Africa: A Comparative Study of the Contribution of Electoral Commissions to the Strengthening of Democracy.* Johannesburg: Open Society Initiative for West Africa.
9. Ibid.

10. Emmanuel Debrah. 2011. "Measuring Governance Institutions' Success in Ghana: The Case of the Electoral Commission, 1993–2008" *African Studies* 70(1): 25–45.
11. International Institute for Democracy and Electoral Assistance (IDEA). 2012. *Electoral Management During Transition: Challenges and Opportunities.* Policy Paper Series.
12. Judith G. Kelley. 2012. *Monitoring Democracy: When International Election Observation Works, and Why It Often Fails.* Princeton: Princeton University Press.
13. See also Mattes, chapter 11 in this volume.
14. Guy S. Goodwin-Gill. 1994. *Free and Fair Elections: International Law and Practice.* Geneva: Inter-Parliamentary Union; Palle Svensson and Jorgen Elklit. 1997. "What Makes Elections Free and Fair?" *Journal of Democracy* 8(3): 32–46; Sarah Birch. 2011. *Electoral Malpractice.* Oxford: Oxford University Press.
15. See Norris, chapter 1 in this volume.
16. Michael Bratton, ed. 2013. *Voting and Democratic Citizenship in Africa.* Boulder: Lynne Rienner Publishers.
17. Pippa Norris, "Are there Global Norms of Electoral Integrity?" *Electoral Studies* 32(4): 576–588.
18. See Kelley, *Monitoring Democracy*; Ari Greenberg and Robert Mattes. 2013. "Does the Quality of Elections Affect the Consolidation of Democracy?" In *Voting and Democratic Citizenship in Africa*, Ed. Michael Bratton. Boulder, CO: Lynne Rienner Publishers.
19. Michael D. Boda. 2005. "Reconsidering the free and fair question" *Representation* 41(3): 155–160.
20. See Norris, Elklit and Reynolds, chapter 3 in this volume.
21. Shaheen Mozaffar and Andreas Schedler. 2002. "The Comparative Study of Electoral Governance—Introduction" *International Political Science Review* 23(1): 5–27.
22. See Sarah Birch. 2008. "Electoral Institutions and popular confidence in electoral processes: A cross-national analysis" *Electoral Studies* 27(2): 305–321; Guillermo Rosas. 2010. "Trust in Elections and the Institutional Design of Electoral Authorities: Evidence from Latin America" *Electoral Studies* 29(1): 74–90.
23. Ibid.
24. Lonna Rae Atkeson and Kyle L. Saunders. 2007. "The Effect of Election Administration on Voter Confidence: A Local Matter?" *Political Science and Politics* 40(4): 655–660; Thad E. Hall, Quin Monson and Kelly D. Patterson. 2009. "The Human Dimension of Elections: How Poll Workers Shape Public Confidence in Elections" *Political Research Quarterly* 62(3): 507–522.
25. International Institute for Democracy and Electoral Assistance (IDEA). 2012. *Electoral Management during Transition: Challenges and Opportunities.* Policy Paper Series.
26. Marie-Soliel Frere. 2011. "Covering post-conflict elections: Challenges for the media in Central Africa" *Africa Spectrum* 46(1): 3–32.
27. Emmanuel Debrah. 2011. "Measuring governance institutions' success in Ghana: The Case of the Electoral Commission, 1993–2008" *African Studies* 70(1): 25–45.
28. Alexander B. Makulilo. 2009. "Independent Electoral Commission in Tanzania: A False Debate?" *Representation* 45 (4): 435–453.
29. Fall et al. *Election Management Bodies in West Africa.*
30. See James A. McCann and Jorge I. Dominguez. 1998. "Mexicans react to electoral fraud and political corruption: An assessment of public opinion and voting behavior" *Electoral Studies* 17(4): 483–503; Michael Bratton. 2008. "Vote buying and violence in Nigerian election campaigns" *Electoral Studies* 27(4): 621–632.
31. Christopher J. Anderson and Andrew J. LoTempio. 2002. "Winning, losing and political trust in America" *British Journal of Political Science* 32: 335–351; Seligson and Maldonado, chapter 11 in this volume.
32. Sarah Birch. 2010. "Perceptions of electoral fairness and voter turnout" *Comparative Political Studies* 43(12): 1601–1622.

33. Devra C. Moehler. 2009. "Critical citizens and submissive subjects: Election losers and winners in Africa." *British Journal of Political Science* 39(02): 345–366; Mattes chapter in this volume.

34. See the Appendix for a description of the data and variable construction.

35. Marco R. Steenbergen and Bradford S. Jones. 2002. "Modeling multilevel data structures" *American Journal of Political Science* 46(1): 218–237.

36. All empirical models using perceptions of electoral integrity as the DV have been estimated using both the dichotomous and ordinal measures, with no substantial differences in the results.

37. Across 28 election periods in the sample, a plurality of citizens (45 percent) rated the elections as completely free and fair, while a further 30 percent of those interviewed believed that the elections only had minor problems. When these two categories were combined, approximately three in four Africans (75 percent) had a positive rating of the elections. Conversely, only 12 percent of those surveyed regarded the most recent elections as "not free and fair," while 14 percent of respondents saw the elections as "free and fair with major problems" (26 percent).

38. Judith G. Kelley. 2012. Monitoring Democracy: When International Election Observation Works, and Why It O#en Fails. Princeton: Princeton University Press.

39. See Martinez i Coma and Frank, chapter 4 in this volume.

40. Judith G. Kelley. 2012. *Monitoring Democracy: When International Election Observation Works, and Why It Often Fails.* Princeton: Princeton University Press.

41. See Birch, "Electoral institutions and popular confidence in electoral processes"; Guillermo Rosas. 2010. "Trust in Elections and the Institutional Design of Electoral Authorities: Evidence from Latin America." *Electoral Studies* 29(1): 74–90.

42. Ryan L. Claassen, David B. Magleby, Quin Monson and Kelly D. Patterson. 2013. "Voter confidence and the Election-Day Voting Experience." *Political Behavior* 35: 215–235.

43. Judith Kelley. 2012. *Monitoring Democracy: When International Election Observation Works, and Why It Often Fails.* Princeton: Princeton University Press.

44. See Paul Collier and Pedro C. Vicente. 2010. "Violence, Bribery, and Fraud: the Political Economy of Elections in Sub-Saharan Africa." *Public Choice* pp. 1–31; Bratton, "Vote Buying and Violence in Nigerian Election Campaigns."

45. Staffan Lindberg. 2006. *Democracy and Elections in Africa.* Baltimore: Johns Hopkins University Press.

46. Table 10.1 reports the maximum likelihood coefficients (represented in log-odds) of citizens' likelihood to consider elections free and fair given a unit change in the main individual-level and election-period predictors.

47. I have calculated the changes in predicted probabilities of a respondent perceiving elections to be free and fair given a minimum to maximum change of specific independent variables, while holding all non-binary independent variables at their mean and while Losing Partisan and Non-Partisan are both set to 0, Gender is set at Female, and Residential Location is set to Urban.

48. See Paul Gronke. 2013. "Are we confident in voter confidence? Observations on perceptual measures of electoral integrity." Paper presented at the 2013 Annual Workshop of the Electoral Integrity Project, Harvard University, Cambridge, MA.

49. See Mattes, chapter 11 in this volume.

50. Eldred V. Masunungure. 2009. Ed. *Defying the Winds of Change: Zimbabwe's 2008 Elections.* Harare: Weaver Press.

11

Electoral Integrity and Democratic Legitimacy in Africa

ROBERT MATTES

Elections are the sine qua non of modern representative democracy. Yet beyond this truism, how important are they to the process of democratization in young multiparty regimes? While virtually all political scientists see elections as a *necessary* element of democracy, an influential line of research has warned against an overemphasis on competitive elections, or what Terry Karl called the "fallacy of electoralism."[1] In a wide-ranging attack on the "transition paradigm," Thomas Carothers argued that many countries that moved away from authoritarianism and hold regular elections are no longer transiting toward democracy, but constitute a new hybrid form of regime that mixes elections with autocratic practice.[2] For Marina Ottaway and for Steven Levitsky and Lucan Way, elections allow "semi-authoritarian" or "competitive authoritarian" regimes—who have no intention of moving toward genuine democracy—to placate domestic opponents and the international community.[3] Indeed, Andreas Schedler, and also Levitsky and Way, highlighted a wide range of democratic shortcomings and abuses that continue even as these countries hold successive, reasonably free and fair elections that sometimes result in defeat of the ruling party.[4] The bottom line, for this school of analysts, is that recurring elections—in and of themselves—generate few if any positive externalities for the larger democratic process. In Carothers' words, "greatly reduced expectations are in order as to what elections will accomplish as generators of deep-reaching democratic change."[5]

A second line of research, however, argues that elections are a *sufficient* condition for popular self-government. Joseph Schumpeter, for example, asserted that competition amongst multiple candidates and political parties for the free votes of the electorate is sufficient to generate a range of democratic externalities beyond the electoral arena, such as increased freedom of speech, association, and news media, as well as greater accountability and responsiveness.[6] Similarly, Carl Freidrich's "law of anticipated reactions" argues that any government whose policies and actions will be subsequently reviewed by an electorate with the power to punish bad actions or reward good ones is likely to consider the opinions and preferences of voters in the policy-making process.[7] Finally, Dankwart Rustow argued that democracy

> is by definition a competitive process, and this competition gives an edge to those who can rationalize their commitment to it, and an even greater edge to those sincerely who believe in it.... In short, the very process of democracy institutes a double process of Darwinian selectivity in favor of convinced democrats: one among parties in general elections, and the other among politicians vying for leadership within these parties.[8]

Staffan Lindberg has provided important empirical support for the Schumpeter thesis that repeated elections may produce other democratic goods.[9] By examining 287 Sub-Saharan African elections between 1989 and 2005, he showed not only that African elections were gradually becoming freer and fairer, but also demonstrated that as the number of unbroken consecutive elections in a given country accumulated, opposition parties were more likely to participate, "old guard" bureaucrats were more likely to retire, presidential (but not legislative) elections became more competitive, electoral losers were more likely to accept the results, campaigns became more peaceful, and multiparty regimes became increasingly stable. More provocatively, he demonstrated that most of these effects existed even where elections were flawed (though the effects were generally smaller than when elections were free and fair).

Most importantly, by examining changes in Freedom House data before and after these 287 elections, Lindberg found that repeated elections did, in fact, produce subsequent incremental advances in the quality of civil liberties. And again, he showed that flawed elections also tended to produce increases in civil liberties, though with smaller effects than with free elections (the only deviation occurred amongst countries holding flawed fourth or subsequent elections, which was largely driven by Zimbabwe).[10] In sum, he concluded that "elections are a powerful force for political change. *They are sometimes the ignition that sparks other processes that tend to cause direct improvements in a country's level of political freedom and rights.*"[11]

The causal mechanisms, according to Lindberg, are multifaceted. By turning citizens into voters, he reasons, elections increase the likelihood that they will exercise and defend other democratic rights and expect elected leaders to defend those rights. Organizations that conduct key services during elections, such as monitoring or voter education, come to apply their skills to other areas of democracy between elections. Authorities, civil servants, security officials, and judges who have to maintain elections will be less likely to engage in anti-democratic behaviors as soon as the campaign is done. Elections also create spaces for news media to push back boundaries on what is permissible, and then defend those boundaries in the post-election period. Finally, elections bring countries under increased international scrutiny, and criticisms may be taken on board and addressed in the subsequent inter-election period.

However, whether or not these really are the relevant causal mechanisms remains open to further empirical test. In this chapter, I focus on the consequences of elections for individual citizens: do elections really change citizens' attitudes and behaviors toward democracy? And if they do matter, is it simply their uninterrupted repetition, or is it their integrity that matters most?

Indeed, previous research has confirmed that the integrity of elections matters for at least some types of attitudes toward democracy. In their analyses of data from Round 1 of the Afrobarometer collected in 12 countries, Michael Bratton, Robert Mattes, and E. Gyimah-Boadi found that people who rated their most recent election as free and fair were far more likely to be satisfied with democracy and feel that they live in a democracy, than those who thought their election had been a charade.[12] However, they found no link between people's ratings of elections and whether or not they supported democracy or rejected non-democratic regime alternatives.[13]

In a more recent analysis, Greenberg and Mattes explored the accuracy of popular evaluations of elections, and whether the micro-level impacts of these evaluations accumulated to produce tangible macro-level shifts in public opinion.[14] Using expert data on the "objective" integrity of elections and aggregated Afrobarometer public opinion across 33 African elections in 18 different countries, they found a very strong, positive correlation, suggesting that African electorates—if not individual voters—pay attention to not only who wins and who loses, but also to the conduct of their national elections.

In a type of natural experiment, Greenberg and Mattes identified 15 overtime pairs, or dyads of Afrobarometer country surveys, that contained an intervening election, of which some were free and some were flawed (as well as a control group of 13 pairs of country surveys in which there was no intervening election). Across the 10 dyads that contained a free election, there was an average *increase* in the perceived supply of democracy of +10 percentage points. In contrast, there was an average *decrease* in the perceived supply of democracy in the five dyads of country surveys that contain a flawed election (−10.2 percentage points) as well as the 13 pairs of country surveys with no intervening election (−8.5 percentage points). They also found that popular demand for democracy appeared to *decrease* after a flawed election (−9.8 percentage points), but held steady after a high integrity election (+1.7 percentage points) or where there was no intervening election (−1.4 percentage points). However, due to the small sample size and large standard errors, the differences in demand were not statistically significant.

Methodology

In this chapter, I extend this research by linking together macro-level data about elections and electoral integrity, with micro-level attitudes and behavior toward democracy and the state, but I also do this across a longer time period and broader range of cases than previous research. I explore two broad issues. First, how do individual Africans form their evaluations about their elections? Second, do people's evaluations of their elections translate into attitudes about the democratic regime or state institutions, or into relevant citizen behaviors such as community activity, contacting representatives and officials, protest, or support of political violence?

In order to measure the integrity of African elections, I use Staffan Lindberg's dataset of elections held between 1989 and 2007, updated by researchers in the Department of Political Science at Michigan State University.[15] Lindberg collected information from domestic monitoring organizations, news media, and academic sources to classify each election across a number of variables, including the freeness and fairness of those elections, the number of consecutive multiparty elections that came before a given election, and whether the election was marred by violence and losing political parties' rejection of the election results.

With Lindberg, I expect to find that elections in Africa's multiparty systems matter, and that they generate externalities for the larger democratic regime. National elections constitute the largest mobilization of the citizenry outside of war, and in the multiparty systems of Sub-Saharan Africa constitute the most salient democratic activity of which citizens may be aware. Thus, elections should have a major impact on people's overall sense of how democracy works in practice. I anticipate that public evaluations of electoral integrity will indeed be related to the actual integrity of that election, at least as measured by independent expert ratings. More importantly, I expect that these evaluations will help shape public attitudes toward the democratic regime.

In contrast to the Lindberg thesis, however, I anticipate finding important differences in the nature of the impact depending on the integrity of those elections. In young, emerging multiparty regimes with relatively low levels of formal education and poorly developed communications infrastructure, a flawed election should lead people to reevaluate and downgrade the perceived supply of democracy. Nevertheless, since demand for democracy is an aspiration, and given that previous research has demonstrated that individual-level differences in demand are based largely on differences in cognitive skills and cognitive awareness of politics, I do not expect electoral integrity to increase or decrease the demand for democracy in any substantial way.

The Sources of Africans' Individual Perceptions of Electoral Integrity

On what basis do Africans form opinions about their elections? Given the low levels of formal education, independent news media, or general communications infrastructure, one might legitimately ask about the accuracy of individual Africans' perceptions of their elections. The Lindberg thesis implies that evaluations improve over time, as long as a country simply keeps repeating competitive elections. Others might expect that people's opinions are just a sense of "whose political ox has been gored," with people who identify with the winning party giving the election an uncritically positive review, and losers an unremittingly negative reading.[16]

To measure public evaluations of electoral integrity, responses are used from the Afrobarometer survey question, "How would you rate the freeness and fairness of the most recent (presidential / parliamentary) election in your country held on (specific date)?"[17] Response ranged from (0) "Not free and fair" and (1) "Free and fair but with major problems" to (2) "Free and fair but with minor problems," or (3) "Completely free and fair."[18]

To assess the impact of repeated elections, Lindberg's data summarizes the number of uninterrupted competitive elections a given election represents. I also use his data on the "objective" freeness and fairness of each election, as well as whether or not the campaign or election was marred by violence, and whether losing parties accepted the results. Lindberg collected information from domestic monitoring organizations, news media, and academic sources to determine the freeness and fairness of those elections. Based on this information, each election is coded as 0 ("No, not at all"—when elections were wholly unfair and an obvious charade orchestrated by the incumbent rulers), 1 ("No, irregularities affected outcome"—when the election has a legal and practical potential to be free and fair but there were numerous flaws or serious frauds that affected the result), 2 ("Yes, somewhat"—where there were deficiencies either unintended or organized but that did not affect the election outcome), and 3 ("Yes, entirely"—where elections were free and fair, even though there might have been human errors or logistical restrictions on the process).

While there is a positive, statistically significant bivariate relationship between the number of consecutive elections and public evaluations, it is relatively weak ($r = .047$, $p < = .001$). In contrast, there is a relatively strong micro-level association between the expert ratings and individual evaluations ($r = .272$, $p = < .-001$). In those country surveys that followed an election judged by observers as completely unfree, the average response was 1.5 (on a scale of 0 to 4), which increased in a stepwise fashion with an average of 3.1 in those surveys that followed an election adjudged to be completely free and fair.

These relationships are then tested after controlling for potentially confounding factors. In order to ensure that we are assessing the impact of repeated elections per se, rather than the larger democratic regime, I add a measure of the number of consecutive years a country had been an electoral democracy (as judged by Freedom House) at a given country survey. I also include measures of voters' *personal electoral experiences* (whether they actually voted, their perceived freedom of the vote, and whether or not they identified with winning or losing parties—with independents as the excluded category), their level of *cognitive sophistication* (formal education, news media use, and cognitive engagement—a construct of political discussion and political interest), as well as a series of *demographic* (age, gender, urban/rural status, and level of lived poverty) controls.

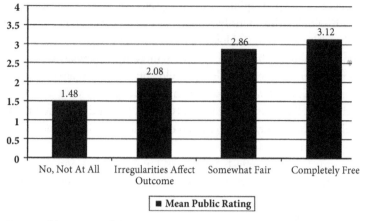

Figure 11.1: Public ratings of electoral integrity. Source: Afrobarometer

Model 1 examines the relative effect of overall electoral integrity on individual perceptions of the recent election, and other electoral characteristics such as the level of violence, whether losing parties accepted the results, and the number of consecutive elections. The model holds constant individual-level demographic characteristics, as well as the number of consecutive years of electoral democracy. The results demonstrate that once we control for the continuous experience with overall democracy, the effect of the number of consecutive elections is quite small, and indeed negative. In contrast, expert ratings of the overall integrity of the election (b = .160), losing party acceptance, and the absence of violence have substantial and positive effects on individual perceptions. However, the overall explanatory power of the mode is quite modest (Adjusted R^2 = .089).

Model 2 adds in the impact of cognitive sophistication and individual electoral experiences. This almost doubles the overall explanatory power but also shows that the impact of overall electoral integrity retains considerable independent impact. But voters' assessment of the freedom of their vote also matters as well as whether or not they actually voted. Cognitive sophistication tends to diminish popular ratings of the election: people with higher levels of formal education are more critical of the freeness and fairness of their election. Partisan considerations also matter—those who identify with the party that won the election have far more positive opinions than those who feel close to a party that lost.

The Consequences of Africans' Individual Perceptions of Electoral Integrity

Thus, not only do the evaluations of whole African electorates correlate strongly with expert observer ratings, but we now have evidence that their individual

Table 11.1: **Explaining the Perceived Freeness and Fairness of Elections**

	Bivariate r	*Model 1*	*Model 2*
Constant		1.57	1.17
Election Characteristics			
Expert Rating	.272	.160	.155
Losing Parties Accept	.227	.075	.045
Elections Peaceful	.228	.056	.055
Consecutive Elections	.043	−.036	NS
Consecutive Years Electoral Democracy	.167	.032	.038
Cognitive Sophistication			
Education	−.098		−.072
Cognitive Engagement	.045		.028
News Media Use	−.020		NS
Election Experiences			
Voted	.129		.095
Perceived Freedom of Vote	.185		.117
Winner	.217		.126
Loser	−.150		−.108
Controls			
Lived Poverty	−.090	−.057	NS
Age	.080	..066	NS
Rural	.032	.NS	NS
Gender	.032	NS	NS
Multiple r		.298	.402
Adjusted R^2		.089	.162
N		59,997	59,997

Note: Cells report standardized OLS regression coefficients (B's). All reported Betas are significant at p = < .001.

Dependent variable is *Perceived Freeness and Fairness of the Election.*

Source: Afrobarometer.

perceptions are also based on the actual integrity of the election, rather than simply the accumulated record of consecutive elections. However, we have also found that Africans have more positive opinions if they actually took part in the election, if campaigns and election days were peaceful, and if opposition parties accepted the results (though, as Lindberg points out, this is often a double-edged sword since opposition parties sometimes reject the results of well-run elections).[19] At the same time, voters still see elections through a partisan lens that distorts their evaluations in the opposite direction depending on whether they identify with winning or losing parties (again, for comparable findings, see Norris 2013 and 2014, as well as the Kerr, Maldonado, and Seligson chapters in this volume).

I now turn to examining whether these perceptions, or any other characteristics of elections, produce positive externalities for democracy in the form of subsequent citizen attitudes and behaviors. First, I investigate whether election characteristics and/or Africans' evaluations of freeness and fairness shape their evaluations of the output of the larger democratic system. Second, I test whether they affect the legitimacy of the democratic system. And third, I look at whether elections and electoral evaluations have any identifiable impact on subsequent political behavior.

Evaluating the Outputs of the Democratic System

Are citizens who live in countries that have had a relatively long unbroken string of competitive elections, or that have just experienced a free and fair election, or who simply think their elections were free and fair, more likely to perceive a high level of *democratic supply*? Are they more likely to see key state institutions as *trustworthy*, and are they more likely to think their elected leaders are *responsive* to public opinion?

Following Bratton, Mattes, and Gyimah-Boadi, I define the perceived *supply of democracy* as a combination of public evaluations of the current level of democracy and their current satisfaction with the way democracy works in their country.[20] The first concept is measured with the Afrobarometer survey item that asks citizens whether "the way" their country is governed is, "on the whole," "a full democracy," "a democracy with minor problems," "a democracy with major problems," or "not a democracy." The second concept is measured by the standard survey item that asks people how "satisfied" they are with "the way democracy works" in their country. A citizen feels fully supplied with democracy if she believes that the country is democratic and if satisfied with the way that democracy works.

To measure the perceived *trustworthiness of key state institutions*, I use the Afrobarometer item that asks citizens, "How much do you trust each of the following, or haven't you heard enough about them to say?" focusing on their responses with regard to the Election Commission, as well as the police and the courts. Furthermore, to measure the *perceived responsiveness of elected leaders*, I use the Afrobarometer item that asks respondents: "How much of the time do you think" members of parliament, and local councilors "try their best to listen to what people like you have to say?"

I then regress the composite construct of perceived democratic supply on the election evaluations and election characteristics that we have already discussed above. But we also know from previous micro-level research that Africans base their estimates of the supply of democracy not only on their assessment of the electoral process but also on the delivery of other "political goods" such as the performance of the president, levels of official corruption, and the availability of civil liberties.[21] Thus, while the following tables display the estimates of the electoral items of interest, the underlying regression analyses include controls for people's *assessments of the current level of civil liberties* and *corruption* in their country, their *performance evaluations of members of parliament and local councillors,* and their *approval of and level of trust in the president,* as well as the standard demographics already included in previous models.

Once we control for a country's experience with electoral democracy, the number of consecutive election has a small—and negative—impact on the perceived supply of democracy and trust in the Electoral Commission. It does, however,

Table 11.2: **Explaining Perception of the Output of the Democratic System**

	Perceived Supply of Democracy	*Trust in IEC*	*Trust in Police and Courts*	*Responsiveness of Elected Officials*
Constant	0.71	0.40	1.26	0.14
Consecutive Elections	.025	−.044	.070	.098
Expert Rating	.030	.089	NS	.091
Losing Parties Reject	−.018	NS	NS	−.055
Electoral Peace	.021	NS	NS	−.025
Perceived Freeness and Fairness of Election	.219	.146	.061	NS
Perceived Freedom of Vote	NS	NS	.018	NS
Winner	.063	.037	.027	.033
Loser	NS	NS	.016	.017
Voted	NS	NS	−.019	NS
Multiple r	.560	.562	.438	.358
Adjusted R²	.314	.304	.192	.128
N	59,997	59,997	59,997	45,997

Note: Cells report standardized OLS regression coefficients (B's). All reported Betas are significant at p = < .001.

Source: Afrobarometer.

make a positive contribution to the popular sense of trust in law enforcement agencies and the perceived responsiveness of elected officials. The actual integrity of the election makes positive contributions to three of these dependent variables (but not to trust in law enforcement agencies). Whether or not elections are peaceful, or whether the losing parties accept the results, has minor and inconsistent effects.

However, confirming earlier findings at both the micro and macro level, individual perceptions of the freeness and fairness of the election make a very substantial contribution to people's sense of whether they are satisfied with, and living in, a democracy.[22] As would be expected, electoral perceptions shape the perceived trustworthiness of the Electoral Commission but also law enforcement institutions.

Evaluating the Legitimacy of the Democratic Political System

In this section, I ask whether citizens who live in countries that have had a relatively long unbroken string of competitive elections, or that have just experienced free and fair elections, or who simply think their elections were free and fair, are more likely to see their *democratic regime,* their *constitution,* and their *state law enforcement institutions* as *legitimate?*

I define *democratic legitimacy* as a combination of explicit support for a democratic regime combined with rejection of authoritarian alternatives to democracy. Support for democracy is measured by the widely used item that asks people to choose from the following three statements: "democracy is preferable to any other kind of government," "in some circumstances, a non-democratic government can be preferable," or "it doesn't matter what kind of government we have." Rejection of authoritarianism is measured by three items that ask people to approve or disapprove systems whereby "only one political party is allowed to stand for election and hold office," "the army comes in to govern the country," and "elections and Parliament are abolished so that the president can decide everything." To assess people's sense of *constitutional legitimacy,* Afrobarometer asks people whether they agree or disagree that "Our constitution expresses the values and hopes of the South African people." And to tap the *legitimacy of the state,* it asks people whether "The courts have the right to make decisions that people always have to abide by," "the police always have the right to make people obey the law," and "the tax department always has the right to make people pay taxes."

Consistent with Lindberg's expectations, an unbroken string of competitive elections is, in fact, associated with higher levels of support for democracy. However, after controlling for the accumulated experience of democracy, repeated elections—in and of themselves—have a negative effect on the legitimacy of the constitution and state institutions. The overall integrity of the election and the acceptance of

Table 11.3: **Explaining the Legitimacy of the Democratic Political System**

	Democratic Legitimacy	Constitutional Legitimacy	State Legitimacy
Constant	2.18	1.50	2.28
Consecutive Elections	.092	−.128	−.024
Expert Rating	NS	NS	NS
Losing Parties Reject	NS	NS	NS
Electoral Peace	−.085	NS	−.037
Perceived Freeness and Fairness of Election	.021	.095	.033
Perceived Freedom of Vote	.018	.038	NS
Winner	NS	.042	.024
Loser	.050	−.020	NS
Multiple r	.367	.388	.201
Adjusted R^2	.134	.150	.040
N	59,997	35,997	45,997

Note: Cells report standardized OLS regression coefficients (B's). All reported Betas are significant at $p = < .001$.

Source: Afrobarometer.

results by losing parties have few important impacts on any of the legitimacy items. Oddly, peaceful election campaigns are negatively related to the legitimacy of both democracy and state law enforcement agencies. Citizens' perceptions of freeness and fairness have minor, positive effects on democratic and state legitimacy, but more meaningful effects on constitutional legitimacy.

Citizen Participation

Finally, I ask whether the characteristics of an election, or citizens' perception thereof, make people any more or less likely to participate in the political process. I focus on four dimensions of conventional and unconventional political participation: communing, contacting, protesting, and the use of political violence. In order to measure participation in collective forms of community politics, Afrobarometer provides respondents with a list of actions and then asks them "whether you, personally, have done any of these things during the past year." *Communing* is tapped by people who say they "attended a community meeting," or "got together with others to raise an issue." *Contacting* is tapped by a separate set of questions that asks people

Table 11.4: **Explaining Citizen Behaviors**

	Contacting	Communing	Protesting	Support for Political Violence
Constant	−.31	−.09	0.30	1.27
Consecutive Elections	NS	.173	NS	NS
Expert Rating	NS	.026	−.023	.123
Losing Parties Reject	.035	.075	.043	−.106
Election Peace	−.045	NS	.059	.030
Perceived Freeness and Fairness of Election	−.019	NS	−.018	−.055
Perceived Freedom of Vote	NS	.040	NS	−.055
Winner	.073	.065	.043	NS
Loser	.051	.036	.036	NS
Voted	.051	.110	.023	NS
Multiple r	.308	.426	.247	.206
Adjusted R²	.195	.181	.061	.041
N	45,997	59,997	59,997	20,597

Note: Cells report standardized OLS regression coefficients (B's). All reported Betas are significant at $p = < .001$.

Source: Afrobarometer.

"During the past year, how often have you contacted" their local councilor, their member of parliament, or a government official "about some important problem or to give them your views?"

As one of the "list of actions," respondents are also asked whether they had "attended a demonstration or protest march" in the previous 12 months: I use this as the measure of *protesting*. Finally, a more intense measure of unconventional behavior is participation in *political violence*. While Afrobarometer has asked about this in the past, the question item did not appear in the same round with the questions on electoral perceptions. Thus, as a proxy measure, I use a different question about political violence that admittedly gets more at their values than actual participation. It asks people to choose between two statements: "The use of violence is never justified in South African politics today" or "In this country, it is sometimes necessary to use violence in support of a just cause."

The Lindberg thesis that elections spur other types of citizen involvement beyond voting receives support from its strong, positive contribution to communing (B =

.173), but otherwise, its impact on behavior is negligible. In countries where losing parties accept election results, people are more likely to report taking part in community affairs, and contacting representatives and officials. The most intriguing set of results in Table 11.4 can be found in the last column, dealing with Support for Political Violence. Popular support for the use of violence in politics declines where all opposition parties have accepted the results, where respondents say the election is free and fair, and where people think their vote is freely given. These results obtain, even though expert ratings of overall electoral integrity are positively linked to support for violence.

Putting It All Together

Iterative single-stage regressions can only provide us with a series of discrete snapshots of a complex reality. In order to get a more synthetic view of the causes and consequences of perceptions of electoral integrity, I have estimated two path models. In Figure 11.2, I produce a model across all three rounds of surveys that assesses

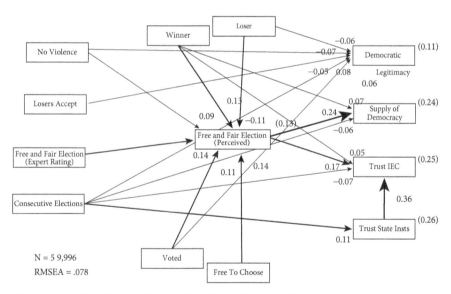

Figure 11.2: Path Model of Regime Supply and Demand. Notes: Structural equation modeling using maximum likelihood estimation. Diagram shows only those paths associated with election variables of interest (B = >.05, p = < .001). However, all estimates are calculated after applying controls for demographics and performance evaluations (not shown). Path coefficients are Standardized Regression Estimates. Coefficients attached to the dependent variables (in parentheses) are Squared Multiple Correlations and analogous to R2. RMSEA is the Root Mean Squared Error of Approximation: a value up to 0.05 indicates a close fit of the hypothesized model with the actual data, with values of up to 0.08 representing a reasonable fit. Source: Afrobarometer.

how the key electoral variables we have thus far discussed combine to shape how individuals assess the freeness and fairness of their election, and how all of these variables simultaneously shape evaluations of the legitimacy and performance of the political system. While the model is estimated with controls for the effect of performance evaluations and demographic factors, only the statistically significant and important effects of the electoral variables are shown (B = >0.05).

What Figure 11.2 demonstrates is that the major sources of popular evaluations of electoral integrity are the same factors that are measured by domestic monitoring organizations and summarized by Lindberg's overall rating of the freeness and fairness of an election, and the extent to which an election was conducted peacefully. Neither the number of consecutive elections nor whether losers accepted the result have any impact. People's own experience of their ability to cast their vote without coercion also contributes to their evaluations of integrity. In addition, people who voted in the election, and those who identified with the winning party, are more positive, while those who identified with losing parties are less so.

Popular perceptions of the freeness and fairness of their election, in turn, have important impacts on their degree of trust in the Electoral Commission, and their sense of the overall level of democracy in their country. Election evaluations, however, have only a very small, positive impact on the perceived trustworthiness of state law enforcement institutions or the legitimacy of democracy.

Yet there is also evidence that corroborates at least part of the Lindberg thesis of repeated elections. Controlling for a country's record of democracy, a longer chain of uninterrupted elections contributes to higher levels of democratic legitimacy, as well as to trust in state institutions. At the same time, a longer chain of uninterrupted elections—independent of the history of democracy—results in lower popular estimates of the supply of democracy, and less trust in the Electoral Commission.

In Figure 11.3, I investigate how these variables in turn shape four political behaviors (communing, contacting, protesting, and support for violence).[23] Figure 11.3 demonstrates that free elections enhance individuals' overall assessments of democracy, and their trust in the Electoral Commission. However, neither of these variables makes any subsequent contribution to the four political behaviors that we have tested. Hence, to the extent that flawed elections lead people to downgrade their perceived supply of democracy, this may increase the gap between aggregate demand for democracy and the aggregate sense of supply, possibly leading to increased societal-wide pressure from "dissatisfied democrats" on the state to bring the level of democracy into line with popular preferences.[24] However, there is no evidence that it will lead those specific people to increase their level of either peaceful or violent political engagement.

Rather, it is those people who see democracy as legitimate, and who see their law enforcement agencies as trustworthy, who are more likely to contact elected representatives and government officials, and, to a lesser extent, refrain from protest and reject the use of political violence. In addition, because a longer chain of

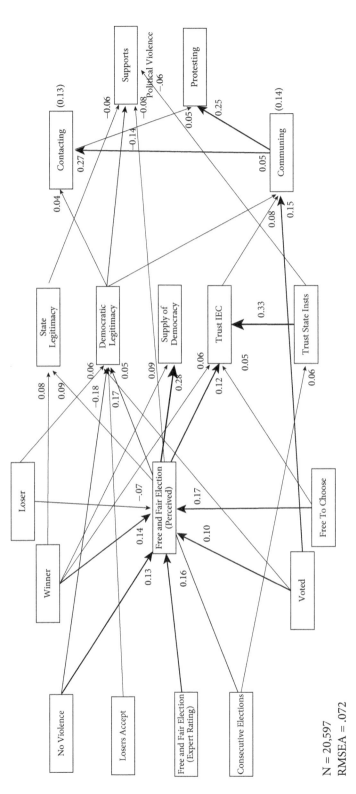

Figure 11.3: Path Model of Behavior Notes: Structural equation modeling using maximum likelihood estimation. Diagram shows only those paths associated with election variables of interest (B = >.05, p = < .001). However, all estimates are calculated after applying controls for demographics and performance evaluations (not shown). Path coefficients are Standardized Regression Estimates. Coefficients attached to the dependent variables (in parentheses) are Squared Multiple Correlations and analogous to R^2. RMSEA is the Root Mean Squared Error of Approximation: a value up to 0.05 indicates a close fit of the hypothesized model with the actual data, with values of up to 0.08 representing a reasonable fit. Source: AfroBarometer.

unanticipated elections has a positive contribution to both democracy legitimacy and the trustworthiness of state law enforcement agencies, it may ultimately have the most important indirect impact of all our election related variables on increasing citizen-leader engagement, and reducing violent protest. Thus, while the impact of the measure of consecutive elections has had inconsistent and often unanticipated impacts throughout our analysis, the Lindberg thesis cannot be rejected out of hand. Repeated elections, independent of their quality, seem to produce—indirectly—a range of positive citizen behaviors.

Conclusions

In contrast to the "electoral fallacy" argument, elections matter—at least with respect to citizens' views of the democratic regime and state, and their level of political engagement. Even in Africa, with low levels of formal education, communications infrastructure, and news media use, people are able to distinguish between low- and high-quality elections. However, Africans are better able to recognize electoral integrity when elections occur without violence and when they themselves actually take part in the election. At the same time, voters still see elections through a partisan lens that distorts their evaluations in an opposite direction depending on whether they identify with winning or losing parties.

In turn, citizens who live in societies in which elections are conducted freely and fairly and are held in peace, and those who think their vote is freely given, are much more likely to feel they live in a democracy. To the extent that popular demand for, and the perceived supply of, democracy and the ratio thereof are important parts of democratic consolidation (Mattes and Bratton 2007), flawed elections weaken the process of democratization.

With respect to the Lindberg thesis, repeated elections—regardless of the history of democracy in a given country—do matter. While their impacts are clearly uneven, they do contribute to higher levels of democratic legitimacy and trust in state institutions. In this way, they also make an important, albeit indirect, contribution to increasing popular engagement with democratic politics, and decreasing protest and support for political violence. This provides at least tentative support for Staffan Lindberg's argument that repeated elections turn voters into citizens, by increasing their commitment to democracy as a legitimate regime and, in turn, the likelihood that they will exercise and defend other democratic rights and expect elected leaders to defend those rights.

Notes

1. Terry Karl. 1986. "Imposing Consent: Electoralism Versus Democratization in El Salvador," in *Elections and Democratization in Latin America, 1990–1985*, eds. Paul Drake and Eduardo

Silva. San Diego, CA: Center for Iberian and Latin American Studies, Center for US/Mexican Studies, University of California, San Diego, pp. 9–36.

2. Thomas Carothers. 2002. "The End of the Transition Paradigm." *Journal of Democracy* 13: 5–21.

3. Marina Ottaway. 2003. *Democracy Challenged: The Rise of Semi-Authoritarianism.* Washington DC: Carnegie Endowment for International Peace; Steven Levitsky and Lucan Way. 2010. *Competitive Authoritarianism: Hybrid Regimes After the Cold War.* Cambridge: Cambridge University Press.

4. Andreas Schedler. 2006. *Electoral Authoritarianism: The Dynamics of Unfree Competition.* Boulder, CO: Lynne Rienner Publishers.

5. Thomas Carothers. 2002. "The End of the Transition Paradigm." *Journal of Democracy* 13: 5–21.

6. Joseph Schumpeter. 1942. *Capitalism, Socialism and Democracy.* London: George Allen & Unwin.

7. Carl Freidrich. 1963. *Man and His Government.* New York: McGraw Hill.

8. Dankwart Rustow. 1970. "Transitions to Democracy: Towards a Dynamic Model." *Comparative Politics* 2(3): 337–363, p. 358.

9. Staffan Lindberg. 2006. *Democracy and Elections in Africa.* Baltimore: Johns Hopkins University Press, 2006; Staffan Lindberg. 2006. "Better Turn the Other Cheek: The Effects of Opposition Behavior on Democratization." *Journal of Contemporary African Politics* 24/1: 123–138; Staffan Lindberg. 2008. *Democratization by Elections in Africa Revisited.* Conference on Elections in West Africa. Miami University, 10–11 April; Staffan Lindberg. ed. 2009. *Democratization by Elections: A New Mode of Transition.* Baltimore: Johns Hopkins University Press.

10. Staffan Lindberg. 2008. *Democratization by Elections in Africa Revisited.* Conference on Elections in West Africa. Miami University, April 10–11.

11. Staffan Lindberg. Ed. 2009. *Democratization by Elections: A New Mode of Transition.* Baltimore: Johns Hopkins University Press. p.45 (emphasis added).

12. Michael Bratton, Robert Mattes and E. Gyimah-Boadi. 2005. *Public Opinion, Democracy and Market Reform in Africa.* Cambridge: Cambridge University Press.

13. For similar findings in other regions, see Sarah Birch. 2008. "Electoral Institutions and Popular Confidence in Electoral Process: A Cross-National Analysis," *Electoral Studies* 27(2): 305–321; Pippa Norris. 2013. "Does the World Agree about Standards of Electoral Integrity? Evidence for the Diffusion of Global Norms," *Electoral Studies* (forthcoming); Pippa Norris 2014. "Electoral Integrity and Political Legitimacy," In *Comparing Democracies 4*, Lawrence Leduc, Richard Niemi and Pippa Norris, eds, (London: Sage), as well as the Maldonado and Seligson chapter in this volume.

14. Ari Greenberg and Robert Mattes. 2013. "Does the Quality of Elections Affect the Consolidation of Democracy?" *Voting and Democratic Citizenship in Africa*, Ed. Michael Bratton. Boulder: Lynne Rienner Publishers.

15. Staffan Lindberg, *Elections and Democracy in Africa, 1989–2007* http://www.clas.ufl.edu/users/sil/downloads.html

16. Anderson, Christopher, Andre Blais, Shaun Bowler, Todd Donavan and Ola Listhaug. 2005. *Losers' Consent: Elections and Democratic Legitimacy.* Oxford: Oxford University Press.

17. In some early surveys in some countries, "freeness and fairness," was replaced by "honest or dishonest."

18. This question was asked in Rounds 1, 3, and 4 of Afrobarometer, providing us with more than 50,000 responses from 40 separate survey conducted in 20 countries.

19. Staffan Lindberg. 2006. "Better Turn the Other Cheek: The Effects of Opposition Behavior on Democratization." *Journal of Contemporary African Politics* 24/1: 123–138. Indeed, while there is a strong correlation of the integrity of an election and whether losing parties accept results (Tau c = .600, p = < .001, N = 344), it is far from perfect.

20. Michael Bratton, Robert Mattes and E. Gyimah-Boadi. 2005. *Public Opinion, Democracy and Market Reform in Africa.* Cambridge: Cambridge University Press.

21. Michael Bratton, Robert Mattes and E. Gyimah-Boadi. 2005. *Public Opinion, Democracy and Market Reform in Africa.* Cambridge: Cambridge University Press.

22. Michael Bratton, Robert Mattes and E. Gyimah-Boadi. 2005. *Public Opinion, Democracy and Market Reform in Africa.* Cambridge: Cambridge University Press; Ari Greenberg and Robert Mattes. 2013. "Does the Quality of Elections Affect the Consolidation of Democracy?" *Voting and Democratic Citizenship in Africa,* Ed. Michael Bratton. Boulder: Lynne Rienner Publishers.

23. However, since several of these variables are only present in Round 3 of the Afrobarometer, the analysis is restricted to 20,597 respondents from 18 Round 3 surveys. I also add in the intermediate variable on the legitimacy of state institutions that was only asked from Round 3.

24. Robert Mattes and Michael Bratton. 2007. "Learning About Democracy: Awareness, Performance, and Experience," *American Journal of Political Science* 51/1: 192–217; Pippa Norris. 2011. *Democratic Deficit: "Critical Citizens" Revisited.* Cambridge: Cambridge University Press.

12

Electoral Trust in Latin America

ARTURO MALDONADO AND MITCHELL A. SELIGSON

Regular, fair, competitive elections are a necessary (but not sufficient) condition of democracy. The Freedom House and Polity IV indexes, two of the best-known measures of democracy in the world, include electoral integrity as a key indicator of a healthy democratic system. Emerging from an era of deeply flawed election mal-practices, Latin America and the Caribbean have improved the quality of their elections since the beginning of the so-called third wave of democratization. However, this improvement has not been achieved equally across all of the Latin American and Caribbean countries. For instance, Hartlyn and McCoy analyze 32 elections in 13 Latin American countries since the end of the 1980s and classify them in a three-fold categorization: successful, flawed, and failures.[1] They find that two-thirds of the elections were successful; four had deficiencies and were flawed; and eight showed serious deficiencies and were failures. Thus, while countries like Chile and Uruguay have positive records in their electoral administration, other countries, like Peru, Venezuela, and Dominican Republic, still have considerable room for improvement. In chapter 6, Ugues also demonstrates mixed performance by EMBs in several Central American cases.

Moreover, uneven levels of electoral integrity among Latin American elections also seem to generate varying levels of citizens' trust across Latin American countries. Carreras and İrepoğlu find that "distrust in elections is much higher in Latin America than in the other world regions" (p.3) using the 2010 wave of the AmericasBarometer surveys and the Comparative Study of Electoral Systems (CSES) survey.[2] Thus, research on electoral integrity should deal with this discrepancy between improved, but not perfect, electoral institutions and mistrustful perceptions about elections. This chapter aims to fill this gap in the literature.

Figure 12.1 presents the average for electoral trust for countries in the 2012 wave of Latin American Public Opinion Project (LAPOP) surveys. Attitudes toward the question *"To what extent do you trust elections?"* were gauged on a scale from "not at all" (1) to "a lot" (7). These responses were then recalibrated to a 0–100 scale,

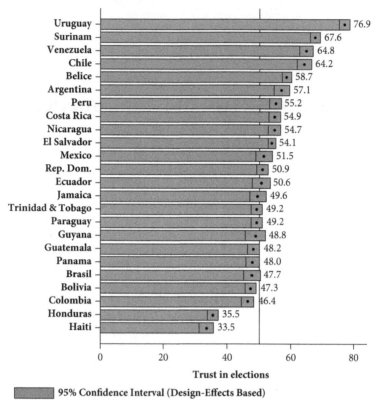

Figure 12.1: Electoral trust in Latin America, 2012 Source: © AmericasBarometer by LAPOP

where we consider the score of "50" to represent the dividing line between average trust and distrust.

Figure 12.1 shows that the difference in electoral trust between the country at the top and bottom is more than 40 points on a 0–100 scale, a large difference. It also spans the continuum from countries in which the mean level of trust is positive and those in which it is negative. Specific distinctions highlight the obvious contrasts, such as the top ranking of Uruguay, a consolidated democracy, and the bottom ranking of Haiti, a fragile democracy recently afflicted by one of the most destructive earthquakes in history. Our results show seven countries (Haiti, Honduras, Colombia, Bolivia, Brazil, Panama, and Guatemala) below the midpoint of 50. Seven countries in the middle cluster hover around the neutral point. Finally, 10 countries are significantly above the midpoint. This group includes well-consolidated democracies like Uruguay and Chile, but also less well-established democracies, such as Peru and Venezuela.

Looking at Figure 12.1, we need to establish how much of the variance across countries is explained by individual factors and how much is accounted for contextual-level factors. This chapter, organized into four sections, attempts to shed light on these questions. The first reviews the literature about electoral trust and develops testable hypotheses. The study focuses on the winners-losers gap in electoral trust by contrasting the views of respondents who supported the winning and losing candidates. It also evaluates a series of moderating factors in this relationship by the level of electoral integrity in a country, time passed since last election, and alternation in power. The second section presents the data and the selected variables. The third reports on the results. The last section sums up and suggests avenues for future research.

Theory and Hypotheses

Elections divide voters into two groups: those who voted for the winner, either for the majority party in Congress or for the presidency, and those who voted for the losing candidates. The literature has established that being either a winner or a loser is an important variable in explaining feelings toward institutions. Anderson et al. find that this affects several outcome variables, such as democratic legitimacy, satisfaction with democracy, evaluations of system responsiveness, and support for democratic principles.[3] On average, for almost all cases, according to their findings, losers exhibit lower levels of legitimacy, satisfaction, evaluation of responsiveness, and support for democratic principles than do winners. They discuss three plausible mechanisms for this to happen. First, the utilitarian mechanism implies that winners would obtain a higher utility than losers. That is, winners may feel better represented and express higher external efficacy. Second, the affective mechanism suggests that winning and losing experiences trigger positive and negative emotions, which also lead to positive and negative moods toward government and institutions. Finally, the cognitive consistency mechanism suggests that losers would become more negative toward the political system to avoid psychological discomfort and restore consistency.

In a subsequent study, Singh, Lago, and Blais examine the impact of winning, competitiveness, and ideological congruence on evaluations of democratic principles, institutions, and performance.[4] They include a set of dependent variables related to democratic principles, including fairness of elections. Their analysis compares Australia, Canada, the United Kingdom, and the United States. In the same line as Anderson et al., they find that "being part of the political majority (or the winning team) leads to support for the system, its institutions, and its authorities." Birch analyzes the effect of individual-level and contextual-level variables on confidence in elections.[5] She includes conventional socioeconomic variables and support for winning/losing party or candidate and finds that this latter variable is a strong predictor of confidence in elections. She also includes contextual-level variables, such as whether the country has a PR system, whether there is public funding for parties, and whether there are independent electoral commissions, to test the hypothesis that "institutional structures that promote a 'level playing field' at each stage of the electoral process will enhance the extent to which voters perceive their elections to be fair." Along the same lines, Banducci and Karp hypothesize that the electoral system mediates between elections and citizens' feelings about institutions.[6] They state that "the electoral system may help to mediate the differences between winners and losers. Systems that distort the translation of votes into seats may serve to alienate segments of the electorate who are not fairly represented." They test for the varying effects of consensual versus majoritarian electoral systems.

In their research, Anderson et al. examine whether and how the winners-losers gap differs between old and new democracies, a further test of the effect of being a winner/loser.[7] Using the 1999 European Values Survey, they find that "the analysis of system support in old and new democracies so far indicates that losing clearly has a negative effect on political support in all systems, but the effect is more pronounced in post-communist countries than in stable democracies in Western Europe." However, they do not specifically consider the interaction between the winning/losing experience and the levels of democracy and trust in elections. In this chapter, we do take such variables into account. They also suggest that repeated losing experiences exacerbate the gap between winner and losers, which is along the same lines as Banducci and Karp suggesting that "dissatisfaction may grow over time among those who do not have political representation or are continually in opposition."[8]

Analyzing the effect of electoral commissions, Rosas tests whether electoral administrations have impact on trust in the elections. He finds that "levels of confidence in the electoral process among political elites are higher in countries with politically autonomous EMBs (electoral management bodies), but this effect is muted in the analysis of citizen attitudes."[9] In this volume, Kerr (chapter 10) also includes in his analysis the effect of the performance of EMBs on citizens' perception of quality of elections in 18 African countries, finding that the performance of electoral tribunals has a significant effect on citizens' evaluations. Also in this volume, Mattes (chapter 11) tests the effect of consecutive elections and expert evaluations about the quality of elections on perceptions of freeness and fairness of African citizens and finds that consecutive elections have a significant but not substantive effect and that expert opinions seem to shape public opinion about electoral integrity. Both Kerr and Mattes examine the winning/losing condition in their models.

Recent research has differentiated certain types of winners and losers. Singh, Karakoç, and Blais distinguish citizens that voted for parties that win more seats in parliament but who are not part of the government, and citizens who voted for parties that lose seats in parliament but are part of the government in an election in a German Länder.[10] They find that "voters react first and foremost on the basis of who gets to form the government. People feel better if their party is in power even if it had lost votes and seats (the case of SPD) and they feel worse if their party enters into the opposition even if gained a few votes (FDP)." Curini, Jou, and Memoli distinguish between winners who have previously lost and losers who have won in previous elections.[11] Their finding is that both groups exhibit higher levels of satisfaction with democracy than voters who had lost in previous elections. Moreover, these scholars also differentiate winners from losers by their ideological proximity to the government. They find that proximity has a direct effect on democratic satisfaction. However, those articles do not test these effects on trust in elections.

In sum, research on elections has found that the contrast between winners and losers has an important impact on several democratic attitudes and behaviors, such as trust in government, feelings about institutions, or importance of democracy, including confidence in elections. In this chapter, we will examine the effect of being a winner or a loser on citizens' levels of trust in elections for all countries in Latin America and the Caribbean (excluding Cuba).

> *Hypothesis 1: Citizens who voted for the winning party or candidate will show, on average, higher levels of trust in elections than citizens who voted for the losing parties or candidates.*

Anderson et al. find that the effect of support for the winning/losing candidate on several variables related to democratic attitudes including satisfaction with democracy depends on the country's level of democracy, measured by the Freedom House index.[12] We hypothesize that the effect of being a winner/loser on trust in elections depends on contextual levels of electoral integrity. In Latin America and the Caribbean, we will only use the component of the Freedom House index that measures to what extent the legislative representatives and the national chief authority are elected through free and fair elections.

> *Hypothesis 2: The gap between winners and losers in their levels of trust in elections will be larger in countries with poorer evaluations of electoral integrity than in countries with better evaluations of electoral integrity.*

Several scholars have argued that the performance of the respective EMBs impacts citizens' confidence and trust in elections. We will test the direct effect of a measure of performance of electoral tribunals on trust in elections and how this variable moderates the gap between winners and losers. In the same manner as with levels of electoral integrity, we argue that the gap between winners and losers decreases as countries have better EMBs.

> *Hypothesis 3: Countries with better evaluations of their electoral tribunals will show, on average, higher levels of trust in elections than countries with poorer evaluation of their electoral tribunals.*
>
> *Hypothesis 4: The gap between winners and losers in their levels of trust in elections is larger in countries with better evaluations of their EMBs than in countries with poorer evaluations of their EMBs.*

Elections are cyclic events every four, five, or six years for presidential contests, and as a result they produce winners and losers only occasionally. The effect of being a winner or a loser may be higher when elections are recent and citizens have this winning/losing experience at the top of their heads. However, as time goes by, citizens may disregard whether they voted for the winning or losing candidate or party and the gap between winners and losers may fade or even vanish entirely. This implies that when estimating the different models, we will use an interactive term between the amount of time elapsed since last election and the winning/losing experience.

> *Hypothesis 5: The more recent the elections are, the higher the gap will be between winners and losers in levels of trust in elections.*

Finally, over time the incumbents may run in subsequent contests and win again, while losers may lose again. As we have explained above, the literature proposes that repeated winning and losing experiences may exacerbate the gap between winners and losers. To address this issue, the model includes an interaction term between a second-level variable that taps whether the country has had alternation in power and being a winner/loser.

> *Hypothesis 6: The gap between winners and losers in their levels of trust in elections will be higher when there is no alternation in power than when an incumbent/party in government changes.*

Data

The present chapter draws upon the AmericasBarometer survey data collected by the Latin American Public Opinion Project (LAPOP). This project has collected survey data systematically every two years since 2004, drawing on national probability samples of voting-age adults.[13]

Variable Measurement

In this chapter, we use the data from the latest round of the 2012 AmericasBarometer survey and from the 2006 wave. Our main dependent variable is worded: "*To what extent do you trust the elections?*" This question was asked on a 1–7 scale from "not at all" to "a lot" and is recalibrated to a 0–100 scale, which is the standard metric used by the LAPOP to standardize all the variables.

In the AmericasBarometer surveys, this question was asked in 15 countries in 2006 and in 24 countries in 2012.

Our main independent variable is voting for the winning candidate or party. The AmericasBarometer surveys ask the following question: *"Who did you vote for in the first round of the last presidential elections of (year)?"* We coded 1 if respondents say they voted for the winning candidate and 0 otherwise.[14] In the pooled sample, the mean value for winners is 34 percent, but it varies from countries like Chile, where around one-fifth voted for the winner, to countries like Ecuador, where just over half voted for the winner.

Figure 12.2 displays the winners-losers gap in electoral trust for the 2006 and 2012 rounds of LAPOP surveys. Most countries were found to exhibit a positive gap between winners and losers, except Paraguay, Peru, and Trinidad and Tobago in 2012. For the same period, the largest gap belongs to Nicaragua (34 points), followed by Venezuela (20). Venezuela and Guyana show consistently high gaps between winners and losers in both rounds and in 2006, and both countries showed the highest gap between winners and losers: a difference of 32 points in Venezuela and 30 points in Guyana.

Hartlyn and McCoy identify Venezuela (in 2000), Guyana (in 1997), and Nicaragua (in 1997) as countries where elections were flawed during the 1990s.[15] Following this line of argument, it seems that those countries that experienced problems with elections are those where the gap between winners and losers is wider.

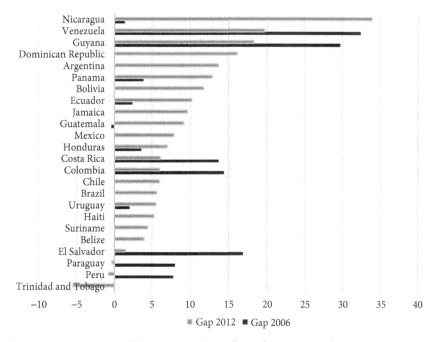

Figure 12.2: Winners and losers gap in electoral trust by country and year

We will test this hypothesis using the electoral integrity component of the Freedom House index, analyzing the gap between different levels of electoral consolidation.

We also add different variables as covariates, including identification with a political party,[16] an index of political knowledge,[17] the traditional left-right self-placement scale,[18] political interest,[19] perception of corruption,[20] and interpersonal trust.[21] The literature has identified and used these variables as predictors of trust or confidence in elections. Moreover, we will include standard socioeconomic controls in the models, such as gender, age, educational level, wealth, and urbanization, to explain trust in elections.

In addition to individual-level variables, we included five contextual-level variables that have been identified in the academic literature as predictors of trust in elections. To gauge the level of electoral integrity, we will use the electoral component of the Freedom House index that ranges from 0 (worst) to 12 (best). In Latin America in 2012, this index goes from 5 (in Venezuela or Haiti) to 12 (in Chile, Uruguay, Costa Rica, El Salvador, and Panama). We include this variable in the analysis for both LAPOP survey rounds in 2012 and 2006. Additionally, for 2006, we also included an indicator about the quality of elections and related aspects of political freedom from the Economist Intelligence Unit.[22]

We also wanted to monitor elite confidence in electoral tribunals. For this, we used data for 17 Latin American countries included in the University of Salamanca's Parliamentary Elites of Latin America (PELA) surveys.[23] These surveys ask representative samples of members of national congresses about their democratic attitudes, opinions, and perceptions. They also include a question that measures how much confidence members of Congress have in electoral tribunals measured on a four-point scale from "a lot" to "none." We aggregate this information by country and recalibrate the scale to 0–100. For the 2012 AmericasBarometer round, we gathered information from the latest wave of PELA surveys, including in all cases the legislators in office in 2012. For the 2006 dataset, we collected information from the congressional period that includes the legislators in office in 2006. The resulting variable measures elite confidence in electoral tribunals and ranges from 38 points in Ecuador in 2006 to 92 points in Chile in 2012, according to the perceptions of the legislators. This is an appropriate measure to tap performance of EMBs because legislators are directly involved in elections and have incentives to be informed about the performance of these institutions.

For economic development, we have also included the 2010 GDP per capita (constant 2000 US$) measure and logged it for the analysis of the 2012 round of the AmericasBarometer. We have not used the 2011 GDP per capita measure because the data excludes Suriname, although we obtained similar results when we used it. For 2006, we use the 2006 GDP per capita (constant 2000 US$).

The AmericasBarometer surveys are fielded every two years and because of this, the time elapsed between the latest presidential election and the survey changes from country to country. We take advantage of this feature of the dataset to test the fifth hypothesis. We have measured time in days between the first round of the last presidential election and the first day of the fieldwork in the country. This measure has an ample variation, going from 2,033 days in Mexico to 38 days in El Salvador in 2012. This is why we use the logged scale that has a mean value of 2.7 (= 479 days).

Finally, we included a measure to tap alternation in power. We focused on the last three elections. The 2012 LAPOP data collects information about the most proximate election that identifies the current incumbent in each country. If the former president/party was different from the current incumbent, this variable has a value of 1. If the last two presidents/parties were different from the president in office, this variable has a value of 2. Thus, this variable has a value of 0 if the same president or party is in power since at least the last three elections. For 2006, we have measured this variable as a dummy. It equals 0 if the current incumbent or party has been reelected and 1 if the current incumbent or party is different from the previous one.

To test hypotheses 2, 4, 5, and 6, we have created interactive terms between voting for the winning candidate and the electoral integrity variable, evaluation of EMBs, time elapsed since the last presidential election, and alternation in power.

Results

We first test whether there are differences between winners and losers in their levels of trust in elections in the 2006 and the 2012 rounds of the AmericasBarometer surveys. Anderson et al. state that "losers are more likely to take a critical view of a process that did not favor them."[24] The AmericasBarometer results illustrated in Figure 12.2 confirm that, on average, those who did not vote for the winning candidate had less trust in elections than those who voted for the winning candidate. In both waves, losers are below the neutral 50-point and fall on the negative side of the 0–100 scale. In contrast, winners are, on average, above the neutral point, on the positive side of trust in elections.

First, we examine gaps between winners and losers depending on the respective levels of electoral integrity of the country and GDP per capita for the 2006 and 2012 rounds of AmericasBarometer. Below, a hierarchical model includes individual-level variables (as in previous analysis) and all contextual-level variables, to test whether the gap remains when controlling for country-level variables.

Anderson et al. find that the gap between winners and losers is larger in new rather than old democracies.[25] We replicated their strategy using the 2006 and the 2012 rounds of LAPOP surveys, and our findings are equivalent. We recoded the electoral integrity variable to a 0–1 measure, where "0" means countries below electoral integrity average and "1" means countries above that average. The gap is 11.3 in countries with low electoral integrity and 11.8 in countries with high electoral integrity in 2006—a small difference. Similar to Anderson et al.'s findings, in 2012, countries with low electoral integrity have a gap almost twice as large as those with high electoral integrity. All differences are statistically significant in both rounds.

In order to test whether the gap is different among countries depending on their levels of wealth, we have divided countries into two groups: those below and those above average GDP per capita in 2010. The GDP per capita measure and the integrity of the electoral process variable—a fundamental component of any measure of democracy—are moderately correlated ($r = 0.17$ in 2006 and 0.48 in 2012); consequently, countries with higher values of electoral integrity are wealthier. Moreover, the gap between winners and losers follows the same trend as for integrity and GDP: wealthier countries and countries with higher values of electoral integrity show a larger gap than below-average countries in 2006. However, we observe an inverse pattern in 2012: wealthier countries and countries with increased electoral integrity display a smaller gap than below-average countries. These results may indicate that both variables are correlated. Given that our interest is in testing the effect of the integrity of the electoral process variable, we will include this variable and GDP to test if the effect of electoral integrity does not vanish when controlling for a country's wealth.

Our measure of the integrity of the electoral process is also highly correlated with the variable that gauges the evaluation of EMBs ($r = 0.47$). Both measures capture distinct but related aspects of the electoral process. The integrity of the electoral process measures whether elections work well in a country, while the evaluation of EMBs measures aspects closer to electoral administration and bureaucracy. To prevent problems of collinearity, we will include either one of them in our models.

Multivariate estimates test whether the gap in electoral trust between winners and losers holds when controlling for standard socioeconomic variables such as age, education, gender, income, and place of residence, and for variables that the literature has identified as having an effect on trust in elections, such as interest in politics, left/right self-placement, political knowledge, vote in the last election, identification with a party, perception of corruption, interpersonal trust, and internal and external efficacy in 2012.

The coefficients shown in Table 12.1 coincide with the simple averages. After controlling for socioeconomic and political covariates, winners display higher levels of trust in elections than do losers. Moreover, those who are interested in politics, those who place themselves on the right in the ideological scale, those who identify with a party, those who perceive less corruption, those who have more interpersonal trust, and those who have more external and internal efficacy are more likely to show higher levels of trust in elections. These results are consistent for both rounds of the AmericasBarometer surveys and are also in accordance with previous findings in the literature about trust or confidence in elections in other regions of the world.

Table 12.1: **Explaining Electoral Trust in Latin America**

Variable	Trust in elections 2006	Trust in elections 2012
Voted for the winning candidate	11.55*	4.24*
	(0.72)	(0.44)
CONTROLS		
Political interest	0.11*	0.07*
	(0.01)	(0.01)
Left-right self-placement	0.67*	0.56*
	(0.13)	(0.07)
Political knowledge	0.01	−0.01
	(0.01)	(0.01)
Voted in the last election	−0.03*	0.01*
	(0.01)	(0.01)
Identification with a party	0.05*	0.03*
	(0.01)	(0.00)
Perception of corruption	−0.14*	−0.12*
	(0.01)	(0.01)
Interpersonal trust	0.10*	0.10*
	(0.01)	(0.01)
External efficacy		0.21*
		(0.01)
Internal efficacy		0.09*
		(0.01)
Age	1.44*	0.86*
	(0.230)	(0.14)
Educational level	2.12*	1.42*
	(0.484)	(0.30)
Gender	−0.45	1.13*
	(0.636)	(0.38)
Quintiles of wealth	0.10	−0.20
	(0.231)	(0.14)
Place of residence	0.293	−0.06
	(0.217)	(0.12)
Constant	37.1*	29.2*
	(2.051)	(1.28)
N	9,652	20,682
R^2	0.09	0.16

Note: OLS regression estimates. * *p < 0.05.*

Source: AmericasBarometer by LAPOP, 2006 and 2012.

Table 12.2: **Hierarchical Analysis of Electoral Trust in Latin America**

Variable	Trust in elections 2006 (Model 1)	Trust in elections 2006 (Model 2)	Trust in elections 2006 (Model 3)	Trust in elections 2012 (Model 4)	Trust in elections 2012 (Model 5)	Trust in elections 2012 (Model 6)
Voted for the winning candidate	51.89*	6.66*	62.51*	19.97*	14.91*	28.26*
	(4.85)	(3.05)	(8.26)	(1.54)	(1.85)	(2.59)
Integrity of the electoral process	5.01*		5.08*	1.45*		1.29
	(1.56)		(1.95)	(0.61)		(0.72)
Winner × Integrity	-3.76*	–	-2.77*	-1.45*		-1.47*
	(0.45)		(0.47)	(0.15)		(0.15)
GDP per capita (logged)	27.73*		23.83*	14.87*		16.06*
	(9.02)		(11.44)	(4.20)		(5.33)
Evaluation of performance of EMBs		0.55*			0.40*	0.18
		(0.23)			(0.10)	(0.11)
Winner × Evaluation of performance of EMBs		-0.01			-0.14*	0.03
		(0.05)			(0.03)	(0.03)
Time			2.42			-1.12
			(7.61)			(2.60)
Winner × Time			-3.69			-1.58*
			(1.90)			(0.68)

	(1)	(2)	(3)	(4)	(5)	(6)
Alternation in power			10.90			1.52
			(7.52)			(1.98)
Winner × Alternation in power			−17.78*			−3.07*
			(1.86)			(0.50)
Constant	−108.31	6.26	−106.66*	−34.39*	10.52	−36.56*
	(33.59)	(14.45)	(45.41)	(13.74)	(6.68)	(16.50)
Random-effects parameter						
Var. (Constant)	47.05	89.31	67.35	34.42	42.81	37.67
Var. (Residual)	855.19	810.54	848.36	659.96	682.44	658.65
N	9,652	8,008	8,563	20,682	15,279	20,682
Countries	11	9	10	23	17	23
Wald chi2	928.65	539.24	964.28	3546.79	2632.6	3593.55
LR test	346.94	546.31	310.44	783.36	724.27	775.62

Notes: * $p < 0.05$.

Source: AmericasBarometer by LAPOP, 2006 and 2012.

The literature has also identified contextual-level variables as predictors of trust in elections. In addition to the individual-level variables used earlier, in Table 12.2 models include the integrity of the electoral process variables, evaluation of EMBs,[26] time elapsed since the last election, and alternation in power. Models 1 and 4 test the direct and conditional effects of the integrity of the electoral process on levels of trust in the elections. Models 2 and 5 assess whether the evaluations of electoral tribunals have any effect on citizens' trust in election and whether this variable moderates the gap between winners and losers. Finally, models 3 and 6 include time, alternation in power, and cross-level interactions between having voted for the winning candidate and time and alternation, in order to test whether the gap decreases in time and whether it diminishes when there is alternation in power.

Table 12.2 presents the results of these hierarchical models for the 2006 and the 2012 rounds of the LAPOP surveys. We use linear random intercept models that allow the coefficient to vary across countries, but fix the slope. We find that levels of trust in elections vary a great deal across countries, justifying the random intercept models. For the sake of brevity, we do not report the coefficients for the individual-level variables, but they are similar to those of Table 12.1.

The results are in accordance with our expectations: those who voted for the winning candidate show higher levels of trust in elections than those who voted for the loser candidates or parties, even when controlling for individual- and contextual-level factors. Countries with higher evaluations of electoral integrity also exhibit, on average, higher levels of trust in elections.

The negative sign of the coefficient of the cross-level interactive term between voted for the winning candidate and integrity of the electoral process indicates that the gap between winner and loser decreases when countries exhibit higher values of electoral integrity. We can predict differences between winners and losers on electoral trust depending on the respective level of electoral integrity of the countries for the 2012 round. The estimates indicate that the gap decreases as the level of electoral integrity increases. Moreover, the difference in citizens' levels of trust in elections between winners and losers is statistically significant for lower values of integrity. As the level of integrity of the country increases, this difference between winners and losers diminishes, virtually disappearing at the higher values. As a robustness check of our results, variants of models 1 and 6 use an alternative measure of electoral integrity—an evaluation of the electoral process from the Economist Intelligence Unit—and we find substantively similar results.

The coefficients for the evaluation of the performance of EMBs are positive and statistically significant in models 2 and 5. They suggest that countries where EMBs are more positively evaluated, on average, show higher levels of trust in elections. These findings are in the same line as Kerr's in chapter 10 of this volume. The coefficient for the interactive term between voted for the winning candidate and evaluation of the performance of EMBs is negative and statistically significant in 2012. These results suggest that the gap between winners and losers in levels of trust in elections seem to decrease as legislators improve their opinion about electoral authorities.

We have also included the time elapsed between the last presidential election and the first day of the fieldwork of the surveys in both LAPOP rounds. Afterward, we have created an interaction term between time elapsed and the gap between winners and losers. We hypothesize that this gap may decrease as time goes by. The sign of the interaction term is negative and may indicate that the more time that elapses between the election and the survey, the smaller the gap. However, this coefficient is significant only in 2012. The lack of significance in 2006 is contrary to our expectations, perhaps indicating an interesting conclusion: that the gap between winners and losers created by elections is not ephemeral.

Finally, we have included a measure to gather alternation in power and an interaction between this variable and being a winner. We expect that countries where there is no alternation in power—where the same ruler is in power for more than one period—show a higher gap than countries where there is alternation. The coefficient for the interaction between being a winner and alternation in power is negative, pointing out that the gap is higher for countries with no alternation. We can predict values of trust in elections by being a winner and loser at different values of alternation in power in 2012. This estimate supports our previous expectations: countries with no alternation in power show a higher gap than countries with more alternation. Moreover, the difference in the level of trust between winners and losers in elections is statistically different from zero at 90 percent of confidence when there is no alternation of power in the last two elections. It is also statistically significant when there is no alternation in the last election (the same president or party in power in the last two terms), but it is not statistically significant when there has been alternation (current president or party in power is different from prior two incumbents).

Conclusions

Overall, being a winner or a loser in an election seems to be a fundamental predictor of trust in elections: in Latin American countries, *winners exhibit higher levels of trust in elections than do losers.* This result increases confidence in the robustness of this widely observed phenomenon.

We also demonstrate, however, that in Latin American countries, *the winners-losers gap in electoral trust varies depending on levels of electoral integrity.* For example, Venezuela and Nicaragua, two countries in which electoral integrity has recently been questioned, show the highest gap between winners and losers in 2012. It seems that the gap is high in Venezuela due to the winners' score (76.5), whereas in Nicaragua it is due to the elevated score of winners (71.1) as well as the diminished score of the losers (37.2). Thus, the gap may arise because winners increase their levels of trust in elections when they win, or because losers have less confidence in elections, or both. Future studies should distinguish the mechanism explaining this effect.

Moreover, we also find that the performance of the electoral management bodies has a direct effect on trust in elections. *When electoral tribunals work well, citizens reward their effort and trust in elections increases.* Thus, an evaluation of a specific institution develops into a diffuse support for the whole process.

Additionally, we examine whether the gap weakens over time. Because elections are periodic events, they create winners and losers, but the effect on political attitudes may be exacerbated just after election day. As time goes by, winners may observe a decrease in their initial enthusiasm and losers may accept that the winner candidate or party is governing. Evidence does not support this expectation; on the contrary, *the gap remains stable over time.* In this case, time may not heal all wounds.

Finally, we test whether repeated winning and losing experiences over successive contests exacerbate the gap between winners and losers in electoral trust. We compare countries with alternation versus countries with no alternation, and find the expected relationship: *the gap between winners and losers in electoral trust is higher in countries without alternation in power.* Thus, it seems that presidents or parties that stay in office for more than one or two terms create more polarization in their societies in several remarkable respects, such as satisfaction with democracy and one of its main mechanisms, elections. In contrast, alternation of power-holders attenuates the differences between winners and losers.

These findings contribute to the general electoral integrity literature. A limited level of citizen trust in elections is a serious challenge for a country. Electoral administration and bureaucracy may organize elections that meet international standards, but if people do not believe in the electoral integrity, this may generate doubts about results, dissatisfaction with the whole process, requests for new elections, and even violence, particularly among those who voted for a losing candidate. The Mexican 2012 election is an exemplary case. The Freedom House webpage states that "the 2012 elections were considered generally free and fair, but complaints persisted, especially by the opposition PRD, concerning media coverage and alleged vote buying."[27] As a result, public demonstrations gathered thousands of protesters demanding an overturn of the vote results. Thus, research on citizens' trust in elections helps to shed light on broader challenges of electoral integrity.

Notes

1. Jonathan Hartlyn and Jennifer McCoy. 2001. "Elections with 'Adjectives' in Contemporary Latin America: A Comparative Analysis." Paper delivered at the 2001 Annual Meeting of the Latin American Studies Association, Washington D.C.
2. Miguel Carreras and Yasemin İrepoğlu. 2013. "Perceptions of Electoral Integrity, Efficacy, and Electoral Participation in Latin America." *Electoral Studies* 32(4): 609–619.
3. Christopher Anderson, André Blais, Shaun Bowler, Todd Donovan and Ola Listhaug. 2005. *Losers' Consent: Elections and Democratic Legitimacy.* Oxford: Oxford University Press.
4. Shane Singh, Ignacio Lago and André Blais. 2011. "Winning and Competitiveness as Determinants of Political Support." *Social Science Quarterly,* 92(3): 695–709.

5. Sarah Birch. 2008. "Electoral institutions and popular confidence in electoral processes: A cross-national analysis." *Electoral Studies* 27: 305–320.
6. Susan Banducci and Jeffrey A. Karp. 2003. "How elections change the way citizens view the political system: Campaigns, media effects and electoral outcomes in comparative perspective." *British Journal of Political Science* 33: 443–467.
7. Christopher Anderson, André Blais, Shaun Bowler, Todd Donovan and Ola Listhaug. 2005. *Losers' Consent: Elections and Democratic Legitimacy.* Oxford: Oxford University Press.
8. Susan Banducci and Jeffrey Karp. 2003. "How elections change the way citizens view the political system: Campaigns, media effects and electoral outcomes in comparative perspective." *British Journal of Political Science* 33: 443–467.
9. Guillermo Rosas. 2010. "Trust in elections and the institutional design of electoral authorities: Evidence from Latin America." *Electoral Studies* 29: 74–90.
10. Shane Singh, Ekrem Karakoç and André Blais. 2012. "Differentiating winners: How elections affect satisfaction with democracy." *Electoral Studies* 31: 201–211.
11. Luigi Curini, Willy Jou and Vincenzo Memoli. 2011. "Satisfaction with Democracy and the Winner/Loser Debate: The Role of Policy Preferences and Past Experience." *British Journal of Political Science*, 42(2): 241–261.
12. Ibid.
13. We thank the United States Agency for International Development, the UNDP, the Inter-American Development Bank, the U.S. National Science Foundation, the CNPq (Brazil), the Tinker Foundation Incorporated, the World Bank and, especially, Vanderbilt University for supporting the collection of these data.
14. We also coded as 0 (losers) those who did not vote. This group is particularly important in non-compulsory voting countries like Chile where 25 percent of respondents say they did not vote. We then replicated the analyses, excluding those who did not vote. The results were substantively similar.
15. Ibid.
16. This question is worded as: "*Do you currently identify with a political party?*"
17. This index is built based on two factual questions: "*What is the name of the current president of the United States of America?*" and "*How long is the presidential term of office in (Country)?*" This index equals 100 if respondent answers two questions correctly, 50 if respondent answers one question correctly, and 0 if respondent does not get any right answers.
18. This question is worded as: "*On this card there is a 1–10 scale that goes from left to right. The number one means left and 10 means right. Nowadays, when we speak of political leaning, we talk of those on the left and those on the right. In other words, some people sympathize more with the left and others with the right. According to the meaning that the terms 'left' and 'right' have for you, and thinking on your own political leanings, where would you place yourself on this scale? Tell me the number.*"
19. This question is worded as: "*How much interest do you have in politics: a lot, some, little or none?*"
20. This question is worded as: "*Taking into account your own experience or what you have heard, corruption among public officials is: very common, common, uncommon or very uncommon?*"
21. This question is worded as: "*And speaking of the people from around here, would you say that people in this community are very trustworthy, somewhat trustworthy, not very trustworthy or untrustworthy?*"
22. We extracted this information from the Quality of Government data, http://www.qog.pol. gu.se/data/ (accessed August 28, 2013).
23. Information available in http://americo.usal.es/oir/elites/eliteca.htm (accessed August 26, 2013).
24. Ibid.
25. Ibid.
26. This variable diminishes the number of countries from 23 to 17. We have replicated all models excluding this variable and the results are substantively similar.
27. The Freedom House project http://www.freedomhouse.org/report/freedom-world/2013/ mexico (last accessed August 28, 2013).

13

American Attitudes Toward Election Fraud

THAD E. HALL AND CHARLES STEWART

Whether an election has been decided fairly is a critical factor in determining if the losers consent to be governed by the winner rather than contesting the winner's legitimacy.[1] The integrity of an election turns on a number of factors, including whether eligible citizens are given unfettered access to the polls, voters are allowed to express a choice that reflected their free will, the voting pool is diluted through double-voting or a flood of ineligible voters, and election officials fairly administer the election laws and accurately canvass the results.

The narrative of the history of voting in the United States has emphasized the expansion of the franchise and efforts to reduce fraudulent elections.[2] In this "Whig history" of election administration, the progressive integrity of American elections has been highlighted. But even within this broader narrative, pockets of fraud have been acknowledged in places like Chicago, Wells County (Texas), and Tammany-era (New York City). Widespread national concern about voter fraud (or at least unfairness) reentered national political discourse in the aftermath of the 2000 presidential election, through episodes such as the 2000 Florida recount, allegations of voting machine tampering in Ohio in 2004, and charges that groups like ACORN were flooding the voter rolls with fictitious registrants.[3]

The salience of fraud as a policy issue has also grown because of the 2008 Supreme Court decision *Crawford v. Marion County Election Board*, in which the Court majority argued that reducing perceptions of the likelihood of fraud provided a rationale for voter identification requirements. The majority opinion asserted that "flagrant examples of such fraud in other parts of the country have been documented throughout this Nation's history... and that Indiana's own experience with fraudulent voting in the 2003 Democratic primary for East Chicago Mayor—though perpetrated using absentee ballots and not in-person fraud—demonstrate that not only is the risk of voter fraud real but that it could affect the outcome of a close election."[4] Furthermore, the Court argued that, "while that interest is closely related to the State's interest in preventing voter fraud, public confidence in the integrity of the electoral process has independent significance, because it encourages citizen participation in the democratic process."[5] The majority opinion asserts that fraud, or the perception of fraud, may discourage individuals from voting.

In light of the rising salience of voter fraud allegations, it is important to understand who feels that fraud is a problem and under what circumstances citizens are the most likely to have their concerns about fraud allayed. In light of the goal of the nation's election administrators to run elections fairly, are voters convinced this goal has been met? If not, who is the most skeptical? Supporters of losing candidates? The perpetually cynical? In addition, in the mind of voters, is election fraud all of a single piece, or do voters distinguish different types of fraud, such as election tampering by officials versus double-voting by individual citizens?

We attempt to answer these questions through considering American attitudes regarding fraud. We focus on six types of behavior that are widely regarded as fraudulent: (1) voting more than once, (2) stealing or tampering with ballots that have been voted, (3) impersonating another voter in order to cast a ballot, (4) voting by non-citizens, (5) voting an absentee ballot that is not one's own, and (6) changing the reported vote count to misrepresent the true results. These forms of election fraud fall along the continuum discussed by Alvarez, Hall, and Hyde.[6] We use data from the 2012 Survey of the Performance of American Elections (SPAE), a national online survey of 10,200 registered voters in the 50 states and the District of Columbia, to perform our analysis.

Previous Research on Fraud in American Elections

As other chapters in this volume demonstrate, public opinion toward the honesty and fairness of elections have been studied in many global regions and contexts, including in Latin America and Sub-Saharan Africa. Here we will focus on research directly related to American attitudes toward election fraud and how these perceptions can be affected by framing.

Much US research has centered on the role that identification can play in deterring election fraud, following the *Crawford* v. *Marion County Election Board* 2008 US Supreme Court case holding that an Indiana law requiring voters to provide photo IDs did not violate the Constitution of the United States. The consideration of public attitudes toward other forms of fraud has been studied much less in the US literature.

Research by Ansolabehere and Persily considers attitudes toward election fraud in the context of the debate over voter identification.[7] They note that the debate over photo ID requirements is predicated on the idea that voter impersonation at the polls is problematic, even though documented cases of such crimes are rare.[8] Despite the implied claim in the *Crawford* decision that the presence of strict ID laws should reassure voters that elections are administered cleanly, Ansolabehere and Persily find that voters in states with strict requirements do not differ in their perceptions of how common fraud is as compared with voters in states without strict requirements. They also find that a person's perception of the frequency of voter fraud does not affect their likelihood of voting.

Others have analyzed public attitudes toward photo identification laws more generally. Two such studies have found that generic photo identification laws are very popular with the public, even among liberal Democrats.[9] In a recent study, Alvarez et al. examine attitudes toward voter identification laws in the context of the tension that may exist between a person wanting (1) to require voter identification to ensure the integrity of an election to prevent fraud and (2) to ensure that all eligible voters can cast ballots.[10] Alvarez and his collaborators find that there is a strong partisan component to the framing issue: Republicans are much more concerned about election fraud and are much less concerned about voter access than are Democrats. They also find that absentee voters are more concerned about issues of access than are early in-person voters. However, all respondents except strong Democrats express support for the idea that voter identification laws do in fact prevent fraud. Respondents with more education are less likely to think ID laws prevent fraud, as are younger respondents. Interestingly, this study, which had a large Hispanic subsample (the data are from New Mexico), finds that Hispanics are more likely than whites to think that ID laws deter fraud.

The *Crawford* decision suggests that variations in legal frameworks across the United States should affect the attitudes of individuals regarding how often certain types of election fraud occur. For example, despite the Ansolabehere and Persily research, the *Crawford* decision strongly implies that voter identification laws should have an effect on the public's views regarding the frequency of certain types of in-person election fraud. Advocates for such laws make explicit claims that voter ID laws are necessary to keep non-citizens from voting and to keep voter impersonation from occurring.[11] It is important to remember that the majority opinion in *Crawford* acknowledges the potential problem of absentee voting fraud. Critics of convenience voting—no-excuse absentee voting laws especially—occasionally argue that such laws increase the possibility of absentee voting fraud.[12]

Related attitudes include confidence in whether votes are counted, which we call "voter confidence." Research on this topic shows that experiential, demographic, and political factors affect voter confidence. By experiential factors, we mean the quality of the experience had by citizens when they vote in a polling place. A series of studies has found that a negative polling place experience—such as having a hard time finding the location or enduring a long wait to vote—reduces voter confidence. The same is true of absentee voters, who are also less likely to be confident their votes are counted as cast, compared to in-person voters.[13] Two studies by Hall and Stewart and one by Hall, Monson, and Patterson find that people who have an excellent experience with their poll workers are also more confident that their vote was counted accurately.[14] There are also certain demographic aspects that come to the fore in evaluations of confidence. For instance, better educated individuals appear to be more confident.[15]

Several studies have also found partisan dimensions to voter confidence. Research conducted in the aftermath of the 2006 midterm election found that Republicans were more confident their votes were counted as cast than were Democrats.[16] More recent work, however, conducted in the wake of the 2008 election, has found that this partisan effect is actually embedded in a more general "winner's effect" related to voter confidence.[17] People who vote for a winning candidate are more confident that their ballot was counted accurately.

Based on these and similar studies, we develop a set of hypotheses regarding American attitudes toward voter fraud. We consider first the attitudes of respondents, then the political characteristics that may affect these attitudes. Finally, we consider how state laws may affect public attitudes toward various types of fraud.

Respondent Characteristics

It has long been accepted that one factor shaping the decision whether to vote is a calculus regarding whether the ballot will matter.[18] Concerns about fraud could diminish the value of one's vote, thus depressing turnout. Attitudes about the fairness of government may also affect citizens' outlooks on voting. Given the history of disenfranchisement that African Americans have faced in the United States, they should have a less positive view of the fairness of the political process. These two factors lead us to hypothesize the following:

- *Hypothesis 1*: Non-voters, more than voters, will think that voter fraud is more likely.
- *Hypothesis 2*: African American voters, more so than whites, will be more likely to be concerned about the frequency of election fraud.

Age is another factor that may influence attitudes about fraud. For instance, recent research has suggested that younger individuals (whether they are voters or not) and inexperienced voters are less likely to believe that ballots are actually cast secretly.[19] Those with more experience voting will understand the process better (or at least will have internalized norms concerning the honesty of the system) and may have more nuanced opinions about the opportunities for fraud to be perpetuated. Similarly, research has found that older voters tend to have better experiences in the voting process than do younger voters, which may carry over to their attitudes toward voter fraud. This observation forms the basis of the third hypothesis.

- *Hypothesis 3*: Older voters will view fraud as less likely than will younger voters.

Voters also bring information and knowledge to the polls. Some of this knowledge comes in the form of education and some in awareness of current events. Here, knowledge could be a double-edged sword. People who are more informed might view fraud as being more likely given the coverage of such issues in the media (especially online media that is more partisan in nature). On the other hand, people who are more educated and informed tend to show more trust in government and less cynicism.[20]

Voters also bring political attitudes to the polls. Activists on both the left—who are concerned about "hackable" voting machines, long lines, and purges of voter lists—and those on the right—who are concerned about voter registration fraud and illegal voters—have expressed apprehensions about election fraud at various times.[21] However, as we noted earlier, we expect that voters who support the winner to take a more rosy view and to be less likely to think that fraud occurs frequently. This "winner's effect" would mean that people who supported the winning candidate in 2012 would be less likely to think that fraud occurs frequently,[22] leading us to propose the following hypotheses:

- *Hypothesis 4*: Voters for Barack Obama (the national winner) will be less likely to think that fraud is common compared to voters for Mitt Romney.
- *Hypothesis 5*: Those who vote for a candidate who does not win the most votes in their county will think that fraud is more common than will those whose candidate won the most votes in the county.
- *Hypothesis 6*: Republican identifiers will think fraud is more common compared to Democrats.[23]

The Quality of the Voting Experience

We expect that voters will evaluate voter fraud in terms of the quality of their most recent voting experience. For in-person voters, we anticipate that those who have a positive voting experience will view fraud as being less common than those who have a negative experience on these dimensions. For absentee voters, we do not have any similar expectations, as their experience is less controlled and few absentee voters reported experiencing a problem casting their absentee ballot.

Even though voter identification has been such an important component of the debate over election fraud, we do not foresee being asked to show identification to reduce one's view that voter fraud is common, based on the findings of Ansolabehere and Persily.[24] However, were we to find that being asked to show photo identification reduced a voter's view that fraud was common, it should affect the questions related to voting twice, non-citizens voting, and voter impersonation—that is, it should affect opinions about in-person voting, but not absentee voting. Given these findings, we propose the following hypotheses.

- *Hypothesis 7:* Voters who encounter problems at the polls will think that fraud is more common than do voters who do not encounter a problem.
- *Hypothesis 8:* Voters who have an excellent experience with poll workers will be less likely to think that fraud is common compared to those with a less-than-excellent experience.
- *Hypothesis 9:* Voters who are required to show a photo ID will not have different attitudes about how common election fraud is compared to those who are not required to show a photo ID.[25]

State Election Laws and Contextual Factors

The debate over minimizing election fraud is largely being fought at the state level, in efforts to change state election laws. The three areas where legal reforms could affect public perceptions of voter fraud are (1) voter identification requirements, (2) convenience voting, and (3) voter registration. There are minimal federal requirements in each of these areas. First, the Help America Vote Act (HAVA) contains a minimum identification requirement; all first-time voters who had registered by mail must show some form of identification when they vote for the first time. Otherwise, a state can have any voting requirement within reason; state laws are highly heterogeneous in what is considered proper for authenticating a voter. The argument contained in the *Crawford* decision and the position advocated by those who support strict photo ID laws is that having such a law reassures voters that the state is taking special precautions to guard against the types of fraud that can occur in physical polling places, particularly voter impersonation.

Second, given the strictness of the rules associated with getting an absentee ballot in states that still require an excuse, voters who live in these states should think that absentee voter fraud is less common than those who live in states with no-excuse absentee voting laws and those who live in states with all vote-by-mail elections (Oregon and Washington).

Third, we do not have expectations about whether voters who live in states with Election Day Registration (EDR) should believe fraud is more or less common than residents in other states. On the one hand, voters in these states will have experience with fixing their registration at the polls if problems arise, and therefore should have fewer negative experiences that lead to questions about fraud. On the other hand, voters in these states may have more reason to wonder whether it is easier to engage in activities such as double-voting (through multiple registrations), due to the unified nature of registering and voting.[26]

Finally, aggregate demographic factors may lead to voters being more or less worried about particular types of fraud based on the demographics of the state. This is particularly true of factors related to non-citizen voting, which is a charge often raised by conservative political groups. Given current demographic trends, we expect concerns over non-citizen voting to be most acute in states with high Hispanic populations.

Based on this analysis, we generate the final four hypotheses:

- *Hypothesis 10*: Individuals who live in states that require a voter to show government-issued photo identification before casting a ballot will be less likely to think fraud is common.
- *Hypothesis 11*: Individuals who live in states with excuse-required absentee voting will be less likely to think absentee voter fraud is common compared to those who live in no-excuse absentee voting or vote-by-mail states.
- *Hypothesis 12*: Individuals who live in states that have large Hispanic/ Latino populations will be more likely to think fraud is common.

For clarity, we define the coding for each independent variable in Table 13.1.

Data and Analysis

This analysis uses data from the *2012 Survey of the Performance of American Elections* (SPAE), which was the second in a series of nationwide polls gauging the quality of the election experience from the perspective of voters. The SPAE is an Internet survey administered by YouGov, with 200 interviews of registered voters in each of the 50 states plus the District of Columbia, for 10,200 observations overall.[27] The core questions focus on the experience voters have voting on Election Day, in early voting, or during postal voting. In addition, the survey asked questions related to attitudes toward voter fraud, which are the primary dependent variables we use in the models. Specifically, respondents were asked this question:[28]

The following is a list of activities that are usually against the law. Please indicate how often you think these activities occur in your county or city:

- *People voting more than once in an election;*
- *People stealing or tampering with ballots that have been voted;*
- *People pretending to be someone else when going to vote;*
- *People voting who are not U.S. citizens;*
- *People voting an absentee ballot intended for another person;*
- *Officials changing the reported vote count in a way that is not a true reflection of the ballots that were actually counted.*

Respondents were provided with five possible responses: (1) it almost never occurs; (2) it occurs infrequently; (3) it occurs occasionally; (4) it is very common;

Table 13.1: .Summary of Variables

Explanatory factor	Hypothesis Number	Variable Name	Definition
Voter Attributes	1	Voter	1 if respondent is a Voter, 0 otherwise
	2	Black	1 if respondent is African American, 0 otherwise
	3	Age (respondent)	Respondent's age in years
	4	Romney vote	1 if respondent voted for Romney, 0 otherwise
	5	Supported Candidate Lost	1 if respondent's candidate lost the county the respondent lives in, 0 otherwise
	6	Democratic Party ID	1 if respondent identified as a Democrat, 0 otherwise
		Republican Party ID	1 if respondent identified as a Republican, 0 otherwise
Voter Experiences	7	Encountered problem	1 if respondent reports encountering at least one of the following problems voting—voter registration, voting equipment, finding the polling place, or waits more than 30 minutes to vote—0 otherwise
	8	Poll Worker Excellent	1 if respondent rates poll worker "excellent," 0 otherwise
	9	Required to show photo ID	1 if the respondent was required to show a photo ID in order to vote, 0 otherwise

(Continued)

Table 13.1: **Continued**

Explanatory factor	Hypothesis Number	Variable Name	Definition
State Election Laws and Contextual Factors	10	Government ID Law	1 if respondent lives in 1 of the 11 states that request or require photo ID, as noted by the National Conference of State Legislatures, 0 otherwise
	11	Excuse Required Absentee Vote	1 if respondent lives in a state that requires an excuse to get an absentee ballot, 0 otherwise
	N/A	EDR (Election Day Registration)	1 if respondent lives in a state with EDR, 0 otherwise
	12	Latino Population	Percentage growth in state's Latino population, 2000–2010
			Overall Percent State Population Latino, 2012
Demographic controls	N/A	Education	Education in years. Recoded from six ordinal response categories into the midpoint of each category: 10, 12, 13, 14, 16, 18
		Male	1 if the respondent is a male, 0 otherwise
		Interest in News	1 = Follows News "Hardly at all;" 4 = Follows News "Most of the Time"

and (5) I'm not sure. For this analysis, we have excluded respondents who answered, "I'm not sure."[29]

In the analysis, we examine three populations. First, we consider all respondents, both voters and non-voters. This allows us to explore attitudes toward fraud generally. Because the larger pool of respondents includes non-voters, we exclude questions about voting experience and vote choice that were not asked of the non-voting population. Second, we next confine the analysis to all voters. By analyzing voters alone, we are able to study the effects of factors that relate to the voting experience, such as the mode of voting and partisan vote choice. Third, we finish by studying only in-person voters, which allows us to focus on factors related to the face-to-face experience of voting. These models exclude absentee voters as well as all respondents from Oregon and Washington State because all, or nearly all, of their voters vote by mail.

In Table 13.2, we show the distribution of responses across all six types of reform that were asked about. We also break the responses down for each of the populations we wish to explore—all respondents, voters only, and in-person voters only.[30] Because the frequencies are so similar across the three populations examined in Table 13.2, here we focus the discussion on Table 13.2a, all respondents.

In general, the type of fraud that is viewed as most likely to be "very common" is non-citizen voting—an answer given by 20 percent of all respondents. This is followed by voting someone else's absentee ballot (14 percent), voter impersonation (13 percent), voting more than once (13 percent), officials changing the tally (12 percent), and tampering with ballots (10.9 percent). One interesting finding across the three populations is that the percentage of voters thinking that each type of fraud is common declines as the population shrinks from all respondents to all voters, and then from all voters to just in-person voters. This tells us that non-voters have larger fraud concerns compared to voters and that absentee voters, overall, worry about fraud somewhat more than do in-person voters.

Multivariate Analyses

Our initial examination of responses to the fraud-frequency questions revealed that there was a significant amount of intercorrelation across responses at the respondent level, despite the fact (discussed immediately above) that some forms of fraud were viewed as slightly more common than others. The average intercorrelation among these six items is 0.73. When we subject answers to the six items to a principal-components factor analysis, we find that they loaded largely on a single factor, with 79 percent of the variance accounted for by this one factor (eigenvalue = 4.72). The second factor has an eigenvalue of 0.52, explaining only 9 percent of the variance.

This high inter-item correlation suggests that, despite the fact that we can identify at least six forms of fraud that are substantively distinct, the average respondent does not make subtle distinctions between, for instance, the frequency of voter impersonation fraud and the frequency of fraud due to multiple voting. Because of

Table 13.2: **Percent of Americans Concerned about Fraud**

a. All Respondents

Frequency of fraud	Type of fraud					
	People Voting More Than Once	Voter Tampering with Ballots	Voter Impersonation	Non-Citizen Voting	Voting Others Absentee Ballot	Officials Changed Ballot Tally
Never	47	47	43	40	34	47
Infrequent	20	22	21	18	24	22
Occasional	18	19	21	20	26	18
Very Common	13	11	14	20	14	12
N	8,121	8,014	8,069	8,093	7,688	7,854

b. All Voters

Frequency of fraud	Type of fraud					
	People Voting More Than Once	Voter Tampering with Ballots	Voter Impersonation	Non-Citizen Voting	Voting Others Absentee Ballot	Officials Changed Ballot Tally
Never	49	49	45	41	35	49
Infrequent	20	21	21	18	24	22
Occasional	18	18	20	20	25	18
Very Common	12	10	13	20	14	10
N	7,539	7,435	7,483	7,503	7,117	7,287

c. All In-Person Voters (Early and Election Day)

Frequency of fraud		Type of fraud				
	People Voting More Than Once	Voter Tampering with Ballots	Voter Impersonation	Non-Citizen Voting	Voting Others Absentee Ballot	Officials Changed Ballot Tally
Never	49	50	46	42	36	50
Infrequent	20	21	20	18	23	21
Occasional	18	18	20	20	25	17
Very Common	11	10	12	19	14	10
N	6,130	6,050	6,064	6,067	5,743	5,924

Note: Columns sum to 100%; deviations from 100% are due to rounding error.

the high inter-correlation among the six items, we tested our hypotheses by creating a single "fraud scale" as the dependent variable, using the predicted factor score for each individual's response to the six fraud questions as the dependent variable. This is the analysis that forms the core of what follows. We did perform auxiliary analysis, in which we analyzed responses concerning each type of fraud separately. We found no substantive differences across fraud type that merited discussion. Therefore, the analysis that follows focuses on the fraud scale we constructed by combining answers as described above.

Table 13.3 presents the results of three OLS regressions, where the dependent variable is the "fraud scale" constructed from the factor analysis.[31] We begin by examining the results for all respondents in Table 13.3. This model does not include vote choice, vote mode, or voting experience questions and our primary interest in these models concerns the independent variable for whether or not a respondent— all of whom were registered voters—voted.

The first finding is that voters are less likely to think that fraud occurs compared to non-voters. Considering the demographic characteristics of respondents, non-whites are more likely to think that fraud occurs, while older and better-educated respondents are less likely to believe fraud is common.

The voter models also show a strong partisan gap in beliefs about the frequency of fraud. Compared to Independents, Republican-identifiers are much more likely to think that fraud occurs often, while Democrats are much less likely to believe that fraud is a frequent occurrence. Turning to the variables that relate to state characteristics, we do see several interesting results. First, respondents in states with strict voter identification laws are not more or less likely to think that fraud is common. Second, respondents in EDR states are less likely to think that fraud is common. Finally, respondents in states with larger Hispanic populations are more likely to think that fraud occurs frequently.

In the "all voters" models, we can compare the attitudes of early and absentee voters to the baseline of election-day voters. We can also now include two measures related to vote choice: if the respondent was a Romney voter and if the voter's candidate choice was not the top vote-getter in the county in which they live.

For the vote mode questions, absentee voters think that fraud is more common than election-day voters do, but not early voters.

The addition of variables to account for vote choice produces interesting results that need to be interpreted carefully. Looking first at the variables that gauge the presidential candidate the voter supported, we see a form of "losers regret" in two ways. First, Romney voters nationwide are much more likely to believe that fraud is common in their own city or county than are Obama voters. In addition, voters were more likely to believe fraud was common when their preferred candidate lost their home county.

However, notice that when we add direct measures for the candidate whom the voter supported, the signs on the partisan variables flip. For instance, in the original

Table 13.3: **Explaining American Attitudes Toward Election Fraud**

	All Respondents		All Voters		In-Person Voters	
	Coefficient	*Standard Error*	*Coefficient*	*Standard Error*	*Coefficient*	*Standard Error*
Voter	-0.292	0.048	—	—	—	—
Absentee voter	—	—	0.142	0.036	—	—
Early voter	—	—	-0.054	0.037	—	—
Romney voter	—	—	0.942	0.041	0.909	0.039
Favored candidate lost respondent's county	—	—	0.165	0.028	0.155	0.026
Encountered problem voting	—	—	—	—	0.216	0.049
Poll worker was excellent	—	—	—	—	-0.197	0.030
Was asked to show ID	—	—	—	—	-0.189	0.095
Black	0.225	0.056	0.325	0.062	0.257	0.065
Other race	0.169	0.046	0.188	0.048	0.187	0.059
Age	-0.0049	0.0008	-0.0077	0.0008	-0.0078	0.0009
Republican	0.323	0.044	-0.085	0.042	0.094	0.047
Democrat	-0.483	0.028	-0.110	0.028	-0.107	0.036
Strict state ID law	-0.044	0.053	-0.066	0.045	-0.067	0.047
State requires excuse to cast absentee ballot	0.088	0.056	0.078	0.042	0.094	0.042

(*Continued*)

Table 13.3: **Continued**

	All Respondents		All Voters		In-Person Voters	
	Coefficient	Standard Error	Coefficient	Standard Error	Coefficient	Standard Error
EDR state	−0.144	0.047	−0.147	0.048	−0.111	0.051
Percent Hispanic state population	0.0060	0.0023	0.0055	0.0021	0.0055	0.0025
Male	−0.053	0.027	−0.079	0.026	−0.087	0.031
Education	−0.053	0.005	−0.040	0.0049	−0.042	0.006
News interest	0.020	0.019	−0.0039	0.0189	0.016	0.020
Constant	1.19	0.085	0.424	0.094	0.493	0.123
N	6,193		5,630		4,293	
R^2	.15		.25		.25	

Note: Ordinary least squares regression. Standard errors clustered at the state level.

analysis that included all respondents, being a Republican was associated with believing fraud was common, while being a Democrat was associated with believing fraud was uncommon. However, once we focus on voters and control for their preferred presidential candidate, partisans are less likely to believe fraud is common than are independents.

Although this may seem an anomalous finding, we argue it is not. What the "all voters" analysis suggests is that attitudes about the frequency of fraud in a presidential election can be divided into two parts. The first is the attitude formed because one is a partisan, rather than an independent. The second is the attitude formed because one is pleased, or disappointed, in the result of the election. As far as the pure influence of partisanship is concerned, voters with any partisan attachment are less likely to ascribe fraudulence to the electoral process than are independents. However, voters with a partisan attachment can be divided into two subgroups — Romney voters, who are overwhelmingly Republican, and therefore are more likely to cry "fraud" because of the outcome, and Obama voters, who are overwhelmingly Democratic, and therefore more likely to believe the electoral contest was fought fair-and-square. As the "all voters" analysis suggests, the size of the candidate-specific effect swamps the pure partisan effect.

The variables that measure state attributes perform nearly identically when we confine ourselves to voters: voters who live in states with strict voter identification laws do not express different attitudes about fraud being common, voters who live in an EDR state are less likely to think that fraud is common, and voters in states with large Hispanic populations are more likely to think that fraud is common.

Finally, we turn to the responses by individuals who voted in person, either in early voting or on election-day. This analysis allows us to focus on three variables that are relevant only to those who voted in person: whether the voter encountered a problem voting, the quality of the poll worker who checked in the voter, and whether the voter showed identification. (We note in passing that the other variables perform identically to the "all voters" model.)

Consistent with intuition and expectations, voters who encountered problems voting (defined as having a problem with voter registration, finding the polling place, or waiting more than 30 minutes to vote) were more likely to believe fraud was common; conversely, voters who encountered excellent poll workers were less likely to believe fraud was common. Voters who showed identification before voting were less likely to believe fraud was common, but the difference just barely missed conventional criteria for statistical significance ($p = -.054$).

Conclusions

In this chapter, we have endeavored to explain the factors that make American voters more or less concerned about election fraud. We posited a dozen hypotheses regarding the factors that would affect how respondents think about the frequency of different types of fraud in their cities and counties. Table 13.4 reviews those hypotheses and the results for each. As a general matter, we find support for hypotheses related to individual demographic and political factors, and only mixed results for the influence of legal factors.

The power of the partisan influences on perceptions of fraud and the weakness of the legal influences have important consequences for thinking about the factors that shape the legitimacy of elected officials—or at least presidents—in this period of heightened partisan polarization. Taking the results of this chapter together with other recent research, there is very strong evidence that voters who support losing candidates in presidential contests often strain to grant the winner legitimacy. This is not to say that most supporters of Mitt Romney regard President Obama as an illegitimate holder of the presidency—nor would most Obama supporters have doubted the legitimacy of Romney had he won the contest. It is to say that supporters of losing candidates, more than supporters of winners, appear to be more likely to conclude that defeat was due to there being an uneven playing field in the electoral arena.

The results of our analysis also bring a note of caution to the desire to use election laws to allay fears about the cleanliness of elections. For instance, just like Ansolabehere and Persily before us, we find, at best, weak (and statistically insignificant) evidence that the presence of strict photo ID laws causes voters to conclude that fraud has become less frequent in their community. The association between having election-day registration and believing that fraud is infrequent is stronger, but the direction of the causal arrows is unclear.

This is a cross-sectional study. In recent years, social scientists have relied more frequently on experimental studies—in the field, laboratory, and survey research setting. That is certainly the direction that we and other scholars need to go, in order to pin down more precisely whether changing the legal regime can, in fact, change the attitudes of citizens about the cleanliness of elections.

We also note in concluding that our analysis has proceeded under an assumption that it is better if American citizens (voters and non-voters) believe that fraud is infrequent. Based on our years of research into the issue, and the research of others, we are convinced that it is, as a general matter. However, despite the fact that it is very difficult, if not impossible, to measure the actual degree of election fraud across the American landscape, it must be the case that fraud is in fact more common in some places than others. The fact that we do not have measures of actual fraud in our multivariate analysis holds open the possibility that we over-attribute influence to political and demographic factors.[32]

Assuming that the outcomes of American presidential elections are in fact only trivially affected by fraudulent activities, but concluding that changes in laws have not been successful in convincing citizens that elections have become cleaner, what are public officials to do in convincing people that fraud is minimal? Our analysis

Table 13.4: **Summarizing the Results**

	Hypothesis	Result
Voter Attributes	1. Non-voters will think that voter fraud is more likely than are non-voters, across all six types of fraud presented.	Supported
	2. African American voters will be more likely than are whites to be concerned about election fraud, especially fraud related to election officials manipulating the results of elections or ballot tampering.	Supported
	3. Older voters will view fraud as less likely than do younger voters.	Supported
	4. Voters for Barack Obama (the national winner) will be less likely to think that fraud is common compared to voters for Mitt Romney.	Supported
	5. Voters who vote for a candidate that does not win the most votes in their county will think that fraud is more common than will those whose candidate won the most votes in the county.	Supported
	6. Republican identifiers will think fraud is more common compared to Democrats.	Supported
Voter Experiences	7. Voters who encounter problems at the polls will think that fraud is more common than do voters who do not encounter a problem.	Supported
	8. Voters who have an excellent experience with poll workers will be less likely to think that fraud is common compared to those with a less-than-excellent experience.	Supported
	9. Voters who are required to show a photo ID when they vote will evaluate their poll workers more positively than those who are not required to show an ID, regardless of state law.	Not Supported
State Election Laws and Contextual Factors	10. Individuals who live in states that require a voter to show a government-issued photo identification before casting a ballot will be less likely to think fraud—especially voter impersonation and non-citizen voting—is common.	Not Supported
	11. Individuals who live in states with excuse-required absentee voting will be less likely to think absentee voter fraud is common compared to those who live in no-excuse absentee voting or vote-by-mail states.	Not Supported
	12. Individuals who live in states that have large Hispanic/Latino populations will be more likely to think fraud—especially voter impersonation and non-citizen voting—is common.	Supported

provides one clear answer: make sure elections are well run. One of the strongest influences on attitudes about the prevalence of fraud is the quality of experience a voter had when he or she went to the polls.

This finding suggests that investing in elections—having well-trained poll workers, ensuring that voters do not have problems with equipment, making sure registered voters are in fact on the rolls, and reducing waiting times to vote—pays off in terms of the legitimacy of elections in the minds of voters, echoing Clark's findings in chapter 9. In an era in which the consideration of election laws is just as contentious as any other policy area, non-partisan attention to the quality of the voter experience is one activity that would benefit candidates of both parties, just as it benefits all voters.

Notes

1. See, for instance, Christopher J. Anderson, André Blais, Shaun Bowler, Todd Donovan and Ola Listhaug. 2007. *Losers' Consent: Elections and Democratic Legitimacy.* New York: Oxford University Press; William H. Riker. 1983 "Political Theory and the Art of Heresthetics," in Ada W. Finifter, ed., *Political Science: The State of the Discipline* Washington, D.C.: The American Political Science Association, pp. 47–65.

2. Alexander Keyssar. 2000. *The Right to Vote.* New York: Basic.

3. Rick Hasen. 2012. *The Voting Wars: From Florida to the Next Election Meltdown.* New Haven: Yale University Press; Walter Mebane. 2004 "The Wrong Man Is President! Overvotes in the 2000 Presidential Election in Florida" *Perspectives on Politics* 2; Robert F. Kennedy, Jr. 2006. "Was the 2004 Election Stolen?" *Rolling Stone,* June issue.

4. Crawford v. Marion County Election Board. 2008. Citation from the slip opinion, which can be found at http://www.supremecourt.gov/opinions/07pdf/07-21.pdf, p.2.

5. Crawford v. Marion County Election Board. 2008. Citation from the slip opinion, which can be found at http://www.supremecourt.gov/opinions/07pdf/07-21.pdf, p.2.

6. R. Michael Alvarez, Thad E. Hall and Susan Hyde. 2008. *Election Fraud: Detecting and Preventing Electoral Manipulation.* Washington, D.C.: Brookings.

7. Stephen Ansolabehere and Nathaniel Persily. 2008. "Vote Fraud in the Eye of the Beholder: The Role of Public Opinion in the Challenge to Voter Identification Requirements" *Harvard Law Review* 121.

8. Lorraine Minnite. 2010. *The Myth of Voter Fraud.* Ithaca, N.Y.: Cornell University Press.

9. R. Michael Alvarez, Thad E. Hall, Ines Levin and Charles Stewart III. 2011. "Voter Opinions about Election Reform: Do They Support Making Voting More Convenient?" *Election Law Journal: Rules, Politics, and Policy* 10, 2: 73–87.; Charles Stewart III. 2013. "A Voter's Eye View of the 2012 Election" in *Annual meeting of the Southwest Social Science Association,* New Orleans.

10. R. Michael Alvarez, Thad E. Hall, Ines Levin, and Charles Stewart III. 2011. "Voter Opinions about Election Reform: Do They Support Making Voting More Convenient?" *Election Law Journal: Rules, Politics, and Policy* 10, 2: 73–87.

11. Jane Mayer. 2012. "The Voter-Fraud Myth" *The New Yorker,* http://www.newyorker.com/reporting/2012/10/29/121029fa_fact_mayer

12. See, for instance, John Fortier. 2006. *Absentee and Early Voting.* Washington, D.C.: AEI Press.

13. R. Michael Alvarez, Thad E. Hall and Morgan Llewellyn. 2008. "Are Americans Confident Their Ballots Are Counted?" *Journal of Politics* 70:3; Lonna Rae Atkeson and Kyle Saunders. 2007. "Election Administration and Voter Confidence: A Local Matter?" *PS: Political Science and Politics* 40: 655–660. Also see Ryan L. Claassen, David B. Magleby, J. Quin Monson and

Kelly D. Patterson. 2008. "At Your Service: Voter Evaluations of Poll Worker Performance" *American Politics Research* 36: 612–634; Ryan L. Claassen, David B. Magleby, J. Quin Monson and Kelly D. Patterson. 2012. "Voter Confidence and the Election-Day Voting Experience" *Political Behavior* 35: 215–235.

14. Thad E. Hall and Charles Stewart III. 2010. "Voter Attitudes toward Poll Workers in the 2008 Election" in *Caltech/MIT Voting Technology Project Working Paper*; Thad E. Hall and Charles Stewart III. 2013. "Voter Attitudes toward Poll Workers in the 2012 Election" in *Caltech/MIT Voting Technology Project Working Paper*; Thad E. Hall, J. Quin Monson, and Kelly D. Patterson. 2009. "The Human Dimension of Elections: How Poll Workers Shape Public Confidence in Elections" *Political Research Quarterly* 62: 3.

15. Alvarez, Hall and Llewellyn. "Are Americans Confident Their Ballots Are Counted?"

16. Ibid; Atkeson and Saunders. "Election Administration and Voter Confidence: A Local Matter?"; Also see Center for the Study of Elections and Democracy at Brigham Young University. 2008. "Evaluating the Quality of the Voting Experience" Provo, Utah: Brigham Young University; Hall, Monson, and Patterson "The Human Dimension of Elections: How Poll Workers Shape Public Confidence in Elections."

17. Alvarez, Hall and Llewellyn. "Are Americans Confident Their Ballots Are Counted?"; Michael W. Sances and Charles Stewart III. 2012. "Partisanship and Voter Confidence, 2000–2010" in *Annual meeting of the Midwest Political Science Association*. Chicago, IL.

18. William H. Riker and Peter C. Ordeshook. 1968. "A Theory of the Calculus of Voting" *American Political Science Review* 62: 1.

19. Alan S. Gerber, Gregory A. Huber, David Doherty and Conor M. Dowling. 2013. "Is There a Secret Ballot? Ballot Secrecy Perceptions and Their Implications for Voting Behaviour" *British Journal of Political Science* 43: 1. Also see Ryan L. Claassen et al. "At Your Service: Voter Evaluations of Poll Worker Performance"; Ryan L. Claassen et al. "Voter Confidence and the Election-Day Voting Experience."

20. Dalton has shown that trust in government in the U.S. is generally positively related to level of education in the post-war era. Relevant to the previous discussion, he also shows that older voters tended to be less trusting in the 1950s, but that the relationship between age and trust had reversed by 2000. See Russell J. Dalton. 2005. "The Social Transformation of Trust in Government" *International Review of Sociology* 15: 1.

21. Rick Hasen. *The Voting Wars: From Florida to the Next Election Meltdown*; Jane Mayer. "The Voter-Fraud Myth" *The New Yorker*.

22. Alvarez, Hall and Llewellyn. "Are Americans Confident Their Ballots Are Counted?"; Sances and Stewart "Partisanship and Voter Confidence, 2000–2010."

23. We operationalize this hypothesis using two dummy variables, the first indicating whether the respondent is a Democrat, the second indicating whether the respondent is a Republican. The test of this hypothesis is whether the coefficient for the Democratic dummy variable is greater than the coefficient for the Republican dummy variable. It is important to note also that Independent voters may feel that the system least considers their views, given that the rules of elections are set by and intended to represent the needs of the political parties. If Independents have such concerns, then we expect both Democrats and Republicans to think fraud is less common compared to the baseline. However, we still expect Republicans to have greater fraud concerns than Republicans.

24. Ansolabehere and Persily. "Vote Fraud in the Eye of the Beholder: The Role of Public Opinion in the Challenge to Voter Identification Requirements."

25. In an earlier draft of this chapter, we attempted to match what identification the voter was asked to produce with the identification the voter should have been asked to produce under their state's law. Unfortunately, the SPAE questions concerning voter identification are not detailed enough to match voter responses with particular state laws, in all their variety.

26. It should also be said that in a cross-sectional analysis, such as we conduct here, if we observe a negative correlation between EDR and beliefs about fraud, we cannot tell whether the experience with EDR is leading to the reduced sense of fraud, as opposed to the dynamic in which

voters who live in a state they believe to be less fraud-prone are more likely to support relaxed registration policies.

27. The SPAE reports, containing all relevant information about each iteration of the survey, can be found at http://vote.caltech.edu/content/2008-survey-performance-american-elections-0 (accessed August 19, 2013) and http://dvn.iq.harvard.edu/dvn/dv/measuringelections (accessed August 19, 2013).

28. The questions were rotated across respondents. The response options were not.

29. The percentage of respondents answering "I'm not sure" ranges from 2,032 (20.34 percent) for the question "people voting more than once in an election" to 2,451 (24.53 percent) for the question "people voting an absentee ballot intended for another person."

30. The frequencies reported in Table 13.2 are based on using the analytical weights provided in the dataset, which attempted to align various demographics to known demographics of each state. Because there are roughly equal numbers of respondents drawn from each state, the weights do not allow us to approximate national norms. Because respondents from large-population states are more likely to respond that they believe fraud (of any type) is frequent in their city or county, this means that the frequencies reported in Table 13.2 are skewed slightly in favor of fraud being viewed as less frequent. (This is because the sample favors respondents from small states.)

31. Standard errors are clustered at the state level.

32. The one major exception to this statement is the measure of Hispanic population that appears in the analysis, which is probably a highly imperfect proxy for non-citizen voting. However, this measure is also a proxy for so many other factors, including out-group suspicion, that we do not wish to make too much of function as a proxy for non-citizen voting.

CONCLUSIONS: WHAT IS TO BE DONE? POLICY INTERVENTIONS

14

Lessons from the Ground

What Have We Learned? What Do We Do Next?

The theories and empirical evidence scrutinized in previous chapters provide insights into the academic research being generated on electoral integrity. But does this agenda match the concerns of practitioners in the international community? What are the most urgent priorities in understanding problems of electoral malpractice? How can links between scholars and practitioners be strengthened?

To address these issues, in June 2013, over 60 academics and policy makers met for two days at Harvard University's Weatherhead Center for International Affairs. Current issues of electoral integrity were discussed at this, the second annual Electoral Integrity Project's workshop. The event culminated with a roundtable discussion of representatives drawn from leading international organizations in the subfield.[1] The session was chaired by Pippa Norris (Sydney and Harvard University) and participants included Staffan Darnolf (the International Foundation for Electoral Systems, IFES, Zimbabwe); Annette Fath-Lihic (International Institute for Democracy and Electoral Assistance, International IDEA); Eric Bjornlund (Democracy international); David Carroll (The Carter Center); Betilde Muñoz-Pogossian (Organization of American States, OAS); Aleida Ferreyra (United Nations Development Program, UNDP); and Chad Vickery (IFES).

Pippa Norris: Welcome to the final session. So far we have learnt from first-class academic research across a wide range of issues. We wanted this final panel to be a roundtable discussing what academics are missing and which areas of research could contribute to the work done by the major organizations focused on strengthening elections. We are going to ask each speaker to suggest what he or she would like to prioritize. What are the urgent problems in the field of electoral integrity where scholars could contribute? What would you prioritize in the research agendas?

Staffan, would you like to kick off?

Staffan Darnolf (IFES): Thank you very much. I have found these last two days to be extremely useful and fascinating. I will return to Zimbabwe tomorrow afternoon with some new arguments for my discussions with Election Monitoring

Bodies [EMBs] about why they need to shape up for the [July 31, 2013] elections in two months' time. From my perspective, there are three areas where we could really benefit and use additional help. One is the issue of election costs, a second area deals with proper indicators for identifying potential electoral fraud, and the third topic is voter education.

First let me mention a few words about *election costs* and follow up on Alistair Clark's paper [chapter 9 of this volume]. When in the field, we are often asked by donors and others whether the budget that they are looking at makes sense or not. Is this an expensive election? Are they trying to introduce things that are unrealistic? Is it sustainable? What it boils down to is: what are the variables that we [should] include when we talk about the costs of elections?

Up to now a lot of attention has been given to election day—perhaps also the campaigning period—but not the full electoral cycle. Also, the costs of having an independent election management body have been neglected. If you have a government-run EMB, a lot of costs are hidden, because it is comprised of civil servants working as election administrators. And what about the costs of security? In some places, police officers are required by law to be outside the polling stations; in other places that is not the case. So sometimes it is difficult to make comparisons of costs because the variables to be included are not standardized. We should have at least some sort of "minimum package" across the electoral cycle that can then be compared. Additionally, there are sometimes major investments in a lot of countries when it comes to, for instance, voter registration. The introduction of biometric voter registers designed to reduce the possibility of multiple registrants is a massive investment that could be up to half of the election budget. That completely skews our data on costs and how we compare it. So I am really interested to see more academic work on election costs and how we measure them properly.

In terms of *detecting fraud*, I have also been fascinated by the workshop discussions about second digits or Benford's Law as indicators.[2] If warning signs appear, administrators need to determine if it is really fraud or rather malpractice. Malpractice may be addressed with better training; for fraud, we may need to change forms, procedures, or regulations in order to close that loophole.

But my question here is how relevant are these [fraud] indicators in a non-Western environment? Are we all the same? Have these indicators been tested in Asian settings, in African settings? Do we all think alike when it comes to numbers? Because when confronted with something like this, a chairperson of an election commission will often say "Well, this comes from the US and Europe. I'm not really sure how applicable this is for my setting." I, as a practitioner, need to be able to say that it has been tested and validated in non-Western settings. Then I have some ammunition in my negotiations.

Finally, my last comment has to do with *voter education*. We often spend tens of millions of dollars on voter education leading up to an election, and we would like to measure whether the voter education activity was good, effective, and reached the stakeholders. We do a lot of voter education, but we do not really know if it works. We spend lots of money on face-to-face activities, public service announcements or billboards, but at best we might have tested this material on staff at the headquarters of the Election Commission. On a few occasions (most recently in the [Democratic Republic of the Congo]) IFES tested educational material with a control group. But we need so much more of your academic thinking when we pilot test materials before we start printing hundreds of thousands, sometimes millions, of these posters. How can we make this more efficient? We have different target audiences for voter education. Sometimes it is elders; sometimes it is people with disabilities, and so forth. We need to be much more methodological and scientific in our approach, and I think there are many ways in which we can benefit from the work of scholars.

Pippa Norris: Thank you very much, Staffan. There was the *"Cost of Election"* handbook produced by UNDP, but that was published a few years ago now, so maybe we need to update it.[3] Please, Annette, tell us your priorities from an International IDEA perspective. You work on so many of these issues. What do you think are the priorities that you would like to see?

Annette Fath-Lihic (International IDEA): I would like to mention the Global Commission on Elections, Democracy, and Security. Kofi Annan led this initiative to put electoral integrity on top of the agenda and International IDEA hosted the Secretariat. A couple of months ago, the Global Commission published its recommendations.[4] I think it really gives a good guidance of what kinds of areas we should look into from different angles. Certainly International IDEA wants to bring some of the points forward and turn them into projects. I would like to mention three of them.

One of the very crucial issues is *election observation*. Nowadays it is done broadly—to a point to where I think it is overcrowded in some elections. But what is often missing is the follow-up on these recommendations, and also the role that civil society is playing as some sort of a watchdog. We should not forget that international observers leave. And even if they stay a couple of months, at some point they have to detach because it is not their country. But at the end of the day, we should focus more on civil society. This would also promote the electoral cycle. Observers come every four years, and often the recommendations are the same because simply no work has been done in between.

The second issue is certainly *electoral violence.* International IDEA is launching the Electoral Risk Management Tool.[5] We have a long list of indicators that enable EMBs to use this as an early warning and mitigation tool for election violence. It is very comprehensive, and I think it is a useful tool; but of course it is not the answer to all questions, and more research is needed in this field.

The last point concerns the role of *social media* in elections. We all have our smartphones, and I have seen people with smartphones in polling stations. Some people tweet results. So I think there is somewhat of a gap between electoral laws and the practice. When it comes to the impact of social media on election integrity, the field changes so fast. So I think we really have to look into this topic, and not too much is out there. Every day a new application is developed, and it has a huge impact on elections.

Pippa Norris: And electoral violence is certainly an issue that we want to take on in the Electoral Integrity Project, as well as social media and crowdsourcing. So they are all important topics. Eric, would you like to tell us from your perspective what you think is most important?

Eric Bjornlund (Democracy International): Thank you very much for the opportunity. I have been to a lot of meetings about election observation over the years, and it is really great to come to one where there is so much focus on research methods, datasets, statistical measures, and rigorous study of election integrity. This is all welcome, and I think it is still relatively new.

As probably no one in this room needs to be reminded, the whole field is really still young. Twenty-five years ago this idea of serious election observation or focus on election integrity around the world really did not exist. Since then—as Susan Hyde has reminded us—it has become an international norm, and it is mostly good. It has made a modest but very real contribution to democratization in certain countries and to the sort of larger public good in the world. And you have things like the *Declaration of Principles on International Election Observation* that is all positive. But that said, I have some serious concerns that in a lot of ways observation—and maybe election assistance as well—is less effective now than it was 10 years ago. There are some problems inherent in the enterprise.

One important issue is how to evaluate elections. How do you avoid this pass/fail assessment, or using the magic words "free and fair elections"? This will not be easily resolved. And there are issues in regards to the different institutions involved in this industry around the world—what their mandates, interests, and biases are. Some of these questions are addressed in the *Declaration of Principles*.

Three issues I would like to address are somewhat new on the agenda, or they have become more serious challenges recently. One is the sense that what we call outcome-based observation runs the risk of calling into question our independence in the process. Because sometimes what we as an international community feel about the political results of an election affects what we say about the process. Low quality of observers and the shadow market for observers allow certain governments to go "shopping" for observers, which might lead to conflicting findings and competition among observer groups. But even the high-quality observer groups—the ones that have committed to principles and are trying to do a good job—still find themselves in this trap where what they say about an election is substantially affected by how they feel about the outcome. A lot of that is subconscious and a lot of it comes out of good motivations, but it makes me worry about the observation enterprise.

I think that we have incentives to cover up flaws sometimes. We have incentives to worry about the reactions to our statements. For example, in Kenya in 2013 we worried about the reactions to our statements. Would there be violence? These considerations have an effect—even subconsciously—on how we assess an election. We are a little bit less focused on finding the truth in exchange for trying to encourage calm and peace. Calm and peace are important values, but they are not necessarily the main focus of election observer groups.

A second concern is *transparency*, in particular of election observers and their methodologies. As we in the observation community become more sophisticated in terms of our methodologies, we also have an obligation to explain that to the audiences that are interested in our findings—because there is a lot of weight put into what we say.

Not to single out any group, but an example that comes to mind is a domestic election observation group in Kenya. They did a parallel vote tabulation, which verified the official results. They called it "verified" and stamped it when it was not the case. There were margin of error issues and the range of results meant that they really could neither verify nor question the official results. But more to the point, we need to know how they had come to those results. They need to tell more about what their methodologies are. This is true about exit polls and many different kinds of methodologies—particularly as there is increasing emphasis on statistically based observation efforts.

Another example of transparency concerns election management bodies. I think the election observation community needs to remember that election management bodies have obligations in terms of transparency. So when the Kenyan Election Commission, for example, does not share their results at the polling station level, it is really hard for us to make an assessment about claims of discrepancies and erroneous tallies.

There is no way for anybody to evaluate these claims if they do not have that information. Therefore, it is important for us to encourage election management bodies in the world to be transparent. One of the key issues is how the vote count works, including access to the tabulations and reporting of the numbers at the polling station level. The international community has not insisted on that. We have been willing to say nice things about the overall effect of the Kenyan elections without much complaining about the lack of transparency.

The final thing that I would like to mention is that we should be careful about the *fixation with technology and technological solutions* to what seem like fundamentally political problems. In the voter registration area, in the quick transmission of vote counting results, in procurement of equipment for elections—technological solutions are very readily sought. But as Staffan said, these things cost a lot of money. They can create distortions in terms of procurement processes and incentives.

Technology can help solve some of these problems. Annette mentioned technology in terms of the crowdsourcing of election observer reports—a really interesting idea. But technology will not fundamentally change how people perceive election processes in cases where they do not already have confidence in them. If we introduce technology, we mostly just change what people do not have confidence in. And again using the Kenya example—the Election Commission might have trouble implementing and using that technology. So not only did they spend the money, they did not even get the expected returns in terms of efficiency and confidence.

Pippa Norris: The point about data is that records are not always available to researchers. So for example, the European Union evaluations have a good statistical methodology, but that data is not available for us to analyze.

Eric Bjornlund: Yes, I realize I am on both sides of this discussion. But I agree that we should push observer organizations to be transparent and provide their data. That is important and is going to improve the enterprise and confidence in it.

Pippa Norris: Any researcher knows the value of data, and realizes that published data will be used by the next generation of researchers. So the easiest way to engage academics is not to give them money but to give them data.

David, your thoughts about where we should be going?

David Carroll (Carter Center): Thank you, Pippa. My comments overlap a bit with what some of the others have said but maybe with a little twist.

First of all, I would say that while there is a convergence on international standards as the basis for assessing elections, there is still a lot of work to be done on spelling out the *methodology of observation*. How can we apply the assessment criteria that exist in international instruments and other sources to our practical work? And importantly, what is the process of drawing overall conclusions about an election in a systematic way?

Secondly, speaking from the perspective of election observer organizations, I would like to see more research similar to Robert Mattes' recent paper [chapter 11 of this volume]. In our work at the Carter Center we see the main objective of election observation as related to shaping public perceptions. It is not necessarily about deterring fraud. Instead, our objective is to provide authoritative assessments that are well grounded and well researched. Therefore, we have a role in mediating how people perceive the quality of elections. So more research on public perceptions would be helpful for us.

Related to Annette's comment is the issue of following up on recommendations, which has been discussed in our Annual Meeting of Election Observation Groups since 2005. I think we are getting a little better at it, but we need to improve as a community. I am sure that there are ways in which we can benefit from more research in this regard.

It would also be helpful for researchers to focus on the impact of the democracy assistance community at large and on the different roles, because there are a lot of misconceptions. Early writing on election observation found that "Election observers came and did not improve the country's democracy." I am sorry, but this is not what election observation should be expected to do—certainly not by itself. Election observation is part of a broader community, which also includes the technical assistance providers, the international donors, the policy community, and national actors. We certainly need more coordination amongst ourselves, but we also need research that parcels out those roles and their effects.

Another area that the previous speakers have mentioned is *election technologies*. I could not agree more in terms of the costs of elections and the obsession with technology. It is a problem that we are very concerned about. Our particular interest relates to the impact on the quality of the elections and the degree to which they meet standards. Sometimes this heavy emphasis on electronic technologies in the election process complicates the task.

And lastly, I would like to point to the question of *domestic observation*, international observation, and the nexus between them. In the democracy promotion community we are increasingly aware that the future is domestic observation—it has to be, and everybody knows that. But I also think there will still be an important role for international observers for quite a while. We need to find ways to more deliberately reinforce each other's work.

Pippa Norris: Just to pick up on the idea of democracy research strengthening the work of the international community, do you think there are enough internal links? Do you think there are enough links to the scholars who are working in this field?

David Carroll: Both are lacking. I think in the practitioner community we do not talk nearly enough to one another across sectoral roles. The technical assistance providers have good links with each other, for example, but the links between them and observers could improve; the observers are doing more information-sharing, but need to do more. The biggest gap, however, is that our connection to the policy community is not very well structured and in some cases does not really exist. The Global Commission's report has rightfully pointed out the need for more coordination on those issues, and to communicate more effectively across the democracy promotion community. Maybe the Global Commission can somehow play a role in that. But as far as the gap between the practitioners and the scholarly world is concerned, the Electoral Integrity Project is filling a huge gap, and I am very excited about what it can bring about.

Pippa Norris: At purely academic events I am always very aware of that gap. How do you start to bridge that? The capacity to bring in practitioners and to involve them in a dialog is incredibly difficult. It needs to be sustained. You cannot just do it once, right? Betilde, your thoughts about where we need to go?

Betilde Muñoz-Pogossian (Organization of American States): The first thing I would like to point out is the value that the Electoral Integrity Project is bringing to this conversation. One of the priorities we want to focus on is to move the discussion from this conceptualization of a positive and negative assessment of an election—or as you said earlier, a black and white definition—to something that is more comprehensive. Something based on the whole of the electoral cycle.

But all of the things that we have been discussing are based on the instruments that—at least in the case of the OAS—states have approved themselves. When we go do election observation, the expectation is that we're going to come up a day or two later and say "Was it good? Yes or no?" We want to push the conversation with the media, with academia, with opposition groups—especially when we are assessing the elections—to a level that is more comprehensive.

I talked earlier about this concept of democratic elections that is shared by all of us. In our view, in Latin America, the challenges linked to election day have by and large been overcome. Massive fraud does not happen anymore—at least not how it used to in the transition to democracy in Latin America and the Caribbean. But we still see some issues that persist and were not addressed during this workshop.

We see violations of the *secrecy of the vote*, and we see a lot of vote buying. I believe it's even more grotesque nowadays for some reason, and I have been doing election observation for 13 years. Electioneering and campaigning on election day around the voting centers still happen and are not being addressed, although they have some influence on how the voters exercise their right on election day.

Another issue linked to technology is the delay in the *transmission of results* that happens frequently. Knowing who the winner on election day is generates certainty and peace and avoids electoral conflicts. There are still challenges to transmission of preliminary results, most related to their efficiency and swiftness.

Are we comfortable with these things happening? Of course not. But we know that we're not going to have perfect elections. So one controversial question that I would like scholars to address is "What level of irregularities are we comfortable with so that we can say that this was still a democratic election?" Andreas Schedler was talking earlier about a reasonable threshold. I do not have the answer, but we should think about whether we can live with a reasonable amount of irregularities while still deeming an election as acceptable.

Another set of issues regards the *competitiveness of elections*. And as David [Carroll] said, this is linked directly to the quality of the election. OAS is working on how to assess the participation of women and men in elections as voters, as candidates, and as members of electoral management bodies—both at the national level as well as in the decentralized entities. In addition, it is important to assess the access to the media by parties and candidates and how vulnerable groups participate in elections. In Latin America this regards, for example, Afro-descendants and indigenous peoples, but also displaced persons. How are they covered by the media, or how do they have access to political financing? In the case of Haiti, for instance, we have found that our methodology was not suited to assess the participation of those who were affected by the earthquake.

Another issue we would like to see more research on is the *use of state resources* by incumbents. We see it happening not only in national elections, but even more so at the municipal level—at least in Latin America. The high costs of political campaigns, the coverage by the media, gender-bias in the media, access to information on the money coming in and out of the campaigns—these are some of the main things that continuously come up in our election observation reports and that are brought to our attention by key stakeholders. And then the big issue of illegal financing, or illegal monies coming into campaigns, is a big challenge in Latin America and the Caribbean.

Finally, the community of scholars can also contribute to the question of *assessing impact of election observation*. In the case of Haiti we did an evaluation of that mission, and we realized that we really do not have a satisfactory way of assessing the impact of our work. This is specifically related to election observation but is also pertinent to electoral technical assistance. Any scholarly work that provides such instruments would be an excellent contribution.

Just to add, we think that international election observations can contribute to the integrity of elections. By making our methodologies and instruments more rigorous, and by documenting what we're seeing in our statements much more rigorously, we would hopefully be able to contribute to more democratic elections. Observer presence throughout the electoral cycle is very important, specifically linked to what some of my colleagues just mentioned—the follow-up to election observation reports. As a community we have realized that we keep producing recommendations, which are not implemented. We do not really have a way to track it at this point.

As a side note on an interesting project that the OAS has been promoting at the global level—we are conveners of a group within the International Organization for Standardization (ISO). We have a working group that is considering the approval of an International Electoral ISO norm, a norm that seeks to improve the quality in the provision of services that EMBs give to electors. It has not been approved yet, but it is an ongoing conversation that perhaps could be of interest to practitioners and scholars alike. So to summarize my remarks, the issue of measuring impact for us is perhaps the most crucial one.

Pippa Norris: Certainly measuring impact is an issue which scholars are greatly interested in now for many reasons; evaluation research is really the cutting edge of a lot of our work. Obtaining access is especially challenging for younger scholars since they must first make connections, so we need a bridge. It can't just be a personal bridge; it needs to be a more structural bridge.

Aleida, UNDP does have a convening role in New York.

Aleida Ferreyra (United Nations Development Program): We have a convening role and in a way we have a different role from some of the other organizations here, such as IFES—we do not do observation. The UN rarely does any electoral observation today, only under the mandate of the Security Council or a General Assembly resolution, which means, in all actuality, that we have not done much electoral observation in at least the last 10 years. This is due to conflict of interests, since we provide electoral assistance in 60 countries a year, where observation will take place. Additionally, there are others who are doing it much better.

Pippa Norris: A division of labor.

Aleida Ferreyra: It is a division of labor. Having said that, I think UNDP has been using the electoral cycle approach since 2005, and when we started in that year, less than half of the projects, about one quarter of them focused beyond the election event. Today, three quarters of the projects focus on the electoral cycle, and only one third of them focus exclusively on the electoral event. In this sense, we really appreciate that your approach is looking at the broader picture. The electoral cycle approach goes beyond the temporal, including other areas of electoral work, and allows us to look at actors other than the EMB, like the media, the police, parliaments, etc.

In the last two years we have gone through a lot of evaluations and lessons learned of our work and confirmed that the electoral cycle approach has been very successful, and it has also emphasized areas where we still have challenges in the field. Those areas, I think, could benefit from your work.

One of those areas is the insufficient links with other areas of governance. One thing that we have found is that we have been very successful in improving the quality of the performance of electoral management bodies, but we have been less successful in affecting the overall democratic environment.

A good example is the case of Georgia, where the electoral management body has substantially improved the quality of its work, and how staffs are trained, with all the support of IFES and UNDP. However, issues such as political party finances and electoral violence may still be a concern. There are a number of issues that are not direct targets of electoral assistance but which are still connected strongly to democratic governance.

One of the things that we have realized in all these processes is that assessments are essential—both the assessments conducted by organizations and the self-assessments by electoral management bodies. We are working on several guidelines and tools, and I think the work that you do can benefit that work, that's one area.

Another area mentioned previously by IFES and the Carter Center concerns the issues of sustainability, cost, and effectiveness. The CORE Report on the cost of elections was a first good attempt but was very limited in its scope, so we are now updating it so it can become a tool that can be used by scholars.

Pippa Norris: It is useful that different EMBs could report the costs in a common place so you could build up cumulative experience and share it.

Aleida Ferreyra: Yes, we need to develop really a solid methodology for collection. For example, we have extensive information on different costs of materials, machines, etc.... but information is dispersed. Thus, trying to come up with a solid methodology on various issues is one of the challenges that we face. It would be good to collaborate with you there.

Pippa Norris: If we can, Aleida, let's bring in Chad because I also want just to have some minutes for the scholars to respond to this list of issues and how they can actually come back and think about real ways to develop these relationships. So let us come back a minute for Chad, for your thoughts about where we should be going and what we should be doing at this particular stage.

Chad Vickery (IFES): Great, I will try to be very brief. We are talking about bridging gaps and I think that my first exposure to this group basically was [the 2011 joint ISPA-ECPR conference] in Brazil. But I think the other leg of the three-legged stool that is missing, and strangely I can be in that world, too, is bar associations. I think the World Justice Forum and the Rule of Law Index is a very interesting aspect of measuring what's happening, too, and I feel like as much as practitioners are different from academics, lawyers are even more different, but I think that there can be lessons learned from all three worlds.

I also think it is interesting to listen to the discussion of causality in trying to explain historical events, but for practitioners in the field we need models that are predictive. Explaining what happened five years ago is very interesting, but when I am on the ground and there is an election happening I need to know where there will be pockets of violence so that we can react to it. So I think models that are more predictive are needed rather than explaining historical events for me, and that is a difficult task, I know. Obviously, monitoring evaluation is something that we can all work together on immediately and is very much needed, and I think assessing the value of the effectiveness of election management bodies is hugely important.

I think one thing we need to consider is technical assistance has had a real sea change. I think at the beginning of EMB management assistance, it was not assistance, we ran elections. Now we are asking the Afghans to run the election, and we are behind providing advice but they make the decisions. We do not make the decisions anymore.

And so it is not a fair comparison trying to say that the effectiveness of domestic groups running an election is the same as when we had internationals actually running elections with unlimited resources. When you are evaluating this you need to ask the question "Who was running the election?"

Two other very quick things. The donor community is all of a sudden very, very excited about giving money directly to local NGOs. I read an article on foreign policy that said that these groups aren't beholden to the local government; so they're less likely to be pressured than the international groups. I think there needs to be studies on the effectiveness of these local groups.

The last thing is there is a body of law developing on the rights of indigenous populations. Mexico is doing a lot of work on when can indigenous populations have communal voting, for example. In Mexico, it is for their own elections they can have communal voting but federal elections they have to follow normal procedures. That is an interesting field where further research can be conducted.

Pippa Norris: I agree there have not been that many people who have followed up on that topic.

We have got a long list of different issues which I think are important and I would really like people to comment on some of these. Please, come back and give us some of your thoughts.

Nahomi Ichino (Harvard University): Thank you for the list of research needs. I would like to throw it back to you and ask for the practitioner community to also take an active part by making your information more accessible, more available, and more transparent in general. I know there's been a lot of work in the past years with UNDP, USAID, and others to quantify analysis, monitoring, and evaluation. Give us more access. There are ad hoc monitoring and evaluation initiatives between academics and the practitioner community. I think there's a lot more potential in that area as well. And in terms of research opportunities and fellowships within these organizations for academics—that's another huge area that could be developed, but at the moment that's really very limited.

Pippa Norris: Fellowships and internships for the younger generation, of course, so they get experience. And again, there are opportunities. It's not that we're reinventing the wheel but whether people know about them and how you get in. This is what my students at the Kennedy School want to know—"How can I get engaged in this work in democratization?"—and they are finding it incredibly hard to do so.

Thad Hall (University of Utah): Building on the previous points, it seems like one of the things that would be very helpful is examining this issue of management—and management changes not necessarily at the legal level but at the procedural level. That requires a different type of study that's much more in-depth and really looks at how the elections are being managed at kind of the ground level; and then how do certain changes affect voter attitudes and the ability of election workers to implement the election. It seems that you all have a lot of the data for that if you do the follow-up work, and that seems to be a very important aspect to all of this.

Pippa Norris: Or making the data available for us to do the follow-up work.

Thad Hall: Exactly.

Pippa Norris: We need that sort of link.

James Long (University of Washington): Thanks for this very good discussion. I am going to push back on two points. One is this monitoring and evaluation point. You have probably 10 PhD students in this room that would get on a plane tomorrow to go do a monitoring and evaluation of what you're doing. It should not take a Susan Hyde every election to do a monitoring and evaluation. Maybe it no longer needs to be on deployment of observers but maybe on something like voter education. I appreciate that everyone up here is saying we need to do monitoring and evaluation but why don't you just do it? Why isn't that a standard part of what you have to do now? The World Bank in its projects has to do monitoring and evaluation, and other development assistance people have to do it really consistently. In international election observation and even domestic, that's not necessarily the case.

Pippa Norris: James, let me just follow up on that one. So where do practitioners go if they want to find help from good students?

Chad Vickery: It's not obvious—where are they? I'd like to know. And I'd like to know how we measure the quality of these folks.

Pippa Norris: That's right.

Susan Hyde (Yale University): Yes, there are a number of research networks. For example, if you're interested in a randomized control trial, there is a wonderful research network that is tasked with this exact problem of [making the link] between practitioners and academics called EGAP, which I just came from yesterday—Experiments in Government and Politics.[6] They have a network, they have places to advertise for these sorts of things and they're pursuing this model of how to best matchmake. But I think you could also email this group with a request for PhD students because there are a lot of people just desperate for access to exactly these types of opportunities.

Pippa Norris: I really think it is helpful to publicize these kinds of practical links so scholars can match against agencies.

James Long (University of Washington): But I mean an easy thing is to say "In every observation that we do we're going to evaluate a part of it," and so that when you are thinking about your response to a request for proposals or you're thinking about how you're going to deploy core staff and long-term observers—that you know you're going to have somebody there who is going to be doing this kind of evaluation. And at some point it doesn't need to be PhD students—it could just be a staff member at your organization where that is their technical expertise—like we have staff members whose technical expertise is to do statistically based sampling.

Staffan Darnolf: When we're doing technical assistance, we usually have to report indicators, which is the monitoring and evaluation. And on a number of occasions, they're not measuring impact. Then we have a rough report saying that the turnout increased from 55 percent to 58 percent and assume that since we spent $20 million on voter education that that was the payoff.

And the problem is that we do not get money to do tests. We cannot afford to have control groups in two constituencies and not to run voter education material there. Hopefully then, we can sometimes link up with research money and marry our access to EMBs and so on with your expertise in designing and running these kinds of tests for us.

Pippa Norris: Susan, do you want to come back on that?

Susan Hyde: Yes. I just wanted to say that I think a productive task that this group could potentially do going forward is to highlight some of the problem statements, things that we all agree on. I mean there were a number of them that were just mentioned, and I think that at this stage what's sometimes missing is a group of interested parties coming together and thinking about how those problems might be addressed in a specific point-by-point, "This is the research agenda moving forward, this is what we can do." Additionally, I think it seems like it would be useful if we came up with a technology to make sharing information more readily available—that's good for everyone.

Sarah Birch (University of Glasgow): It would be great if the Electoral Integrity Project website could have a forum where practitioners could outline their research needs and researchers could outline their data needs.

Pippa Norris: Can I just bring Carolien, though, on just that question of access because we are having problems still in getting access to the observational reports from the EU.

Carolien van Ham (University of Twente): Actually the OSCE has two statisticians on all of their missions. Together they have data on the majority of OSCE missions at the observer report level. The OSCE has been hesitant to make these data public, but hopefully it will become available at some point. It's an incredibly rich source.

Fabrice Lehoucq (University of North Carolina, Greensboro): There is a study about the impact of international observation and that's Judith Kelly's study, which is very systematic. And the overall news is that there is an impact. We don't want to overestimate it but there is an impact. And one thing I would suggest that perhaps people on your side do is: I'd like to know predictors of when I'm going to have a problem election. I think it would be interesting every so often for you to get on the phone and to call a couple of people and say "Do you have 40 minutes to talk?" or "Can I give you X amount of money and you write something in five pages, document where this is going on?" And then we could facilitate that information because I think that question we could answer.

Now, it can be hard if you're in the midst of organizing missions or providing technical assistance to actually take the time to read this stuff. But I think one thing to facilitate this is to call, or talk, to people every so often and say: "I would like to have a short academic paper on this question—I want five pages." And I think a lot of us would rise up to the challenge.

Andreas Schedler (CIDE): I wish to introduce another polemical note, probably reinforcing what I understand James to have said. When you were asking us to evaluate or measure impact, I think either you should do it yourselves—that's what bureaucracies under the pressure of new public management demands do: evaluate results—or ask public administration people to take care of it. We don't do that. We're political scientists. Our key interest is in power, strategic interaction. We can't provide the certainties you're asking us for. We can't be predictive. Rather, if we're good for something, we're good for introducing uncertainty. Don't ask us for administrative certainties—we cannot deliver that.

Chad Vickery: But I think in regards to the actual impact of long-term evaluation, practitioners need help, donors need help. They've developed log frames and you should see, I have three large projects in Pakistan—each one of them has an extensive log frame—and does any of it really show that there's been extensive impact? I don't know. And so I think the donors require things from us that probably aren't effective, and I think you could probably help us illustrate that. I think it brings some credibility when we have an outside party involved.

Adrián Gimate-Welsh Hernandez (CILUAMI-UAM-Iztapalapa): I like your idea of a predictor model. Secondly, one of the constant points that the policy makers do make is that there is no dialogue between academics and the policy makers.

I think this group of us—we have to have much more presence within the areas where legislatures take decisions, because much of this is very, very important and they have to know much of the ideas expressed here, especially in the process of designing institutions.

I think this is one of the manners in which the impact can be more real and concrete. In Mexico, for example, the legislature has relations with the national university, but it's not often that they have a discussion with other academics, except recently that the UAM has been doing it through the Center for Legislative Research. I think one of the ways to have more impact is to have dialogues with policy makers, so that the conclusions that you're arriving at in this kind of a meeting—will somehow be incorporated in the institutional design in which they are engaged.

Pippa Norris: And of course political scientists have to translate their work into real, clear, and effective work in our journals—so that people read them.

Matt Golder (Pennsylvania State University): Just very quickly, there's a lot of requests for practitioners to release the data, but at the same time you've indicated that there are strategic reasons why you wouldn't want to reveal that data. And so for us, on the other end, I think we need to be careful that you guys are being strategic. We need to model that strategic nature and recognize that the data that we receive is going to be a selection of the data that sort of fits certain patterns. So we need to be careful.

Aleida Ferreyra: I think it will be a little different with the observer groups, because the data that you will get from an electoral assistance provider is completely different from an observer. So in our case, all the project documents, all the project evaluations—even the thematic evaluation that I mentioned that evaluates our work for the last 25 years—are on the website. The problem is that you need to know where the information is on the massive website. It's not user friendly. Just finding our information for UNDP can be extremely complicated.

Pippa Norris: To wrap up, I'd just again like to thank everybody. This panel has been terrific and I think that we need to continue the dialogue, so really I'd like to invite everybody to come to our future workshops as well. Great panel, great papers, and thanks for coming.

Notes

1. A video of the roundtable can be seen at http://youtu.be/zQeByeHARfc. The transcript has been edited for space and clarity.
2. See, for instance, Walter R. Mebane Jr. 2008. "Election Forensics: The Second Digit Benford's Law Test and Recent American Presidential Elections." In *Election Fraud: Detecting and Deterring Electoral Manipulation*. Eds., R. Michael Alvarez, Thad E. Hall, and Susan D. Hyde. Washington D.C.: Brookings Institution.
3. Rafael López-Pintor and Jeff Fischer. Eds. 2006. *Getting to the CORE—A Global Survey on the Cost of Registration and Elections*. New York: UNDP/IFES.
4. Global Commission on Elections, Democracy, and Security. 2012. *Deepening Democracy: A Strategy for Improving the Integrity of Elections Worldwide*. Stockholm: International IDEA.
5. International IDEA. http://www.idea.int/elections/conflict.cfm.
6. http://e-gap.org/.

INDEX

Note: Material in figures or tables is indicated by italic page numbers. Endnotes are indicated by n after the page number.